Lecture Notes in Computer Science 4473

Commenced Publication in 1973
Founding and Former Series Editors:
Gerhard Goos, Juris Hartmanis, and Jan van Leeuwen

Dirk Draheim   Gerald Weber (Eds.)

Trends in Enterprise Application Architecture

2nd International Conference, TEAA 2006
Berlin, Germany, November 29 - December 1, 2006
Revised Selected Papers

 Springer

Volume Editors

Dirk Draheim
Software Competence Center Hagenberg
Austria
E-mail: draheim@acm.org

Gerald Weber
The University of Auckland
Department of Computer Science
New Zealand
E-mail: g.weber@cs.auckland.ac.nz

Library of Congress Control Number: 2007937136

CR Subject Classification (1998): C.3, C.4, D.2, F.2

LNCS Sublibrary: SL 3 – Information Systems and Application, incl. Internet/Web
and HCI

ISSN   0302-9743
ISBN-10   3-540-75911-5 Springer Berlin Heidelberg New York
ISBN-13   978-3-540-75911-9 Springer Berlin Heidelberg New York

Springer is a part of Springer Science+Business Media

springer.com

© Springer-Verlag Berlin Heidelberg 2007
Printed in Germany

Typesetting: Camera-ready by author, data conversion by Scientific Publishing Services, Chennai, India
Printed on acid-free paper   SPIN: 12179268   06/3180   5 4 3 2 1 0

Preface

Enterprise applications range from simple Web shops to complex enterprise resource planning systems. In the area of enterprise applications, interesting research questions arise with regard to software development, system performance, stability, scalability, security, usability, and maintainability.

The purpose of this conference was to bring together researchers and practitioners in the field of enterprise application architecture. In TEAA 2006, the authors presented a wide range of contributions to current fields of research in enterprise applications. We would like to thank our invited speaker, Bernhard Thalheim, for his inspiring keynote, as well as all the speakers and participants for their contributions and discussions. We are grateful to our sponsor IBM for supporting the conference.

January 2007
Dirk Draheim
Gerald Weber

Organization

General Chair

Hans-Joachim Lenz   Freie Universität Berlin, Germany

Program Committee Co-Chairs

Dirk Draheim   SCCH, Austria
Gerald Weber   The University of Auckland, New Zealand

Local Organizing Co-Chairs

Dirk Draheim   SCCH, Austria
Marten Schönherr   Technische Universität Berlin, Germany

TEAA 2006 Program Committee

Ilkay Altintas   University of California, San Diego, USA
Jose Enrique
  Armendariz-Inigo   Universidad Pública de Navarra, Spain
Colin Atkinson   University of Mannheim, Germany
Sandrine Balbo   University of Melbourne, Australia
Phil Bernstein   Microsoft Corporation, USA
Jim Bezdek   University of West Florida, USA
Behzad Bordbar   University of Birmingham, UK
Rajendra Bose   University of Edinburgh, UK
Myra B. Cohen   University of Nebraska - Lincoln, USA
Judith Cushing   The Evergreen State College, USA
Hendrik Decker   Ciudad Politecnica de la Innovacion Valencia,
                             Spain
Klaus R. Dittrich   Universität Zürich, Switzerland
Gill Dobbie   University of Auckland, New Zealand
Jürgen Ebert   Universität Koblenz, Germany
Robert Franz   University of Applied Sciences Brandenburg,
                             Germany
James Frew   University of California, Santa Barbara, USA
Avigdor Gal   Technion Haifa, Israel
Vahid Garousi   Carleton University, Canada
Martin Gogolla   Universität Bremen, Germany

Norbert Gronau	Universität Potsdam, Germany
Martin Große-Rhode	Fraunhofer ISST, Germany
Richard Hall	Laboratoire LSR-IMAG, France
Olaf Herden	Berufsakademie Stuttgart, Germany
Igor Ivkovic	University of Waterloo, USA
Raj Jain	Washington University in St. Louis, USA
Seon Ho Kim	University of Denver, USA
Josva Kleist	Aalborg University, Denmark
Evangelos Kotsovinos	Deutsche Telekom Laboratories, Germany
Hermann Krallmann	Technical University Berlin, Germany
Gunther Lenz	Siemens Corporate Research, USA
Wolfgang Lindner	MIT, USA
Giuseppe A. Di Lucca	University of Sannio, Italy
Christof Lutteroth	University of Auckland, New Zealand
Teresa Mallardo	Universita degli Studi di Bari, Italy
Hermann Maurer	Universität Graz, Austria
Josephine Micallef	Telcordia Technologies Inc., USA
Roland Mittermeir	Universität Klagenfurt, Austria
Roland M. Müller	Free University Berlin, Germany
Jan Newmarch	Monash University, Australia
Toyohiro Nomoto	Hitachi Systems Development Lab, Japan
Klaus-Dieter Schewe	Massey University, New Zealand
Marten Schönherr	Technische Universität Berlin, Germany
Douglas C. Schmidt	Vanderbilt University, USA
Alan P. Sexton	University of Birmingham, UK
Marcin Sikorski	Gdansk University of Technology, Poland
Dennis Smith	Carnegie Mellon University, USA
Il-Yeol Song	Drexel University, USA
Bernhard Thalheim	Christian-Albrechts-Universität Kiel, Germany
Dan Toft	IBM Rochester, USA
Can Türker	ETH Zürich, Switzerland
Mark van den Brand	Technical University of Eindhoven, Netherlands
Hans Vangheluwe	McGill University, Canada
Marlon E. Vieira	Siemens Corporate Research, USA
Gerd Wagner	Universität Cottbus, Germany
Rajeev Wankar	University of Hyderabad, India
Rainer Weinreich	Johannes Kepler Universität Linz, Austria
Yun Yang	Swinburne University of Technology, Australia
Byunggu Yu	University of Wyoming, USA
Yanchun Zhang	Victoria University, Australia

Table of Contents

Engineering Database Component Ware

Bernhard Thalheim

Christian Albrechts University Kiel, Department of Computer Science, 24098 Kiel, Germany
thalheim@is.informatik.uni-kiel.de

Abstract. Large database applications often have a very complex structuring that complicate maintenance, extension, querying, programming. Due to this complexity systems become unmaintenable. We observe, however, that large database applications often use an implicit structuring into connected components. We propose to initially use this internal structuring for application development. The application architecture is based on database components. Database components can be composed to an application system. This paper shows how components may be developed, composed and applied.

1   Towards Information Systems Engineering

Component-Based Application Engineering
Software engineering is still based on *programming in the small* although a number of approaches has been proposed for *programming in the large*. Programming in the large uses strategies for programming, is based on architectures, and constructs software from components which collaborate, are embedded into each other, or are integrated for formation of new systems. Programming constructs are then pattern or high-level programming units and languages.

The next generation of programming observed nowadays is *programming in the world* within a collaboration of programmers and systems. It uses advanced scripting languages such as Groovy with dynamic integration of components into other components, standardisation of components with guarantees of service qualities, collaboration of components with communication, coordination and cooperation features, distribution of workload, and virtual communities. Therefore, component engineering will also form the kernel engineering technique for programming in the world. The next generation of software engineering envisioned is currently called as *programming by composition* or construction. In this case components also form the kernel technology for software and hardware.

Software development is mainly based on stepwise development from scratch. Software reuse has been considered but never reached the maturity for application engineering. Database development is also mainly *development in the small*. Schemes are developed step by step, extended type by type, and normalized locally type by type. Views are still defined type by type although more complex schemata can be easily defined by extended ER schemata [Tha00].

Therefore, database engineering must still be considered as *handicraft* work which require the skills of an *artisan*. Engineering in other disciplines has already gained the maturity for industrial development and application.

D. Draheim and G. Weber (Eds.): TEAA 2006, LNCS 4473, pp. 1–15, 2007.
© Springer-Verlag Berlin Heidelberg 2007

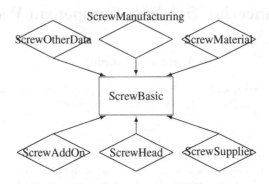

Fig. 1. HERM Representation of the Star Type *Screw*

Engineering applications have been based on the simple *separation principle*: *Separation of elements which are stable from those elements which are not*. This separation allows *standardization* and *simple integration*. An example is the specification of screws as displayed in Figure 1[1]. Screws have a standardized representation: basic data, data on the material, data on the manufacturing, data on specific properties such as head, etc.

Complex Applications Result in Large Schemata

Monographs and database course books usually base explanations on small or 'toy' examples. Reality is, however, completely different. Database schemata tend to be large, not surveyable, incomprehensible and partially inconsistent due to application, the database development life cycle and due to the number of team members involved at different time intervals. Thus, consistent management of the database schema might become a nightmare and may lead to legacy problems. The size of the schemata may be very large.

It is a common observation that large database schemata are error-prone, are difficult to maintain and to extend and are not surveyable. Moreover, development of retrieval and operation facilities requires highest professional skills in abstraction, memorization and programming. Such schemata reach sizes of more than 1000 attribute, entity and relationship types. Since they are not comprehensible any change to the schema is performed by extending the schema and thus making it even more complex. Database designers and programmers are not able to capture the schema.

Application schemata could be simpler only to a certain extent if software engineering approaches are applied. The repetition and redundancy in schemata is also caused by

- different usage of similar types of the schema,
- minor and small differences of the types structure in application views, and
- semantic differences of variants of types.

Therefore, we need approaches which allow to reason on repeating structures inside schemata, on semantic differences and differences in usage of objects.

---

[1] We use the extended ER model [Tha00] that allows to display subtypes on the basis of unary relationship types and thus simplifies representation.

Large schemata also suffer from the *deficiency of variation detection: The same or similar content is often repeated in a schema without noticing it.*

Techniques to Decrease Complexity in Applications

Large database schemata can be drastically simplified if techniques of *modular modelling* such as *modular design by units* [Tha00] are used. It is an abstraction technique based on principles of hiding and encapsulation. Design by units allows to consider parts of the schema in a separate fashion. The parts are connected via types which function similar to bridges.

Data warehousing and user views are often based on *snowflake or star schemata*. The intuition behind such schemata is often hidden. Star and snowflake schemata are easier to understand, to query, to survey and to maintain. At the same time, these structures are of high redundancy and restricted modelling power. For instance, the central type in a star or snowflake schema is a relationship type which has attributes that use only numerical types. We may wonder, however, why we need to apply these restrictions and why we should not use this approach in general.

Co-design [Tha00] of database applications aims in consistent development of all facets of database applications: structuring of the database by schema types and static integrity constraints, behavior modelling by specification of functionality and dynamic integrity constraints and interactivity modelling by assigning views to activities of actors in the corresponding dialogue steps. Co-design, thus, is based on the specification of the the database schema, functions, views and dialogue steps. At the same time, various abstraction layers are separated such as the conceptual layer, requirements acquisition layer and implementation layer.

Software becomes surveyable, extensible and maintainable if a clear separation of concerns and application parts is applied. In this case, a skeleton of the application structure is developed. This skeleton separates parts or services. Parts are connected through interfaces. Based on this *architecture*, an application can be developed part by part.

We *combine* modularity, star structuring, co-design, and architecture development to a novel framework based on components. Such combination seems to be not feasible. We discover, however, that we may integrate all these approaches by using a component-based approach. This skeleton can be refined during evolution of the schema. Then, each component is developed step by step. Structuring in component-based co-design is based on two constructs:

Components: Components are the main building blocks. They are used for structuring of the main data. The association among components is based on 'connector' types (called hinge or bridge types) that enable in associating the components in a variable fashion.

Skeleton-based construction: Components are assembled together by application of connector types. These connector types are usually relationship types.

Goals of the Paper

The paper surveys our approach [Tha02, Tha03a, Tha05] for *systematic development of large database schemata* and applies it for database construction based on components and for collaborating component suites. The paper is based on [Fey03, FT02, ST06a,

ST04]. We introduce first the concept of database components and then discuss engineering of database applications based on components.

2 Database Components and Construction of Schemes

Database Schemes in a Nutshell
We use the extended ER model for representation of structuring and behavior generalizing the approach of [PBGG89]. The extended ER model (HERM) [Tha00] has a generic algebra and logic, i.e., the algebra of derivable operations and the fragment of (hierarchical) predicate logic may be derived from the HERM algebra whenever the structure of the database is given.

A database type $\mathfrak{S} = (S, O, \Sigma)$ is given by

- a structure S defined by a type expression defined over the set of basic types B, a set of labels L and the constructors product (tuple), set and bag, i.e. an expression defined by the recursive type equality
  $t = B \,|\, t \times ... \times t \,|\, \{t\} \,|\, [t] \,|\, l : t$,
- a set of operations defined in the ER algebra and limited to S, and
- a set of (static and dynamic) integrity constraints defined in the hierarchical predicate logic with the base predicate P_S.

Objects of the database type $\mathfrak{S}^C$ are S-structured. Classes $\mathfrak{S}^C$ are sets of objects for which the set of static integrity constraints is valid.

Operations can be classified into "retrieval" operations enabling in generating values from the class $\mathfrak{S}^C$ and "modification" operations allowing to change the objects in the class $\mathfrak{S}^C$ if static and dynamic integrity constraints are not invalidated.

A database schema $\mathfrak{D} = (\mathfrak{S}_1, ..., \mathfrak{S}_m, \Sigma_G)$ is defined by

- a list of different database types and
- a set of global integrity constraints.

The HERM algebra can be used to define (parameterized) views $\mathfrak{V} = (V, O_V)$ on a schema $\mathfrak{D}$ via

- an (parameterized) algebraic expression V on $\mathfrak{D}$ and
- a set of (parameterized) operations of the HERM algebra applicable to V.

The view operations may be classified too into retrieval operations O_V^R and modification operations O_V^M. Based on this classification we derive an *output view* O^V of $\mathfrak{V}$ and an *input view* I^V of $\mathfrak{V}$.

In a similar way (but outside the scope of this paper) we may define transactions, interfaces, interactivity, recovery, etc.

Obviously, I^V and O^V are typed based on the type system. Data warehouse design is mainly view design [Tha00].

Database Components and Component Algebra
A database component is *database scheme that has an import and an export interface for connecting it to other components by standardized interface techniques.* Components are defined in a data warehouse setting. They consist of input elements, output

elements and have a database structuring. Components may be considered as input-output machines that are extended by the set of all states S^C of the database with a set of corresponding input views I^V and a set of corresponding output views O^V. Input and output of components is based on channels K. The structuring is specified by S_K. The structuring of channels is described by the function $type : C \rightarrow V$ for the view schemata V. Views are used for collaboration of components with the environment via data exchange. In general, the input and output sets may be considered as abstract words from M^* or as words on the database structuring.

A **database component** $\mathcal{K} = (S_K, I_K^V, O_K^V, S_K^C, \Delta_K)$ is specified by

$\bigl(\text{static}\bigr)$ schema S_K describing the database schema of $\mathcal{K}$,

syntactic interface providing names (structures, functions) with parameters and database structure for S_K^C and I_K^V, O_K^V ,

behavior relating the I^V, O^V (view) channels
$$\Delta_K : (S_K^C \times (I_K^V \rightarrow M^*)) \rightarrow \mathcal{P}(S_K^C \times (O_K^V \rightarrow M^*)).$$

Components can be associated to each other. The association is restricted to domain-compatible input or output schemata which are free of name conflicts.

Components $\mathcal{K}_1 = (S_1, I_1^V, O_1^V, S_1^C, \Delta_1)$ and $\mathcal{K}_2 = (S_2, I_2^V, O_2^V, S_2^C, \Delta_2)$ are free of name conflicts if the set of attribute, entity and relationship type names are disjoint.

Channels C_1 and C_2 of components $\mathcal{K}_1 = (S_1, I_1^V, O_1^V, S_1^C, \Delta_1)$ and $\mathcal{K}_2 = (S_2, I_2^V, O_2^V, S_2^C, \Delta_2)$ are called *domain-compatible* if $dom(type(C_1)) = dom(type(C_2))$.

An output O_1^V of the component $\mathcal{K}_1$ is *domain-compatible* with an input I_2^V of the component $\mathcal{K}_2$ if $dom(type(O_1^V)) \subseteq dom(type(I_2^V))$

Component operations such as merge, fork, transmission are definable via application of **superposition operations** [Kud82, Mal70]: Identification of channels, permutation of channels, renaming of channels, introduction of fictitious channels, and parallel composition with feedback displayed in Figure 2.

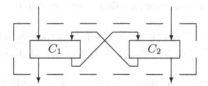

Fig. 2. The Composition of Database Components

Thus, a **component schema** is usually characterized by a kernel entity type used for storing basic data, by a number of dimensions that are usually based on subtypes of the entity type which are used for additional properties. These additional properties are clustered according to their occurrence for the things under consideration. Typically, the component schema uses four dimensions: subtypes, additional characterization, versions and meta-characterizations.

The star schema is the main component schema used for construction.

A **star schema** for a database type C_0 is defined by
- the (full) (HERM) schema $S = (C_0, C_1, ..., C_n)$ covering all types on which C_0 has been defined,
- the subset of *strong types* $C_1, ..., C_k$ forming a set of keys $K_1, ..., K_s$ for C_0, i.e., $\cup_{i=1}^{s} K_i = \{C_1, ..., C_k\}$ and $K_i \rightarrow C_0$, $C_0 \rightarrow K_i$ for $1 \leq i \leq s$ and $card(C_0, C_i) = (1, n)$ for $(1 \leq i \leq k)$.
- the extension types $C_{k+1}, ..., C_m$ satisfying the (general) cardinality constraint $card(C_0, C_j) = (0, 1)$ for $((k + 1) \leq i \leq n)$.

The extension types may form their own $(0, 1)$ specialization tree (hierarchical inclusion dependency set). The cardinality constraints for extension types are partial functional dependencies.

There are various variants for **representation** of a star schemata:

- Representation based on an entity type with attributes $C_1, ..., C_k$ and $C_{k+1}, ..., C_l$ and specialisations forming a specialization tree $C_{l+1}, ..., C_n$.
- Representation based on a relationship type C_0 with components $C_1, ..., C_k$, with attributes $C_{k+1}, ..., C_l$ and specialisations forming a specialization tree $C_{l+1}, ..., C_n$. In this case, C_0 is a *pivot element* [BP00] in the schema.
- Representation by be based on a hybrid form combining the two above.

Star schemata may occur in various variants within the same conceptual schema. Therefore, we need variants of the same schema for integration into the schema. We distinguish the following variants:

Integration and representation variants: For representation and for integration we can define views on the star type schema with the restriction of invariance of identifiability through one of its keys. Views define 'context' conditions for usage of elements of the star schema.

Versions: Objects defined on the star schema may be a replaced later by objects that display the actual use, e.g., *Documents* are obtained and stored in the *Archive*.

Variants replacing the entire type another through renaming or substitution of elements.

History variants: Temporality can be explicitly recorded by adding a history dimension, i.e., for recording of instantiation, run, usage at present or in the past, and archiving.

Lifespan variants of objects and their properties may be explicitly stored. The lifespan of products in the acquisition process can be based on the *Product-Quote-Request-Response-Requisition-Order-InventoryItem-StoredItem* cycle displayed in Figure 6

Meta-Characterization of Components, Units, and Associations

Utilization information is often only kept in log files. Log files are inappropriate if the utilization or historic information must be kept after the data have been changed. Database applications are often keeping track of utilization information based on archives. The same observation can be made for schema evolution. We observed that database schemata change already within the first year of database system exploitation. In this case, the schema information must be kept as well.

The skeleton information is kept by a meta-characterization information that allows to keep track on the purpose and the usage of the components, units, and associations. Meta-characterization can be specified on the basis of dockets [SS99] that provide information. The following frames follows the co-design approach [Tha00] with the integrated design of structuring, functionality, interactivity and context. The frame is structured into general information provided by the header, application characterization, the content of the unit and *documentation* of the implementation.

- on the content (*abstracts* or *summaries*),
- on the delivery instruction,
- on the parameters of functions for treatment of the unit (opening with(out) zooming, breath, size, activation modus for multimedia components etc.)
- on the tight association to other units (versions, releases etc.),
- on the meta-information such as resources, restriction, copyright, roles, distribution policy etc.
- on the content providers, content reviewers and review evaluators with quality control policies,
- on applicable workflows and the current status of completion and
- on the log information that enable in tracing the object's life cycle.

Dockets can be extended to general descriptions of the utilization. The following definition frame is appropriate which classifies meta-information into mandatory, good practice, optional and useful information.

3   Non-invasive Database Component Composition

Construction Requirements
Component construction is based on a general component architecture or a skeleton. Each component is developed in separate. The advantage of the strict separation is an increase of modularisation, parameterisability and conformance to standards.

We derive now a none-invasive construction approach which does not change components used for construction. Due to this restriction we gain a number of properties such as *adaptivity*, *seemless gluing*, *extensibility*, *aspect separation*, *scalability*, and *metamodelling* and *abstraction*.

Components and Harnesses
The construction is based on harnesses and the application skeleton. The skeleton is a special form of a meta-schema architecture. It consists of a set of components and a set of harnesses for superposition operations. Harnesses are similar to wiring harnesses used in electrotechnics. A harness consists of a set of input-output channels that can be used to combine wrapped components.

Given a sets of components $\mathfrak{K} = \{\mathcal{K}_1, ..., \mathcal{K}_m\}$ and labels $\mathfrak{L} = \{L_1, ..., L_n\}$ with $n \geq m$. Given furthermore a total function $\tau : \mathfrak{L} \rightarrow \mathfrak{K}$ used for assigning roles to components in harnesses. The triple $(\mathfrak{K}, \mathfrak{L}, \tau)$ is called harness skeleton $\mathfrak{H}$. The arity of the skeleton is n.

The skeleton is graphically represented by doubly rounded boxes. Components are graphically represented by rounded boxes. The construction may lead to complex components called *units*.

The example in Figure 3 has been used in one of our projects. Parliamentarians and inhabitants are combined into a component *Users*. We may use a large variety of positions. A user may use a certain service through some devices. Appointments are based on the usage of services. Tools vary depending on services and on equipment. The final schema contains more than 2.500 attribute, entity, cluster and relationship types. The skeleton of the application is rather simple.

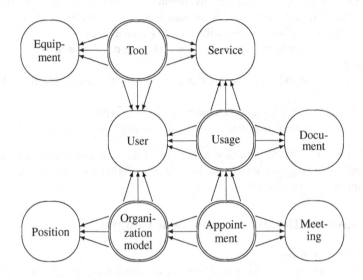

Fig. 3. Skeleton of a Schema for *e-Government Service* Applications

Harness Filters

Components may be associated in a variety of ways. In the application in Figure 3 the usage of services depends on the properties of parties, the tools they may use, and the services provided. Services, parties, and tools have their own dimensionality. If we use the classical approach to schema development each subtype may cause the introduction of a new usage type. The schema explodes due to the introduction of a large variety of usage type. To overcome this difficulty we introduce filters.

Given component schemata of an n-ary harness skeleton. A filter of an n-ary harness is an n-ary relation defined of the multi-dimensional structure of the components, i.e. on the views defined for the components.

Filters may be represented either graphically or in a tabular form. In our example, we obtain the following filter. Components are already presented in Figure 3. We develop a number of services which might be used depending on the role, rights, and positions of the users. For instance, the parliamentarian is interested in search of related documents in the role of an inhabitant and in search of related meetings.

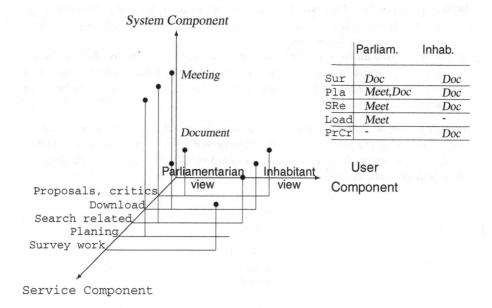

The table shown in the figure:

	Parliam.	Inhab.
Sur	*Doc*	*Doc*
Pla	*Meet,Doc*	*Doc*
SRe	*Meet*	*Doc*
Load	*Meet*	-
PrCr	-	*Doc*

The implementation of filters is rather straightforward. Each harness has a filter. Since views are defined together with their identification mechanism, an n-ary harness may be represented by an $(n+1)$-ary relationship type associating the components with their roles and extended by the filter.

A **harness** consists of the harness skeleton $\mathfrak{H} = (\mathfrak{K}, \mathfrak{L}, \tau)$ and the harness filter $\mathfrak{F} = \{(L_i, \mathcal{V}^{L_i}) \mid 1 \leq i \leq n, L_i \in \mathfrak{L}, \mathcal{V}^{L_i} \subseteq \mathcal{V}_{\tau(L_i)}\}$ for a set of wrapped components $(\mathcal{K}_i, \mathcal{V}_i)$.

Operators Used For Non-Invasive Schema Construction

In [Tha03b] a number of composition operators for construction of entity and relationship types has been introduced: constructor-based composition, bulk composition, lifespan composition (architecture-based composition, evolution composition, circulation composition, incremental composition, network composition, loop composition), and context composition.

We generalize now these composition operators to component-based schema construction.

Constructor harnesses are based on composition operations such as *product*, *nest*, *disjoint union*, *difference* and *set* operators.

Bulk harnesses allow to bound components, types or classes which share the same skeleton. Two harness skeletons $\mathfrak{H}_1 = (\mathfrak{K}_1, \mathfrak{L}_1 \tau_1)$ and $\mathfrak{H}_2 = (\mathfrak{K}_2, \mathfrak{L}_2 \tau_2)$ are called unifiable if they are defined over the same set of components, $|\mathfrak{L}_1| = |\mathfrak{L}_1| = n$, and there exists a permutation ρ on $\{1, ..., n\}$ such that $\mathcal{K}_{\tau_1(i)} = \mathcal{K}_{\tau_2(\rho(i))}$. The bulk harness of unifiable harnesses $\mathfrak{H}_1, ..., \mathfrak{H}_p$ is constructed by renaming the labels L_j of each harness $\mathfrak{H}_i$ to $L_{i,j}$ and combining the label functions τ_i.

Application-separating harnesses: An enterprize is usually split into departments or
units which run their own applications and use their own data. Sharing of data is
provided by specific harnesses.

Distribution-based harnesses: Data, functions and control may be distributed. The exchange is provided through specific combinations which might either be based on
exchange components that are connected to the sites by harnesses or be based on
combination harnesses.

Application-separation-based harnesses have been widely used for complex structuring. The architecture of SAP R/3 often has been displayed in the form of a waffle.
For this reason, we prefer to call this composition *waffle composition* or architecture
composition displayed in Figure 4.

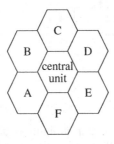

Fig. 4. The Waffle Architecture Composition

An Application of Component Composition

A typical lifespan construction is the *Order* chain displayed in Figure 6. We discover a
chain in the ordering and trading process: *Quote, Request, Response, Requisition, Order, Delivery, Billing, Payment.* Within this chain, parameters such as people responsible in certain stages are inherited through the components. They are included into the
type for the purpose of simpler maintenance. They cannot be changed within the type
inheriting the component. Thus, we use an extended inheritance of structuring beyond
the inheritance of identification.

At the same time, this schema can be constructed on the basis of components. We
may distinguish only four basic parts. Parties are either organisations or people. Products have a number of properties that are independent on parties. The two components
are associated within the ordering and trading process. The parties may play different roles within this process. The parties act based on these roles. So, the component
schema is given in Figure 5.

The roles of parties in the ordering and trading process can be unfolded. We observe a
role of a supplier, of a requestor, of a responding party, of a requisition party and finally
the role of the orderer. At the same time, the final order has a history or a lifespan.
We may apply the lifespan constructor as well. The application can be either based on
collaborating components are can be condensed to the schema given in Figure 6. This
schema combines components and unfolds roles and expands the ordering and trading
activities. We notice that this schema is not necessarily the solution for the ordering and

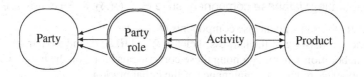

Fig. 5. Component Schema for Product Acquisition Activities

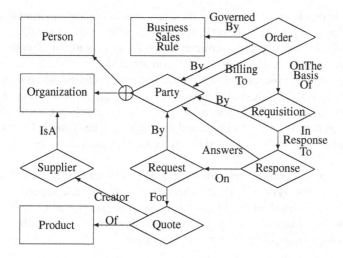

Fig. 6. The Database Schema of the Ordering and Trading Process After Composition

trading process. We may use the components instead and explicitly model component collaboration. In this case the components may stay non-integrated.

4   Collaborating Database Component Suites

Services Provided By Components For Loosely Coupled Suites
A service consists of a wrapped component $(\mathcal{K}_i, \mathcal{V}_i)$, the competencies $\Sigma_{(\mathcal{K}_i, \mathcal{V}_i)}$ provided and properties $\Psi_{(\mathcal{K}_i, \mathcal{V}_i)}$ guaranteeing service quality. Wrapped components offer their own data and functions through their views. The *competence of a service* manifests itself in the set of tasks $\mathcal{T}$ that may be performed and in the guarantees for their quality.

Database Component Collaboration
Instead of expanding and unfolding the component schema in Figure 5 we may follow a different paradigm. The four basic parts are loosely associated by a collaboration, are supported by component databases and communicate for task resolution. This approach has already been tried for distributed databases. Our approach is far more general and provides a satisfying solution.

A collaborating database component suite $\mathfrak{S} = (\mathfrak{K}, \mathfrak{H}, \mathfrak{F}, \Sigma)$ consists of

- an set $\mathfrak{K}$ of wrapped database components $(\mathcal{K}_i, \mathcal{V}_i)$
- a harness consisting of the harness skeleton $\mathfrak{H} = (\mathfrak{K}, \mathfrak{L}, \tau)$ and the harness filter $\mathfrak{F}$,
- an collaboration schema $\mathfrak{F}$ among these components based on the harness, and
- obligations Σ requiring maintenance of the collaboration.

The *collaboration schema* explicitly models collaboration among components. We distinguish three basic processes of component collaboration:

Communication is defined via exchange of messages and information or simply defined via services and protocols [Kön03]. It depends on the choice of media, transmission modes, meta-information, conversation structure and paths, and on the restriction policy. Communication must be based on harnesses.

Coordination is specified via management of components, their activities and resources. It rules collaboration. The specification is based on the pre-/post-articulation of tasks and on the description management of tasks, objects, and time. Coordination may be based on loosely or tightly integrated activities, may be enabled, forced, or blocked. Coordination is often specified through contracts and refines coordination policies.

Cooperation is the production of work products taking place on a shared space. It can be considered as the workflow or life case perspective. We may use a specification based on storyboard-based interaction that is mapped to (generic and structured) workflows. The information exchange is based on component services [ST06a] for production, manipulation, organization of contributions.

This understanding has become now a folklore model for collaboration but has not yet been defined in an explicit form. We use the separation of concern for the specification of component collaboration.

Collaboration obligations are specified through the collaboration style and the collaboration pattern.

The *collaboration style* is based on four components describing

supporting programs of the connected component including collaboration management;

data access pattern for data *release* through the net, e.g., broadcast or P2P, for *sharing* of resources either based on transaction, consensus, and recovery models or based on replication with fault management, and for *remote access* including scheduling of access;

the style of collaboration on the basis of component models which restrict possible communication;

and the coordination workflows describing the interplay among parties, discourse types, name space mappings, and rules for collaboration.

Collaboration pattern generalize protocols and their specification [Kön03]. They include the description of components, their responsibilities, roles and rights. We know a number of collaboration pattern supporting *access and configuration* (wrapper, facade, component configuration, interceptor, extension interface), *event processing* (reactor, proactor, asynchronous completion token, accept connector), *synchronization* (scoped locking, strategized locking, thread-safe interface, double-checked locking optimization) and *parallel execution* (active object, monitor object, half-sync/half-async, leader/followers, thread-specific storage).

Exchange frames combine the collaboration schema with the collaboration obligations. The collaboration schema can be considered to be an exchange architecture that may also include the workplace of the client using the component suite.

Supporting Collaboration Schemata By Service Managers

The abstraction layer model [Tha00, ST06b] distinguishes between the application domain description, the requirements prescription, the system specification, and the logical or physical coding. The specification layer typically uses schemata for specification. These schemata may be mapped to logical codings. The mapping of services to logical database components is already given by classical database textbooks. We map collaboration schemata to service managers. This mapping provides also a framework for characterisation of competencies and quality.

The *service manager* $\mathcal{M}an$ supports functionality and quality of services and manages sets of wrapped components. The manager supports a number of features for collaboration. The architecture of the services manager follow the separation of concern into communication, coordination, and cooperation. We may thus envision the architecture in Figure 7.

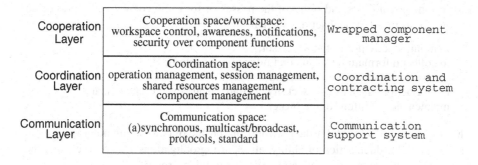

Cooperation Layer	Cooperation space/workspace: workspace control, awareness, notifications, security over component functions	Wrapped component manager
Coordination Layer	Coordination space: operation management, session management, shared resources management, component management	Coordination and contracting system
Communication Layer	Communication space: (a)synchronous, multicast/broadcast, protocols, standard	Communication support system

Fig. 7. Layers of a services manager for typical collaborating components

Collaborating services are defined by the quadruple $\mathcal{S} = (\mathfrak{S}, \mathcal{M}an, \Sigma_\mathcal{S}, \Psi_\mathcal{S})$ describing   (Collaborating Suite, Service Manager, Competence, Characteristics). The competence is derived from the competence of the services. The quality of collaborating services may also be derived from the quality properties of components in the suite based on the properties of the harnesses, their collaboration schema, and the corresponding obligations. Typically, quality heavily depends on the suite properties. For instance, reliability of a suite may be less than the reliability of its components.

Concluding by Demonstrating the Potential of Privacy Supporting Suites

Let us show the potential of loosely coupled database component suites for privacy workbenchs. Privacy research is becoming the "poor cousin" among the mainstream research. Novel applications such as Web2.0 have created a new rush towards social networking and collaborative applications. This enables new possibilities, but also is a threat to users' privacy and data. On the surface, many people seem to like giving away their data to others in exchange for building communities or like to get bribes from companies in exchange of privacy. A number of hidden privacy implications of some Web2.0 and Identity2.0 services, standards and applications can be observed here. At the same time, it is often stated that there is no way to properly preserve privacy.

We show the potential of collaborating databases based on the infon model of [AFFT05]. An infon is a discrete item of information of an individual and may be parametric. The *parameters* are objects, and the so-called *anchors* assign these objects such as agents to parameters.

We may distinguish four relationships between infons and individuals (people), institutions, agencies, or companies: An infon may be possessed by an individual, institution, agency, or company. For example, an individual may possess private information of another individual or, a company may have in its database, private information of someone. Individuals know that an infon is in possession of somebody else. Infons may belong to individuals. Finally, an infon is owned by an individual. The ownership is the basis for the specification of privacy.

The **owner sovereignty principle** restrains the right or sovereignty of people over their owned infons. A *policy* supporting the owner sovereignty principle restrains the possessor in the role of 'content and topic observer' and preserves the owner in the role of 'informed owner' and 'refresher'. The contract between owner and possessor restricts the possibilities and rights of the possessor for using content and topics on an ongoing basis by additional actions such as

- to monitor activities of the possessor,
- to collect information (about conditions of possession),
- to give a warning to the owner, and
- to take actions such as use, security, welfare, accuracy, correctness, and maintenance of infons to the owner.

The collaboration is *faithful* if the portfolio and profile of contracting possessor do not include any forbidden action or ability, all reporting obligations are observed, and the proprietor is able to observe obligations applied to the possessor.

The private database is called *information wallet* if it is a component service with the following additional function enhancements for owners o, possessors p, infons i, infon requests r_i, time stamps t, delivered infon streams identifiers s_i, public keys $puk(r_i, o, p, t)$ for p, private keys $prik(i, o, p, t)$ for o, records of delivered infons by the owner $store(o, i, p, s_i)$, and encoding and decoding relations $encrypt(i, prik, s_i)$, $decrypt(p, r_i, s_i, puk, t)$ extended by steganographic watermarking $mark(i, o, p)$ for infons:

- $satisfy(request(r_i, o, p, t)) \Rightarrow$
  $\quad encrypt(i, prik(i, o, p, t), s_i)) \wedge deliver(p, o, s_i)) \wedge store(o, i, p, s_i))$
- $decrypt(p, r_i, s_i, puk(s_i, o, p, t), t') \Rightarrow$
  $\quad inform(o, Act(p, s_i, decrypt), t') \wedge mark(i, o, p)$
- $read(p, mark(i, o, p), t') \Rightarrow inform(o, Act(p, s_i, read), t')$
- $send(p, mark(i, o, p), p', t') \Rightarrow inform(o, Act(p, s_i, send(p, p')), t') \wedge$
  $\quad \neg send(p, mark(i, o, p), p', t') \wedge send(p, r_i, p', t')$

$$- \; satisfy(request(puk(s_i, o, p, t), o, p, t')) \Rightarrow$$
$$deliver(p, o, puk(s_i, o, p, t)) \wedge store(o, i, p, puk(s_i, o, p, t)) \, .$$

We assume that watermarked infons cannot be changed by anybody. We can show now that information wallets preserve the owner sovereignty principle.

References

[AFFT05]   Al-Fedaghi, S.S., Fiedler, G., Thalheim, B.: Privacy enhanced information systems. In: Proc. EJC'05. Informaton Modelling and Knowledge Bases, Tallinn. Series Frontiers in Arificial Intelligence, vol. XVII, IOS Press, Amsterdam (2005)

[BP00]   Biskup, J., Polle, T.: Decomposition of database classes under path functional dependencies and onto contraints. In: Schewe, K.-D., Thalheim, B. (eds.) FoIKS 2000. LNCS, vol. 1762, pp. 31–49. Springer, Heidelberg (2000)

[Fey03]   Feyer, T.: A Component-Based Approach to Human-Computer Interaction - Specification, Composition, and Application to Information Services. PhD thesis, BTU Cottbus, Computer Science Institute, Cottbus (Dezember 2003)

[FT02]   Feyer, T., Thalheim, B.: Many-dimensional schema modeling. In: Manolopoulos, Y., Návrat, P. (eds.) ADBIS 2002. LNCS, vol. 2435, pp. 305–318. Springer, Heidelberg (2002)

[Kön03]   König, H.: Protocol Engineering: Prinzip, Beschreibung und Entwicklung von Kommunikationsprotokollen. Teubner, Stuttgart (2003)

[Kud82]   Kudrjavcev, V.B.: Functional systems (in Russian). Moscov Lomonossov University Press, Moscow (1982)

[Mal70]   Malzew, A.I.: Algebraic systems. Nauka, Moscow (1970)

[PBGG89]   Paredaens, J., De Bra, P., Gyssens, M., Van Gucht, D.: The structure of the relational database model. Springer, Heidelberg (1989)

[SS99]   Schmidt, J.W., Schering, H.-W.: Dockets: a model for adding vaulue to content. In: Akoka, J., Bouzeghoub, M., Comyn-Wattiau, I., Métais, E. (eds.) ER 1999. LNCS, vol. 1728, pp. 248–262. Springer, Heidelberg (1999)

[ST04]   Schmidt, P., Thalheim, B.: Component-based modeling of huge databases. In: Benczúr, A.A., Demetrovics, J., Gottlob, G. (eds.) ADBIS 2004. LNCS, vol. 3255, pp. 113–128. Springer, Heidelberg (2004)

[ST06a]   Schewe, K.-D., Thalheim, B.: Component-driven engineering of database applications. In: APCCM'06, vol. CRPIT 49, pp. 105–114 (2006)

[ST06b]   Schewe, K.-D., Thalheim, B.: Usage-based storyboarding for web information systems. Technical Report 2006-13, Christian Albrechts University Kiel, Institute of Computer Science and Applied Mathematics, Kiel (2006)

[Tha00]   Thalheim, B.: Entity-relationship modeling – Foundations of database technology. Springer, Heidelberg (2000)

[Tha02]   Thalheim, B.: Component construction of database schemes. In: Spaccapietra, S., March, S.T., Kambayashi, Y. (eds.) ER 2002. LNCS, vol. 2503, pp. 20–34. Springer, Heidelberg (2002)

[Tha03a]   Thalheim, B.: Database component ware. ADC'2003, Australian Computer Science Communications 25(2), 13–26 (2003)

[Tha03b]   Thalheim, B.: Database component ware. Proc. ADC'2003, Journal on Research and Practice in Information Technology 17, 1–13 (2003)

[Tha05]   Thalheim, B.: Component development and construction for database design. Data and Knowledge Engineering 54, 77–95 (2005)

An Architecture for Integrating Heterogeneous University Applications That Supports Monitoring

Dhiah el Diehn I. Abou-Tair and Jörg Niere

Software Engineering Group
University of Siegen
aboutair@informatik.uni-siegen.de
joerg.niere@uni-siegen.de

Abstract. Within a company or a university different organization units need their own information system to perform their business tasks. There is also a massive need of integration in order to optimize the processes. Integration usually means to wrap the applications or couple them via technologies such as CORBA. Especially when applications are coupled, it is hard work to get an overview over the whole system or to establish common data-consistency rules or to monitor privacy issues. In this paper we present an approach in which we model the data-models of the independent applications and connect them by pre-defined integration connections. Upon our common business model we are able to establish data-consistency rules or monitor, e.g., privacy issues or data-flow. Therefore, our solution presents a smart integration without loosing the application's independence.

1 Introduction

During the last years the business processes within German universities have raised dramatically. On the one hand the change from the 'diploma' to a consecutive 'bachelor/master' program challenges administrative processes. On the other hand the universities legal form has changed and universities got a so-called global budget. Due to the newly gained autonomy of universities, the government demands a huge amount of reports, e.g. acquired third party projects, number of students, lectures, graduates and their relations, etc. In addition to the newly gained responsibilities, a university has and in the future will also have a number of traditional services and tasks such as, creation of the program of lectures, assigning lecturers and rooms, maintaining a library and a refectory, staff management, etc.

Usually German universities are structured in organization units, like other universities. The structure differs from university to university, but there are basic common structures. Usually a university has a library, a computer center, an overall administration, etc., which are independent from the scientific organization such as institutes, faculties and research groups. Research groups

D. Draheim and G. Weber (Eds.): TEAA 2006, LNCS 4473, pp. 16–24, 2007.

maintain specific laboratories for their research area, whereas the computer center maintains common labs. Research groups provide lectures, seminars, project groups, practical trainings, and they are responsible for the organization of exams corresponding to the offered lectures. The coordination of exams in a certain course of study is the duty of the student registration office organizationally located in a faculty or institute, which usually consists of a number of research groups.

Nearly each organization unit in a university maintains its own information system. The computer center manages logins for their laboratories or MAC-addresses to access the public WLAN net. Each student, who wants to lend out a book from the library needs a certain access to the library's information system, which also manages the states of the books. Sometimes information systems store data redundantly, e.g. exam results, which exist in the faculty located office's information system and in the information system of certain research groups. In principle, collecting information, which is stored locally in one information system does not require much effort, but collecting information, spread over a number of different information systems means much effort usually because the identity in the different systems is not common. An example of such a problematic task is the government report each year or half a year.

In this paper we present the current business and the existing heterogeneous information systems at the University of Siegen in more detail. The business model is transferable to other universities so we are able to derive requirements for the integration of different information systems at universities in general. Afterwards we assess the performance of currently existing systems and present current research activities in this area. Our solution is currently under development and uses an intelligent integration channel. The architecture of the system is presented in section 4. Finally we figure out current and future work.

2 Today's Universities Business and IT-System Requirements

This section describes the organizational structure and the current IT situation at the University of Siegen more detailed and we will derive requirements for an integration of the different used information systems.

2.1 Heterogeneous Information Systems

Within the university the different organization units use different information systems. Some units use modules of the the current market leader HIS-GX-Software. For example the university administration as well as the student registration office in the computer science department use specific modules from HIS-GX-Software. An alternative software for student registration offices is FlexNow! [1], which is used in other departments. Public information such as lectures, room, staff etc, are available via web access and underlying is a software called UnivIS (University Information System), cf. [2]. In order to input data into UnivIS, the system provides web forms in contrast to the HIS modules, which provides a platform dependent client to input and export data. The university library uses the Aleph-Software, [3], which use nearly all university libraries in the German state Northrhine-Westfalia. There also exists a central e-learning platform called Moodle [4], which comes from the CampusSource-Initiative [5]. Last but not least, each department uses its own information systems, e.g. the electrical engineering and computer science department uses a proprietary system to manage how many students take a certain lecture and to manage the room capacities and evaluation forms appropriately.

The reason for such a heterogeneous information system structure mainly results from missed investments in the past. 20 years ago most administrative processes worked with paper and pencils. Coming along with computers also the information systems have been established and especially in the beginning those systems where handmade. In addition, the university's organization structure without a leading IT department was another reason for the heterogeneous structure.

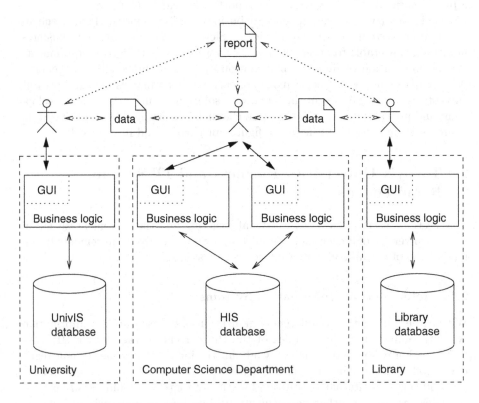

Fig. 1. Universities' heterogeneous IT-landscape example

2.2   Business Processes

Assume a lecturer wants to publish his/her a lecture announcement in the next semester. Such a task includes diverse data, e.g. the content of the lecture, the prerequisites, references etc. In this case, the lecturer has to input the lecture announcement itself into the UnivIS system, and the Moodle e-learning platform together with the references and links to other lectures or material. Hence the lecturer needs a room he/she has to input the data into the proprietary system of the department and finally the lecturer must inform the student registration office in a written form, because the system is only accessible by certain persons due to data protection laws. In addition, the lecturer will publish the announcement on his/her research groups' web pages. Concluding, the lecturer has to input the data into different isolated systems manually, if possible. This holds some problems if changes occur, e.g. the room or time schedule has changed.

Evermore, tasks such as creating of reports will be done manually. E.g. in order to generate the government report the lecturer respectively the department secretary, at first requires the data from the actual system separately and after that he/she assembles the report, manually. Unfortunately, the process to gather the data is quite extensive when we consider that every application needs own identification data, there is no standard export format for the data. Most users do this using the traditional 'copy and paste' even if some screened systems such as the HIS software do not allow it. In addition, if a lecturer wants to know if some students have done the required lectures to enter some exam, he/she must send a list of all students who wanted to attend to the examination office.

The information systems used at the University of Siegen are mostly not connected to each other and also incompatible concerning the data exchange format. The systems also provide less interfaces and are maintained by different organization units. This results in redundant data and complex business processes such as described above. E.g. a student has usually more than four different logins to different systems such as the computers in the laboratories, email account, library authentication and a login for the e-learning platform, access to certain machines, rooms, etc. The same problem occurs during other administrative processes within the university such as providing the program of lectures or the reports to the government.

Figure 1 shows the current situation of heterogeneous systems. Data exchange is done manually by the users of the individual information systems and performed only if necessary. For example, a research group, who wants to perform an exam, retrieves a list of all registrated students from the students registration office. In the preparation phase of the exam, the data will be stored in the research group's information system and a copy will be send back to the office which includes the results. In general, Information, which must be collected from more than one information system, usually means to ask the corresponding persons and assemble the data afterwards.

2.3   IT-System Requirements

Based on our own analysis we can derive the following requirements for the integration of information systems at universities:

- single sign-in systems
- distributed maintained sub-systems
- data-consistency
- no violation of data protection and privacy laws
- comfortable collection of system spread information
- flexible system extension

3   Related Work

By searching the IT-Landscape a variety of possible IT solutions are found. The middleware platforms, Enterprise Application Integration, and Web Services belong to this category.

Approaches such as the traditional middleware platforms and CORBA are heavily used for the implementation of complex distributed applications[6]. Unfortunately, for our domain such architectures are insufficient because they need knowledge of the nature of the core systems before the implementation[7]. Enterprise Application Integration technology provides a possible solution, the problem with this being that in a huge domain such as a university, it is difficult to keep an overview on the interfaces between the diverse application – $n*(n-1)/2$ interfaces where n is the number of applications. Even more, the implementation of such a solution is complex, not easy to maintain, and prone to bugs. The Service Oriented Architecture and the Web Services provide a possible solution, but in the case of our domain by using such a technology we could not trace who uses the data anymore, which is an essential requirement of the German Federal Data Protection Act (Bundesdatenschutzgesetz) (BDSG). In fact, we need a solution that integrates the diverse heterogeneous systems and monitors the data to consider the BDSG.

Approaches which are based on a mediator architecture where the diverse heterogeneous systems are unified under one big data schema are not sufficiently efficient for our domain, so that our aim of coupling the systems is not only to gain a common ground, but also to keep their independence. In other words, we want to have integration on the common layer only. Other integration architecture like the Import/Export-Schema architecture are less helpful because of the previously mentioned problem of privacy.

During the last years a number of projects have been instantiated to solve the problem of Universities' heterogeneous systems. For example the KII (Karlsruhe Integrative Information Management), which is mainly used to evaluate the excellence in teaching, cf. [8]. The IntegraTUM project [9,10] tries to integrate different isolated systems within one portal. Such huge projects carry a certain feasibility risk, which the Campus Management project at the FU Berlin has shown, cf. [11].

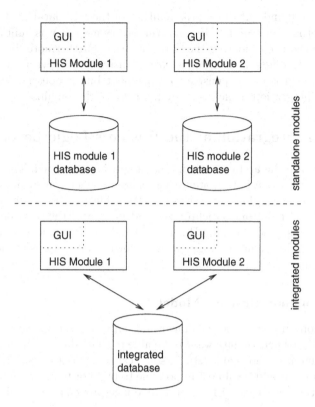

Fig. 2. Varieties between standalone and integrated mode of HIS Modules

Most software used in German universities is a product made by Hochschul-Informations-System GmbH (HIS) [12]. HIS is Germany's market leader in building Information Systems for university needs. Over the years the products of HIS where expanded to cover all administrative areas of universities. These products are divided in modules where every module covers an administrative area, e.g. student registration office. These modules use a two tier client/server architecture. On the one hand this architecture decision provides limited flexibility. On the other one, the only integration possibility works right on the database management system.

Figure 2 illustrate two of the varieties of HIS modules in a standalone mode as in integrated mode. Even though the presented approach is one of the established solutions for the integration, it has disadvantages and troubles figured out during the practical adoption of the HIS products. E.g. continuous data redundancy, data inconsistencies through switching between the modes, no encapsulation of the modules functionality, no access control to sensitive data and it does not provide a standardized integration solution between all modules either.

Moreover, we found out during the analysis of the HIS database layer that it lacks a conceptual construction. It seems that every module was built as the need for it arose without considering the data integrity. Furthermore, by developing new modules HIS offers asynchronous data transmission between them. In fact, such a mechanism is not expensive to implement but it does not provide any form of data integration, which is a key point for such domains.

4   System Integration at the Business Logic Level

Figure 3 illustrate the architecture of our integration approach. The main component of our approach is the integration channel, where all extant systems in the university domain dock to it through their business logic. In fact the integration channel monitors, synchronizes and integrates the data flow between those applications. The Common Business Model consists of the domain knowledge in form a lightweight ontology. In the following subsections we describe the Common Business Model in detail.

4.1   The Common Business Model

Our integration approach does not mean full data integration. Such integration is infeasible, "... owners of data want to be able to share data without any central authority (even at the logical level). In some cases, the data is so diverse that a mediated schema would be almost impossible to build or to agree upon, and very hard to maintain over time"[13]. Therefore, our approach consists of a Common

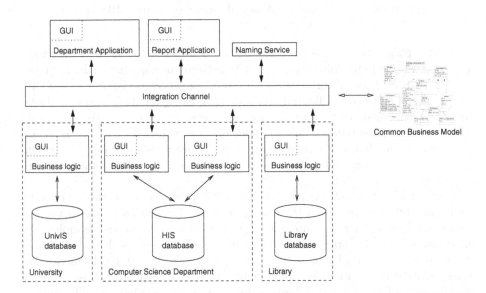

Fig. 3. Integration solution of diverse applications in the same domain

Business Model, which consists of the domain knowledge in form a lightweight ontology.

The Common Business Model is the brain of the Integration Channel. In difference compared to middleware platforms and CORBA is that the common business logic supplies the integration channel with domain knowledge about the diverse systems in the domain independently of the docking instant. On the one hand, the need of specific domain knowledge, especially about the data sources encapsulated in the domain are a key point of the development of a particular system that exploits previously accumulated domain demands. It is an essential point to obtain a well defined domain analysis, which evolves continuously within the systems. On the other hand, the Common Business Model does not provide a full integrated schema for every data source in the domain. In contrast, it just consist of the common interfaces of the diverse systems in the domain whichinput are essential for the integration process. Firstly, this guarantees that other system have only access to common data. Secondly, every system keeps it independency.

Furthermore, by docking the existing systems to our integration channel, every application holds its own graphical user interface (GUI). Thus, the existing applications will not loose their stand-alone properties. No visible changes will occur for the users whom are already using them. By doing so, we do not provide an integration solution which is limited to systems within a single company; our aim is to integrate heterogeneous systems only in their common parts to perform common tasks and to maintain their independency. Moreover, the diverse services provided by the applications will be registered in the Naming Service component to make them available for other applications.

5   Conclusion

This paper presents our novel architecture of an integration channel, that allows for integrating previously independent applications. The main and also the most different part to existing approaches is our common business model, which we call 'the brain' of the integration channel. The brain is a lightweight ontology and consists of the integrated parts of the applications docked on to the channel. In addition, we allow the users of the different applications to access them independently and our integration channel monitors and manages the common integrity. This feature makes our approach more flexible and extensible than traditional ones.

References

1. University of Bamberg, Germany: FlexNow! (2005) (last visited, January 2006), online available http://flexnow.uni-bamberg.de
2. Config Informationstechnik eG, Germany: UnivIS (University Information System) (2006) (last visited, January 2006), online available http://www.univis.de/
3. Ex Libris Ltd., Germany: Aleph Software by Ex Libris Ltd. (2006) (last visited, January 2006), online available http://www.exl.de/aleph.htm

4. Moodle, Germany: Moodle E-Learning-Plattform (2006) (last visited, January 2006), online available http://moodle.org/
5. CampusSource, Germany: CampusSource Initiative (2006) (last visited, January 2006), online available http://www.campussource.de
6. Hauck, F.J., Kapitza, R., Reiser, H.P., Schmied, A.I.: A flexible and extensible object middleware: Corba and beyond. In: SEM '05: Proceedings of the 5th international workshop on Software engineering and middleware, pp. 69–75. ACM Press, New York, NY, USA (2005)
7. Alonso, G., Casati, F., Kuno, H.: Web Services: Concepts, Architectures, Applications. Springer, Heidelberg (2004)
8. Universität Karlsruhe (TH), Germany: Karlsruhe Integrative Information Management (2006) (last visited, January 2006), online available http://www.kim.uni-karlsruhe.de
9. Technische Universität München, Germany: CIO TU München (2006) (last visited, January 2006), online available http://portal.mytum.de/cio/projekte/integratum/dokumente/index_html
10. Technische Universität München, Germany: TU München Porta (2006) (last visited January 2006), online available http://portal.mytum.de/campus/folder_listing
11. Freie Universität Berlin, Germany: Campus Management (2006) (last visited, January 2006), online available http://www.fu-berlin.de/campusmanagement/
12. HIS GmbH, Germany: HIS (2006) (last visited, January 2006), online available http://www.his.de
13. Tatarinov, I., Halevy, A.: Efficient query reformulation in peer data management systems. In: SIGMOD '04: Proceedings of the 2004 ACM SIGMOD international conference on Management of data, pp. 539–550. ACM Press, New York (2004)

On the Specification of Parameterizable Business Components

Jörg Ackermann and Klaus Turowski

Chair of Business Informatics and Systems Engineering,
University of Augsburg, Universitätsstr. 16, 86135 Augsburg, Germany
{joerg.ackermann,klaus.turowski}@wiwi.uni-augsburg.de

Abstract. To build enterprise applications out of software components promises more flexible and adaptable information systems. In practice it turns out
that the business components to be used must be themselves adaptable. Parameterization is an adaptation technique which is well-suited for adaptation on
business level. Successful reuse of business components requires techniques to
specify the components. In this paper we discuss how the parameterization
properties of a component can be included in its specification – this includes parameters themselves and their effect on the components functionality.

Keywords: Component-Based Enterprise Application Systems, Specification of
Business Components, Parameterization.

1 Introduction

Many information systems currently in use are monolithic, integrated applications that
are hard to maintain and hard to adapt to changing requirements [23]. One solution to
these problems is to follow a component-based approach where it becomes easier to
change system parts (by replacing components). Exchanging components alone, however, can not solve all variability issues because it is not efficient for frequent smaller
changes. Parameterization is a common technique that is well-suited when used for
smaller non-technical adaptations. This is the reason why we study parameterizable
business components.

A crucial prerequisite for third-party component reuse is the comprehensive and
standardized specification of software components [21]. How to include parameterization options in a component specification was earlier not addressed but is now topic
of a research project (Sect. 2). After introducing an exemplary component (Sect. 3)
we develop proposals how parameter settings and parameterization effects can be
included in the component specification and describe consequences for the specification of terminology, tasks, interfaces and behavior (Sect. 4). The paper concludes with
a discussion of related work (Sect. 5) and a summary (Sect. 6).

This paper makes the following contributions: We address the (so far unsolved) issue how to specify the parameterization properties of business components. For that
we propose how to specify parameters and parameterization tasks themselves and
additionally we show how the effects parameterization has on the components functionality can be specified. These results by itself form an important building block for

D. Draheim and G. Weber (Eds.): TEAA 2006, LNCS 4473, pp. 25–39, 2007.

the complete specification of parameterizable components. Moreover, the results are interesting for any software using parameterization (like standardized business application suites as SAP R/3) because our approach is a first step towards general specification of parameterization effects. This paper extends earlier project results [1,2] in two ways: specification of the domain perspective is novel and results for the technical perspective [2] were updated and aligned with the domain perspective.

2 Specification of Parameterizable Software Components

A comprehensive and standardized specification of software components is prerequisite for a composition methodology [21] and supports reuse of components by third parties [10]. With *specification* of a component we denote the complete, unequivocal and precise description of its external view - that is which services a component provides under which conditions [24].

Currently there exists no generally accepted and supported specification standard covering all aspects relevant to component-based software engineering (see Sect. 5). We base our work on the specification framework "Standardized Specification of Business Components" [24] which defines different specification levels (for terminology, tasks, interfaces, behavior, coordination, quality, marketing), identifies the objects to be specified and proposes for each level a specific notation language.

Adaptation is of great importance in component-based application systems because components can rarely be reused without being adapted [4]. (For a short overview on adaptation see Sect. 5.) One adaptation technique is the so called *(data-based) parameterization* [2]. It is a technique for planned adaptation where the component producer defines parameters (which influence structure and behavior of the component) and the component consumer chooses parameter settings that are suitable for his requirements. Parameter values are assumed to be data-like and non-executable – in difference to situations where programs or whole components are expected as parameter values (*program-based parameterization*). Main advantages of data-based parameterization are that adaptation can be easily performed and does not require implementation knowledge because no coding modifications are necessary. One disadvantage is that adaptation is limited to use cases foreseen by the component producer. Another disadvantage stems from the way parameterization is often used: many software systems like SAP R/3 allow complex parameterization without providing an adequate parameter specification – correlations between parameters and the components functionality become almost impossible to trace [15].

Parameter settings typically change structure and behavior of a component – that is they influence the components external view. Consequently parameterization aspects must be part of a components specification. This earlier unsolved issue is currently under investigation in our research project.

3 Exemplary Component *WarehouseManagement*

In this section we introduce an exemplary component *WarehouseManagement* that will be used throughout the rest of the paper. To be as realistic as possible design and terminology of the example were influenced by real business application products like SAP R/3. To be suitable as example, however, we simplified the component substantially – real applications are typically more complex. The business task of the component is to manage a simple warehouse complex. Fig. 1 shows the information objects belonging to the component. (More details about the role of the model in the specification and the meaning of the notations can be found in Sect. 4.)

The component *WarehouseManagement* allows to define several warehouses which might differ in their warehouse handling (e.g. fixed bin picking area or hall with high rack shelves). Each warehouse consists of different storage bins (storage places) where the goods are physically stored. An entity of *WarehouseStock* represents one unit of a material stored at a specific storage bin. The type *Material* stands for the warehouse specific properties of a material. To simplify matters we assume that each material will be stored at exactly one warehouse (real business applications might support complex warehouse determination strategies.)

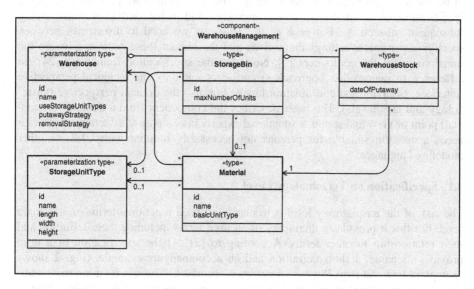

Fig. 1. Conceptual data model for component *WarehouseManagement*

The component allows parameterization by providing several parameters (data fields used for parameterization) as e.g. *putawayStrategy*. Parameters are typically grouped by parameter groups as e.g. *Warehouse*. Note that these groups can have several instances and therefore allow different behavior in parallel.

The exemplary component has two parameter groups: *StorageUnitType* and *Warehouse*. Storage unit types define the unit size in which materials are stored (e.g. a euro palette or a fixed size box). The organizational unit *Warehouse* offers several control parameters. The parameter *putawayStrategy* (*removalStrategy*) defines how to find a suitable storage bin in which to store (from which to retrieve) a unit of material. The following putaway strategies are supported: each material is assigned to fixed bins (static putaway), the system looks for a suitable bin optimizing e.g. storage space (dynamic putaway) or a storage bin is selected by the operator (manual putaway).

The Boolean parameter *useStorageUnitTypes* controls how the size of a storage bin is described. If true, then each storage bin is assigned to the unit type it stores, each material is assigned to the unit type it is delivered in and storage is only allowed if they correspond. If false, then a storage bin can be directly assigned to a material.

To fulfill its business tasks the component offers several interfaces: The interfaces *IWarehouse* and *IStorageUnitType* are used to set parameters and the interfaces *IStorageBin* and *IMaterial* manage corresponding master data. Additionally there is the interface *IStockManagement* which is used for the actual stock management activities as storing und retrieving stock and determining the number of available stock units.

4 Specification Proposals for Parameterization Properties

In this section we develop specification proposals for the parameterization properties of business components. Following the specification framework [24] we discuss the specification of terminology, tasks, interfaces and behavioral constraints in the subsequent subsections. For each of these aspects we need to distinguish between specifying parameter settings themselves and the impact these settings have on the functionality of the component [1]. Note that the specification framework [24] (in difference to many other approaches) considers not only the technical perspective (interface, behavior and coordination levels) but also the domain perspective (terminology and task levels). The latter describes the component from a domain (conceptual) point of view and supports functional experts in component selection – for this it needs a notation suitable for persons not necessarily familiar with UML or other modeling languages.

4.1 Specification on Terminology Level

The task of the terminology level is to clarify all used functional terms on a domain level. For this it provides a dictionary of all used terms including their definition and their relationship to other terms. According to [21,24] the specification of a term provides its name, a short definition and an accompanying example. (Fig. 2 shows exemplary how the term *Putaway Strategy* is specified.) The specification must additionally include the relationship to other terms: In our example putaway strategy is a property of a warehouse and putaway strategy is specialized into manual, static and dynamic putaway strategy. Additionally one can supplement constraints the term or its properties need to adhere to.

The notation used on terminology level is normative language, which is an ontology definition language that is both machine- and human-understandable [20]. Its idea is to use a standardized form of natural language to reduce disambiguities. To specify the relationship between terms one can distinguish between four relationship types: decomposition (A consists of B), association (A is related to B), property (A has property B) and specialization (A is a B or a C). For each of them a sentence building pattern (as shown in parentheses) is predefined that standardizes the relationship specification [21].

Using sentence building patterns has two advantages compared to natural language: Specifications become less ambiguous und the resulting dictionary structure forms a light-weight ontology allowing an easy way to automatically retrieve relation-ship information (e.g. find all terms related to a certain term). The advantage of using normative language compared to other ontology notations or UML lies in the fact that it is understandable for functional experts who in general do not have knowledge of formal modeling or ontology notations. (Note that it is possible to automatically trans-form normative language expressions into other ontology notations.)

Term: PUTAWAY STRATEGY
Short definition: PUTAWAY STRATEGY defines which strategy is used within one WAREHOUSE to put away stock. Supported strategies are manual, static and dynamic.
Example: Dynamic putaway strategy
Relationships: PUTAWAY STRATEGY is a MANUAL PUTAWAY STRATEGY or a STATIC PUTAWAY STRATEGY or a DYNAMIC PUTAWAY STRATEGY. WAREHOUSE has property PUTAWAY STRATEGY. PUTAWAY STRATEGY is a parameter.

Fig. 2. Specification of parameter term *Putaway Strategy*

To specify parameter settings we start with the fact that the top-level specification objects are parameters and parameter groups [2]. Parameters and their groups typi-cally have a domain meaning and therefore must be specified on terminology level. Next we observe that parameterization objects have a structure similar to other infor-mation objects and in borderline cases it is not always possible to clearly distinguish between them [1]. Therefore we propose to specify parameter and parameter groups similarly to other domain terms. Parameters need, however, to be clearly recognizable for component users because parameters often influence component functionality substantially and moreover must be set at configuration time. Therefore we propose to identify parameters and parameter groups by an additional statement in the collection of relationships. To improve intelligibility and allow for automatic processing we define two new sentence building patterns: "X is a parameter." and "Y is a parameter group.". The last line of Fig. 2 shows an example how such a pattern is applied and specifies that *Putaway Strategy* is a parameter. As a result parameters are specified analogously to other domain terms but are recognizable by an additional annotation.

Next we discuss how to specify the effects parameterization can have on domain terms. Specification objects on terminology level are term definitions, relationships and constraints. If the meaning of a term is variable (depending on a parameter), all variants need to be described in the terms short definition. (For reasons of clarity, however, one should avoid making the meaning of a term parameter dependent. In-stead one could define separate terms for each variant using specialization.) Depend-encies of a constraint on a parameter must be explicitly covered in the constraint.

From domain analysis [7], reference data modeling [22] and an analysis about parameterization effects on component specifications [2] we know that parameters often influence relationships between terms. Domain analysis identifies five *variability types* (mandatory, optional, alternative, optional alternative, (inclusive) or) which are used in feature modeling [7]. Experience has shown that these five variability types are sufficient to model structural variability in domain analysis.

The sentence building patterns introduced earlier (e.g. "A consists of B" for decomposition) describe must-relationships and thus correspond to the mandatory variability type. To express variability we propose to define additional patterns. Fig. 3 shows five sentence building patterns resulting from applying the five variability types to the decomposition relationship. (Note that the sentence building patterns were designed to be easily extendable to more terms. Example: "A consists of exactly one of B or C or D." To keep the presentation simple we used at most three terms.) Similar sentence building patterns are defined for relationship types *association* and *property*. Sentence building patterns for *specialization* are slightly different and will be discussed in section 4.2.

Mandatory decomposition:	A consists of B.
Optional decomposition:	A can consist of B.
Alternative decomposition:	A consists of exactly one of B or C.
Optional alternative decomposition:	A consists of at most one of B or C.
Or-decomposition:	A consists of one or more of B or C.

Fig. 3. Variability types and associated sentence building patterns for decomposition

It must be explicitly specified if a relationship variability depends on parameters. For this we follow two approaches in parallel: First we just denote on which parameters a variability depends using predefined sentences – for an example refer to the third relationship in Fig. 4. Second we specify detailed which parameter settings result in the occurrence of which relationship variant. Such specifications are included in the specification category *constraint* which is done in natural language (see also Fig. 4).

The detailed specification is necessary because only so the exact effects of parameterizations can be described. As these dependencies can be arbitrarily complex it is not possible to define sentence building patterns for them. Therefore we utilize – as for all other constraints – natural language specification. Declaring additionally the parameter dependency using sentence building patterns provides a crucial advantage: Parameter dependencies can be automatically retrieved – so it becomes possible to search for all effects one particular parameter has. This is a big advantage compared to current business applications where such information can not be captured easily [2]. Additionally it is shown that a variable relationship is parameter dependent (this corresponds to so-called build-time operators in reference data modeling [22]).

Fig. 4 shows how parameter dependent variability is described in the specification of the term *Storage Bin*. The third relationship specifies that *Storage Bin* is either related to *Storage Unit Type* or to *Material* or to none of them. Which relationship is allowed is defined by the parameter *Use Storage Unit Types*. This dependency is

Term: STORAGE BIN
Short definition: A STORAGE BIN (also storage slot) is the smallest available unit of space within a WAREHOUSE that can be separately addressed.
Example: Storage bin 015-07-02 located at lane 015, shelf 07, area 02 of Warehouse 001
Relationships: WAREHOUSE consists of STORAGE BIN. STORAGE BIN consists of WAREHOUSE STOCK. STORAGE BIN is related to at most one of STORAGE UNIT TYPE or MATERIAL – variability depends on parameter USE STORAGE UNIT TYPES of parameter group WAREHOUSE. STORAGE BIN has property MAXIMAL NUMBER OF UNITS.
Constraints: If USE STORAGE UNIT TYPES is true for the WAREHOUSE the STORAGE BIN belongs to, then STORAGE BIN is related to a STORAGE UNIT TYPE and is not related to a MATERIAL. If USE STORAGE UNIT TYPES is false for the WAREHOUSE the STORAGE BIN belongs to, then STORAGE BIN is not related to a STORAGE UNIT TYPE and can be related to a MATERIAL.

Fig. 4. Specification of business term *Storage Bin*

detailed in the constraints where it is specified how the parameter *Use Storage Unit Types* (of the *Warehouse* the *Storage Bin* belongs to) restricts the allowed associations.

Our specification proposals on terminology level were verified as follows: We confirmed that the sentence building patterns are powerful enough to express variability types of feature models and so-called build-time operators in reference data modeling [22]. Moreover we checked that the approach can express all (terminology relevant) parameterization effects identified in [2]. Finally, specifying all terms of the exemplary component *WarehouseManagement* was satisfactorily possible.

4.2 Specification on Task Level

The duty of a business component is to support or execute certain business tasks within an application system. For a functional expert to determine if a component is suitable for his requirements it is necessary to analyze the business tasks supported by the component on a domain (conceptual) level. All necessary information is provided on the task level of the component specification [24].

According to [21] terms and tasks are specified in the same way (both considered as instances of a more general idea *concept*). Therefore our specification proposals for the task level are similar to the terminology level – we do not introduce new specification techniques but transfer the proposals from Sect. 4.1 to the task level.

Task: DEFINE PUTAWAY STRATEGY
Short definition: The task of DEFINE PUTAWAY STRATEGY is to define for a WAREHOUSE which PUTAWAY STRATEGY will be employed and if STORAGE UNIT TYPEs shall be used.
Example: Choose for warehouse 001 (High rack storage) dynamic putaway strategy and the use of storage unit types.
Relationships: MANAGE WAREHOUSES consists of DEFINE PUTAWAY STRATEGY. DEFINE PUTAWAY STRATEGY is a parameterization task.
Constraints: Choosing DYNAMIC PUTAWAY STRATEGY requires choosing true for USE STORAGE UNIT TYPES.

Fig. 5. Specification of parameterization task *Define Putaway Strategy*

Analogously to terms the specification of a business task contains its name, a short definition and an accompanying example. If applicable, one additionally specifies relationships between tasks and supplements constraints that need to be adhered to when executing the task. Specification on task level uses again normative language to specify all related business tasks. For tasks the relationships of type specialization and decomposition are specification relevant [21]: A specialization allows distinguishing between different forms (variants) of a task ("A is B or C") and decomposition allows describing which subtasks form the task ("A consists of B").

To specify parameter settings at the task level we note that parameterization tasks (without its runtime effects) are the top-level specification objects. Parameterization tasks are specified analogously to business tasks. To distinguish between parameterization tasks and normal business tasks the new sentence building pattern "Z is a parameterization task." is introduced. As an example Fig. 5 shows the specification for the parameterization task *Define Putaway Strategy*. This task sets the related parameters *Putaway Strategy* and *Use Storage Unit Types* of a *Warehouse*. The dependency between these two parameters is shown in the constraint category of Fig. 5. Moreover the specification shows that *Define Putaway Strategy* is a subtask of the task *Manage Warehouses*.

Next we discuss how to specify the effects parameterization can have on business tasks. Parameters can influence business task definitions, relationships and constraints. Specification of such parameterization effects will be analogously to the specification on terminology level. Variations in the definition (again not recommended) or in constraints have to be included into the natural language specification. For variable relationships between different tasks we use again special sentence building patterns – for decomposition we reuse the results from Fig. 3 and variants in a specialization are discussed below. If the variability depends on a parameter, this is again denoted using a special sentence building pattern (for an example see Fig. 7).

Mandatory one-subtype specialization:	A is B.
Optional one-subtype specialization:	A can be B.
Alternative specialization:	A is exactly one of B or C.
Optional alternative specialization:	A is at most one of B or C.
Or-specialization:	A is one or more of B or C.
Optional or-specialization:	A is none or one or more of B or C.

Fig. 6. Variability types and associated sentence building patterns for specialization

Applying the earlier introduced variability types to the specialization relationship yields the sentence building patterns in Fig. 6. The first two patterns describe the special case of a specialization with only one subtype. The other four patterns describe the different variants a specialization can occur in. (Note that feature modeling knows a sixth variability type *optional or* which can be normalized to several optional features [7] – assuming that the relationship is composite. As a specialization is of abstractive nature this normalization is here not possible.) Note that these four patterns (deduced from feature types) exactly correspond to the following specialization types (in this order): disjoint total, disjoint partial, non-disjoint total, non-disjoint partial.

Task: PUTAWAY STOCK
Short definition: The task of PUTAWAY STOCK is to find suitable STORAGE BINs for a number of units of MATERIAL and store them there physically.
Example: Store one euro palette of material ABC-XYZ – system assigns storage bin 015-07-02
Relationships: PUTAWAY STOCK is exactly one of MANUAL PUTAWAY or STATIC PUTAWAY or DYNAMIC PUTAWAY – variability depends on parameter PUTAWAY STRATEGY of parameter group WAREHOUSE.
Constraints: The parameter PUTAWAY STRATEGY of the WAREHOUSE the MATERIAL is stored in decides which task to perform. If this parameter is set to DYNAMIC (STATIC / MANUAL) PUTAWAY STRATEGY, then DYNAMIC (STATIC / MANUAL) PUTAWAY is performed.

Fig. 7. Specification of business task *Putaway Stock*

How the variability in the task *Putaway Stock* is specified can be seen in Fig. 7. The component supports three variants (*Dynamic Putaway, Static Putaway, Manual Putaway*) how the task can be performed – these variants are specified as subtasks. (It is a modeling decision to decide if the differences in task variants are big enough to justify defining separate subtasks.) In the specialization it is specified that exactly one of the three subtasks is performed when executing *Putaway Stock*. Which one will be picked depends on the parameter *Putaway Strategy*. By using sentence building patterns it becomes again easy to retrieve the parameterization information (e.g. which tasks are influenced by a given parameter). The constraint in Fig. 7 describes the strategy finding: the material decides in which warehouse to store a charge and the parameter *Putaway Strategy* of that warehouse decides the used strategy.

4.3 Specification on Interface Level

The specification on *interface level* contains the signature of the components interfaces (operations, fault messages, data types) – common notation techniques are interface definition languages like OMG IDL [17] or UML interface diagrams [19]. For an example see the UML specification of the interface *IStockManagement* in Fig. 8. The interface level is more technical compared to terminology and task levels and is mainly intended for a technical expert who integrates the component into an enterprise application system.

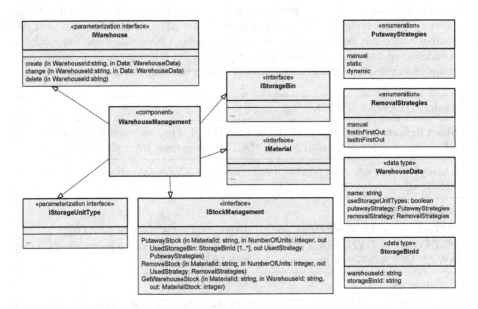

Fig. 8. (Partial) Interface specification of component *WarehouseManagement*

There can be two strategies how to assign values to the parameters of a component: As strategy one the component could use XML configuration files provided by most component frameworks (as Enterprise Java Beans or OMG CCM [18]) and parameters are set by directly editing the configuration file. In this case the XML schema of the configuration file provides the technical specification necessary for setting parameters. As strategy two the component could allow setting parameters via interfaces – the component might store the values either in configuration (or other) files or in data base tables. In this case it is highly desirable that the component provides separate interfaces for parameterization and does not mix parameter settings with regular components operations [18]. Reasons for such a separation are the requirement for an easy identification of parameterization features and the fact that operations used for parameterization are typically not intended for use by other components of an application system. As there are technically no differences we propose to specify parameterization interfaces in the same way as and together with regular interfaces. To clearly identify parameterization interfaces we use for them an additional annotation. For an example compare Fig. 8 which shows the interface specification of our exemplary component: It contains the interface *IWarehouse* which is annotated with the UML stereotype «parameterization interface».

A parameterization effect on interface level would be given if a component signature varies depending on parameter settings. The dynamic change of a component signature, however, is not possible in mainstream component technologies and therefore there is no need for such a specification. Note in this context that the interface level is only concerned with the signature elements that are physically present – the fact that an operation or an operation parameter is not allowed for use (although present) for certain parameter settings must be specified on behavioral level.

4.4 Specification on Behavioral Level

Behavioral specifications describe how the component behaves in general and in borderline cases. This is achieved by defining constraints (invariants, pre- and postconditions) based on the idea of designing applications by contract [16]. The UML Object Constraint Language (OCL) is one of the most used techniques to express such constraints and is often employed for component specifications [6,9,21,24]. The behavioral level contains two types of information: an optional specification data model (realized as UML type diagram – see Fig. 1) which shows the information objects stored by the component [1] and OCL constraints that specify restrictions when using the interfaces.

To specify parameters and parameter groups on the technical level we proceed as follows: Parameter values are stored by the component – therefore parameters should be included in the specification data model. As parameterization objects are structurally similar to other information objects and sometimes not clearly distinguishable [1] they are specified analogously to other information objects. Fig. 1 shows the specification of the parameter group *Warehouse* as an UML type and its parameters (e.g. *putawayStrategy*) as attributes of this type. To distinguish between parameterization objects and regular information objects we introduce a special annotation by using the UML stereotype «parameterization type».

Besides specifying the parameters themselves we need to describe dependencies between parameters by OCL constraints. Fig. 9 shows an OCL constraint that specifies the following: If a warehouse puts away stock dynamically (parameter *putawayStrategy*) then it must use storage unit types (parameter *useStorageUnitTypes*).

```
context Warehouse
  inv: putawayStrategy = PutawayStrategies::dynamic
                    implies useStorageUnitTypes = true
```

Fig. 9. Specification of a parameter dependency

A parameterization effect on behavioral level is given if the structure of information objects in the specification data model or OCL constraints vary depending on parameter values. Structural variability in the data model can be expressed in the model itself (as far as UML allows) and by accompanying constraints. Variability in OCL constraints is expressed in the constraints themselves by including the parameter dependency. As an example we consider the effect of the parameter *useStorageUnit-Types* on a *StorageBin*. In the specification data model (see Fig. 1) the type *Storage-Bin* has optional associations to both types *Material* and *StorageUnitTypes*. To express the exact interdependency between these two associations one additionally needs the OCL constraints shown in Fig. 10.

```
context Storage Bin
  inv: self.Warehouse.useStorageUnitTypes = true implies
            self.StorageUnitType->size() = 1 and
            self.Material->size() = 0
  inv: self.Warehouse.useStorageUnitTypes = false implies
            self.StorageUnitType->size() = 0 and
            self.Material->size() <= 1
```

Fig. 10. Specification of parameterization effect on *Storage Bin*

As verification of our approach we checked that all possible parameterization effects on behavioral level (as identified in [2]) can indeed be specified in the proposed way. This was supported by the successful specification of the exemplary component *WarehouseManagement*.

Note that the specification of a business component contains a domain perspective (terminology and tasks) and a technical perspective (interfaces and behavior). Some of the specified information appears on both perspectives – one might argue that they are redundant. We do not think so as both perspectives describe the component from different angles and for a different audience: The domain perspective describes the components functionality conceptually – for this it targets functional experts and uses normalized language. The technical perspective describes the component from a composition point of view – it addresses technical experts and uses standard development notations as UML. Moreover, it is rather common to specify constraints simultaneously in formal and natural language [6,24] because natural language specification alone might be ambiguous and formal OCL specification alone is hard to understand (especially for functional experts). To ease the maintenance of constraints one could utilize automated translations between formal and informal specifications [11].

Finally it shall be mentioned that the specification framework [24] allows defining mappings between specification objects on domain and technical perspectives. In our example the term *Warehouse* is mapped to the UML type *Warehouse* (cf. Fig. 1), the term *Putaway Strategy* (cf. Fig. 2) is mapped to the attribute *putawayStrategy* of type *Warehouse* (cf. Fig. 1) and the decomposition between the terms *Warehouse* and *Storage Bin* (cf. Fig. 4) is mapped to the aggregation between the corresponding types. The parameter dependencies described as constraints in Fig. 4 are mapped to UML OCL invariants on behavioral level which are shown in Fig. 10. (Due to a top-down approach and the intended simplicity the specification objects on domain and technical perspectives of our example use the same names and stand in one-to-one relationships – note that this might not always be the case.) A specification tool can use such mappings to allow for a simple navigation between related concepts on domain and technical perspectives.

5 Related Work

Currently there exists no generally accepted and supported specification standard for software components covering all relevant aspects. Various authors addressed specifications for specific tasks of the development process as e.g. design and implementation [6,9]. Approaches towards a comprehensive specification are few and include [3,12,21,24]. Its consideration of technical and domain aspects in one unified proposal is the main advantage of [24] (and the later work of [21]). Parameterization aspects are not discussed in the literature about component specification.

Adaptation is an important aspect of component-based software engineering because in practice components can rarely be reused without being adapted [4]. Consequently adaptation in component-based application systems is discussed by many authors – for an overview see e.g. [4]. Important adaptation techniques include: copying code, inheritance, aggregation, wrapping, superimposition, adaptation interfaces, parameterized contracts and several types of parameterization. Parameterization is identified as an adaptation technique by most authors, but not discussed in detail. Specification aspects are not covered in the literature about component adaptation.

Integrated standard application suites like SAP R/3 allow complex parameterization (also called *customizing*). Although customizing is discussed frequently, little attention has been paid to the detailed description of parameter settings. In practice the quality of parameter documentation is often not sufficient – correlations between parameters and the components functionality become almost impossible to trace [15]. There are some works containing detailed recommendations for parameter settings specific for a software suite and a functional area (e.g. [8]). A general approach towards specification of parameters and parameterization effects does not exist.

Variability is an important issue in software engineering and e.g. relevant for configurable reference models [22], software reuse [13], generic programming [7] and the related product-line approach [5], as well as for modern Business Process Management [14]. We use their results as a methodical foundation.

6 Summary

In this paper we discussed how parameterization properties of a business component can be included in the components specification. We proposed how to specify parameters and parameterization tasks themselves and additionally we showed how the effects parameterization has on the components functionality can be specified. These results are not only interesting for the specification of parameterizable business components but present also a first step towards general specification of parameterization effects. This paper concentrated on the components functionality (terminology, tasks, interfaces and behavior) – non-functional aspects (as quality and general commercial information) were not considered and are direction of future research.

References

1. Ackermann, J.: Specification Proposals for Customizable Business Components. In: Over-hage, S., Turowski, K. (eds.) Proceedings 1st International Workshop Component Engineering Methodology, Erfurt, pp. 51–62 (2003)
2. Ackermann, J.: Zur Beschreibung datenbasierter Parametrisierung von Softwarekomponenten. In: Turowski, K. (ed.) Architekturen, Komponenten, Anwendungen - Proceedings zur Tagung AKA 2004, Augsburg. LNI issue P-57, pp. 131–149 (2004) (in German)
3. Beugnard, A., Jézéquel, J.-M., Plouzeau, N., Watkins, D.: Making Components Contract Aware. IEEE Computer 7, 38–44 (1999)
4. Bosch, J.: Adapting Object-Oriented Components. In: Proceedings of the 2nd International Workshop on Component-Oriented Programming (WCOP '97), Turku, Finland (1997)
5. Bosch, J., Florijn, G., Greefhorst, D., Kuusela, J., Obbink, H., Pohl, K.: Variability Issues in Software Product Lines. In: van der Linden, F.J. (ed.) PFE 2002. LNCS, vol. 2290, pp. 13–21. Springer, Heidelberg (2002)
6. Cheesman, J., Daniels, J.: UML Components. Addison-Wesley, Boston (2001)
7. Czarnecki, K., Eisenecker, U.W.: Generative Programming: Methods, Tools, and Applications. Addison-Wesley, Boston (2000)
8. Dittrich, J., Mertens, P., Hau, M.: Dispositionsparameter von SAP R/3-PP: Einstellungshinweise, Wirkungen, Nebenwirkungen. Vieweg Verlag, Wiesbaden (1999) (in German)
9. D'Souza, D.F., Wills, A.C.: Objects, Components, and Frameworks with UML: The Catalysis Approach. Addison-Wesley, Reading (1998)
10. Geisterfer, C.J.M., Ghosh, S.: Software Component Specification: A Study in Perspective of Component Selection and Reuse. In: Proceedings of the 5th International Conference on COTS Based Software Systems (ICCBSS), Orlando, USA (2006)
11. Hähnle, R., Johannisson, K., Ranta, A.: An Authoring Tool for Informal and Formal Requirements Specifications. In: Kutsche, R.-D., Weber, H. (eds.) ETAPS 2002 and FASE 2002. LNCS, vol. 2306, pp. 233–248. Springer, Heidelberg (2002)
12. Han, J.: A Comprehensive Interface Definition Framework for Software Components. In: Proceedings of 1998 Asia-Pacific Software Engineering Conference, Taipei, pp. 110–117 (1998)
13. Jacobson, I., Griss, M., Jonsson, P.: Software Reuse. ACM Press /Addison Wesley Longman, New York (1997)
14. Ly, L.T., Rinderle, S., Dadam, P.: Semantic Correctness in Adaptive Process Management Systems. In: Dustdar, S., Fiadeiro, J.L., Sheth, A. (eds.) BPM 2006. LNCS, vol. 4102, pp. 193–208. Springer, Heidelberg (2006)
15. Mertens, P., Wedel, T., Hartinger, M.: Management by Parameters? Zeitschrift für Betriebswirtschaft 61, 569–588 (1991) (in German)
16. Meyer, B.: Applying "Design by Contract". IEEE Computer 10, 40–51 (1992)
17. OMG (ed.): The Common Object Request Broker: Architecture and Specification (2001)
18. OMG (ed.): CORBA Components Specification. Version 3.0 (June 2002) (Date of Call: 2006-02-02) URL: http://www.omg.org/
19. OMG (ed.): Unified Modeling Language: UML 2.0 Superstructure Specification July 4, 2005) (Date of Call: 2005-09-09) (2005) URL: http://www.omg.org/technology/documents

20. Ortner, E., Schienmann, B.: Normative Language Approach: A Framework for Under-standing. In: Thalheim, B. (ed.) Conceptual Modeling, pp. 261–276. Springer, Heidelberg (1996)

21. Overhage, S.: UnSCom: A Standardized Framework for the Specification of Software Components. In: Weske, M., Liggesmeyer, P. (eds.) Object-Oriented and Internet-Based Technologies, Proceedings of the 5th Net'Object Days, Erfurt (2004)

22. Schütte, R.: Grundsätze ordnungsmäßiger Referenzmodellierung. Ph.D. thesis. Gabler Verlag, Wiesbaden (1998) (in German)

23. Szyperski, C., Gruntz, D., Murer, S.: Component Software: Beyond Object-Oriented Pro-gramming, 2nd edn. Addison-Wesley, Harlow (2002)

24. Turowski, K. (ed.): Standardized Specification of Business Components: Memorandum of the working group 5.10.3 Component Oriented Business Application Systems. University of Augsburg (2002) (Date of Call: 2005-09-09) URL: http://www.fachkomponenten.de

Implementing Non-functional Service Descriptions in SOAs

Stephan Aier[1], Philipp Offermann[2], Marten Schönherr[2], and Christian Schröpfer[2]

[1] Institut of Information Management, University of St. Gallen,
Mueller-Friedberg-Strasse 8, 9000 St. Gallen, Switzerland
stephan.aier@unisg.ch
[2] Berlin University of Technology, Faculty of Computer Sciences and
Electrical Engineering, Franklinstr. 28/29, 10587 Berlin, Germany
{philipp.offermann,marten.schoenherr,
christian.schroepfer}@sysedv.tu-berlin.de

Abstract. This article describes a framework for extended service descriptions based on OWL-S (Web Ontology Language for Services) focusing on non-functional criteria. Necessary service management tasks will be introduced and extended by corresponding data elements and statements for its automated support. After a short comparative description of several existing approaches to semantic service descriptions the paper addresses the actual extension of OWL-S. Non-functional extensions as service lifecycle elements and Quality of Services (QoS) are added. To extend QoS capabilities, the approach combines the common extension mechanism with UML (Unified Modeling Language) Profile for QoS. A prototype delivers the proof-of-concept for the first part of the extension. The prototype implements SOA-specific authentications and all basic features for a tool-supported service management using extended semantic service descriptions by defining an ontology-based service taxonomy and service annotation.

Keywords: SOA, Protégé, OWL-S, QoS, UML Profile for QoS, service management, ontology, service lifecycle.

1 Service Management as a Key Issue in SOAs

Scientists and practitioners emphasize the potential of SOAs (service-oriented architectures) especially by reconciling business requirements and IT infrastructures. SOA definitions range from a solely technology-driven approach to a new management school approach on how to run the whole enterprise. Gold et al. consider technological aspects focusing on standardized interface descriptions.

> "[A service oriented architecture is] a set of components which can be invoked, and whose interface descriptions can be published and discovered." [1]

McCoy and Natis take into account aspects of stakeholder, granularity, reuse and agility:

D. Draheim and G. Weber (Eds.): TEAA 2006, LNCS 4473, pp. 40–53, 2007.
© Springer-Verlag Berlin Heidelberg 2007

> "SOA is a software architecture that builds a topology of interfaces, interface implementations and interface calls. SOA is a relationship of services and service consumers, both software modules large enough to represent a complete business function. So, SOA is about reuse, encapsulation, interfaces, and ultimately, agility." [2]

Furthermore issues as service management and optimization are being addressed:

> "SOA is the concept of service-enabling new and existing software; linking internal and external service-enabled software systems; and implementing an enterprise-wide infrastructure to enable, manage, and optimize services use and interaction" [3] (see also [4, 5])

A common understanding of further SOA characteristics are the distributed manner of SOAs, the aspect of service orchestration, loose coupling of applications, and the standardization of interface descriptions [4, 6, 7]. Lubinsky and Tyomkin focus on the business process-driven integration and therefore derive the following three main aspects of an SOA [4]:

- Service descriptions
- Business processes
- Service management

A proper description of services is a fundamental precondition for a service management. While various research activities deal with aspects of functional service description, we will focus on non-functional elements of a service description in order to enable a *service lifecycle management (SLM)* and aspects of *quality of service (QoS)*.

Modeling functional and non-functional information in a machine-readable and semantically enriched way is a basis for a highly automated service management framework. In web services technology, UDDI (Universal Description, Discovery, and Integration) repositories and WSDL (Web Services Description Language) are used for service publication, discovery, and description but do not provide the necessary semantic functionality for service management aspects.

Our approach builds on OWL-S (Web Ontology Language for Services), a well established ontology framework, and existing tools to construct the necessary extensions. The two aspects that need to be covered in the non-functional area are service lifecycle information and offered QoS guarantees by a service. Hence, it is necessary to look at semantic web service description standards in general as well as description standards in the QoS domain.

2   Requirements for Non-functional Service Description

In order to support service management activities, like semi-automatic discovery, service level management, and service migration, several types of information need to be modeled within the service description. The following two sections describe requirements for service description regarding information relevant for service life cycle management and QoS guarantees. The lists contain the most obvious points in both categories. However, they can not be regarded as complete. A future-proof approach must allow for extension of ontological terms used for description. Building on this extensibility, domain-specific models can be build that capture most requirements relevant in the domain.

2.1 Additional Description for Service Lifecycle Management

In the area of lifecycle management, the following information should be covered. The information can be categorized as organizational aspects and technical aspects.

Organizational aspects include information like *service name*, *service category*, *versioning information*, *variant information*, and *links to further business description* of the service. However, the most important organizational aspect for a service lifecycle management is the *lifecycle status* of a service. Possible states are "Planned", "Design", "Test", "Pilot", "Active–intensive maintenance", "Active–regular maintenance", "Sunsetting candidate", "Sunsetting in progress", and "Sunsetted". Especially for the operational management of active services information about the *service provider*, different *responsibilities*, *roles*, *persons* (e.g. for maintenance), and *pricing* (depending on QoS class) are of importance.

Technical aspects include information on the *infrastructure* the service runs on like server name, configuration management ID, etc. and a link to *source code* of the service. For managing *service dependencies* information about other services used as well as services depending on a certain service are necessary.

These statements are not very complex. It will be shown that they can be easily realized as OWL-S extensions.

2.2 QoS Guarantees

Quality of service aspects can be categorized in a *general dimension*, *cost dimension*, *performance dimension*, *reliability dimension*, and other *boundary conditions*.

The *general dimension* includes the overall *QoS-Level*. The service level regarding performance, quality ("Gold", "Silver", "Bronze") are defined in a separate SLA document. Furthermore services belong to a certain *service category* which may be derived in a service domain analysis [8] and a *communication pattern*, e.g. real time or batch.

The *cost dimension* specifies tariff models. Services may be paid, e.g. per period of time, per service call, or for volume of traffic.

The performance dimension includes primarily technical values. Specified values may be service response *time*, *data capacity* of an underlying database (normal/max after extension), *accuracy* of the result of a calculation, *arrival patterns* describing jitter and arrival distributions, and certain *performance ratios* like number of service requests per period of time (throughput of data sets, calculations per time, normal/max after extension) etc.

The *reliability dimension* includes aspects of *functional correctness* of services, their *availability* (business hours, weekdays/time, and incident resolution time), end-user usability, and aspects of *security* like security level, encryption standard, access rights, authenticity etc.

Other *boundary conditions* describe *organizational aspects* like promoters/opponents for certain activities, *cultural aspects* like different languages needed for end-user communication and *normative aspects* like compliance with laws/regulations and certification.

3 Relevant Standards

A number of standards have evolved in the area of semantic service description. A selection of them most relevant from a content and time perspective is being discussed in this section: OWL-S, WSMO (Web Service Modeling Ontology), and WSDL-S (Web Services Description Language – semantically enriched). For the QoS part we will discuss UML (Unified Modeling Language) Profile for QoS.

3.1 OWL-S

OWL-S (Web Ontology Language for Services) [9] is an upper ontology language developed by the semantic web services arm of the DAML (Darpa Agent Markup Language) program [10]. It uses the OWL (Web Ontology Language) ontology language. OWL-S supplies a core set of markup language constructs for describing the properties and capabilities of web services in unambiguous, computer-interpretable form and facilitates the automation of web service tasks including automated service discovery, execution, interoperation, composition, and execution monitoring [9].

OWL-S uses four classes to describe web services: *Service, ServiceProfile, ServiceGrounding*, and *ServiceModel. Service* is a reference point for the other elements. *ServiceProfile* facilitates service discovery and describes functional and non-functional aspects. It is the part where OWL-S can be extended. *ServiceProfile* is therefore described in detail in section 4. Figure 1 depicts all its elements. *ServiceModel* is targeted at in depth analysis once the service has been discovered. It describes in detail how to use the service, the semantics of requests, responses, pre- and post-conditions (effects), as well as optionally even the process. *ServiceGrounding* describes how the actual instance of a service can be accessed, i.e. protocol, message format, serialization, transport, and addressing.

We have chosen OWL-S as the basis for our service description approach for two reasons. First of all, it is based on OWL, a well established ontology language. Secondly, there are tools available for working with OWL ontologies as well as with OWL-S service descriptions.

3.2 WSMF/WSMO/WSML

WSMO is another upper ontology for describing web services semantically. It has been submitted to the W3C (The World Wide Web Consortium). WSMO represents a meta-model for web service description and is compatible to MOF (Meta-Object Facility). Basis for WSMO is WSMF (Web Service Modeling Framework) [11]. WSML (Web Services Modeling Language) which is used in WSMO provides a rule-based language for the semantic web [12]. As defined in WSMF, WSMO uses four main components: *ontologies, goals, mediators*, and *web services*.

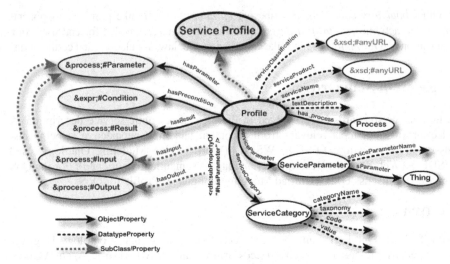

Fig. 1. Overview ServiceProfile [1]

Ontologies can be imported for the description of individual elements. In WSMO, they are used to define an agreed common terminology by providing concepts, and relations between the concepts [13].

Goals describe the functionality and interfaces of the web services from a user perspective. This is the section that can very well be used for discovery by potential service requestors.

Mediators describe the elements mediating between different *ontologies*, *goals*, and *web services*. They refer to external web services providing transformation services. The concept of *mediators* makes WSMO interesting for the description of heterogeneous web services.

Web services are among others described by *non-functional properties* and a *capability*, describing its functionality from a provider's perspective. *Non-functional properties* describe additional information about the web service, e.g. *owner*, *contributor*, *rights*, and *scalability*. They can be defined also for other elements and extended by using terms imported with ontologies.

Like OWL-S, WSMO only contains rather generic elements to describe web services. Some elements for service lifecycle management and QoS elements are included but seem rather ad hoc. That is why OWL-S has been chosen as the basis for the approach described here. However, we assume that a similar approach can be developed based on WSMO using *non-functional properties*.

3.3 WSDL-S

WSDL-S is a standard for a semantically enriched web services description. It is an extension of WSDL (Web Services Description Language). With this incremental approach it has been possible to add semantics to service descriptions without having to redefine the standard. [14]

In WSDL-S, the actual ontology representation can be done with an ontology language chosen by the user, e.g. OWL, WSML, or UML. In WSDL-S semantic description is done in the following way. Three new elements are added as extensibility elements to WSDL: *category* (extension to *interface*), *preconditions*, and *effects* (extensions to *operation*). Service categorization can be done using *category*. The actual semantic annotation to the service and its elements input, output, operation, precondition, effect, and category is done by referring via URIs (Uniform Resource Identifier) to an externally defined ontology. Two extension attributes specify the association and schema mapping between WSDL elements and ontologies.

Summing up, WSDL-S is a standard for semantic description of web services which heavily leverages existing standards and is very flexible with respect to ontology and mapping languages.

3.4 UML Profile for QoS

UML Profile for QoS is a comprehensive framework for modeling QoS requirements and offerings. It extends the reference UML 2.0 meta-model mainly by using the stereotype concept. It allows for the modeling of QoS properties in UML models [15].

UML Profile for QoS uses the following approach. It describes a QoS model specific to the respective domain separated from the actual elements to be annotated. In the actual UML model the elements can be annotated using terms defined in this QoS model. UML profile is based on a QoS meta-model and comprises the three sub-profiles *QoS Characteristics*, *QoS Constraints*, and *QoS Levels*.

The QoS model is defined by using *QoS Characteristics*. Among others, it uses the stereotypes *QoS Characteristic* and *QoS Dimension* to specify respectively quantify aspects of QoS. It is possible to use statistical values (maximum, minimum, range, mean, variance, standard deviation, percentile, frequency, moment, and distribution) to express preferences about the direction when comparing or optimizing parameters. The relationship between several *QoS Characteristics* and elements that are part of one QoS statement can be described by *QoS Context*.

Annotating the elements with QoS requirements/offerings is done with *QoS Values* or with *QoS Constraints*. *QoS Values* specify values for QoS dimensions available at modeling time. *QoS Constraints* describe limitations of *QoS Characteristics* for annotated elements, either by listing the allowed elements or by stating the limits. Three types of constraints exist: *QoS Required*, *QoS Offered*, and *QoS Contract*. For service description in most cases *QoS Offered* will be used. However, using *QoS Required* it is possible to specify constraints the provider has towards the requestor, e.g. invocation/arrival patterns. *QoS Contract* can be used for specifying service level agreements. Different levels supported by a system with regard to QoS can be defined by *QoS Level*. A *QoS Level* is described by an allowed space for the values of the QoS characteristics. The different levels can be used in SLAs.

There are several reasons for choosing UML Profile for QoS for the extension of OWL-S. Firstly, it comes with its own general catalog of QoS characteristics which is neither domain- nor project-specific. Although it is not complete, it is an excellent basis for a common understanding of the most important QoS parameters. Secondly, it can be well integrated with business process modeling, which is the counterpart of the web services matching problem to the service description. For service matching and service level negotiation this offers the advantage of having both the description of offered QoS and the description of required QoS in the same logical format. Thirdly, compared to other specifications, UML Profile for QoS is quite mature. A lot of other QoS-related work and frameworks where considered already during its first definition. Summarizing, UML Profile for QoS is a comprehensive framework for modeling QoS requirements and offerings and is therefore well suited to add comprehensive QoS capabilities to OWL-S.

4   Extending OWL-S for Non-functional Service Description

The following section describes the proposed extension to OWL-S with respect to service lifecycle management and QoS.

4.1   Extensions for Service Lifecycle Management

Extension of OWL-S happens in the *ServiceProfile*. For the functional description *Parameter*, *Input*, *Output*, *Condition*, *Result*, and *Process* are used. The first five refer to the process description in *ServiceModel*. For the non-functional description the following properties/classes are interesting: *serviceClassification*, *serviceProduct*,

```
<owl:Class rdf:ID="ServiceVersion">
  <rdfs:subClassOf rdf:resource=
  "http://www.daml.org/services/owl-s/1.2/Profile.owl#ServiceParameter"/>
</owl:Class>
<owl:Class rdf:ID="ServiceVersionInfo"/>
<owl:DatatypeProperty rdf:ID="VersionName">
  <rdfs:domain rdf:resource="#ServiceVersionInfo"/>
  <rdfs:range rdf:resource="http://www.w3.org/2001/XMLSchema#string"/>
</owl:DatatypeProperty>
<owl:DatatypeProperty rdf:ID="VersionNumber">
  <rdfs:domain rdf:resource="#ServiceVersionInfo"/>
  <rdfs:range rdf:resource="http://www.w3.org/2001/XMLSchema#float"/>
</owl:DatatypeProperty>
```

Fig. 2. Definition of *Service Version* in OWL-S

```
<ServiceVersion rdf:ID="ServiceVersion_10">
  <profile:sParameter>
    <ServiceVersionInfo rdf:ID="ServiceVersionInfo_11">
      <VersionName rdf:datatype="http://www.w3.org/2001/XMLSchema#string"
      >Snake</VersionName>
      <VersionNumber rdf:datatype="http://www.w3.org/2001/XMLSchema#float"
      >5.1</VersionNumber>
    </ServiceVersionInfo>
  </profile:sParameter>
  <profile:serviceParameterName rdf:datatype=
  "http://www.w3.org/2001/XMLSchema#string"
  >ServiceVersion</profile:serviceParameterName>
</ServiceVersion>
<profile:Profile rdf:ID="CalculateRoute_Profile">
  <profile:serviceParameter rdf:resource="#ServiceVersion_10"/>
[…]
</profile:Profile>
```

Fig. 3. Instance of a service description for *CalculateRoute* with details for *ServiceVersion*

Table 1. Additional elements defined for service lifecycle management

Additional service lifecycle parameter	Explanation	
Properties/ subclasses	**Data type**	**Explanation**
ServiceVersion	Versioning information	
VersionName	String	Version name described as literal
VersionNumber	Float	Version number x.x
ServiceVariant	Variant information	
Variant	Integer	Variant number
ServiceLifecycle-Status	Lifecycle status of service component	
LifecycleStatus (subclass of owl:Thing)	(Enumerated instances)	Enumerated instances: "Planned", "Design", "Test", "Pilot", "Active_intensive_maintenance", "Active_regular_maintenance", "Sunsetting_candidate", "Sunsetting_in_progress", "Sunsetted"
ServiceProvider	Service provider information	
ProviderLink	anyURI	Link to external information (name, address, contacts, credentials, etc.) in provider database
ServiceInfrastructure	Infrastructure the service runs on	
ServerID	anyURI	List of Server IDs the service runs on
ResourceID	anyURI	List of Resource IDs the service uses
SourceCodeLink	Link to source code in code repository	
SourceCode	anyURI	Link to source code
ServiceResponsibility	Responsibility for service from business and technical perspective	
BusResponsibility	anyURI	Link to organization/person with business responsibility
TechResponsibility	anyURI	Link to organization/person with technical responsibility
BusinessDescription	Information about business background	
BusDescription	String	Textual description of business background
BusInfLink	anyURI	Link to further information resources
ServicePricing	Pricing information	
PricingModelQ1	anyURI	Link to pricing model for QoS level 1
...	...	...
PricingModelQn	anyURI	Link to pricing model for QoS level n

serviceName, textDescription, ServiceCategory, and *ServiceParameter*. The first five can be used for the requirements mentioned as they are. The web service can be classified using *serviceClassification* (mapping to an OWL ontology of services, e.g. NAICS) and *serviceProduct* (mapping to an OWL ontology of products, e.g. UNSPSC), as well as *ServiceCategory* (mapping to taxonomies potentially outside of

OWL or OWL-S). Using *serviceName*, a semantic name can be given to a service. Free text descriptions can be represented with *textDescription*.

The element *ServiceParameter* is especially important for the extension. Here the remaining additional service lifecycle characteristics are defined (Table 1). Future extensions also can be realized using *ServiceParameter*.

ServiceParameter consists of the *serviceParameterName*, the actual name of the parameter, defined as literal or URI, and *sParameter*, a link to the value within an OWL ontology. Figure 2 shows the definition of *ServiceVersion* in OWL-S as an example. *VersionName* (type *xsd:string*) and *VersionNumber* (type *xsd:float*) are defined as datatype properties of the class *ServiceVersionInfo* (subclass of *owl:Thing*). Figure 3 shows the *ServiceVersion* information in OWL-S in a service description for a logistics web service *CalculateRoute*. *ServiceVersion_10* and *ServiceVersion-Info_11* are instances that contain the actual version information "snake" and "5.1".

4.2 Extensions for QoS

Section 2.2 gives a flavor of what the level of complexity is when describing QoS offerings. It shows that a comprehensive and extensible QoS framework that builds on extensive experience needs to be leveraged. UML Profile for QoS is such a framework that suffices these requirements.

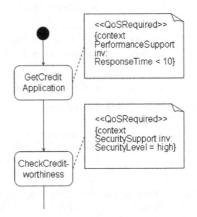

Fig. 4. Example QoS requirements in an UML activity diagram

Hence we propose to use UML Profile for QoS together with OWL-S to bring QoS functionality to web services description. To achieve this, it is not necessary to develop the whole QoS model in OWL-S. It is sufficient to introduce the QoS annotations to the services to be described. The QoS model does not have to be defined in OWL-S. This description remains in UML and can be reused for other service descriptions. This is very much in line with the idea of using the same QoS notation on the business process side as well as on the service description side to facilitate service level negotiation. Introducing the QoS annotations into the OWL-S service descriptions can again be easily done by adding *QoSCharacteristics* as a new

```
<profile:Profile
  rdf:ID="GetCreditApplication_Profile">
  <profile:serviceParameter>
    <QoSCharacteristics rdf:ID="QoSCharacteristics_14">
      <profile:sParameter>
        <QoSStatement rdf:ID="QoSStatement_15">
          <Statement rdf:datatype="http://www.w3.org/2001/XMLSchema#string">
          &lt;&lt;QoSOffered>> {context PerformanceSupport inv: ResponseTime
          &lt; 8}</Statement>
        </QoSStatement>
      </profile:sParameter>
      <profile:serviceParameterName rdf:datatype=
      http://www.w3.org/2001/XMLSchema#string>
      QoSCharacteristics </profile:serviceParameterName>
    </QoSCharacteristics>
  </profile:serviceParameter>
  [...]
</profile:Profile>
```

Fig. 5. QoS offering for *GetCreditApplication* in the service description

ServiceParameter. QoSStatement is defined as a subclass of *owl:Thing* with the data type property *statement* of the type string. This field contains the QoS constraints in OCL (Object Constraint Language) of the element to be annotated. Figure 4 shows example QoS requirements on the demand side in a UML activity diagram. *ResponseTime* of *GetCreditApplication* is required to be lower than 10 ms. Figure 5 shows the corresponding QoS offering in the service description of *GetCreditApplication*.

5   Prototyping a Service Management

In order to support the mentioned features we have prototyped a service management framework. It consists of a system architecture mainly integrating open source features and a methodology describing how to use the prototype to introduce a service management in an SOA.

5.1 Architecture

The architecture consists of a modeling approach using Protégé (extended by an OWL plug-in) to edit an OWL-S ontology. The Jena framework is being used to integrate and search the models. Furthermore there is a relational database (MySQL) representing the ontology attributes and integrating the UDDI taxonomy. The logic and GUI implements a service management-specific authentication approach differentiating roles as "Service Architect", "Service Programmer", and "Business Process Owner". A role-specific GUI shows relevant issues depending on the roles' tasks and interests only. For example a programmer needs to have detailed information about finding and binding of services which a business process owner will never need. Figure 6 gives an overview of the prototypical architecture and its three-layered structure.

Protégé is a free, open source ontology editor from Stanford University [16]. Protégé with Protégé-OWL, a plug-in for defining ontologies in OWL also from Stanford University (available at [17]), is used for taxonomy definition. OWL-S Editor is a Protégé plug-in developed at SRI International (available at [18]). It helps to define

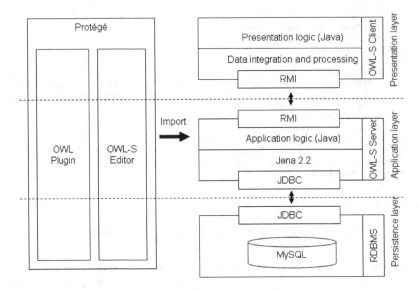

Fig. 6. Overview of service management prototype

services in OWL-S by making available the OWL-S ontology with its predefined elements and a special view on the service, profile, grounding, and process instances. The prototype itself is written in Java. It uses RMI (Remote Method Invocation) for communication between the Java components and builds on Jena, a semantic web service framework, for the semantic support. Jena facilitates the usage of internal and external reasoners and access to the database via RDQL (Resource Description Framework Query Language) [19]. The prototype uses it for interfacing with the database where the semantic description is stored and for performing several operations on the ontology database, in this case MySQL.

5.2 Methodology

The first version of the prototype supports basic tasks for a service management. The following tasks are being implemented:

Taxonomy/Ontology Definition. The mentioned additions to the OWL-S ontology can be made with the OWL Editor adding new *ServiceParameter* and *owl:Thing* sub-classes. Later service descriptions and ontology extensions can be done using the OWL file. Also, a taxonomy for the service category field and input/output parameters can be developed with Protégé OWL.

Service Description and Annotation. Service annotation and changes to existing annotations are done with the OWL-S Editor by loading the OWL file that contains the ontology extended by the above mentioned elements. It is possible to import existing WSDL descriptions.

Once the extended OWL-S ontology is loaded the services can be described. For specifying a parameter for a service the predefined *ServiceParameter* has to be used.

There are two ways of doing this. If the parameter contains listed elements, e.g. *ServiceLifecycleStatus*, a link to an existing instance can be used. If the parameter contains an element with free content like a number or a text field (e.g. *ServiceVersion*), a new parameter value instance has to be created.

For the service description Protégé and the web-based GUI can be used. Protégé does not support the service management-specific authentication system. Therefore the use of the prototyped GUI should be preferred.

Apart from the non-functional elements, it is possible to semantically describe the input/output parameters using normal OWL-S functionality and the service parameter ontology defined.

Service Registration. Service registration is done by importing the OWL-S service description into the prototype and its database. This is necessary in the case of changing attributes. The prototype then performs the search activities laid out in the next part.

Service Discovery and Review. The main functionality of the prototype is search functionality across the services registered and described. There are several possibilities for performing searches using the additional semantic information:

1. Simple queries – searching for services, input/output parameters, taxonomy expressions, etc. using the full names of these elements
2. Semantic queries for services using their input and output parameters
3. Semantic queries for services that match other services' input or output parameters
4. Semantic queries for services using taxonomy elements
5. Semantic queries using the other additionally defined parameters such as *ServiceVariant*, *ServiceResponsibility*, and *ServiceLifecycleStatus*

Queries can be combined by limiting the search space by an outcome of a previous search operation. For service management in complex environments it is absolutely necessary to support role-specific views combined with access rights management. The architect for example does not necessarily need to know all the details about the pricing scheme. Business owners are not interested in technical details about invocation. Hiding unnecessary information improves usability, reduces the number of errors, and is sometimes a must when it comes to confidentiality. The prototype is currently being extended by this functionality.

The main feature is the generic way of defining/redefining service taxonomy and the permanent annotation of existing and new services. It is a matter of fact that there is no stable service description in complex environments. Therefore the change of taxonomy in a distributed SOA is a must when it comes to a huge number of implemented services, different service lifecycle stages, and an existing role-based service governance approach.

6 Conclusion

Sustainability as the most important characteristic of an integrated architecture needs to be considered in an SOA, too. Changes in the design- and runtime of an SOA will be represented by changes in service taxonomy – changes regarding service management requirements by changes in the specific OWL-S ontology. The effort of handling changes and the methodology of staying up-to-date in the annotation using the actual taxonomy needs more than known web service standards offer. The contribution of the work related to this article is a hands-on approach to service descriptions that is extensible regarding additional future requirements. The article shows that it is possible to build a semantically enriched service repository with OWL-S that supports several tasks that are the basis for higher level service management activities. Therefore it is evolutionary and a compatible upgrade of the existing web service description standards.

The current prototype will be extended regarding several issues. On the conceptual level, the integration with a UDDI registry has to be improved. With this respect, the role of WSDL-S for integration has to be examined. In addition, further work is necessary to check whether similar extensions can be made with WSMO.

The presented approach is extendable. A valuable field for further research on the business level is therefore a more structured examination of the content and the statements related to service lifecycle management and QoS. For real world applicability, it is important to have ready-to-use de facto standardized QoS models and extensions to OWL-S.

References

1. Gold, N., Knight, C., Mohan, A., Munro, M.: Understanding Service-Oriented Software, pp. 71–77. IEEE Computer Society Press, Los Alamitos (2004)
2. McCoy, D., Natis, Y.: Service-Oriented Architecture: Mainstream Straight Ahead. Gartner Research (2003)
3. New Rowley Group: Building a more flexible and efficient IT infrastructure - Moving from a conceptual SOA to a service-based infrastructure (2003),
   http://www.newrowley.com/reseach.html
4. Lubblinsky, B., Tyomkin, D.: Dissecting Service-Oriented Architectures. Business Integration Journal, 52–58 (2003)
5. Roth, P.: Moving to A Service Based Architecture. Business Integration Journal, 48–50 (2003)
6. Sleeper, B., Robins, B.: The Laws of Evolution: A Pragmatic Analysis of the Emerging Web Services Market. The Stencil Group, San Francisco (2002)
7. Weinreich, R., Sametinger, J.: Component Models and Component Services: Concepts and Principles. In: Council, W.T., Heinemann, G.T. (eds.) Component-Based Software Engineering: Putting Pieces Together, pp. 22–64. Addison Wesley, Boston (2001)
8. Aier, S.: How Clustering Enterprise Architectures helps to Design Service Oriented Architectures. In: IEEE SCC2006, IEEE, Chicago, USA (2006)
9. Martin, D., Burstein, M., Hobbs, J., Lassila, O., McDermott, D., McIlraith, S., Narayanan, S., Paolucci, M., Parsia, B., Payne, T., Sirin, E., Srinivasan, N., Sycara, K.: OWL-S: Semantic markup for Web services (2006),
   http://www.ai.sri.com/daml/services/owl-s/ 2/ overview/
10. DAML: DAML Services (2006), http://www.daml.org/services/owl-s/
11. Fensel, D., Bussler, C.: The Web Service Modeling Framework WSMF. In: Electronic Commerce: Research and Applications, pp. 113–137 (2002)

12. Feier, C., Domingue, J.: D3.1v0.1 WSMO primer. DERI (2005),
    http://www.wsmo.org/TR/d3de.1/v0.1/
13. de Bruijn, J., Bussler, C., Domingue, J., Fensel, D., Hepp, M., Keller, U., Kifer, M.,
    König-Ries, B., Kopecky, J., Lara, R., Lausen, H., Oren, E., Polleres, A., Roman, D., Sci-
    cluna, J., Stollberg, M.: Web Service Modeling Ontology (WSMO) - W3C Member sub-
    mission 3 June 2005 (2005), http://www.w3.org/Submission/WSMO/
14. Akkiraju, R., Farrell, J., Miller, J., Nagarajan, M., Schmidt, M.-T., Sheth, A., Verma, K.:
    Web service semantics - WSDL-S - W3C member submission 7 November 2005 - Version
    1.0 (2005), http://www.w3.org/Submission/2005/SUBM-WSDL-S-20051107/
15. OMG: UML Profile for Modeling Quality of Service and Fault Tolerance Characteristics
    and Mechanisms - OMG available specification - Version 1.0 - formal/06-05-02. OMG
    (2006), http://www.omg.org/cgi-bin/apps/doc?formal/06-05-02.pdf
16. Welcome to Protégé. Stanford Medical Informatics (2006), http://protege.stanford.edu/
17. What is Protégé-OWL? Stanford Medical Informatics (2006),
    http://protege.stanford.edu/overview/protege-owl.html
18. The OWL-S Editor (2004), http://owlseditor.semwebcentral.org/
19. Jena - A Semantic Web Framework for Java. sourceforge.net, http://jena.sourceforge.net/

Industrializing Software Development:
The "Factory Automation" Way

N. Ilker Altintas[1,2], Semih Cetin[1,2], and Ali H. Dogru[2]

[1] Cybersoft Information Technologies,
Ata Plaza 3/3, Kat:3, 34758, Istanbul, Turkey
{ilker.altintas,semih.cetin}@cs.com.tr
[2] Department of Computer Engineering
Middle East Technical University, Ankara, Turkey
dogru@ceng.metu.edu.tr

Abstract. Improving the productivity by means of systematic reuse has been a major challenge particularly for the last decade in software industry. Following the individual techniques like Architecture-Based Development, Model-Driven Development and Software Product Lines, Software Factories have eventually come to the stage as an umbrella solution to software productivity problem by assembling the applications with frameworks, patterns, models and tools. While this theoretically seems quite suitable, it still needs practical guidance at certain points such as defining and orchestrating reusable assets for setting up distinct software factories. This paper proposes a methodical way for such difficulties in establishing software factories as the way other manufacturing industries have been doing for several decades, which is known to be "factory automation". We articulate the "software factory automation" for managing reusable assets across distinct software product lines based on an architecture-driven software factory meta-model and tailoring them to form directly executable software assets.

1 Introduction

The vision of improving reusability and hence quality is critical for increasing the productivity of software teams as well as decreasing the cost and time to market of software products. Boehm put special emphasis on software productivity management through systematic reuse leveraged by three basic strategies: working faster via tools to automate the labor-intensive tasks, working smarter with process improvement, and working less via reuse of software artifacts [7]. The question is which strategy will produce the highest payoff? An extensive analysis addressed this question for the US Department of Defense and concluded that "working less" is more valuable three times than "working smarter" and six times than "working faster" [8].

Mainly for past two decades, software industry has demanded personal productivity and now it turns its vision to the technologies that automate business processes. As the industry matures, businesses look for much richer functionalities and quicker response times. Accordingly, software industry should surpass the techniques that brought it to this point, and embrace the industrialization best practices achieved by manufacturing. These include product assembly from

D. Draheim and G. Weber (Eds.): TEAA 2006, LNCS 4473, pp. 54–68, 2007.

components, reducing labor-intensive tasks with automation, setting up the software product lines and supply chains, formalizing the interfaces, and standardizing architectures and processes. In short, such a vision is known to be the "software factory" approach. Although this approach is not new and addressed by many researchers and industry experts, it still needs formal models and practical assistance for establishing them across different business domains.

This paper presents a methodical approach to set up software factories based on an architecture-driven "software factory meta model", defining factory assets accordingly and tailoring them for creating actual software factories in diverse product lines. This proposition is inspired by the "programmable logic controller" approach applied in other industries for many years, however explicitly adapted to building software factories. Establishing software product lines so far on different business domains such as banking, insurance, enterprise resource planning and e-government, we concluded that reusable assets can be designed for functional and non-functional requirements even across these diverse business domains by modeling a generic software factory schema and then tailoring to directly executable software assets.

The paper continues with brief explanation of comparable studies in the next section. Then, we shall introduce the overview of our software factory automation model. Followed by explaining the practical implementation aspects of our proposed approach, the paper ends with conclusions and future work.

2 Background and Related Work

Some have claimed so far that software cannot be manufactured, hence automating the software development process is not that much viable for reuse. Meanwhile, the skilled labor bottleneck in software industry has led to rapidly increasing costs, time to market delays, and common problems like reliability, security, and performance. Early projects for the industrialization of software development had come in late 80's like European [32], Japanese [1], or Brazilian [33] models. However these attempts were too early to be successful without the help of contemporary research in systems modeling and software reuse.

Different software reuse techniques have been devised so far, which resulted in reasonable savings by using prefabricated parts for higher productivity [4, 26]. Specifically, Component-Oriented Software Engineering (COSE) puts software reuse within an architectural framework to produce a set of reusable components that are composed to obtain a high level of reuse while developing members of an application family [13]. Architecture-Based Development (ABD) shows a clear understanding of domain architecture by separating design from implementation issues, which makes the reusable aspects explicit [36]. Service-Oriented Architecture (SOA) leverages a logical framework by decoupling several logical units of functionality, i.e. services, which facilitates the software reuse by eliminating the recreation of common services [3, 37]. Frameworks are providing software reuse by hiding the composition details from component implementers through the use of proper patterns [16, 17].

Aspect-Oriented Software Development (AOSD) introduced new techniques for the separation and composition of scattered and tangled concerns in a way that recurring aspects can be easily modeled for reuse [15, 24]. Model-Driven Development (MDD) uses models to automate development and achieve the software reuse by automatically generating executable parts whenever and wherever needed. MDD exploits Domain Specific Languages (DSL) to write higher-level specifications of software that capture developer intent in computational forms [30, 35, 38].

While the aforementioned methods enable software reuse, they do not present a complete roadmap. Software Product Line (SPL) has been the first complete approach for systematic reuse by sharing a common and managed set of features that satisfies the specific needs of a particular market segment or mission and that are developed from a common set of core assets in a prescribed way [4, 12]. SPL is a conceptual baseline and organizations should realize their own implementations accordingly [28].

The concept of SPL has been extended to define Software Factories that configure extensible tools, processes, and content using a software factory template based on a software factory schema to automate the development and maintenance of variants of an archetypical product by adapting, assembling, and configuring framework based components [18, 20, 25, 38]. Like SPL, Software Factory is also a logical baseline, but there exist some implementations such as ISpySoft in .NET environment [23]. While they exist, there has been no mutual understanding yet to generalize the establishment of Software Factories as the way manufacturing industry has been doing. Some efforts like PuLSE by Fraunhofer [29] and Kulkarni et al [22] share the concerns similar to our proposal, but the former is concentrated on individual setup of SPLs with reference architectures and methodic processes whereas the latter proposes a completely model-driven way. We differ from PuLSE primarily by using isolated building blocks for seamless integration, and from Kulkarni et al by being more architecture-driven.

3 The "Software Factory Automation" Way

It has been typically recognized in many industries that recurring and labor intensive tasks were left to machines with automatic processes for maximizing the productivity. Industrial automation such as controlling machines or factory assembly lines is done through the use of small computers called Programmable Logic Controller (PLC). A PLC has three basic building blocks: Programmable Processor (PP) to be programmed with a Computer Language (CL) using a dedicated Development Environment (DE).

Our Software Factory Automation (SFA) approach is principally inspired by the PLC concept. Fig. 1 shows this one-to-one correspondence: Domain Specific Engine (DSE) is paired with PP, Domain Specific Language (DSL) with CL, and Domain Specific Tool (DST) with DE. The encapsulation of DSE, DSL, and DST is called as Domain Specific Kit (DSK) to be paired with PLC in analogy. As the way PLCs are used for abstracting a wide range of functionalities like basic relay control or motion control, DSKs in SFA approach can be designed specifically to abstract certain things such as screen/report rendering or business rule execution in software factories.

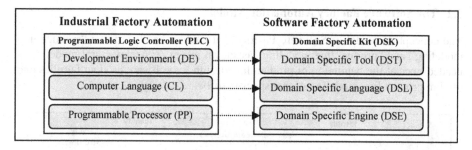

Fig. 1. Software Factory Automation and PLC Analogy

SFA has further commonalities with PLC. Specifically, PLC is typically a Reduced Instruction Set Computer (RISC) based and contains a variable number of I/O ports. So does our SFA model. DSK has logical I/O ports to have seamless connection with each other for context propagation. DSLs are kept in higher-level abstractions so that the design and transformation can be easily accomplished as in the concept of RISC in PLCs. Moreover, DSE has inherent execution monitoring features in design as PP has extensions for Supervisory Control and Data Acquisition (SCADA) monitoring.

3.1 Basic Definitions and Stakeholders

Before giving the details, we present the basic definitions and identify stakeholders in Table 1 for better understanding of our SFA model.

Table 1. Basic Definitions and Stakeholders of SFA Model

Term (Acronym)	Definition
Software Factory Automation (SFA)	A collection of best practices, software assets, and architectural frameworks out of which it enables the creation of a software factory.
SFA Architectural Hyperframe	A template for defining the composability of DSEs to form SPL reference architecture (a sort of software factory schema).
SPL Reference Architecture	SPL reference architecture is the generalized architecture of several end products, and it defines the infrastructure common to the end systems and the interfaces of components that will be included in the end systems [19].
Product Architecture	A specialization of the SPL reference architecture for a specific product.
Domain Specific Language (DSL)	A programming language dedicated to a particular domain or problem with appropriate built-in abstractions and notations.
Domain Specific Engine (DSE)	An engine specifically designed and tailored to execute a specific DSL.
Domain Specific Tool (DST)	An environment to develop software artifacts of a specific DSL.
Domain Specific Kit (DSK)	A collective name for DSL, DSE and DST.
Asset Meta Model (AMM)	A meta-meta-modeling language, which allows us to define an asset modeling language for a specific product line.
Asset Modeling Language (AML)	A meta-model, derived from AMM, to define all software artifacts to be used in a particular product line.
Asset Model	The model of any specific software artifact, which is defined by using AML.
Executable Asset	The runtime object built from an asset model after tailoring.
Stakeholder	Responsibility
SFA Engineer	Development of Software Factory Automation model.
SPL Engineer	Design of a specific SPL, DSEs, and its SFA-based asset model, as well as management of product line and its assets, which is in charge of product line management and core asset development compliant with general SPL model.
Product Engineer	Management of a specific product in an individual product line.
Product Line Staff	People responsible for all other product line activities including business domain modeling and asset tailoring for a specific product.

3.2   The Software Factory Automation Model

The conceptual model of Software Factory Automation has two parts: "architectural modeling" and "product line modeling" as shown in Fig. 2. Architectural modeling is needed once at the beginning of product line design for software product families and used in product line modeling of that specific software factory.

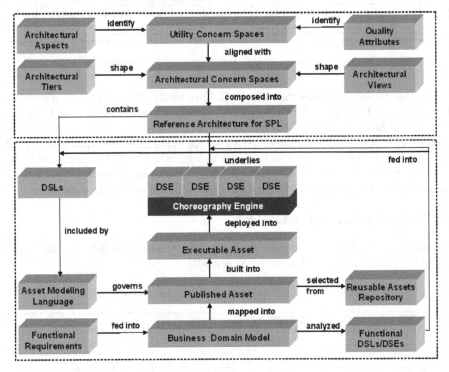

Fig. 2. The Conceptual Model of Software Factory Automation

Architectural Modeling

Architecture modeling is expected to relate architectural aspects and quality targets to running components and connectors. SFA uses an architectural modeling approach first to localize these concerns in multiple concern spaces and then relate them from problem to solution domain. This approach identifies the problem domain in Utility Concern Spaces by correlating the Architectural Aspects and Quality Attributes, and solution domain in Architectural Concern Spaces by correlating the Architectural Tiers and Architectural Views.

Architectural aspects are the required set of architectural issues like authentication, authorization, and logging whereas quality attributes are product quality issues such as scalability, performance, and flexibility. Architectural tiers are well-known tiers of "n-tier" architectural model such as presentation, Web, application and data tiers whereas architectural views are different viewpoints of stakeholders like functional, process, design, and system views. Classical approaches map these problem domain concerns to design decisions of solution domain, which may end up with crosscutting concerns.

SFA prefers to address problem and solution domain concerns in isolated concern spaces and map these concern spaces into each other instead of mapping individual architectural concerns. This mapping technique is called "symmetric alignment" [9] and assisted by a methodical approach to identify components (DSEs), and connectors (composition of DSEs) in the solution domain, which constitutes the SPL Reference Architecture (Software Factory Template) in our SFA model. Moreover, identification of architectural properties facilitates the definition of SPL Contextual Information, which contains the stateful/stateless information to connect individual DSEs, and is needed for independent design and implementation of these individual DSEs through a standard communication schema across DSLs. At the end of this step, DSEs and DSLs have been identified within the solution domain (target scope of the software factory).

SFA architectural modeling identifies the set of DSEs and associated DSLs with the composability rules under an "SFA Architectural Hyperframe", which is a sort of software factory schema that can later form SPL Reference Architectures. SFA model needs a way to define this architectural hyperframe through an XML-based meta-model, which is called Asset Meta Model (AMM). AMM is a meta-modeling language to define the Asset Modeling Language (AML) of a distinct SPL.

Accordingly, AML includes the set of required DSLs to define reusable assets of an individual SPL. The common asset definition at a meta-level enables the design and cross-utilization of reusable software assets across multiple factories. Embedding the selected DSLs into AMM together with defining choreography and variability points of assets constitute an AML for the target software factory. AML defines how DSLs will be composed to form the assets of a software factory by defining the composability rules and constraints. AMM also provides proper means to define variability points and parameterizations of assets whereby the resulting AML has specific definitions for the management of commonality/variability in domain assets.

Product Line Modeling

Apart from this architectural modeling process, functional requirements of business domain for a product family need another modeling process, which is called "product line modeling" in SFA approach and illustrated in the lower part of Fig. 2. Executed from the bottom up, this process starts with a domain analysis to form a Business Domain Model for the specific software factory. Domain analysis is performed in two ways: one for understanding the functional requirements specific to a product family, and the other for defining common/variable points among the current DSEs/DSLs dedicated to functional items.

Business domain model is then mapped into Published Assets in the second phase. Published assets are the meta-level specialization of reusable assets for the particular functional requirements of a software factory. Towards publishing reusable assets for a particular business domain, this step selects proper assets from Reusable Assets Repository under the supremacy of Asset Modeling Language previously introduced in architectural modeling. Published assets are semantically expressed and accessible specifications that can be generated into actual Executable Assets. Formally, these two steps depend on a semantically expressed notation known as Business Process Modeling Notation (BPMN), which is a methodology independent and unambiguous notation to express any business process with semantics apart from being a visual notation [6]. Since BPMN is a notation that business process analyst uses to design executable business processes, it is selected as the modeling notation for representing business domain and publishing assets for SFA approach.

After representing the Published Assets, SFA needs another expression language to specify the Executable Assets. SFA anticipated the use of Business Process Modeling Language (BPML) [6] extended with DSL abstractions for several reasons. First, BPMN directly translates into BPML, which thoroughly assists our transformation approach from Published Assets to Executable Assets. Furthermore, BPML provides an abstracted execution model for collaborative and transactional business processes based on a transactional finite-state machine, which is quite suitable for the expression of executable assets in terms of DSLs and for the deployment to DSEs managed by a Choreography Engine.

However, there are some drawbacks as well. BPML adopts a monolithic execution model where every sort of detail should be specified at once, which is contradictory to the "deferred encapsulation" [20] of DSEs. In SFA approach, choreography engine requires the separation of concerns across different DSEs and thus deferred encapsulation can be achieved through plugging in and out any DSE as needed. That is why BPML needs extensions to support DSLs with higher levels of abstraction.

3.3 SFA Architectural Hyperframe

The features mapped into specific DSLs are going to be executed by corresponding DSEs. Therefore, dynamic plugging and context-awareness of DSLs are crucial for the runtime execution model. However this is not enough, a central authority is needed for the seamless integration. SFA Architectural Hyperframe (through a Choreography Engine) enables this communication and coordination among DSEs. It ensures context management, state coordination, communication, produce/consume messaging, nested processes, distributed transactions, and process-oriented exception handling.

Dynamically assembling the parts in software factories is a must and this can be achieved only by "deferred encapsulation" [20] that can be modeled in different ways such as Inversion-of-Control or Mediator Patterns [17]. Another systematic approach for that is known to be "Feature-Oriented Programming/Development (FOP/D)". The features are first class entities to be used in the design of more capable SPLs, since dynamically adding and removing features may facilitate the flexibility of designing products and empower the commonality and variability management [14]. Our SFA approach anticipates feature-driven specification with dynamically composable basic aspects, which is called "Rule-Based Model for Basic Aspects (RUMBA)" [2, 10].

RUMBA basically enables the design of any entity with the dynamic composition of feature-driven "basic aspects". Moreover, every basic aspect may contain other basic aspects recursively to form the "features". RUMBA is a versatile component for modeling the SFA Architectural Hyperframe. It has been used as a separate DSE for business rule management in modeling insurance applications. Furthermore, it can be used in the design and implementation of very flexible DSEs for any feature set such as content management and workflow management.

SFA Architectural Hyperframe needs a formal composition model like the way PLCs can be composed to have the complete factory automation in other industries. A DSL either may have a textual or graphical representation (concrete syntax) [38]. In our approach, DSLs are required to comply with certain standards to be plugged into the Choreography Engine. Each DSL defines artifact names, external references (referred artifact names from the outer world), composition rules and constraints (like connector types), and variability points specifically applicable for the domain. In such a way, DSEs are declarative, context-free and loosely coupled to each other; hence we can easily apply the golden principle of separation of concerns for different domains. Therefore, each concern has been expressed and executed by different DSL and DSE combination like PLCs are controlling certain concerns in industrial automation.

4 Software Asset Model for Software Factory Automation

A software asset model that will enable the cross-utilization of reusable assets is the key concept in SFA approach. These software assets will then be applicable across various software factories. In this section, the asset definition and corresponding meta-levels are presented as well as the asset meta-model and specification of distinct assets is discussed with a simplified example.

4.1 Understanding Software Asset

In product line approach, the definition of asset is left to the SPL Engineer. In factory automation model we propose a semantic model for assets as shown in Fig. 3. Our asset model is focused on the definition and management of all software artifacts, rather than other process assets such as design artifacts, test scenarios, procedures, etc. However, this does not imply that process-oriented product line assets are not critical for the success of setting up SPL (see Section 5).

Different software factories can be instantiated from Software Factory Automation model. Therefore, we devise a modeling language, AMM, to define the factory and its asset model. Fig. 3 depicts this relation on the right of the figure.

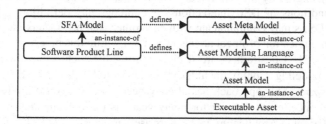

Fig. 3. Four Levels of Software Asset Models

AMM is a meta-meta-modeling language to allow us to define an AML. For each software factory, an AML is defined using the meta-meta-model of AMM. AML is a meta-model to define all software artifacts to be used in a particular software factory. Notice that different product lines imply the use of different modeling languages. In a software factory, software assets are modeled with corresponding AML. Finally, within a product line, different products can be assembled using the reusable software assets by means of tailoring. The term "tailoring" is used to cover all activities such as parameterization and customization of existing assets and development of new ones.

4.2 Software Asset Meta Model

AMM is an XML-based specification language to support the definition of a software factory and its asset model. Fig. 4 shows the overview model of AMM.

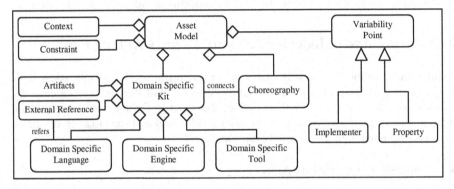

Fig. 4. Software Asset Meta Model (AMM)

The main block of AMM is the DSKs, which are formed by defining DSLs, DSEs and DSTs. For instance, if business rule segregation is needed for the domain, then:

– DSL is an XML-based rule specification language, e.g. RuleML [31],
– DSE is the corresponding rule execution runtime environment, e.g. RUMBA,
– DST is the accompanied rule definition editor, e.g. RUMBA RuleEditor.

The domain specific needs of different software factories can be plugged into the choreography engine by this approach. "Choreography" block in Fig. 4 defines the rules and conditions of DSE interactions. A choreography definition indicates that two specific DSEs may communicate with each other, and parameters like connection type and communication protocol are also specified within this block.

"Context" and "Constraints" are decided during the architectural modeling and product line modeling. Context includes all variables to be shared by DSEs through a global namespace. This approach has already been used in several product lines for banking, insurance, e-government for many years as the fundamental mechanism in our Service-Oriented Architecture and Enterprise Service Bus [2, 3]. Context includes not only architectural variables such as "session_identifier", "user_id" etc., but also business domain variables such as "branch_code" or "customer_id" for banking. Both architectural and business domain definitions are product line specific extensions, and resulting AML describes such extensions. Domain specific constraints are expressed as part of AML and they will be applicable to all assets defined by that AML.

Management of "Variability Points" is the key discriminator between conventional software engineering and software product line engineering [21, 27]. The proposed asset model provides means to define variability points. Variability point definitions include variable items, variants, constraints, visibility, binding properties, and the likes.

4.3 Working with Assets

In this section, we discuss how software assets are specified, instantiated and assembled as major concepts of software factories. During our discussion we shall give the simplified version of a real life software asset from our banking product line.

Using the techniques discussed in Section 3, the resulting architectural model has five Domain Specific Kits, which are listed in Table 2. From the asset management point of view, it contains the components (DSE) that have software artifacts to be managed collectively as software assets. For instance, the screen pages and regions are defined in Enhanced Bean Markup Language (EBML: a DSL for content specification [2, 3, 5]); all content and service rules are defined in RUMBA [2, 10]; etc.

Table 2. DSKs in Example Architecture

DSL	DSE	DST	Purpose and Comments
EBML (Enhanced Bean Markup Language) [3,5]	ERE (EBML Rendering Engine)	EDS (EBML Development Studio)	Facilitates rich client presentation
Service XML [3,5]	Service Executor	Service Editor and Eclipse IDE	Realization of the service-oriented architecture. Enables the services to be callable with uniform interfaces
BPML (Business Process Markup Language)	BPML Engine	Process Designer	Definition of business processes and flows.
RUMBA [2,10]	RUMBA Runtime	RUMBA Design Environment	RuleML like syntax to define content, service and business rules
POM (Persistent Object Model) XML [3,5]	POM Runtime	POM Eclipse Plug-in	O2R definitions to access RDBMS

Some descriptive parts of the AML for banking are given in Fig. 5. Major sections of AML are context, domain specific kits, choreography of domain specific kits and variability points. The context definition contains several architectural and functional variables. Domain Specific Kit specification includes the DSL, DSE and DST specifications, artifact names expressed with that DSL and external references to other DSLs to access their artifacts. Name of the artifacts and external references are similar to output and input ports of PLCs, respectively.

```
<asset-meta-model name="Banking">
     <context>
          <var name="session_id"/>
          <var name="user_code"/>
          <var name="brach_code"/>
          ...
     </context>
     <domain-specific-kits>
          <domain-specific-kit>
               <domain-specific-language name="ebml"/>
               <domain-specific-engine name="ere"/>
               <domain-specific-tool name="eds"/>
               <domain-specific-artifacts>
                    <domain-specific-artifact name="page"/>
                    <domain-specific-artifact name="region"/>
                    <domain-specific-artifact name="popup"/>
               </domain-specific-artifacts>
               <external-references>
                    <ref-type name="process"/>
                    <ref-type name="service"/>
                    <ref-type name="rule"/>
               </external-references>
          </domain-specific-kit>
          <domain-specific-kit>
               <domain-specific-language name="servicexml" />
               <domain-specific-engine name="service executor" />
               <domain-specific-tool name="service editor" />
               <domain-specific-artifact name="service"/>
               <external-references>
                    <ref-type name="rule"/>
                    <ref-type name="pom"/>
               </external-references>
          </domain-specific-kit>
          ...
     </domain-specific-kits>
     <choreography>
          <link source="ebml" dest="service" connection-type="sync" .../>
          ...
     </choreography>
     <variability-points>
          <properties>
               <rule name="reasoning">
                    <val>forward</val>
                    <val>backward</val>
               </rule>
          </properties>
          <implementers>
               <service name="body"/>
          </implementers>
     </variability-points>
</asset-meta-model>
```

Fig. 5. An Example Asset Model for Banking Software Factory

After the specification of Domain Specific Kits, choreography rules and variability points are defined. In the sample choreography definition, it is stated with the <link> tag that EBML calls a service synchronously. Variability point example is the one that some rules may have "reasoning" properties with values "forward" or "backward". The rules that will be using such an option are specified while defining an asset. Similarly, service body definitions can be changed dynamically using implementers. The new implementers can be plugged in using bytecode engineering facilities. The RUMBA framework has dedicated architectural patterns for such kind of reflectivity [2, 10].

After briefly discussing the sample AML, we present a definition of a sample asset, the "Document". "Document" is an asset to be used in preparing, displaying, printing and storing transactional documents such as bill payments and account statements. The simplified definition of "Document" is given in Fig. 6.

```
<asset name="document" asset-meta-model="Banking">
     <parts>
          <ebml artifact="page">Register_Document</ebml>
          <ebml artifact="page">Display_Document</ebml>
          <ebml artifact="page">Save_Document</ebml>
          <ebml artifact="region">Show_Document</ebml>
          <service>GenerateDocument</service>
          <service>SaveDocument</service>
          <service>UpdateMetaData</service>
          <service>
               <name>Get_Document</name>
               <use type="rule">isAuthorized</use>
          </service>
          <rule>
               <name>isAuthorized</name>
               <use type="service">getUserInfo</use>
          </rule>
          <rule>isDocumentAvailable</rule>
          ...
     </parts>
     <export-parts>
          <ebml>Show_Document</ebml>
          <service use-property="template-name">GenerateDocument</service>
          <service>SaveDocument</service>
          <rule use-property="reasoning">isDocumentAvailable</rule>
          ...
     </export-parts>
     <external-references>
          <service>getUserInfo</service>
     </external-references>
     <variability-points>
          <properties>
               <template-name/>
          </properties>
     </variability-points>
</asset>
```

Fig. 6. Definition of "Document" Asset (Simplified)

An asset contains artifacts (`<parts>` tag) that are defined by DSLs included in the AML. Those parts may depend on parts from other asset definitions; hence these parts are defined as external references. Similarly, the parts available to other assets are declared in "export-parts" section to make them accessible. Variability points for assets are defined as part of the asset definition as well.

The reusability of software assets directly depends on the existence of common DSLs for different software factories. An asset can be reused across different factories only if the necessary DSEs required by the asset specification exist in software factory definition. The complete version of the given "Document" asset definition has been used in two distinct product families. In banking, it is used to generate and store the statements of the transactions whereas it is used as the means to generate and save the policies in an insurance domain.

5 Setting up a Software Factory

The roadmap for setting up a software factory based on SFA is presented in Fig. 7. The figure describes high-level activities while sieving most of the details. An architecture-based domain modeling instantiates the SPL reference architecture. SFA architectural hyperframe enables the construction of reference architecture by embedding several DSEs. SPL setup will be completed by building and publishing the assets, and importing the product line practices such as asset, configuration and product management.

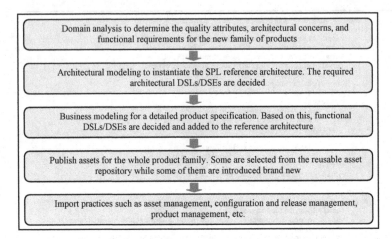

Fig. 7. Setting up a Software Factory Based on SFA

In order to achieve high levels of systematic software reuse and interoperability, the hyperframe provides specifications for both DSE and product engineers, and it enables the creation of SPL reference architecture. SPL reference architecture is the generalized architecture of a product family, and it defines the infrastructure common to end products and interfaces of components that will be included in the end products [19]. Then, concrete architecture is instantiated for a specific product. Product architecture is a specialization of the SPL reference architecture, which includes the considerations such as hardware, operating systems, system software vendors, etc. Fig. 8 depicts the relationship of SFA model approach with levels of architectures.

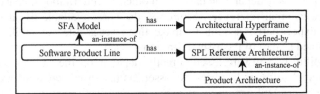

Fig. 8. Software Factory Model and Architectures

The hierarchy of architectures through asset management makes "configuration management" the most critical activity from the management perspective. We learned from lessons that such an activity must be supported with well-organized repositories, automated tools and managerial/organizational processes [11, 34]. In fact, any software factory should have detailed processes complying with Software Process Improvement (SPI) frameworks such as Capability Maturity Model Integration (CMMI), Software Process Improvement and Capability Determination (SPICE) and Allied Quality Assurance Publications (AQAP). Regardless of the SPI standard the organization has to comply with, it is expected to be transparent to software factory automation. Hence, a separate SPI Hyperframe so-called "Lighthouse" in our SFA approach has uniquely achieved such a transparency [11], which is also fully compatible in its design to be integrated with our DSK encapsulation. This is something like PLCs are configured in factories without affecting the ISO compliance of the actual manufacturing processes.

6 Conclusions and Future Work

Starting with SPLs, the Software Factory concept is the new trend to look for more methodical ways to maximize productivity by means of automated efforts wherever possible. However, establishing software factories is not trivial and still needs formal ways and practical assistance. Even more, the reuse is still a meta-level concern in setting up software factories across different business domains as well.

This paper introduced an approach for such difficulties, which is inspired by the way other industries have been successfully realizing factory automation for decades. Initiated from the simple PLC concept, the SFA approach proposed here has a similar baseline to abstract the specialized functionalities in Domain Specific Kits and later compose them according to a software factory meta-model. Authors presented the idea and gave examples accordingly to show the applicability of it. In fact, the authors have already applied the theory and practices given here for several years individually or together, and decided to compile them towards a systematic SFA model. The approach needs further work such as definition of asset ontology, smart repositories recommending the selection of common/varying composition of reusable assets, and tool support in many parts of the modeling and transformations.

References

1. Akima, N., Ooi, F.: Industrializing Software Development: A Japanese Approach. IEEE Software 6(2), 13–21 (1989)
2. Altintas, N.I., Cetin, S.: Integrating a Software Product Line with Rule-Based Business Process Modeling. In: Draheim, D., Weber, G. (eds.) TEAA 2005. LNCS, vol. 3888, pp. 15–28. Springer, Heidelberg (2006)
3. Altintas, N.I., Surav, M., Keskin, O., Cetin, S.: Aurora Software Product Line, TSAD 2005 (2005), http://trese.cs.utwente.nl/TSAD/Papers/aurora.pdf
4. Atkinson, C., Muthig, D.: Enhancing Software Reusability Through Product Line Technology. In: Gacek, C. (ed.) Software Reuse: Methods, Techniques, and Tools. LNCS, vol. 2319, pp. 93–108. Springer, Heidelberg (2002)
5. Aurora Software Product Line (2000), http://www.cs.com.tr/english/products/aurora.html
6. Business Process Management Initiative. http://www.bpmi.org/
7. Boehm, B.W.: Managing Software Productivity and Reuse. IEEE Computer 9, 111–113 (1999)
8. Boehm, B.W.: Analytic Methods in Software Engineering Economics. Springer, Heidelberg (1993)
9. Cetin, S., Altintas, N.I., Sener, C.: An Architectural Modeling Approach with Symmetric Alignment of Multiple Concern Spaces. In: Int. Conf. on Software Engineering Advances, IEEE Computer Society Press, Los Alamitos (2006)
10. Cetin, S., Altintas, N.I., Solmaz, R.: Business Rules Segregation for Dynamic Process Management with An Aspect-Oriented Framework. In: Eder, J., Dustdar, S. (eds.) Business Process Management Workshops. LNCS, vol. 4103, pp. 193–204. Springer, Heidelberg (2006)
11. Cetin, S., Tufekci, O., Karakoc, E., Buyukkagnici, B.: Lighthouse: An Experimental Hyperframe for Multi-Model Software Process Improvement. In: EuroSPI2 Conference (2006)

12. Clements, P., Northrop, L.: Software Product Lines: Patterns and Practice. Addison Wesley, Reading, MA (2001)
13. Dogru, A.H., Tanik, M.M.: A Process Model for Component-Oriented Software Engineering. IEEE Software 20(2), 34–41 (2003)
14. Batory, D.: Feature Oriented Programming for Product-Lines, European Conference on Object Oriented Programming (2006)
15. Elrad, T., Aksit, M., Kiczales, G., Lieberherr, K., Ossher, H.: Discussing Aspects of AOP. Communications of the ACM 44, 33–38 (2001)
16. Fayad, M., Schmidt, D., Johnson, R.: Building Application Frameworks: Object-Oriented Foundations of Framework Design. John Wiley & Sons, Chichester (1999)
17. Fowler, M.: Patterns of Enterprise Application Architecture. Addison-Wesley, Reading (2002)
18. Frankel, D.S.: Business Process Platforms and Software Factories, An Idea Paper, International Workshop on Software Factories (2005)
19. Gallagher, B.P.: Using the Architecture Tradeoff Analysis Method to Evaluate a Reference Architecture: A Case Study, Technical Note CMU/SEI-2000-TN-007 (2000)
20. Greenfield, J., Short, K.: Software Factories: Assembling Applications with Patterns, Models, Frameworks, and Tools. John Wiley & Sons, Chichester (2004)
21. Krueger, C.W.: Practical Strategies and Techniques for Adopting Software Product Lines. In: Workshop on Industrial Experience with Product Line Approaches (2002)
22. Kulkarni, V., Reddy, S.: Enterprise Business Application Product Line As a Model Driven Software Factory. In: International Workshop on Software Factories (2005)
23. Lenz, G., Wienands, C.: Practical Software Factories in.NET. Apress (2006)
24. Nechypurenko, A., Lu, T., Deng, G., Turkay, E., Schmidt, D.C., Gokhale, A.S.: Concern-Based Composition and Reuse of Distributed Systems. In: Bosch, J., Krueger, C. (eds.) ICOIN 2004 and ICSR 2004. LNCS, vol. 3107, pp. 167–184. Springer, Heidelberg (2004)
25. Neema, S., Scott, J., Karsai, G.: Architecture Analysis in Software Factories. In: International Workshop on Software Factories (2005)
26. Peters, J.F., Pedrycz, W.: Software Engineering: An Engineering Approach. John Wiley & Sons, Inc., Chichester (2000)
27. Pohl, K., Böckle, G., Van Der Linden, F.: Software Product Line Engineering: Foundations, Principles, and Techniques. Springer, Heidelberg (2005)
28. Product Line Hall of Fame: http://www.sei.cmu.edu/productlines/plp_hof.html
29. PuLSE: Product Line Software Engineering: http://fogo.iese.fraunhofer.de/PuLSE/
30. Rothenberger, M.A., Hershauer, J.C.: A Software Reuse Measure: Monitoring an Enterprise-Level Model Driven Development Process. Information & Management 35(5) (1999)
31. Rule Markup Initiative. http://www.ruleml.org/
32. Schäfer, W., Weber, H.: European Software Factory Plan-the ESF profile, Modern software engineering, foundations and current perspectives, pp. 613–637 (1989)
33. Sobrinho, F.G., Ferraretto, M.D.: Software plant: the Brazilian software consortium. In: Proceedings of the 1987 Fall Joint Computer Conference on Exploring technology: today and tomorrow, Dallas, US, pp. 235–243. IEEE Computer Society Press, Los Alamitos (1987)
34. Tufekci, O., Cetin, S., Altintas, N.I.: How to Process [Business] Processes, Integrated Design and Process Technology (2006), http://www.cs.com.tr/free/publications/H2PP.pdf
35. Voelter, M.: Model-Driven Software Development Tutorial (2005), http://www.voelter.de/services /mdsd-tutorial.html
36. White, S.A., Lemus-Olalde, C.: Architectural Reuse in Software Development. ASME-ETCE98 (1998)
37. Wong-Bushby, I., Egan, R., Isaacson, C.: A Case Study in SOA and Re-architecture at Company ABC. HICSS (2006)
38. Zdun, U.: Concepts for Model - Driven Design and Evolution of Domain Specific Language. In: International Workshop on Software Factories (2005)

A Closer Look at Database Replication Middleware Architectures for Enterprise Applications[*]

J.E. Armendáriz-Iñigo[1], H. Decker[1], F.D. Muñoz-Escoí[1],
and J.R. González de Mendívil[2]

[1] Instituto Tecnológico de Informática, Campus de Vera, 46022 Valencia, Spain
[2] Universidad Pública de Navarra, Campus Arrosadía, 31006 Pamplona, Spain
{armendariz,hendrik,fmunyoz}@iti.upv.es, mendivil@unavarra.es

Abstract. Middleware-supported database replication is a way to increase performance and tolerate failures of enterprise applications. Middleware architectures distinguish themselves by their performance, scalability and their application interface, on one hand, and the degree to which they guarantee replication consistency, on the other. Both groups of features may conflict since the latter comes with an overhead that bears on the former. We review different techniques proposed to achieve and measure improvements of the performance, scalability and overhead introduced by different degrees of data consistency. We do so with a particular emphasis on the requirements of enterprise applications.

1 Introduction

Although middleware-based replication has been widely discussed in the literature for quite some time [1,2,3], such architectures are only recently emerging as a promising approach to raise the performance and availability of web services for enterprises operating across geographically distant sites [4]. Apart from the usual delay of technological innovations to gain commercial appeal, this is mainly due to two factors: the lack of support from established DBMS vendors, and unsatisfactory solutions for the key challenge of guaranteeing a sufficient degree of consistency and up-to-dateness of replicated data for enterprise applications.

We are confident that the database industry will sooner or later buy into middleware replication technology, since otherwise, the high availability and performance of replicated servers equipped by different vendors would remain an untapped bounty. Hence, we deal in this paper with the remaining issue, viz. the provision of adequate consistency guarantees that are tuned to the requirements of enterprise applications, which may vary from case to case.

There are two canonical alternatives to achieve database replication: by extending the DBMS core code [5,6,7,8], or using a middleware layer [1,2,3,9,10,11]. The former has an immediate performance advantage due to a low overhead, but is vendor-specific and hence handicapped in terms of system interoperability, application portability and migration to new versions or other installations [6,7]. The latter is vendor-independent,

---

[*] This work is supported by the Spanish government under research grants TIC2003-09420-CO2 and TIN2006-14738-C02.

D. Draheim and G. Weber (Eds.): TEAA 2006, LNCS 4473, pp. 69–83, 2007.

hence it is straightforwardly interoperable, facilitates the portability of applications and is easily migrated. It may compensate its higher overhead by an elegant use of built-in SQL constructs, such that concurrency and transaction control is delegated back to where it belongs, i.e., the DBMS core. Enterprise applications clearly benefit from vendor-independent middleware solutions, on which we therefore shall focus in the remainder.

Given the DBMS core vs middleware tradeoff as highlighted above, overhead reduction is clearly the prime goal for middleware architectures. Early solutions have been encumbered by concurrency control tasks that natively belong to the underlying DBMS, and by the necessity to modify given enterprise applications in order to support the middleware's replication management [1,12]. Both issues have rightfully been perceived as burdens or even bugs, rather than features [9]. Further development has then brought forward standardized application interfaces, usually based on JDBC, that offered predefined procedures for web applications (e.g., automated form dialogues) to be called through applications [2].

This move towards application independence is taken a step further by permitting applications to execute any kind of statement. Concurrency control then is delegated to the underlying DBMS while consistency management is left to a given replication protocol, as in RJDBC [11] and C-JDBC [10]. However, both solutions suffer from scalability problems, since an update statement must be executed at all available network nodes before the next statement can be executed. Scalability is enabled in the MADIS architecture [3], which realizes concurrency delegation exclusively by using SQL constructs, and in MIDDLE-R [2,9], which, apart from also using SQL statements, also uses the write-ahead log to propagate updates.

Applications access the distributed system data transparently by way of transactions. All accessible data are persistently stored in an underlying DBMS, the replication of which is hidden from the applications' interface. The transaction isolation level provided by the DBMS co-determines the degree of consistency obtainable in replicated systems. Most commercial DBMSs provide Snapshot Isolation (SI) [13]. It relaxes serializability and thus gains in performance, while concurrency anomalies that cannot easily be worked around are avoided by weakening the SQL-92 standard's definition of isolation levels [13]. This clearly amounts to an immense advantage for web-based applications, since read operations never get blocked with SI [14].

A de-facto standard notion for ensuring transaction correctness in replicated databases is One-Copy Serializability (1CS) [15]. Essentially, it means that the interleaved execution of transactions must be equivalent to some sequential execution. In [14,16], a theory for achieving 1CS using SI has been developed. Moreover, the notion of SI has been extended to Generalized SI (GSI) [14] and One-Copy SI (1CSI) [9], thereby clarifying the notion of *system snapshot* in the context of replicated systems.

The overhead introduced by a middleware architecture is of course determined by its design and implementation, i.e., by the underlying DBMS, the manner by which messages are propagated, how transaction operations are intercepted and managed, etc. However, besides such comparatively superficial technicalities, the overhead is perhaps influenced most crucially by the deployed kind of replication strategy [17,18]. Replication is usually classified by the orthogonal distinctions of: eager or lazy update propagation; executing updates in a dedicated "primary copy" node or permitting update execution everywhere in the network; the degree of communication among sites which may be of constant or linear interaction; and, whether transactions terminate either voting or non-voting. These binary classification criteria span a space of replication protocols with combinations of properties that can be tailored to the specific needs and requirements of various kinds of enterprise applications, that differ with regard to latencies, abortion rates and overhead/performance tradeoff.

In this paper, we propose different transaction correctness criteria in replication architectures that may be satisfied by given enterprise applications. Correlated to the overhead introduced by the architecture, we also review different performance measures. In particular, we review metrics proposed for MIDDLE-R and metrics developed by the DBMS community such as TPC-W [19], which also serves as a benchmark for web transactions. The workload for which the performance is measured is generated in the framework of a controlled internet commerce environment that simulates the activities of a transactional web-based enterprise server.

The rest of the paper is organized as follows: Section 2 paradigmatically describes the main components of a prototypical middleware-based database replication architecture. Its interaction with client applications is described in Section 3. System performance is discussed in Section 4. Section 5 concludes the paper.

2   System Model

Figure 1 shows a typical generic configuration of a replicated database middleware architecture. It is composed of N nodes which communicate among each other via message exchanges. For that, they use a group communication subsystem (GCS), which provides a membership service, i.e., knowledge about live and crashed nodes [20]. Applications submit transaction requests to the system. The database replication middleware (DRM) intercepts these requests and manages the execution of remote transactions at all DBMS replica. The replication protocol, embedded inside the DRM, coordinates the execution of transactions at all nodes in order to ensure data consistency [9,14,15]. Concurrency control, however, is delegated to the DBMSs.

2.1   Protocols for Transaction Execution

Database replication protocols have been classified according to [17]: who can perform updates (*primary copy* [2] and *update everywhere* [9]) and the instant when a transaction update propagation takes place (*eager* [9] or *lazy* [21]). In eager replication schemes, updates are propagated inside the context of the transaction. On the other hand, lazy replication schemes follow the next sequence: update a local copy, commit the transaction and propagate changes to the rest of available replicas. Data consistency is straightly forward by eager replication techniques although it requires extra messages. On the contrary, data copies may diverge on lazy schemes and, as there is no automatic way to reverse committed replica updates, a program or a person must reconcile conflicting transactions. Regarding to who performs the updates, the primary copy requires all updates to be performed on one copy and then propagated; whilst update everywhere allows to perform updates at any copy but makes coordination more complex [22]. Another parameter considered for replication protocols is the degree of communication

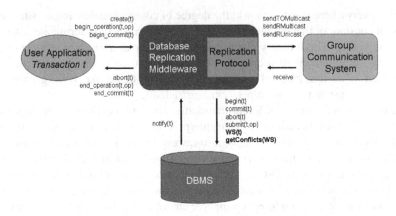

Fig. 1. Sample node of a replicated database middleware architecture

among sites [22]: *constant interaction* [5], where a constant number of messages are exchanged between sites for a given transaction, and *linear interaction* [15], where a site propagates each operation of a transaction to the rest of sites. The last parameter is how a transaction terminates [22]: *voting*, when an extra round of messages are required to coordinate replicas such as the 2-Phase-Commit (2PC) [15] protocol or *non voting*, when a site decides on its own whether a transaction commits or is rolled back, like the certification process [14].

In fixed, tightly connected networks, eager update-everywhere replication is the pre-ferred kind of protocol [17]. Transactions are firstly executed at the node which is close to where they were requested. Updates are then regrouped and sent to the rest of nodes. Once they are delivered, usually in total-order form, the commit phase is started, either with some coordination among nodes (such as in the 2-Phase-Commit protocol (2PC) [15]) or without node interaction but with a certification phase, i.e., a test that decides if a transaction may or may not commit [7,9,14,15]. In loosely connected networks a sim-ilar approach could be taken if all sites directly serve application transactions. However, this replication technique must be enhanced by GCS multicast protocols with optimistic delivery [23] in order to reduce the additional communication latency. In this environ-ment, it could also be used a lazy primary-copy approach [17], since this ensures a faster transaction completion. In general, it is always necessary to take care of possibly conflicting transactions [24] and to re-attempt execution of successfully certified trans-actions until they have been scheduled and committed [9]. This can be accomplished by the DRM, along with schema modifications and stored procedures as described in [25].

2.2 Group Communication

As already indicated, virtual synchrony [20] is supported by a GCS which supports com-munication and membership services. For the model sketched in Figure 1, we assume a system with virtual synchrony, a communication service with reliable multicast for message exchange, and a *partial amnesia crash* [26] failure model (this latter assump-tion is convenient since it is very interesting to deal with node recovery after failure).

The virtual synchrony assumes the notion of a *view*, the set of current active nodes, which is provided by the membership service of GCS. Any change in the composition of a view by entry or exit of a node is supposed to be reported to the recovery protocol (firing a view change event). We assume a primary component membership[1] [27], views installed by all sites are totally ordered (there are no concurrent views), and for every pair of consecutive views there is at least one process that remains operational in both views. Further, *strong* virtual synchrony will be used, to ensure that messages are delivered in the same view they were multicast, and that two nodes exiting view V_1 for entering consecutive view V_2 have delivered the same set of messages in V_1 [20,28].

2.3   The Underlying Database System

At each node, the DBMS stores a physical copy of the replicated database. It executes transactions as specified by the given replication protocol, guaranteeing the well-known ACID transaction properties. With regard to a given node, a transaction is either local or remote, i.e., its write set may originate from a transaction requested at some other node. Moreover, the DRM may modify the database schema, so as to support the automated storage of replication metadata, as well as the triggering of stored procedures to process these metadata.

Instead of the previously mentioned, yet outdated default 2PC locking protocol, commercial DBMSs nowadays usually support Snapshot Isolation (SI), i.e., a kind of multiversion concurrency control [15]. An SI-controlled transaction always reads data from a snapshot of the committed data as of the time the transaction started. It is never blocked from attempting reads as long as its snapshot data is still valid. The writes (updates, inserts and deletes) of a transaction T will also be reflected in this snapshot, to be consulted again if T reads or updates the data another time. Updates by other transactions active after T was initiated are invisible to T. However, a serializable isolation level can be achieved by using SI, as shown in [14,16]. Different isolation levels may be achieved by selecting different replication protocol strategy variants: 1CS [15] (for serializable) and GSI [14], 1CSI [9] for SI. Thereby, they are classified into two families of replication protocols and will be outlined in more detail in Section 3.

2.4   Replication Support

A by now tried-and-tested manner of reducing the overhead of replication protocols is to store and process transaction metadata in the underlying DBMS. However, middleware architectures differ in the way the transaction data are collected and transferred. In MADIS, the transaction report is built by DRM-generated triggers and stored procedures. Although this option is advantageous because it depends on nothing but standard SQL, it involves more write accesses to the database than is necessary if the required information is obtained from the write-ahead log, which is provided in most, if not all DBMSs. This latter option reduces write operations, as observed in [2,9].

The latter paper also pointed out that replication protocols using certification may suffer from aborts caused by the DBMS while applying the write set of already certified

---

[1] We say that a view will satisfy the primary component membership if there are at least half of the pre-configured nodes active in the system.

transactions. A remedy would be to detect conflicting local transactions. Below, we describe a technique for managing concurrency control which combines the simplicity of using DBMS core support with maintaining the product independence of a middleware solution. Instead of having to request and wait for the termination of transactions, conflicting transactions may be aborted immediately. By reducing the abortion delay, the system becomes ready faster for processing other active transactions. We have implemented and tested our approach in PostgreSQL. Our solution needs to scan the system's locking tables. Similar tables are used in virtually all DBMSs (e.g., the V$LOCK view in Oracle 9i, the DBA_LOCK in Oracle 10g r2, the sys.syslockinfo table of Microsoft SQL Server 2000 - converted into a system view in SQL Server 2005 -, etc.), so that this solution is easily portable to all of them, since only standard SQL constructs are used.

Serializability may be obtained also with SI [14], either by modifying the application or considering the readset of transactions. As read-only transactions are only executed at the site they are submitted to, we assume that they read data from a snapshot, and hence do not need to be isolated with regard to update transactions. As a result, it seems appropriate to design a mechanism that notifies write-write conflicts of transactions to the replication protocol. As for conflict detection, the main advantage of our approach is the use of the concurrency control support of the underlying DBMS. Only the system's locking tables need to be scanned for that, so that, again, seamless portability is warranted, since only standard SQL constructs are used. Thus, the middleware is enabled to provide row-level control at each node (as opposed to the usual coarse-grained table control), while all transactions (even those associated to remote write sets) are subject to the underlying concurrency control support. Its implementation is based on the following two elements:

- The database schema is enhanced by the stored function getBlocked(). It looks up blocked transactions in the DBMS metadata (e.g., in the pg_locks view of the PostgreSQL system catalog). It returns a set of pairs consisting of the identifiers of a blocked transaction and of the transaction that has caused the block. If there is no conflict when this function is called, it returns the empty set. In short, getBlocked() reads a system catalog table in which the DBMS keeps information about transaction conflicts. Such a table is maintained by most DBMSs. Thus, this function is easily portable to most of them. Moreover, these DBMSs only provide read access to this system table. So, reading such views or tables does not compromise the regular activity of the DBMS core nor the activity of other transactions.
- An execution thread per database is needed that cyclically calls getBlocked(). Its cycle is configurable and is commonly set to values between 100 and 1000 ms. It runs on the middleware layer. Once this thread has received a non-empty set of conflicting pairs of transactions, it may request the abortion of one of them. For this purpose, each transaction has a priority level assigned to it. By default, it aborts the transaction with smaller priority but takes no action if both transactions have the same priority level.

This mechanism should be combined with a transaction priority scheme in the replication protocol. For instance, we might define two priority classes, with values 0 and 1. Class 0 is assigned to local transactions that have not started their commit phase.

Class 1 is for local transactions that have started their commit phase and also for those transactions associated to delivered write sets that have to be locally applied. Once a conflict is detected, if the transactions have different priorities, then the one with the lowest priority will be aborted. Otherwise, i.e., when both transactions have the same priority, no action is taken and they remain in their current state until the lock is released. Similar, or more complex approaches might be followed in other replication protocols that belong to the update everywhere with constant interaction class [18].

2.5 Replication Middleware

The DRM is the core of the middleware system. It is independent of the underlying DBMS. In [3], we have described a Java implementation, to be used by client applications as a common JDBC driver. It facilitates the plugging and swapping of replication protocols chosen according to given needs and requirements. DRM may act as an interceptor for applications the transactions of which are executed locally at the nearest alive node, while monitoring remote update messages coming in via the GCS. For example, when a commit statement is issued, an eager protocol will start the commit process right away, interacting with the rest of the nodes by transferring the transaction updates. Thereafter, a 2PC protocol or a certification process starts to globally commit the transaction.

3   Middleware Layout for Enterprise Applications

The replication middleware architecture, as outlined in Section 2, is of generic character. In this section, we are going to specialize its layout with regard to typical requirements marked out by applications of enterprises. These enterprises are assumed to consist in a topology of multiple branches and operating in different areas. Needless to say, the enterprise branches and operation areas are supposed to be distributed over geographically disparate locations. In particular, we are going to touch upon application interfaces, load balancing, fault tolerance and tailoring the middleware with regard to different degrees of consistency, as required by different application profiles.

3.1   Interfaces for Communication and Coordination

Most middleware systems that comply with the model as characterized in section 2 export a standard JDBC interface [2,3,10,11]. Hence, applications that already exist do not have to be re-programmed to become usable on top of the middleware. In particular, this means that they can remain completely unaware of the underlying replication, conforming to the ideal of full transparency. Systems such as MADIS, MIDDLE-R, CJDBC and RJDBC merely act as interceptors for invocations performed by clients. Local transactions are forwarded to the underlying DBMS by means of SQL statements. Commit invocations initiate interaction with the remaining nodes. A Read One Write All Available (ROWAA) approach is assumed, with eager update-everywhere replication protocols [17].

Each node has to apply remote transactions coming from other nodes, which mainly consist of writesets of committing transactions. Such remote transactions may abort current active local transactions in case the latter causes any conflict. Then, the middle-ware must notify local transactions about that. The amount of such transaction abortions strongly depends on the degree of consistency as required by the application and on the deployed replication protocol. These abortions have to be done transparently, so that the application perceives them as database rollbacks instead of protocol-driven aborts.

3.2   Load Balancing

Transactions may be redirected to the least loaded node or, more generally, where net-work conditions are optimal. The node to which the transaction is (re-)directed and ini-tially executed is called the *local replica*. Locality of data access supports the decrease of transaction response time. That, however, also depends on the chosen replication protocol (we shall come back on this in Subsection 3.4). Anyway, read operations are always performed on the local node, and no interaction with remote nodes is needed.

Enterprise applications can be classified as services for either internal or external purposes. Internal applications typically are intranet enterprise applications, e.g., IT-based collaboration between different business units, or knowledge management, which is open for internal use but hidden to the outside world. Typical external applications are extranet services, provided via an enterprise web portal to customers and clients. A good intranet replication policy for intranet application is to replicate the database at each site. Such configurations can be likened to peer-to-peer applications. On the other hand, for data replication of extranet enterprise services means that external users access a virtual database which does not belong to their own site. Thus, extranet users behave as clients of a virtual server which actually is a transparently distributed system the high availability, performance, fault tolerance and dependability of which is supported by a transparent replication architecture. This has been outlined in some more detail in [3].

3.3   Fault Tolerance and Recovery

It is important that recovery of crashed or disconnected nodes is fast and does not block the whole system [29]. This permits reducing the workload of alive nodes, as more nodes will recover the replicated database state and will be able to attend new incom-ing transactions. Structurally the same situation is faced with new nodes joining the distribution topology on an ad-hoc basis. Most database replication approaches include a recovery protocol for crashed nodes. In our model architecture, applications may be redirected to an alive node in case its local replica fails. As long as the application is served in a primary component, it will be able to continue its execution. Thus, the high availability of application data is assured. Moreover, thanks to virtual synchrony, a transaction may finally commit even if the serving node of that application crashes during its execution.

3.4   Consistency Levels

Enterprise applications cover a very wide range of different scenarios: Examples can be given that range from grocery chain websites, over web collaboration between customer and e-service centers, to online flight booking and scheduling. A common denominator, however, is that they all share the need to work with consistent, up-to-date data. However, consistency requirements may vary from application to application. For example, web-based flight booking is in need of accurate 24/7 up-to-dateness of data about available flights and seats transactional access with different levels of data consistency. On the other hand, the reporting service applications of interactive data warehousing of grocery chains certainly will not need to take into account the latest updates of the day for their quarterly or annual stock-keeping statistics. With regard to choosing, plugging and swapping of appropriate replication protocols for adapting to changing consistency requirements. This has been looked at in more detail in [3].

Applications may manipulate stored data by SQL statements, including stored procedures. The set of data items read or written by a stored procedure can be anticipated at schema specification time. In particular, the related accesses may be adjusted so as to guarantee a serializable behavior, which clearly is more advantageous than to rely at execution time on the SI provided by the DBMS. Hence, for each stored procedure, a dedicated node can be determined as the owner of that procedure at the time it is compiled. With the knowledge about which data are accessed upon execution of the stored procedure, its owner node can anticipate control strategies and execution plans so as to avoid unnecessary conflicts. This has been looked at in more detail in [2]. In general, however, the data access patterns of user-driven applications are ad-hoc, i.e., unknown in advance. Hence, special attention has to be paid to intersecting read- and writesets of transactions in order to achieve a given level of consistency. The following item points distinguish three characteristic and often encountered levels of consistency requirements, to be adopted for different enterprise applications with corresponding consistency requirements.

- **1CS.** This is the strongest correctness criterion for replicated databases. Replication is transparent to the execution of a transaction. Its interleaved execution among other transactions in the system is equivalent to a serial execution of the transactions in a centralized database. This was introduced in [15] and it supposed that all underlying DBMS were implemented using 2PL.

  This data consistency level is appropriate for applications interested in reading the latest version of data, ensuring that no other transaction will modify the value read until the transaction commits. However, this isolation level does not prevent missing concurrent insertions that satisfy the "WHERE" clause in a "SELECT" statement, thus allowing *phantom reads*.

- **GSI.** This concept has been proposed recently [14], in order to provide a suitable extension of conventional SI for replicated databases. In GSI, transactions may use older snapshots instead of the latest snapshot required in SI. In [14], an impossibility result is stated which justifies the use of GSI in database replication: "there is no non-blocking implementation of SI in an asynchronous system, even if databases never fail". In a non-blocking replication protocol, transactions can start at any time without restriction or delay (even those delays produced by group communication primitives).

  This data consistency level is appropriate for generating dynamic web content. It is typically generated by a combination of a front-end web server, an application server and a back-end database. The possibly dynamic content of the web site is stored in the database of the site's host server. The application server provides methods that implement the business logic of the application. As part of that, the application typically accesses the database. The three servers (web, application and database server) may all execute on a single machine, or each one of them may execute on a separate machine or on a cluster of machines, or various combinations thereof.

– **1CSI.** Simultaneously to the GSI definition, 1CSI was introduced in [9]. It can be viewed as the counterpart of 1CS with serializable SI. A transaction uses the *"latest"* system snapshot which may imply blocking certain read operations as they are not going to see the latest snapshot. A new snapshot version is installed in the system as soon as the transaction installing the new version is firstly committed at any node. Hence, one of the main advantages of SI, viz. non-blocking read operations, is lost.

4 Performance

What makes the use of a given database replication middleware attractive for user applications is its performance. We do not pursue DBMS-core solutions any further, although they will always tend to be somewhat better [7]. But the advantage of our middleware solution is to be independent of the underlying database and to be easily portable to other DBMSs.

The standard way to measure the performance of an application is its transaction response time, i.e. how long it takes to commit a transaction in the system. Measuring the behavior of the system may be done by checking the scalability and overall response time for our application. It is easy to see that the performance of the solution will depend on the kind of applications considered as benchmarks, such as the TPC-W [19] standard benchmark.

4.1 Scalability Through Response Time

We may analyze the scalability and overall performance of the algorithms and the implementation we propose. Moreover, we may study the overhead introduced by the middleware and the GCS. It is important to emphasize that the absolute values of the results are only meaningful to a certain degree. They could be improved by simply using faster machines or by using a different DBMS. The important aspect of these results is the trends they show in terms of behavior as the number of sites and the load in the system increases.

4.1.1 Comparison with Traditional Distributed Locking. A first question that needs to be addressed is whether the middleware we propose really solves the limitations of conventional replication algorithms (e.g., those described in [15]). Gray et al. [17] showed that these conventional algorithms do not scale and, in particular, that increasing the number of replicas would increase the response time of update transactions and produce higher abort rates. We have compared the scalability in terms of response time of our solution with the standard distributed locking implementation of a commercial product, Oracle. The test scenario is fixed to a model of update transactions with the same and fixed number of updates and repeating this pattern of transaction as the number of sites increases [2].

4.1.2 Throughput Scale-out. The main motivation for this work is to provide a replication algorithm that can scale in a cluster based system. Some approaches [2,9,24] have to execute all update transactions at all sites since they do not have any additional knowledge about the database system. As a result, adding new sites in an update intensive environment might help for fault-tolerance, but cannot be used to scale up the system. Using alternative approaches [1], it may be more feasible achieve both fault-tolerance and scalability. Hence, this experiment analyzes how the throughput scales up when we increase the number of sites. It will be very interesting to run three sets of tests: read only, write only, and a mixture of both workloads. The scale-out for a given number of nodes (which is varied in determined range) is obtained as dividing the maximum throughput that can be achieved in this setting by the maximum throughput in a single-site system.

4.1.3 Response Time Analysis. This is pretty similar to the previous point. The same set of transactions acts as a benchmark and we analyze the response time behavior by increasing the load, and determine at which throughput the system saturates (i.e., response times deteriorate).

4.1.4 Communication Overhead. When using group communication primitives, the system built can only scale as much as the underlying communication tool. One of the typical problems of conventional replication algorithms is that they easily overload the network by generating too many messages (e.g., distributed locking generates one message per operation per transaction per site; a 10 site system running transactions of 10 operations at 50 transactions per second generates 5,000 messages per second). Hence 2PC protocols require two multicast messages per transaction whilst certification-based protocols need only one message.

4.2 Transactional Web E-Commerce Benchmark TPC-W

TPC-W [19] is a standard tool proposed by the research and industrial community to measure the performance of DBMSs. It simulates the behavior of users accessing an online bookstore where they search for and buy books. TPC-W has been used by [7,9,14] so as to measure the performance of their different replicated data solutions which are implemented over SI DBMS replicas. TPC-W has different purchase behavior options, but the selection criteria of these options are exclusively based on randomly generated data.

However, although characterizing consumer behavior is a difficult task, the way consumers behave cannot be said to be totally defined by a random pattern. That is why marketing research has tried to describe consumer behavior patterns so as to help firms and practitioners to develop better marketing strategies. Nevertheless, consumer behavior online does not necessarily mimic that observed at physical stores, which has been the one traditionally analyzed. There are important differences between physical and virtual stores that make consumers behave differently. For instance, the amount and quality of the information that is available at each channel, the perceived risk or the possibility of using or not personal purchase lists are not the same at these two shopping environments [30,31,32]. The amount of information available online is said to be extremely high, but this information is always visual, neither tactile nor from the sense of smell [31,33]. So, for products such as towels, in which softness is a valued characteristic, online shopping seems not to be the best shopping option. Thus, a consumer purchasing a towel online will probably show a different behavior than the one he would have had at a physical store — it would be logical to think that he could be more loyal to some brand he had previously purchased.

TPC-W is a transactional web benchmark designed to evaluate e-commerce systems. It specifies a workload that simulates the activities of an online bookstore. Three separate components take part in the interaction: The System Under Test, SUT, comprises all components which are part of the application being simulated; the Remote Browser Emulator, RBE drives the TPC-W workloads creating an Emulated Browser, EB, for each user interacting with the system; and the Payment Gateway Emulator, PGE, represents an external system which authorizes payment of funds.

TPC-W specifies 14 different web pages which must be implemented in the SUT. Moreover it defines the schema of the database where data will be stored. There are described 8 tables: CUSTOMER, ORDER, ADDRESS, COUNTRY, ORDER_LINE, CC_XACTS, ITEM and AUTHOR.

An EB emulates the communication between the customers and the system. The interaction is done through sessions, which are a set of consecutive requests to execute some function. The session duration is controlled by a User Session Minimum Duration (USMD) time, defined as the minimum duration for which a session must last. Between two requests, the EB waits for a period of time, called Think Time.

After each interaction the EB must decide which of the navigation options will be chosen. In the TPC-W specification the probabilities of these navigation options are well defined for each of the pages. TPC-W provides three diverse patterns of behavior for the EBs, called web mixes, varying the ratio of read-only transactions vs. update transactions. The Browsing Mix presents the 95% of read-only transaction as opposed to the 5% of update transactions. The Shopping Mix specifies 80% vs. 20% and the Ordering Mix 50% vs. 50% respectively.

The workload can be adjusted by modifying the values of the mean think time and the number of EBs which take part in the simulation. The size of the database tables is calculated in function of the number of items that the system offers and the number of EBs that participates in the interaction, in order to maintain the scalability of the system.

The TPC-W primary metrics are the Web Interactions Per Second (WIPS) and system cost per WIPS, $/WIPS, calculated using the Shopping Mix. There are also defined another two secondary metrics, corresponding with the Browsing Mix, WIPSb, and with the Ordering Mix, WIPSo. TPC-W establishes a response time requirement for each type of web interaction. At least 90% of each type of web interaction must be returned in the time specified.

During the session, the item selection (that guides the TPC-W requests) can be done from three different webs or by clicking at promotional items:

- *The Best Seller Web Interaction*: it shows the 50 most popular items for a concrete subject among the 3333 most recent orders sorted by descending number of ordered items. The item is selected using a uniform random distribution.
- *The New Products Web Interaction*: it shows the list of the 50 newest products for a concrete subject sorted by descending release date. The item is selected from the list as before.

- *The Search Result Web Interaction*: it shows the list of items which match the criteria given on the previous page, Search Request Web Interaction. There the user selects a search type and defines a search string. TPC-W chooses the search type from a uniform distribution over the values author, title and subject. The search string is filled in function of the selected search type so that a specific match rate is guaranteed. This is achieved by using similar generation functions in the search string and in the field when the database is populated.
- *The Promotional Items*: the promotional items are 5 items whose images are shown on the top of some pages.

5 Conclusion

Middleware database replication architectures are becoming increasingly attractive for enterprise applications, due to their independence of the underlying DBMS. To a large extent, that independence facilitates the modularity, maintenance, migration and portability of applications. Multiple copies of application data are stored at distributed sites and are accessed transparently by way of transactions. Hence, data locality, availability, fault-tolerance and performance are increased, at the cost of maintaining replicated data consistency. However, that may introduce an undue overhead. A focal point of this paper has been the minimization of that overhead.

Existing applications face the problem of having to adapt themselves to these architectures. Some applications even have to be completely rewritten [1], while others may remain the same [2,3,10,11], thanks to a JDBC interface. However, an issue of which application designers and users are not sufficiently taking into account is the required degree of consistency. We have reviewed different levels of data consistency that depend to a significant extent on the isolation level offered by the underlying DBMS: serializable or SI.

Another important aspect considered in this paper is the measurement of the overhead as introduced by replication middleware architectures. A key indicator for the overhead is measured by the transaction response time. That is parameterized by the kind of application and the desired degree of data consistency. That, in turn, is influenced, if not determined, by the chosen replication protocol. We have reviewed two different approaches for measuring the overhead introduced by a middleware architecture. The first one is based on measuring the response time compared to a centralized solution and its scalability. The second one consists in defining an e-commerce bookstore application and run the well-known TPC-W benchmark. The first alternative may fit a given application very well but it does not give any indication about how attractive it may or may not fit to other applications. The second approach is not very attractive either. Although it offers a rich environment for emulating many web service applications, it does not reflect the entire range of web service or application server requirements [19]. Moreover, the extent to which an application can achieve the results enabled by a middleware is highly dependent on how closely TPC-W approximates the customer application. The relative performance of systems derived from this benchmark does not necessarily hold for other workloads or environments. This is to say that extrapolations to any other environment are not recommended.

References

1. Irún, L., Muñoz, F., Decker, H., Bernabéu-Aubán, J.M.: COPLA: A platform for eager and lazy replication in networked databases. In: ICEIS'03, vol. 1, pp. 273–278 (2003)
2. Patiño-Martínez, M., Jiménez-Peris, R., Kemme, B., Alonso, G.: MIDDLE-R: Consistent database replication at the middleware level. ACM Trans. Comput. Syst. 23, 375–423 (2005)
3. Armendáriz, J.E., Decker, H., Muñoz, F.D., Irún, L., de Juan, R.: A middleware architecture for supporting adaptable replication of enterprise application data. In: Draheim, D., Weber, G. (eds.) TEAA 2005. LNCS, vol. 3888, pp. 29–43. Springer, Heidelberg (2006)
4. Gao, L., Dahlin, M., Nayate, A., Zheng, J., Iyengar, A.: Improving availability and performance with application-specific data replication. IEEE Trans. Knowl. Data Eng. 17, 106–120 (2005)
5. Carey, M.J., Livny, M.: Conflict detection tradeoffs for replicated data. ACM Trans. Database Syst. 16, 703–746 (1991)
6. Kemme, B., Alonso, G.: Don't be lazy, be consistent: Postgres-R, a new way to implement database replication. In: Abbadi, A.E., Brodie, M.L., Chakravarthy, S., Dayal, U., Kamel, N., Schlageter, G., Whang, K.Y. (eds.) VLDB, pp. 134–143. Morgan Kaufmann, San Francisco (2000)
7. Wu, S., Kemme, B.: Postgres-R(SI): Combining replica control with concurrency control based on snapshot isolation. In: ICDE, pp. 422–433. IEEE-CS, Los Alamitos (2005)
8. Holliday, J., Steinke, R.C., Agrawal, D., Abbadi, A.E.: Epidemic algorithms for replicated databases. IEEE Trans. Knowl. Data Eng. 15, 1218–1238 (2003)
9. Lin, Y., Kemme, B., Patiño-Martínez, M., Jiménez-Peris, R.: Middleware based data replication providing snapshot isolation. In: SIGMOD Conference (2005)
10. Cecchet, E., Marguerite, J., Zwaenepoel, W.: C-JDBC: Flexible database clustering middleware. In: USENIX Annual Technical Conference, FREENIX Track, USENIX, 9–18 (2004)
11. Esparza-Peidro, J., Muñoz-Escoí, F., Irún-Briz, L., Bernabéu-Aubán, J.: Rjdbc: a simple database replication engine. In: Proc. of the 6th Int'l Conf. Enterprise Information Systems (ICEIS'04) (2004)
12. Armendáriz, J., González de Mendívil, J., Muñoz-Escoí, F.: A lock-based algorithm for concurrency control and recovery in a middleware replication software architecture. In: HICSS, p. 291a. IEEE-CS, Los Alamitos (2005)
13. Berenson, H., Bernstein, P.A., Gray, J., Melton, J., O'Neil, E.J., O'Neil, P.E.: A critique of ANSI SQL isolation levels. In: SIGMOD Conference, pp. 1–10. ACM Press, New York (1995)
14. Elnikety, S., Pedone, F., Zwaenopoel, W.: Database replication using generalized snapshot isolation. In: SRDS, IEEE-CS, Los Alamitos (2005)
15. Bernstein, P.A., Hadzilacos, V., Goodman, N.: Concurrency Control and Recovery in Database Systems. Addison-Wesley, Reading (1987)
16. Fekete, A., Liarokapis, D., O'Neil, E., O'Neil, P., Shasha, D.: Making snapshot isolation serializable. ACM Trans. Database Syst. 30, 492–528 (2005)
17. Gray, J., Helland, P., O'Neil, P.E., Shasha, D.: The dangers of replication and a solution. In: SIGMOD Conference, pp. 173–182. ACM Press, New York (1996)
18. Wiesmann, M., Schiper, A., Pedone, F., Kemme, B., Alonso, G.: Database replication techniques: A three parameter classification. In: SRDS, pp. 206–217 (2000)
19. TPC-W: Transaction processing performance council (2006), Accessible in URL, http://www.tpc.org
20. Chockler, G., Keidar, I., Vitenberg, R.: Group communication specifications: a comprehensive study. ACM Comput. Surv. 33, 427–469 (2001)

21. Petersen, K., Spreitzer, M., Terry, D.B., Theimer, M., Demers, A.J.: Flexible update propagation for weakly consistent replication. In: SOSP, pp. 288–301 (1997)
22. Wiesmann, M., Pedone, F., Schiper, A., Kemme, B., Alonso, G.: Understanding replication in databases and distributed systems. In: ICDCS, pp. 464–474 (2000)
23. Rodrigues, L., Miranda, H., Almeida, R., Martins, J., Vicente, P.: The globdata fault-tolerant replicated distributed object database. In: Shafazand, H., Tjoa, A.M. (eds.) EurAsia-ICT 2002. LNCS, vol. 2510, pp. 426–433. Springer, Heidelberg (2002)
24. Armendáriz, J., Juárez, J., Garitagoitia, J., de Mendívil, J.R.G., Muñoz-Escoí, F.: Implementing database replication protocols based on O2PL in a middleware architecture. In: IASTED DBA, pp. 176–181 (2006)
25. Muñoz, F.D., Pla, J., Ruiz, M.I., Irún, L., Decker, H., Armendáriz, J.E., de Mendívil, J.R.G.: Managing transaction conflicts in middleware-based database replication architectures. In: SRDS, pp. 401–410. IEEE Computer Society Press, Los Alamitos (2006)
26. Cristian, F.: Understanding fault-tolerant distributed systems. Commun. ACM 34, 56–78 (1991)
27. Ricciardi, A., Schiper, A., Birman, K.P.: Understanding partitions and the "no partition" assumption. In: Fourth Workshop on Future Trends of Distributed Systems, IEEE Computer Society Press, Los Alamitos (1993)
28. Jiménez-Peris, R., Patiño-Martínez, M., Alonso, G.: Non-intrusive, parallel recovery of replicated data. In: SRDS, pp. 150–159. IEEE-CS, Los Alamitos (2002)
29. Kemme, B., Bartoli, A., Babaoglu, Ö.: Online reconfiguration in replicated databases based on group communication. In: DSN, pp. 117–130. IEEE-CS, Los Alamitos (2001)
30. Burke, R., Harlam, B., Kahn, B., Lodish, L.: Comparing dynamic consumer choice in real and computer-simulated environments. Journal of Consumer Research 19, 71–82 (1992)
31. Alba, J., Lynch, J., Weitz, B., Janiszewski, C., Lutz, R., Sawyer, A., Wood, S.: Interactive home shopping: Consumer, retailer and manufacturer incentives to participate in electronic marketplaces. Journal of Marketing 61, 38–53 (1997)
32. Otto, J., Chung, Q.: A framework for cyber-enhanced retailing: Integrating e-commerce retailing with brick-and-mortar retailing. Electronic Markets 10, 185–191 (2000)
33. Degeratu, A., Rangasway, A., Wu, J.: Consumer choice behavior in online and traditional supermarkets. the effects of brand name, price, and other search attributes. International Journal of Research in Marketing 17, 55–78 (2000)

Using Rules and R2ML for Modeling Negotiation Mechanisms in E-Commerce Agent Systems*

Costin Bădică[1], Adrian Giurca[2], and Gerd Wagner[2]

[1] Software Engineering Department, University of Craiova,
Bvd.Decebal 107, Craiova, 200440, Romania
`badica_costin@software.ucv.ro`
[2] Internet-Technology Department,
Brandenburg University of Technology at Cottbus,
Walther Pauer Str. 2, 03046 Cottbus, Germany
`{Giurca, G.Wagner}@tu-cottbus.de`

Abstract. With the spread of e-commerce on a global scale, the development of truly open semantic descriptions of negotiation mechanisms for agent systems generated a lot of interest in the research community. This paper proposes the use of the REWERSE rule-markup language R2ML for semantic modeling of negotiation mechanisms to enable agents to engage in more flexible and open negotiations. Rules are developed on top of an ontology of negotiation concepts and define a *lingua franca* for all software agents participating in negotiation.

1 Introduction

Global information networks are described as open collaborative environments hosting intelligent and autonomous services that are able to dynamically discover each other and engage in business transactions, possibly involving automated negotiations. E-commerce is seen as a key service of modern information society and therefore, the ability of software agents to discover remote markets and engage in commercial transactions governed by market mechanisms unknown in advance, is of primary importance.

We understand automated negotiations as a process by which a group of software agents communicate with each other to reach a mutually acceptable agreement on some matter [11]. In this paper we focus our attention on *auctions* – a particular form of negotiation that spread during the last years with the advent of the Internet and the Web. Auctions are negotiations where resource allocations and prices are determined by bids exchanged between participants according to a given set of rules [15].

In automated negotiations (including auctions) it is important to distinguish between *negotiation protocols* (or *mechanisms*) and *negotiation strategies*. The protocol comprises public "rules of encounter" between negotiation participants by specifying the requirements that enable them to interact and negotiate. The strategy defines the private behavior of participants aiming at achieving their desired outcome. This behavior must be consistent with the protocol and is chosen to optimize participant welfare ([26]).

---

* Work of A. Giurca and G. Wagner was partially funded by European Commission and by the Swiss Federal Office for Education and Science within the 6th Framework Programme projects REWERSE (IST-2004-506779) cf. http://www.rewerse.net.

D. Draheim and G. Weber (Eds.): TEAA 2006, LNCS 4473, pp. 84–99, 2007.

A key aspect that generated a lot of interest is the development of a truly open semantic description of negotiation mechanisms [2,1,17,16,19,18]. As our literature overview indicates, we are still quite far from the vision of software agents needing only little compiled knowledge to enable "sensing" the negotiation mechanism and "tuning" their strategy accordingly. As an attempt to narrow this gap, we propose the use of R2ML markup language for semantic modeling of negotiation mechanisms in agent systems. Our proposal builds over existing works [27,2,1] on rule modeling of agent auctions and therefore it is expected to cover at least the auction types discussed there.

Before proceeding let as note that the use of semantic markup languages for modeling negotiation mechanisms is not entirely new; several approaches have already been proposed in the literature ([17,16,19,18]).

The proposal for formalizing negotiations introduced in [18] goes beyond the generic software framework of [2] and implemented in [1]. Its authors suggest the use of an ontology for representing negotiation protocols. Whenever an agent is admitted to negotiation it also obtains a specification of the negotiation mechanism in terms of the shared ontology. The ontology approach introduced in [18] is taken further in [19] by investigating how the ontology can be used to tune the negotiation strategy of participant agents. Note that authors of [19] point out that the ontology approach is still far from the vision where agents need only little hard-coded knowledge about the negotiation mechanism and this is due to the limitations of ontology languages to capturing explicitly the semantics of the rules that govern the negotiation. In this paper we address this issue thus making our work different from existing related works [19,18].

The open environment for automated negotiations specifically targeted to auctions ([16,17]) comprises: i) the *auction reference model* – ARM and ii) the *declarative auction specification language* – DAL. Note that, while not explicitly using rules, a DAL specification models in fact the auction flow using a rule-based approach. DAL uses the following constructs: views, validations, transitions and agreement generators ([16]). Views are analogous to visibility rules, validations are analogous to bidding rules, transitions are analogous to update rules and agreement generators are analogous to clearing rules. Finally, DAL provides also an explicit, implementation-level separation of the specification of auction flow from the auction data. For this purpose, a DAL specification comprises a set of SQL queries that provide access to the market data. While SQL has a declarative semantics and it is useful for the implementation side of DAL, we believe that this feature is less significant as concerning the portability of the language, as compared with the rule-based representation using R2ML.

The paper is structured as follows. Section 2 briefly presents the agent negotiation model and proposes a vocabulary of negotiation concepts. Section 3 discusses a taxonomy of negotiation rules and applies it to English auctions. Section 4 shows how sample rules can be mapped to R2ML constructs and formulates general criteria of such a mapping. Last section concludes and points to future work.

2   Negotiation Model and Vocabulary

The starting point of our work is the rule-based framework for enforcing specific negotiation mechanisms proposed by [2]. Note that details of its implementation using

JADE [5] and JESS [8] including initial experimental results for English auctions were reported in [1]. So, our work can be also seen as an attempt to provide a portable R2ML representation of the auction mechanism that could be reused by that implementation.

Authors of [2] sketched a software framework for implementing agent negotiations that comprises: (1) negotiation infrastructure, (2) generic negotiation protocol and (3) taxonomy of declarative rules. The *negotiation infrastructure* defines roles of negotiation participants (eg.*buyer* or *seller* in an auction) and of a negotiation host. Participants exchange proposals within a negotiation locale managed by the host.

According to the *generic negotiation protocol* ([2]), negotiation is seen as the process of exchanging proposals (or bids) via a common space (also known as market [16,17]) that is governed by an authoritative entity – the negotiation host (or market maker). Status information describing negotiation state and intermediary information is automatically forwarded by the host to all entitled participants according to the information revealing policy of that particular negotiation ([2,1]).

Negotiation rules are used for enforcing the negotiation mechanism. Rules are organized into a taxonomy: rules for participants admission to negotiations, rules for checking the validity of proposals, rules for protocol enforcement, rules for updating the negotiation status and informing participants, rules for agreement formation and rules for controlling the negotiation termination ([2,1]).

We model the basic negotiation vocabulary with the class diagram from Figure 1.

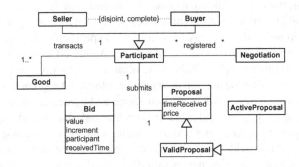

Fig. 1. An excerpt of the negotiation vocabulary

This vocabulary corresponds to an OWL [22] ontology that is used by agents involved in negotiations. *Participant, Seller, Buyer, Negotiation, Good, Proposal, ValidProposal, ActiveProposal*, and *Bid* are OWL classes. *transacts* is an OWL object property corresponding to the many-to-many association between classes *Participant* and *Good*, and *registered* is an OWL object property corresponding to the inverse functional association between classes *Participant* and *Negotiation*. Note that this vocabulary addresses the Platform-Independent Model[1] of a business system and therefore it is independent of the specific technological platform used to implement it.

---

[1] The term platform-independent model (PIM) is most frequently used in the context of the Model Driven Architecture (MDA) approach which corresponds the Object Management Group (OMG) vision of Model Driven Engineering (MDE). The main idea is that it should be possible to use a model transformation language (MTL) to transform a Platform-Independent Model (PIM) into a Platform-Specific Model (PSM).

3   Rules in Agent Negotiation

The aim of this section is to discuss the main types of rules needed to parameterize a negotiation mechanism with a focus on auctions. Our approach is exemplified with a sample set of rules that we have devised for describing single-item English auctions. We have chosen English auctions because they are a non-trivial and easy to understand auction mechanism that became popular because of the establishment of many online auction houses like eBay.

In order to make this presentation independent of a particular rule representation formalism, we have chosen to express our rules in an informal pseudo-code notation. The description is supplemented with a discussion of the intended semantics of the rules that govern a typical single-item English auction.

Technically, English auctions are single-item, first-price, open-cry, ascending auctions ([10],[26]). In an English auction there is a single item sold by a single seller and many buyers bidding against one another for buying the item until the auction terminates. Usually, there is a time limit for ending the auction, a seller reservation price that must be met by the winning bid for the item to be sold and a minimum value of the bid increment. A new bid must be higher than the currently highest bid plus the bid increment in order to be accepted. All the bids are visible to all the auction participants, while seller reservation price is private to the auction.

3.1   Categories of Negotiation Rules

Based on analysis performed in [2,28,27] and our own experience [1] we have concluded that the following categories of rules are necessary for configuring a negotiation mechanism (auction in particular): *bidding rules*, *information rules* and *clearing rules* (terminology is borrowed from [28,27]). Rules are activated when certain events occur during the negotiation (eg. when a participant proposal is received by the host or when a given time period without any bidding activity is observed).

Bidding Rules. These rules are responsible for handling proposals submitted by negotiation participants to determine if these proposals are correct according to the syntactical and semantical requirements of the negotiation mechanism.

This is a two-step process. Firstly, it involves checking if a proposal is valid – i.e. if the proposal is syntactically correct (for example if it specifies an amount to be paid and a transacted product). This check is performed by *rules for proposal validity*.

Secondly, the process involves checking if the bid is in accordance with the semantical requirements of the negotiation mechanism. This check is performed by *rules for protocol enforcement*. For example: i) *posting rules* check the conditions when a participant is allowed to submit a bid; ii) *improvement rules* check if a participant's proposal is an improvement over its own previous proposal or over the proposal that is currently revealed by the negotiation; iii) *withdrawal rules* check if and when a proposal can be withdrawn (for example a proposal can be active only for a fixed amount of time or until it is explicitly withdrawn by a participant).

Information Rules. The negotiation host is essentially a data processor. It is responsible with processing proposals submitted by participants, with updating the state of the negotiation process and with informing participants according to the information revealing policy of the negotiation. *Information rules* govern the policies for generating all this intermediate information that is necessary for running the negotiation. Typically, this information includes negotiation state information (eg.negotiation stage or round, currently highest price, etc.) and information revealed to participants.

For example: i) *update rules* specify how negotiation data (including negotiation parameters or negotiation stage) is updated in case certain events occurred; ii) *visibility rules* specify what negotiation information is visible to which participants; iii) *display rules* specify if and how a specific information about the negotiation should be notified to (some of) the participants.

Clearing Rules. The negotiation goal is to produce one or more deals between the negotiation participants. Clearing rules are responsible with detecting and computing negotiation deals and controlling negotiation life-cycle.

For example: i) *agreement formation rules* determine when an agreement can be reached and what is the corresponding set of deals made; ii) *termination rules* specify when the negotiation terminates.

Rule Activation. Rule activation is triggered by the occurrence of certain events during the negotiation. Usually, the activation of bidding rules is triggered when the negotiation host receives a new proposal. However, information and clearing rules can be triggered by other events, as well, including: lack of bidding activity for a given time, timer events, admission of a new proposal, certain updates of the negotiation state (like changing the round), etc. Note that by combining negotiation activities using associated triggering events and conditions may result in a great variety of negotiations.

3.2   Intended Semantics of Negotiation Rules for English Auctions

In this section we describe a sample set of negotiation rules for single-item English auctions. Rules are written using an intuitive pseudo-code notation, while their intended interpretation is described in natural language.

Bidding Rules for English Auctions handle proposals submitted by negotiation participants and check their correctness according to the English auction mechanism.

VALIDITY rule checks if a proposal is well formed, i.e. if it specifies transacted good and amount to be paid and if it comes from a registered participant (*seller* or *buyer*). In case of success the proposal is recorded as valid together with the time it was received by the negotiation host – *submission time*.

VALIDITY
   IF
      S is a participant registered with negotiation **AND**
      S transacts good A **AND**
      A new proposal Pr was submitted by S **AND**
      S has role $R \in \{buyer, seller\}$ **AND**
      Proposal Pr contains amount to be paid P
   THEN
         Proposal Pr is valid **AND**
         Submission time T is recorded with proposal Pr

Posting rules check if a valid proposal can be posted depending on the type of proposals that were previously posted by the other participants. POSTING-BUYER rule specifies that a *buyer* participant can post a proposal whenever there is a matching offer already posted by a *seller* participant. POSTING-SELLER rule specifies that the *seller* must be the first participant that posts a proposal. Therefore the *seller* is called *market initiator*. Every negotiation mechanism usually specifies a market initiator that is responsible with the initiation of a negotiation process. Posting rules collectively specify that in an English auction the participant with role *seller* must be the first to submit a proposal (with the intention to sell) and only then participants with role *buyer* will submit their proposals (usually called bids, with the intention to buy).

POSTING-BUYER
   IF
      There is a valid proposal Pr of a participant with role *buyer* on good A **AND**
      There is an active proposal of a participant with role *seller* on good A
   THEN
         Proposal Pr is posted

POSTING-SELLER
   IF
      There is a valid proposal Pr of the participant with role *seller* on good A **AND**
      There are no active proposals on good A
   THEN
         Proposal Pr is posted

Improvement rules check if a valid proposal can be posted depending on the content of proposals that were previously posted. IMPROVEMENT-BUYER enforces a new valid proposal to specify a price higher than the currently highest bid plus a give increment. ACTIVATE-SELLER just activates a valid bid posted by the *seller* (note that this rule was added to preserve the symmetry of treating *buyer* and *seller* proposals).

IMPROVEMENT-BUYER
   IF
      Negotiation is on good A **AND**
      Bid increment is Inc **AND**
      Currently highest bid is B **AND**
      Proposal Pr on good A with amount to be paid P was posted by this *buyer* **AND**
      $P \geq B + Inc$
   THEN
         Proposal Pr is active

ACTIVATE-SELLER
   IF
      Proposal Pr was posted by this *seller*
   THEN
         Proposal Pr is active

Note that posting and improvement rules actually check dynamic constraints of the negotiation mechanism, i.e. what sequences of proposals are allowed. Also note that a proposal that passed the validity tests is called *valid*, a proposal that passed the posting tests is called *posted* and a proposal that passed the improvement tests is called *active*.

Information Rules for English Auctions specify the processing applied to an active proposal. This usually results in updates of the negotiation state and notifications sent by negotiation host to negotiation participants.

Update rules specify the necessary updates of the negotiation state when a new active proposal is posted. UPDATE-BUYER rule performs the update of the currently highest bid after a new active proposal was posted by a *buyer* participant (note that rule IMPROVEMENT-BUYER only checks the *buyer* proposal, but does not update the negotiation state). UPDATE-SELLER rule initializes the negotiation state when an active proposal with an offer was posted by a *seller* participant.

UPDATE-BUYER
> **IF**
>> There is an active proposal Pr posted by participant S with role *buyer* **AND**
>> Proposal Pr has price P and was received at time T **AND**
>> Currently highest bid is B
> **THEN**
>> Currently highest bid becomes P and was submitted by S at time T

UPDATE-SELLER
> **IF**
>> There is an active proposal Pr posted by participant with role *seller* **AND**
>> Proposal Pr has price P and refers to good A **AND**
> **THEN**
>> Negotiated good are set to A **AND**
>> Seller reservation price is initialized to P **AND**
>> Currently highest bid is initialized to a default value (0) **AND**
>> Termination time window is initialized to a default value

INFORM rule specifies that whenever the currently highest bid is updated, all the negotiation participants must be notified accordingly. This notification contains the value of the highest bid, the identity of the submitter and the time when it was submitted (actually received by the negotiation host).

INFORM
> **IF**
>> Currently highest bid has been updated
> **THEN**
>> Notify accordingly all the negotiation participants

Visibility rules specify what negotiation information is disclosed to which participants, and what negotiation information is private to the negotiation.

VISIBILITY-SELLER-PROPOSAL rule specifies that good, submission time and participant name of an active proposal submitted by a *seller* are public to all *buyer* participants, while the price is private to the unique *seller* participant.

VISIBILITY-SELLER-PROPOSAL
IF
> There is an active proposal submitted by participant S with role *seller* **AND**
> This proposal is on good A and was recorded at time T

THEN
> S, A and T are visible to all participants

VISIBILITY-BUYER-PROPOSAL rule specifies that all the parameters of an active proposal submitted by a *buyer* (i.e. participant name, price, good and submission time) are public to all negotiation participants.

VISIBILITY-BUYER-PROPOSAL
IF
> The currently highest bid is B and is on good A **AND**
> The currently highest bid was submitted by a participant S at time T

THEN
> S, A, T and B are visible to all participants

Clearing Rules for English Auctions determine negotiation outputs and control negotiation termination.

AGREEMENT-FORMATION rule specifies that whenever agreement formation is triggered, if the currently highest bid is greater than the *seller* reservation price, an agreement is formed between the *buyer* that submitted the highest bid and the *seller*.

AGREEMENT-FORMATION
IF
> The currently highest bid is B and was submitted by *buyer* $S1$ **AND**
> There is an active proposal of *seller* $S2$ with price P **AND**
> Negotiation is on good A **AND**
> $B \geq P$

THEN
> An agreement of $S1$ with $S2$ to transact good A at price $P1$ is formed

TERMINATION rule dictates auction termination whenever a given period of bidding inactivity is observed.

TERMINATION
IF
> Termination time window is W **AND**
> Active proposal that generated currently highest bid was recorded at time Ta **AND**
> Current time is Tc **AND**
> $Tc > Ta + W$

THEN
> Negotiation is declared terminated **AND**
> Negotiation participants are notified accordingly

4 Representing Negotiation Rules in R2ML

Representing negotiation rules in a global information network (eg. an agent environment) requires a commonly agreed rule interchange format. This format must be able to support different rule languages within a single representation framework shared by all parties.

General purpose rule interchange formats, such as RuleML [21] and R2ML [20], address the Platform-Independent Model level (PIM) of a software or business system. One of their goals is to support a PSM[2] to PSM rule interchange via the PIM level. Expressing negotiation rules at PIM level is a significant advantage since the business system does not require any conceptual changes when it is implemented in different specific technological platforms.

RuleML Initiative [21] aims at providing such a general purpose format. The SWRL [3] rule language tries to combine the rule concept from RuleML with the knowledge representation support of OWL [22]. However, both languages have limitations regarding the representation of well known concepts from software engineering: data types, operation calls, etc that are usually needed in real applications. Moreover, none of them supports Event-Condition-Action (ECA) rules that are basic kind of rules in agent negotiations (as seen in the previous section of this paper). The first ideas of a general rule language that will support not only the power of logic programming concepts, but also the widely used object oriented programming paradigm come from 2003 (see [23]). Following this work, proposal of R2ML rule markup language was recently launched [20]. R2ML supports ECA rules and provides markup for rules written in various rule languages including: Prolog, F-Logic [9], SQL, OCL [12], Jena [7], Jess [8], ILR [4], RuleML [21], SWRL [3].

Let us note that our negotiation rules are reaction rules (ECA rules) that follow the event-condition-action model. Therefore, we start with a brief description of the R2ML model of ECA rules and then we provide details of our proposed mapping.

4.1 R2ML ECA-Rules

A R2ML reaction rule is a statement of programming logic that specifies the execution of one or more actions in the case of a *triggering event* occurrence and if its *conditions* are satisfied. *Post-conditions* may be optionally required to be satisfied after the *action* execution. Reaction rules therefore have an operational semantics (formalizing state changes, e.g., on the basis of a state transition system formalism). The execution effect of reaction rules may depend on the rules order (note that the order is defined by the rule execution mechanism or by the rules representation).

The R2ML Events Metamodel specifies the core concepts required for dynamic behavior of rules and provides the infrastructure for more detailed definition of this behavior. Basic properties of an R2ML event expression are: *startDateTime*, *duration* (defines a value specification of the temporal distance between two time expressions that specify time instants) and *occurDateTime* (a derived property given by the addition of duration

---

[2] PSM stands for Platform-Specific Model i.e. a business system level that is dependent of the specific technological platform used to implement it.

to the existent start date time). For the purpose of encoding the agent negotiation rules we utilize only message event expressions. A *message event expression* is an atomic event described by two properties: i) *sender* which is the same with the actor (inherited from *ActionEventExpr*) and ii) *receiver*, an URI reference describing the receiver of the event. See [20] for more details on the R2ML event model.

4.2 Mapping Examples

This section is devoted to the description of the mapping to R2ML of agent negotiation rules presented in Section 3. Because of space limitation, the mapping is illustrated by means of few examples involving R2ML representations of vocabulary, rules, events, conditions and actions.

As R2ML is a rule-based language (other examples are Jess [8], JBoss Rules [6], Oracle Business Rules [14]), it provides the concept of *rule set*. Recall that our negotiation rules are based on the vocabulary described in Section 2. Vocabularies can be referred in R2ML rule sets and, moreover, for simplicity of implementation, R2ML provides its own markup for vocabularies. At the *rule set* level a *specific vocabulary* for the entire set of rules can be encoded.

For example, the *Bid* class from our vocabulary can be represented as:

```
<r2mlv:Class r2mlv:ID="v:Bid">
 <r2mlv:Attribute r2mlv:ID="v:value">
  <r2mlv:range>
   <r2mlv:Datatype r2mlv:ID="xs:positiveInteger"/>
  </r2mlv:range>
 </r2mlv:Attribute>
 <r2mlv:Attribute r2mlv:ID="v:increment">
  <r2mlv:range>
   <r2mlv:Datatype r2mlv:ID="xs:decimal"/>
  </r2mlv:range>
 </r2mlv:Attribute>
 <r2mlv:Attribute r2mlv:ID="v:receivedTime">
  <r2mlv:range>
   <r2mlv:Datatype r2mlv:ID="xs:time"/>
  </r2mlv:range>
 </r2mlv:Attribute>
 <r2mlv:ReferenceProperty r2mlv:ID="v:participant">
  <r2mlv:range>
   <r2mlv:Class r2mlv:ID="v:Participant"/>
  </r2mlv:range>
 </r2mlv:ReferenceProperty>
</r2mlv:Class>
```

The *registered* association is represented as:

```
<r2mlv:ReferenceProperty r2mlv:ID="v:registered">
 <r2mlv:domain>
  <r2mlv:Class r2mlv:ID="v:Participant"/>
 </r2mlv:domain>
 <r2mlv:range>
```

```
  <r2mlv:Class r2mlv:ID="v:Negotiation"/>
 </r2mlv:range>
</r2mlv:ReferenceProperty>
```

Notice that r2mlv is the standard namespace notation for R2ML vocabulary[3] and v is a user-defined notation for his specific namespace of concepts[4].

We detail the mapping of the VALIDITY rule as example. The reader may consult Appendix 5 for the complete R2ML markup of another example rule – IMPROVEMENT-BUYER.

The *triggering event* of this rule is the submission of a new proposal by a registered participant. We consider this event to be *atomic* i.e with *no duration*. This is represented in R2ML by a MessageEventExpression:

```
01  <r2ml:triggeringEvent>
02    <r2ml:MessageEventExpression r2ml:sender="http://www.example.org/eshop"
03          r2ml:startTime="2006-04-21T09:00:00"
04          r2ml:duration="P0Y0M0DT0H0M0S"
05          r2ml:eventType="e:submitProposal">
06     <r2ml:arguments>
07      <r2ml:ObjectVariable r2ml:name="N" r2ml:classID="v:Negotiation"/>
08      <r2ml:ObjectVariable r2ml:name="S" r2ml:classID="v:Participant"/>
09      <r2ml:ObjectVariable r2ml:name="Pr" r2ml:classID="v:Proposal"/>
10     </r2ml:arguments>
11    </r2ml:MessageEventExpression>
12  </r2ml:triggeringEvent>
```

Note that object variables S and Pr are instantiated by matching with the content of the incoming event and they are already bound when rule conditions are evaluated.

The conditions part of the rule is a conjunction of three atoms and it can be expressed in R2ML as follows:

```
13  <r2ml:conditions>
14    <r2ml:ReferencePropertyAtom r2ml:referencePropertyID="v:registered">
15     <r2ml:subject>
16      <r2ml:ObjectVariable r2ml:name="S"/>
17     </r2ml:subject>
18     <r2ml:object>
19      <r2ml:ObjectVariable r2ml:name="N" r2ml:classID="v:Negotiation"/>
20     </r2ml:object>
21    </r2ml:ReferencePropertyAtom>
22    <r2ml:ReferencePropertyAtom r2ml:referencePropertyID="v:transacts">
23     <r2ml:subject>
24      <r2ml:ObjectVariable r2ml:name="S"/>
```

---

[3] The R2ML vocabulary schema URL is
    http://oxygen.informatik.tu-cottbus.de/R2ML/0.4/Vocabulary/r2mlv.xsd
[4] For illustration purposes the vocabulary can be found at http://www.example.org/ecommerce/.
    agents/negotiation/vocabulary.

```
25    </r2ml:subject>
26    <r2ml:object>
27     <r2ml:ObjectVariable r2ml:name="A" r2ml:classID="v:Good"/>
28    </r2ml:object>
29   </r2ml:ReferencePropertyAtom>
30   <r2ml:AttributionAtom r2ml:attributeID="v:price">
31    <r2ml:subject>
32     <r2ml:ObjectVariable r2ml:name="Pr" r2ml:classID="v:Proposal"/>
33    </r2ml:subject>
34    <r2ml:dataValue>
35     <r2ml:DataVariable r2ml:name="P" r2ml:datatypeID="xs:positiveInteger"/>
36    </r2ml:dataValue>
37   </r2ml:AttributionAtom>
38  </r2ml:conditions>
```

First atom (lines 14–21) is a R2ML *reference property atom* that models the condition "S is a participant registered with negotiation N". This atom is true if participant denoted by variable S" is registered with the current negotiation denoted by variable N".

The second atom (lines 22–29) is also a *reference property atom* describing the condition "S transacts good A".

The third atom (lines 30–37) is a R2ML *attribution atom* implementing the condition "Proposal Pr has price P". The execution model consists in computing the value of the attribute price" in the context of the object variable Pr" (the proposal).

The reader may notice that the condition "S has role $R \in \{buyer, seller\}$" is already implemented at the vocabulary level (classes Seller" and Buyer" are a complete partition of Participant").

Since the action part of the rule ("Submission time T is recorded with proposal Pr") denotes an update that invokes a "recording operation", it will go into an R2ML *invoke action expression*. The action receives as argument a R2ML *attribute function term* that evaluates to the value of the attribute v:timeReceived of proposal Pr. Note that this corresponds to an UML-like operation call recordSubmissionTime (Pr.timeReceived). The resulting R2ML markup of the action is:

```
39  <r2ml:producedAction>
40   <r2ml:InvokeActionExpression r2ml:operationID="a:recordSubmissionTime">
41    <r2ml:arguments>
42     <r2ml:AttributeFunctionTerm r2ml:attributeID="v:timeReceived">
43      <r2ml:contextArgument>
44       <r2ml:ObjectVariable r2ml:name="Pr" r2ml:classID="v:Proposal"/>
45      </r2ml:contextArgument>
46     </r2ml:AttributeFunctionTerm>
47    </r2ml:arguments>
48   </r2ml:InvokeActionExpression>
49  </r2ml:producedAction>
```

The VALIDITY rule has also a postcondition – "Proposal Pr is valid". This postcondition corresponds to a R2ML *object classification atom*:

```
50  <r2ml:postcondition>
51   <r2ml:ObjectClassificationAtom r2ml:classID="v:ValidProposal">
```

```
52   <r2ml:ObjectVariable r2ml:name="Pr"/>
53   </r2ml:ObjectClassificationAtom>
54  </r2ml:postcondition>
```

4.3   General Mapping Criteria

Business rules (including those presented in Section 3) are not usually captured using a formal representation. Instead, they are natural language descriptions based on core ontological concepts (eg. variable and class) and have the usual meaning of IF ... THEN programming constructs. It is the role of the rule engineer to map them onto a formal representation. Below we describe the general mapping criteria of such a formalization using R2ML:

1. Rule variables are mapped onto object variables or data variables according to their values types:
   - *Object variables*, if they instantiate classes;
   - *Data variables*, if they instantiate datatypes;
2. UML properties are mapped onto different kinds of atoms according to their ranges:
   - Attributes i.e. UML properties that have data as values are mapped onto *attribution atoms* or *attribute function terms* depending of the context of usage. For example the UML expression Pr.price=P is mapped onto the attribution atom from lines 29–36. See also the attribute function term from lines 41–45 in the example.
   - Object properties i.e. UML properties that have objects as values are mapped onto R2ML *reference property atoms* or *reference property function terms* depending of the context of usage. For example, the reference property atom from lines 21–28 encodes the UML expression S.transacts=A;
3. Actions are mapped onto one of:
   - *InvokeActionExpression*, corresponding to an operation call;
   - *AssignActionExpression*, corresponding to assignment of values to different UML attributes;
   - *CreateActionExpression*, corresponding to a constructor-call;
   - *DeleteActionExpression*, corresponding to a destructor-call;
4. Because the negotiation rules are triggered by instantaneous events (like request-response of a message), events are mapped onto the subclass of R2ML message events that represents atomic events (events without duration).

In Appendix 5 we present another complete example expressed in R2ML for the IMPROVEMENT-BUYER rule.

5   Conclusions and Future Work

This paper proposes the use of R2ML rule-markup language for expressing rule-based representations of agent negotiation mechanisms. Our proposal is demonstrated with an example comprising an R2ML rule model of single item English auctions.

As future work we plan to: (i) analyze how the R2ML representation of negotiation mechanisms can be implemented using a rule engine in a system for agent negotiation; (ii) asses the generality of this proposal by applying it to other price negotiations.

References

1. Bădică, C., Bădiţă, A., Ganzha, M., Iordache, A., Paprzycki, M.: Rule-Based Framework for Automated Negotiation: Initial Implementation. In: Adi, A., Stoutenburg, S., Tabet, S. (eds.) RuleML 2005. LNCS, vol. 3791, pp. 193–198. Springer, Heidelberg (2005)
2. Bartolini, C., Preist, C., Jennings, N.R.: A Software Framework for Automated Negotiation. In: Choren, R., Garcia, A., Lucena, C., Romanovsky, A. (eds.) Software Engineering for Multi-Agent Systems III. LNCS, vol. 3390, pp. 213–235. Springer, Heidelberg (2005)
3. Horrocks, I., Patel-Schneider, P.F., Boley, H., Tabet, S., Grosof, B., Dean, M.: SWRL: A Semantic Web Rule Language Combining OWL and RuleML. In: W3C Member, submission (May 2, 2004), http://www.w3.org/Submission/SWRL/
4. The ILOG Rule Language. http://www.ilog.com/
5. JADE: Java Agent Development Framework. http://jade.cselt.it2
6. JBoss Rules (Drools). http://www.drools.org
7. Jena The Semantic Web Framework. http://jena.sourceforge.net/
8. Jess, Sandia Lab., http://herzberg.ca.sandia.gov/jess/
9. Kifer, M., Lausen, G., Wu, J.: Logical Foundations of Object-Oriented and Frame-Based Languages. Journal of the ACM 42(4), 741–943 (1995)
10. Laudon, K.C., Traver, C.G.: E-commerce. business. technology. society, 2nd edn. Pearson Addison-Wesley, London (2004)
11. Lomuscio, A.R., Wooldridge, M., Jennings, N.R.: A classification scheme for negotiation in electronic commerce. In: Sierra, C., Dignum, F.P.M. (eds.) Agent Mediated Electronic Commerce. LNCS (LNAI), vol. 1991, pp. 19–33. Springer, Heidelberg (2001)
12. Object Constraint Language (OCL), v2.0. http://www.omg.org/docs/ptc/03-10-14.pdf
13. Object Management Group (OMG), http://www.omg.org
14. Oracle Business Rules. http://www.oracle.com/technology/products/ias/business_rules/index.html
15. McAfee, R.P., McMillan, J.: Auctions and bidding. Journal of Economic Literature 25(2), 699–738 (1987)
16. Rolli, D., Luckner, S., Gimpel, A.: A Descriptive Auction Language. Electronic Markets 16(1), 51–62 (2006)
17. Rolli, D., Eberhart, A.: An Auction Reference Model for Describing and Running Auctions. In: Internationale Tagung Wirtschaftsinformatik, Bamberg, Germany, pp. 289–308 (2005)
18. Tamma, V., Phelps, S., Dickinson, I., Wooldridge, M.: Ontologies for Supporting Negotiation in E-Commerce. In: Engineering Applications of Artificial Intelligence, vol. 18, pp. 223–238. Elsevier, Amsterdam (2005)
19. Tamma, V., Wooldridge, M., Dickinson, I.: An Ontology Based Approach to Automated Negotiation. In: Padget, J.A., Shehory, O.M., Parkes, D.C., Sadeh, N.M., Walsh, W.E. (eds.) Agent-Mediated Electronic Commerce IV. Designing Mechanisms and Systems. LNCS (LNAI), vol. 2531, pp. 219–237. Springer, Heidelberg (2002)
20. R2ML - The REWERSE I1 Rule Markup Language. http://oxygen.informatik.tu-cottbus.de/rewerse-i1/?q=node/6
21. The Rule Markup Initiative, RuleML. http://www.ruleml.org
22. Patel-Schneider, P.F., Horroks, I.: OWL Web Ontology Language Semantic and Abstract Syntax., http://www.w3.org/2004/OWL
23. Wagner, G.: Seven Golden Rules for a Web Rule Language. Invited contribution to the Trends & Controversies section of IEEE Intelligent Systems 18(5) (2003)
24. Wagner, G., Giurca, A., Lukichev, S.: R2ML: A General Approach for Marking up Rules. Dagstuhl Seminar Proceedings 05371. In: Bry, F., Fages, F., Marchiori, M., Ohlbach, H. (eds.) Principles and Practices of Semantic Web Reasoning (2005)

25. Wagner, G., Giurca, A., Lukichev, S.: A Usable Interchange Format for Rich Syntax Rules Integrating OCL, RuleML and SWRL. In: Proc. RoW2006, Edinburgh, UK, May 22nd (2006)
26. Wooldridge, M.: An Introduction to MultiAgent Systems. John Wiley & Sons, Chichester (2002)
27. Wurman, P.R., Wellman, M.P., Walsh, W.E.: Specifying Rules for Electronic Auctions. AI Magazine 23(3), 15–23 (2002)
28. Wurman, P.R., Wellman, M.P., Walsh, W.E.: A Parameterization of the Auction Design Space. Games and Economic Behavior 35(1/2), 271–303 (2001)

Appendix A

R2ML markup for IMPROVEMENT-BUYER rule:

```
<r2ml:ReactionRule  r2ml:id="IR-BUYER001">
 <r2ml:triggeringEvent>
  <r2ml:MessageEventExpression r2ml:sender="www.example.org/eshop"
          r2ml:startTime="2006-04-21T09:00:00"
          r2ml:duration="P0Y0M0DT0H0M0S" r2ml:eventType="s:submitProposal">
   <r2ml:arguments>
    <r2ml:ObjectVariable r2ml:name="S" r2ml:classID="v:Buyer"/>
    <r2ml:ObjectVariable r2ml:name="Pr" r2ml:classID="v:Proposal"/>
   </r2ml:arguments>
  </r2ml:MessageEventExpression>
 </r2ml:triggeringEvent>
 <r2ml:conditions>
  <r2ml:ReferencePropertyAtom r2ml:referencePropertyID="v:registered">
   <r2ml:subject>
    <r2ml:ObjectVariable r2ml:name="S"/>
   </r2ml:subject>
   <r2ml:object>
    <r2ml:ObjectVariable r2ml:name="N" r2ml:classID="v:Negotiation"/>
   </r2ml:object>
  </r2ml:ReferencePropertyAtom>
  <r2ml:ReferencePropertyAtom r2ml:referencePropertyID="v:transacts">
   <r2ml:subject>
    <r2ml:ObjectVariable r2ml:name="S"/>
   </r2ml:subject>
   <r2ml:object>
    <r2ml:ObjectVariable r2ml:name="A" r2ml:classID="v:Good"/>
   </r2ml:object>
  </r2ml:ReferencePropertyAtom>
  <r2ml:DatatypePredicateAtom r2ml:datatypePredicateID="swrlb:greaterThan">
   <r2ml:dataArguments>
    <r2ml:AttributeFunctionTerm r2ml:attributeID="v:price">
     <r2ml:contextArgument>
      <r2ml:ObjectVariable r2ml:name="Pr"/>
     </r2ml:contextArgument>
    </r2ml:AttributeFunctionTerm>
    <r2ml:DataOperationTerm r2ml:operationID="op:numeric-add">
     <r2ml:arguments>
      <r2ml:AttributeFunctionTerm r2ml:attributeID="v:value">
       <r2ml:contextArgument>
        <r2ml:ObjectVariable r2ml:name="B" r2ml:classID="v:Bid"/>
       </r2ml:contextArgument>
      </r2ml:AttributeFunctionTerm>
      <r2ml:AttributeFunctionTerm r2ml:attributeID="v:increment">
       <r2ml:contextArgument>
        <r2ml:ObjectVariable r2ml:name="B" r2ml:classID="v:Bid"/>
       </r2ml:contextArgument>
      </r2ml:AttributeFunctionTerm>
     </r2ml:arguments>
```

```
    </r2ml:DataOperationTerm>
   </r2ml:dataArguments>
  </r2ml:DatatypePredicateAtom>
 </r2ml:conditions>
<r2ml:producedAction>
 <r2ml:InvokeActionExpression r2ml:operationID="a:assert">
  <r2ml:arguments>
   <r2ml:ObjectVariable r2ml:name="Pr"/>
  </r2ml:arguments>
 </r2ml:InvokeActionExpression>
</r2ml:producedAction>
<r2ml:postcondition>
 <r2ml:ObjectClassificationAtom  r2ml:classID="v:ActiveProposal">
   <r2ml:ObjectVariable r2ml:name="Pr"/>
 </r2ml:ObjectClassificationAtom>
</r2ml:postcondition>
</r2ml:ReactionRule>
```

Dealing with Scalability in an Event-Based Infrastructure to Support Global Software Development

Rubby Casallas, Oscar González, and Nicolás López

University of Los Andes, Department of Systems and Computing Engineering, Bogotá,
Colombia
{rcasalla,o-gonza1,ni-lopez}@uniandes.edu.co

Abstract. Scalability is a challenging issue in the context of an infrastructure based on asynchronous events to support integration and cooperation between distributed applications. Furthermore, if an infrastructure of this kind supports the execution of processes in a global software development environment, we have to deal with an enormous amount of Internet-scale events passing through the infrastructure diminishing performance. In this paper, we present an approach to treat this problem based on a network of interconnected nodes. At any given moment, each node executes a process while maintaining the scope of the local events and propagating only the events needed to synchronize broader processes. To support cooperation between applications, we use an ECA rules mechanism, which we have extended to enable the infrastructure to identify a process executing in a node, as an application that can cooperate with other processes using a similar mechanism.

Keywords: Event-based Middleware, Scalability, Monitoring systems, Application Integration and Cooperation, Asynchronous Events.

1 Introduction

In a Global Software Development (GSD) scenario, many difficulties arise caused by the geographical dispersion of several teams. These teams perform diverse activities simultaneously to accomplish a common goal. The ways in which these activities have to be coordinated and synchronized depend on business processes that should be defined and managed.

Each process can be supported by a variety of different distributed applications, or at least, by different instances of the same application at different places. In this context, necessarily, a schema to integrate the applications involved has to materialize the high-level business rules. This integration has to preserve the intention of the business rules: this includes the exchange of information and the actions executed to produce the expected results. We need to provide enterprise application architectures with integration mechanisms that support complementary processes and update information automatically to offer an integral vision of business processes and the consistency of information throughout these applications.

We have developed a distributed, event-driven infrastructure and an integration mechanism based on Event Condition Action (ECA) rules, called Eleggua [7]. This

D. Draheim and G. Weber (Eds.): TEAA 2006, LNCS 4473, pp. 100–111, 2007.
© Springer-Verlag Berlin Heidelberg 2007

infrastructure is currently under usage in a software house [11] that faces the problems of global software development[1]; this house has clients and development teams in 4 countries and over 300 developers. Throughout this experience, we have overcome many difficulties in the integration process, beginning with the definition of business rules up to implementation on Eleggua, deployment, and testing. One important issue has emerged related to the scalability of a highly distributed asynchronous event-based middleware even though Eleggua is an appropriate solution for the automation of actions that represent application cooperation in a real world context.

One of the main reasons for congestion in an event-based integration is the traffic of events through the whole geographically disperse infrastructure. However, in a GSD context, some processes are local to a site and need to coordinate only with one or two other local processes in other sites. This means that, by definition, the process that launches each event can limit its scope.

The different levels of activities executed within a process provide a delimitation of their scope. In the same way that there are, in organizations, local domain groups that perform local processes and general groups that perform widespread processes, the events that occur within the processes have a local or a broad range.

In addition to the scalability issue, the management and monitoring of the infrastructure is a very complex task, because of the integration of applications and the high volume of distributed data.

In this paper, we propose a solution to the scalability problem. The solution takes advantage of the fact that there are local and general business processes. The administrator can configure the scope of events based on the definition of the business processes. We have extended Eleggua to manage the scope of events and the diverse network configurations of nodes that have to communicate to synchronize processes. Additionally, we extended the Eleggua monitor to guarantee the administrator a visibility of both local and general state of the infrastructure. J2EE technology is the base of the proposed solution.

The organization of this paper is as follows: the second section presents some basic concepts of the Eleggua middleware and an example scenario useful to illustrate both the problem and the solution. The third section enumerates the requirements we have to satisfy to guarantee scalability. The fourth section presents our proposed solution. The fifth section briefly explains the technologies used to implement the solution. The final section mentions some works related to ours and finally, gives some conclusions and illustrates some possible future works.

2 Background

This section presents some basic concepts of Eleggua and then, we present an example scenario to illustrate the needs in a global software development context.

Systems based on event generation, observation and notification are a widely used architectural style for distributed, loosely coupled systems in a variety of domains [16]. On top of an Event Notification Service (ENS), we defined a mechanism

---

[1] The project is supported and partially financed by the "Instituto Colombiano para el Desarrollo de la Ciencia y la Tecnología Francisco José de Caldas" - COLCIENCIAS.

supported by Event-Condition-Action rules as a strategy to achieve cooperation between applications. Eleggua is a middleware that we have developed as part of a research project[1] [7] [8]. It uses asynchronous event communication at an Internet-scale and the execution of cooperation rules that automate actions that correspond to high-level business processes.

An Eleggua node has two main responsibilities: to offer basic functionality of a publish/subscribe ENS (asynchronous messaging, event generation and event processing) and to execute cooperation rules. A cooperation rule is associated to how an application produces events as a result of the interaction of users and how other applications process and react to the reception of these events.

For each external application, needed to support a business activity, we provide a Cooperation Proxy (CP) component. A CP is responsible of the subscription/generation to events of interest to the application and of the execution of rules required to enable the cooperation of the application within the infrastructure. Figure 1 shows, in a simplified way, an Eleggua node with three external applications, their Cooperation proxies and the relation of these with the event notification service.

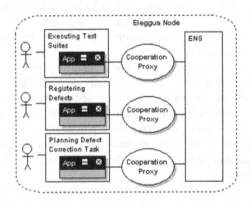

Fig. 1. An Eleggua Node

2.1 Example Scenario

Our example relates to a software testing process. Figure 2 shows the definition of a very simplified testing process. There are four main activities: unit, integration, load and stress, and usability testing. In an independent way, various teams have to perform unit testing for each software component. Once unit testing is finished for all components, integration testing is the next activity executed. Finally, teams perform, simultaneously usability testing, and load and stress testing.

In our example, we can assume that the testing process is accomplished by two geographical disperse teams. Each team is responsible for the execution of some of the activities and uses its own applications to perform these activities (see fig. 3). We need to manage the interaction between the sites to maintain the integrity and completeness of the general process.

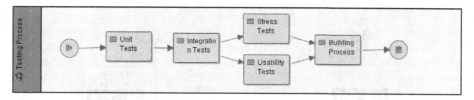

Fig. 2. A Testing Process Definition

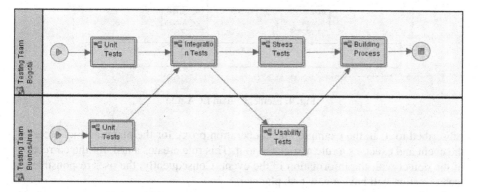

Fig. 3. A Testing Process Execution

When the process starts, each team has to test independently its own components. Thus, there are two instances for the unit testing activity, one for each team. Then, when all unit-testing activities are finished, an integration testing activity initializes on a single site. Once the previous testing activity finishes successfully, an instance of the usability testing activity launches on a site, and an instance of the load and stress-testing activity launches simultaneously on the other site.

Finally, one of the sites, determined by business conditions, consolidates the results of the activities to continue development of the software. Each site should work independently with its own resources to accomplish an activity with a specific purpose, but once the activity is finished, one of the sites must synchronize the general process.

An Eleggua node enables the integration and cooperation of individual applications supporting activities of a business process. For instance, in our example scenario, there can be many applications supporting the tasks performed by developers during a unit testing activity: an application to run the test suites, another to register the defects found, if any, and another to plan the correction of the defects. Using ECA rules, we can define the cooperation between these applications. For example, a cooperation rule can guarantee that, when a defect is found, it is planned automatically a task to correct it. Figure 4 shows the elements involved in the execution of an ECA rule.

The cooperation proxy of the application responsible of registering defects publishes an event called "*defectAssign*". Each time a user registers a defect, the cooperation proxy, which is observing the application, generates an instance of the "*defectAssign*" event. The ENS notifies the event to each application that previously

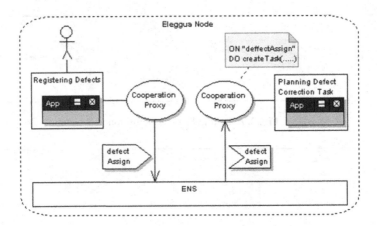

Fig. 4. Elements in an ECA rule

subscribed to it. In the example, the cooperation proxy for the planning tool receives the event and executes a rule associated to it. This rule creates a task for the correction of the defect with the information in the event. Consequently, the user responsible of the correction will have a new task planned.

An Eleggua node executes on a local network; nevertheless, users access most of the external applications via Internet. The performance of an Eleggua node depends on the amount of events passing through the diverse components of the node. On a single process site, over five applications can interact; they exchange events defined on over 40 cooperation rules such as the one described previously. Daily over 300 users interact with these applications passing over a 1000 events.

When the number of events increases, due to a growth in users, applications or both, there is a delay in the communication, diminishing the performance. This scalability problem is in part consequence of the fact that there is a single dispatching event component on each ENS of a node.

3   Requirements for Scalability

This section presents the requirements to achieve scalability in the context of our event-based infrastructure.

3.1   Specific Requirements

According to the scenario presented, above the infrastructure should offer services to achieve scalability, these are:

1. Support the decomposition and synchronization of business processes to execute them on separate nodes.
2. Limit the scope of events according to the process that generates it and the processes interested on it.

3. Provide an Internet-scale communication mechanism between nodes that overcomes the security issues of local nodes.
4. Assure the integrity of the general process.
5. Monitor and control each node to offer a view of the whole process, i.e., a consolidation of the individual state of the nodes into a bigger picture.

4 Proposed Solution

Our approach is to use Eleggua nodes to support independent processes. Each node acts as a logically integrated application; this application interacts with other nodes using a global cooperation proxy. Figure 5 exemplifies an Eleggua network consisting of three Eleggua nodes; each node has its global cooperation proxy (shaded) that communicates with proxies to form the Eleggua network.

The following subsections present how our solution fulfills each requirement.

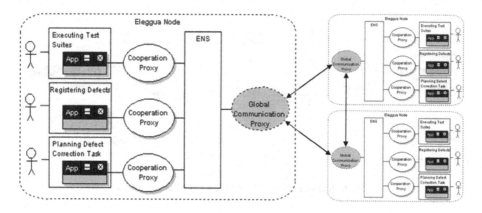

Fig. 5. An Eleggua network

4.1 Processes Synchronization

The basic strategy to limit the amount of events handled by an Eleggua network is to restrict the scope of events according to business processes. Event propagation is limited to the node executing the process where the event occurs, and is only propagated outside if it is necessary to processes executing on other nodes.

As we stated before, cooperation rules achieve the cooperation between applications. Each rule is a set of actions executed because of the occurrence of an event. Each Eleggua node executes local processes for an organization. A LAN network supports the communication between the components of a node. An event-notification-service is in charge of asynchronous messaging. We define the scope of an event as local if only components on one node produce and consume it. In contrast, we define the scope of an event as broad if components on one node produce it and components on various different nodes consume it. Business users defining the cooperation rules establish the scope of the events.

Cooperation rules responsible for the cooperation between processes instead of between applications produce broad events. We have added services to our ENS to achieve the propagation of events according to their type. These services enable the ENS to identify the scope of events and to behave consequently. In the case of broad events, the ENS propagates these outside the node to the neighbor nodes that are interested in the occurrence of the event. This interest is not part of the event; the business rules define it and the nodes are configured to have this information.

In fact, we use the same mechanisms of ECA rules to implement the new services, i.e., each node has its own global cooperation proxy. This new special proxy has to:

– subscribe to broad events produced within its node but consumed outside,
– propagate broad events to neighbors which require it
– subscribe to broad events produced outside
– react to reception of broad events

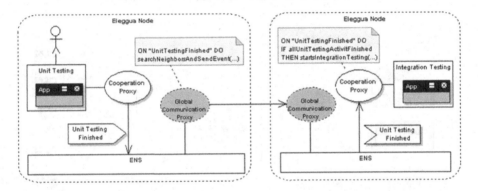

Fig. 6. A cooperation rule between two Eleggua nodes

For instance, in our example, the process in charge of the integration tests cannot start until the termination of each instance of unit testing processes. Let assume that the application that supports unit testing has a service to enable the user to indicate that the unit testing activity finished successfully. Using the ECA rules mechanism the infrastructure observes the user action and generates an event "*UnitTestingFinished*". The cooperation proxy of the unit testing application publishes the "*UnitTestingFinished*" event. The global cooperation proxy of the node where the unit testing activity is running subscribes to the event and has a cooperation rule related to this event. The associated action in the rule identifies all the outside neighbors interested in the event and sends it to each node. In our example, the notification reaches the global cooperation proxy of the integration testing activity. Let us assume that the application supporting integration testing has a cooperation rule that will be activated when an event is received notifying the termination of a unit testing activity. The action of this rule verifies if every unit testing activity is finished to continue the process. Figure 6 illustrates this behavior.

4.2 Network Topology

The system administrator is in charge of configuring the topology for communication of an Eleggua network according to the business processes. The limits of LAN/WAN networks should determine the boundaries of local nodes. Nodes that exchange information according to the business process should be neighbors. The result is a graph as arbitrary as the relations between the activities in a business process are. We need to define the responsibilities of synchronization in the same way that we need to define the decomposition of the processes.

The global cooperation proxy of each node has to publish and subscribe to broad events. Furthermore, the global cooperation proxy has to have the cooperation rules needed for the synchronization. As we mentioned previously, when a global cooperation proxy receives a broad event, the associated rule starts by identifying the interested neighbors. This is easily done, because during the configuration task, a component of the system was in charge of registering this information on the node. In other words, each Eleggua node has a reference to the node responsible for the synchronization of the general process. Additionally it stores information about its neighbors, and the events it publishes and subscribes.

4.3 Fault Tolerance

Each Eleggua node stores the events produced locally and the trace of the broad events propagated outside. If a failure of an Eleggua node occurs, broad events not propagated during that time are stored. Once the administrator solves the problem, the first task of the node is notifying these pending events.

If a node fails, all the others can continue to work in an independent manner. The general process can wait until the administrator restores its state. Eventually, the administrator can recover general consistency.

4.4 Process Monitoring

The most important requirement to monitor an Eleggua network is to offer the administrator a view of the state of the participating nodes. The main requirement for the monitor of a single node is to offer a high-level view of its state. Within a node, we achieve this requirement by showing the administrator the general state of a rule. If something goes wrong, the user can easily identify the source of the problem and from there, understand the causes and make a decision.

Each Eleggua node has its own monitor component. This component has in charge the consolidation of the current state and communication with the general monitor. A set of sensors enables the monitor component, on each node, to notify the state of execution of the rules. The general monitor receives a notification about a problem. Based on the network topology, the general monitor updates the general state view of the process.

The node specific monitoring system has distributed components that communicate with a monitoring client using channels independent from those used by Eleggua. This monitoring system has an approach based on collecting monitoring information on demand from the components of the distributed event middleware. To achieve this, it uses non-intrusive monitoring components for queries that involve high volumes of data; synchronous monitoring of each component of the distributed event middleware; and the distributed event middleware for asynchronous notifications of critical process errors.

5 Implementation

Eleggua has been implemented using J2EE technology [14]. We are using JBoss as the application server. Besides the application server, we use some other standards such as JMS, JBoss AOP, JBossRemoting, Javagroups, and Peer to Peer technology.

We have implemented the node ENS using JMS (Java Message Service) [2]; JMS is a messaging standard that enables application components based on the J2EE to create, send, receive, and read messages. JBossMQ is the JMS provider used in our implementation.

Aspects are used to generate events, specifically, JBossAOP [17], the JBoss solution to implement the aspect-oriented programming paradigm. JBossAOP enables us to intercept any calls to the API of an external application.

A peer-to-peer mechanism enables the communication of nodes in the Eleggua network. This architecture enables sharing of computational resources using direct exchange without a central party involved. In peer-to-peer systems, all components are equivalent in functionality and tasks executed. This architecture facilitates fault tolerance maintaining acceptable performance and connectivity without the need of a centralized global server [1].

We are using JBossRemoting to achieve the communication among Eleggua nodes [10] [12]. This framework permits remote communication both synchronic and asynchronic. JBossRemoting supports several protocols like RMI, HTTP, Multiplex, etc; it uses multicast or JNDI for remote discovering services.

The other technology in use is Javagroups [3] to perform the multicasting over independent channels used to monitor the system. Using Javagroups it is possible to create and manage a group of distributed processes that communicate by means of message exchange. Javagroups is based on IP multicast extended to offer services for management of groups [4].

6 Related Work

This section briefly reviews some known Event Notification Systems that have elements to tackle the scalability issue. JEDI is an event-based generic infrastructure that supports a workflow management system called OPSS (ORCHESTRA Process Support System) [9]. Siena is an internet-scale event Notification service [5]. The key idea of Siena, related to scalability, is the use of a data model to represent events, as the basis for optimizing notification delivery. Hermes is a middleware system for design and execution of activity-based applications in distributed environments [13]. ELVIN is a generic service middleware designed for distributed systems [15].

We now discuss three basic aspects for each system to appreciate the similarities and differences with ours: network topology, event scope and communication.

Network Topology. Refers to how servers are interconnected. JEDI uses dispatching servers (DSs) to communicate applications. An Active Object represents one application in the system. The topology of the DSs is hierarchical; each DS propagates subscriptions to its ancestor. A DS propagates events to its ancestor, its descendents and every Active Object that declared interest for it.

Differing from JEDI, Siena adopted a general graph as network topology where the communication is peer-to-peer. Hermes defines event channels (brokers) interconnected in a topology based on a routing network. Hermes distributes brokers arbitrarily. The system uses hash tables and routing algorithms to deal with the scalability requirement.

An Eleggua Network can adopt any topology, this has as main advantage that it reflect business needs. However, the administrator has to perform some verification to avoid cycles.

Event Scope. Refers to the level of notification associated to an event, which can be local or broad domain. The scope determines how each system routes and propagates events to increase performance. For some solutions, this refers to sending routing information with the event, applying filters, or executing ECA rules.

SIENA tries to maximize the expressive power of the data model to define filters and patterns on events. A filter is a set of attributes and relationships between the values of the attributes. Patterns are sequences of filters joined by a temporal sequence of notifications. By means of the filters and patterns, SIENA can guarantee that only interested nodes will receive messages reducing traffic over the network.

HERMES implements an algorithm of content-based routing [6]. The events are filtered as close to their sources as possible to reduce the bandwidth and increase scalability. Each channel supports requests <message, destiny>, i.e., it is possible to send events between channels. Each channel receives the messages and applies its own filters.

ELVIN includes characteristics such as security, internationalization, and adaptable transport protocols. Similarly to HERMES, the system was extended to provide content-based routing.

Analogous to other solutions, we identified the necessity of sending the minimum information between nodes. The basic difference resides on the fact that the scope of events is associated to the business process definition.

Communication. Refers to the communication between event servers and the information exchanged between them. The architecture of Hermes consists of two main components: event clients and brokers. The communication between the clients is done using an xml protocol. A routing topology based on communication peer-to-peer interconnects the brokers. The routing network guarantees the availability of the system in case of failure of one or more brokers. Each channel maintains a set of application objects to help deciding with which other nodes to route the information.

ELVIN defines events as pairs <attribute, value> using a subscription language based on predicates. The publishers of events can request information about the subscriptions to their events. ELVIN enables a reduction of costs in communication because events publishers do not send events without subscriptions.

In the same way than in Hermes, our solution defines a peer-to-peer architecture to guarantee the independence and a minimum level of failure tolerance of the Eleggua nodes supporting each process. We additionally consider the need for communication protocols between nodes without interfering with the security policies of the organizations.

7 Conclusions and Future Work

In this paper, we presented some considerations for scaling an event-based middleware to an Internet context. Our solution is composed of distributed Eleggua nodes that represent the distribution of the process. Each node treats events on its local domain while specific communication among nodes consolidates the general process. Each node performs particular processes at a given moment. The logic for synchronization of those processes resides on the special cooperation proxies of the nodes.

We have defined a strategy to scale users and tools to support the decomposition of the processes in a global scenario. The definition of an Eleggua network that interconnects nodes and a mechanism limits the scope of events to manage local and broader events enables the scalability of the infrastructure to an Internet-scale. Broad events provide the information to synchronize processes in execution over different nodes. The most relevant result of our investigation is the integration of several approaches and technologies to achieve a useful solution to a concrete problem.

However, we have many works in progress related to our solution. Some of them are extensions to the infrastructure to facilitate the configuration, testing and monitoring of the network. Our main line of research is the integration between a workflow management system and our infrastructure. As we mentioned in the paper, the administrator must manually configure the nodes, the definition and instantiation of each business process could generate this configuration. On this same line of work, the monitor should represent the state of the process according to the instantiation performed.

References

1. Androutsellis-Theotokis, S., Spinellis, D.: A Survey of Peer-to-Peer Content Distribution Technologies. ACM Computing Surveys 36(4), 335–371 (2004)
2. Barcia, R.: JMS Application Architectures. Published on TheServerSide.com (2003)
3. Bela, B.: Adding Group Communication to Java in a Non-IntrusiveWay Using the Ensemble Toolkit, tech. rep., Dept. of Computer Science, Cornell University (November 1997)
4. Bela, B.: JavaGroups - Group Communication Patterns in Java. Technical report, Dept. of Computer Science,Cornell University (July 1998)
5. Carzaniga, A., Rosenblum, D., Wolf, A.: Design and Evaluation of a Wide-Area Event Notification Service. ACM Transactions on Computer Systems 19(3), 332–383 (2001)
6. Carzaniga, A., Wolf, A.: Content-based networking: A new communication infrastructure. In: Workshop, N.S.F. (ed.) NSF Workshop on an Infrastructure for Mobile and Wireless Systems, Scottsdale, AZ, October 2001 (2001)

7. Casallas, R., Lopez, N., Correal, D.: Eleggua: An Event Infrastructure for Application Cooperation. Lecture Notes in Informatics, vol. P-70, pp. 109–123. Springer, Heidelberg (2005)

8. Casallas, R., Acero, C., Lopez, N.: From high level business rules to an implementation on an event-based platform to integrate applications. In: proceedings of the International EDOC Workshop on Vocabularies, Ontologies and Rules for The Enterprise (VORTE 2005), September 20, 2005, Enschede, The Netherlands (2005)

9. Cugola, G., Di Nitto, E., Fuggeta, A.: The Jedi event-based infrastructure and its application to the development of the opss wfms. IEEE Transactions on Software Engineering, 27(9) (2001)

10. Elrod, T., Haynie, J., Sigal, R., Suconic, C.: JBossRemoting. JBoss Group Available on http://labs.jboss.com/portal/jbossremoting

11. Heinsohn Software House. (Last visited: June 2006), Web site: http://www.heinsohn.com.co/

12. Mazzitelli, J.: Introducing JBoss Remoting. Published by ONJava (February 2005)

13. Pietzuch, P.: Hermes: A Scalable Event-Based Middleware. A dissertation submitted for the degree of Doctor of Philosophy. Queens' Collage, University of Cambridge (2004)

14. Roman, Ambler, S., Jewell, T.: Mastering Enterprise Java Beans, 2nd Edition, Copyright 2002 by The Middleware Company

15. Segal, B., Arnold, D., Boot, J., Henderson, M., Phelps, T.: Content based routing with elvin4. In: Proceedings of the AUUG2K Conference (2000)

16. Silva, R., De Souza, C., Redmiles, D.: The design of a configurable, extensible and dynamic notification service. In: Proceedings of the 2nd International Workshop on Distributed Event-Based Systems (DEBS'03) (June 2003)

17. The JBoss, A.O.P.: Group.: JBoss AOP - Aspect-Oriented Framework for Java, JBoss AOP Reference Documentation. (2006), Available online http://labs.jboss.com/portal/ jbossaop/docs/1.5.0.GA/docs/aspect-framework/ reference/ en/ html/index.html

Models and Tools for SOA Governance

Patricia Derler[1] and Rainer Weinreich[2]

[1] Paris-Lodron University of Salzburg, Austria
[2] Johannes Kepler University of Linz, Austria
patricia.derler@sbg.ac.at, rainer.weinreich@jku.at

Abstract. Organizations are moving rapidly towards Service-Oriented Architectures (SOAs). Benefits include cost reduction through reuse, better integration through standardization, and new business opportunities through agility. The successful implementation of an SOA requires not only protocols and technologies like SOAP and WSDL but also support for the processes of creating, validating and managing services in an enterprise. Tools for SOA governance and management are evolving to be the heart of enterprise SOAs. We present an approach for supporting SOA governance activities. Notable aspects of our approach are an extensible model for describing service metadata of arbitrary service types (not only Web services), the concept of service proposals for the process of service specification and service creation, a service browser for service reuse, and support for service evolution through information about service versioning, service dependencies and service installations.

Keywords: Service-Oriented Architecture (SOA), SOA governance, service metadata, service repository, service life cycle.

1 Introduction

Organizations are adopting Service-Oriented Architecture (SOA) as the central principle for structuring their enterprise-wide software system architectures. SOA is both a business strategy and an architectural principle [1]. The business strategy aligns the software infrastructure with the business processes of the organization by modeling business processes as high-level services. From the architectural viewpoint, SOA is a means of partitioning the functionality of a software system into reusable and composable software components (services).

The frequently mentioned benefits of an SOA include cost reduction through cross-organizational reuse of services, agility through alignment with business processes, new business opportunities through agility, independent development through separation of concern, better scalability through isolation, and integration of legacy systems through the additional service layer [4]. The last aspect is especially attractive, since existing legacy systems can be wrapped and reused by services instead of being replaced.

Typically, the term SOA goes hand in hand with Web services [5]. Web service specifications such as SOAP [17], WSDL [18], UDDI [13], the WS-* family [3],

D. Draheim and G. Weber (Eds.): TEAA 2006, LNCS 4473, pp. 112–126, 2007.
© Springer-Verlag Berlin Heidelberg 2007

and BPEL [19] are important prerequisites for business to business (B2B) and enterprise application integration (EAI).

For this reason, the focus of much work in this area has been (and still is) on Web services and related standards. However, standards for interoperability are not sufficient for realizing the benefits of SOA. In addition, activities for creating, validating, deploying and managing services need to be supported. Therefore, approaches for SOA governance and management are emerging [4].

We present an approach for supporting the specification, reuse, creation, deployment and evolution of enterprise services. The approach is based on an extensible model for service metadata and includes tools for describing services, creating service proposals, browsing and searching a service repository, and analyzing service dependencies. The approach is the result of analyzing the requirements of the IT infrastructures of cooperating financial institutions in Austria.

2   Overview

This paper is structured as follows: In Section 3 we describe the organizational processes and system structure for which we developed our approach; this includes a description of service-related artifacts and their relationships. In Section 4 we describe the process for identifying, specifying, creating, developing and deploying enterprise services; this section gives an impression of various activities and roles and presents a typical service life cycle. Section 5 contains an overview of our model and shows how the requirements and the processes described in the previous sections are represented in the model. In Section 6 the developed tools are described along with how selected activities and processes that are important in a typical service life cycle are supported. Section 7 contains a discussion of our approach. In Section 8 we comment on related work. Finally, the paper concludes with a summary and a description of the main points in Section 9.

3   Organizational Processes and System Structure

The presented models and tools were developed for a particular organization in the financial domain. The organization provides and manages the IT infrastructure of financial institutions (banks, insurance companies) and cooperates with other IT organizations and departments in this domain. For this purpose, the organization develops and deploys services.

As the following description shows, the system structure and requirements are generally applicable to many commercial organizations and the example is fairly typical for the application of a service-oriented approach.

To explain the processes involved in creating, deploying, hosting, and managing services, we need to elaborate on service development and service operation.

For a number of institutions, the organization develops and deploys applications and services which it operates in its own computing center. Those applications and services might use services operated by partner institutions, and services operated by the organization itself might be used by applications and services of partner institutions (B2B integration). In addition, services developed by the organization might also be operated by partner organizations and vice versa. This leads to rather complex application and service relationships that need to be managed. Important questions include the following:

(q1) Which services are available?
(q2) Where is a service deployed?
(q3) Which organization is the service provider?
(q4) Who is responsible for service development and evolution?
(q5) Which other services does a service need?
(q6) Which (external) applications and services depend on a service?

The first question (q1) focuses on service (re)use and is important during service specification and development. The questions about service dependencies (q5 and q6) are especially important for service evolution and release management. They help to determine how customers and partners are affected by a new version and which clients are affected (q3 and q4): a customer who simply uses a service might need to update his software (depending on compatibility issues); while a partner who operates a service needs to be informed that a new version is available (q2).

The system structure of the organization contains typical elements of an SOA. Business logic and processes are distilled into services that typically integrate legacy systems. In this context, a huge part of the organization's business rules are implemented on a mainframe and can be used via Customer Information Control System (CICS) [6] transactions, which are encapsulated resource adaptors that are used via transaction codes (TRACOS). The mapping from services to CICS transactions is an important aspect during service definition and design and is supported by our approach.

From a development and release management perspective, it is interesting to describe how products are structured and how services are packaged. Products consist of clients and services and are the units of release planning. Service modules are the units of deployment and versioning. Services are typically implemented using J2EE. Some of the services are published as Web services. Aside from typical Web service clients using WSDL and SOAP, clients can also be implemented in Java accessing the services via IIOP; this is typically the case for Java web clients.

4   Service Life Cycle

This section describes part of a service life cycle, in particular activities and roles from service identification to deployment. Three roles that participate in the life cycle are the product manager, the service developer, and the administrator.

The product manager determines customer requirements, specifies a service for the business logic needed and is responsible for associating the service with a product. The developer is responsible for implementing the service and decides how the service is structured on a technical level, which might include the

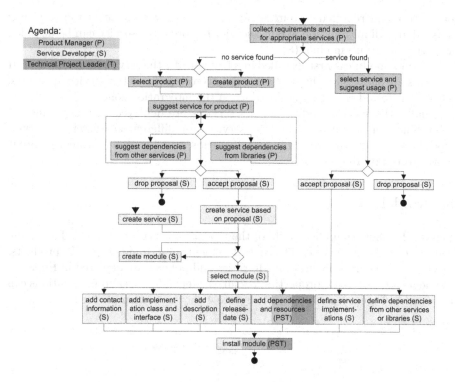

Fig. 1. Service identification, creation and deployment

assignment of a service to a service module. After the development, a service enters a multistage testing and release process.

Figure 1 shows the process in more detail. First, the requirements for the new software are collected by the product manager (1), who organizes the required functionality into services and clients. During specification, the product manager checks whether a service with the required functionality already exists. If an appropriate service is found, this task is complete (3). If no appropriate service is found, the product manager creates a service proposal and assigns it to an existing product (2). The product manager might also propose already existing services that could or must be used for implementing the new functionality.

The created service proposals are forwarded to the development team for the specified product. The development team decides whether to reject, accept or modify a proposal (4). If a proposal is accepted (5), the service enters the development process. The process of service creation can also start with the service developer creating a service without a service proposal (5). This is usually the case for general services that are used in multiple products.

After development has started, the service can be assigned to a service module (6) and details of a service are defined. Examples include contact information, details of a particular service implementation, the service interface, an informal description, the planned release date, dependencies on other services or libraries, properties, and required resources (7). After the development of the service is finished and all information about a service is stored, the service can be installed as part of a service module (8).

A service module is first installed in a test zone by the service administrator. If the tests are successful, the service module is rolled out to the service operators, where it is tested with production data in the integration zone.

Finally, the service module and its services are deployed to the production zone. Since an operator might host services for different customers, a service module is installed and tested in an integration zone for each customer before it moves to the production zone.

5   Model

Figures 2-5 show simplified parts of the model for service metadata. The model consists of eight main areas. The central elements describing proposals, products, services, service implementations, libraries and policies are depicted in Figure 2. Elements for describing properties, resources, dependencies and installations can be found in Figure 3 and Figure 5; Figure 4 shows an example for properties.

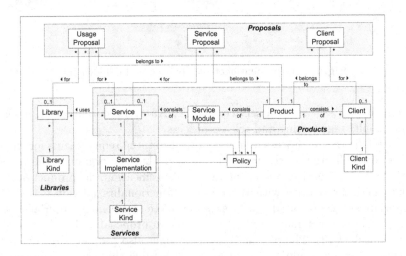

Fig. 2. Proposals, Products, Services, and Libraries

Proposals. Proposals can be created for services and clients (*ServiceProposal*, *ClientProposal*) or for the usage of services or libraries (*UsageProposal*). A proposal contains information about the proposed client, service, or library and status information that indicates whether the proposal has been accepted, realized or rejected.

Products. A product consists of clients and service modules. A service module contains one or more services. The version of a service module defines the version of all contained services. Different versions of a service are part of different service modules, which indicates that the service module is the smallest unit of deployment. If a service needs to be deployed and versioned separately, it can be packaged into a separate service module. A service module has an owner attribute that defines the organization responsible for service development and maintenance. The attribute *deactivationDate* shows how long the service module and its services are supported by the service producer. A service element might have one or more associated tags, which can be used for browsing and searching services in the repository.

Libraries. The *Library* element is used to model the relationship of services to other software artifacts that are not services. Libraries are software components that are not reusable via a network connection like services; instead, they are typically bound to the service (or service module) that uses the library. A library might represent an adapter to an external resource like a CICS transaction. The *LibraryKind* defines the properties and resources that are required to define a specific library. For example, a special instance of a *LibraryKind* describes CICS transactions.

Service implementations. The service implementation element describes how a particular service is implemented. In our case, a service can be implemented as a Web service, an EJB service or a JMS service. A service can have zero or more service implementations.

Policies. Policies define the access level and quality of service indicators for an SOA resource. A user name defines the person, user group or company and a role indicates the access or quality-of-service level. Policies can be defined on the level of products, service modules, clients or services.

Properties, resources, and contacts. Services and service implementations have various properties and resources. For example, a service property could describe the security mechanism for accessing the service. The documentation for a service is a typical service related resource while the EJB home interface of an EJB Service is a resource of the service implementation.

We chose a generic mechanism to store properties and resources of model classes. The model classes *Property* and *Resource* describe kinds of properties and resources (see Figure 3). Concrete values for properties and resources are stored in *PropertyInstances* and *ResourceInstances*. Properties and resources are connected to many classes in the model. The attribute *datatype* for a property

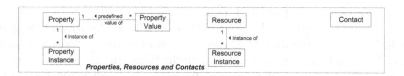

Fig. 3. Properties, Resources and Contacts

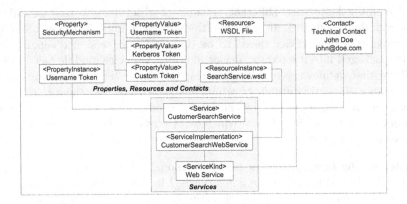

Fig. 4. Property Example

and the attribute *resourcetype* for a resource enable the validation of resources and properties. The attributes *min_occurence* and *max_occurence* define how many instances of a property or resource are required and allowed. *Property-Values* define possible values for the property. The contact element is used for describing persons responsible for specific products, clients and services.

An example for a property is the security mechanism which is used for the authentication of a service and the authorization of the usage of a service (see Figure 4). Possible values for the security mechanism are the Username Token [24] which authenticates the service consumer with a username and optionally a password to the service provider, the Kerberos Token [25], a generated token for authentication which is used by Windows, or custom binary security tokens. Those security mechanisms are stored as *PropertyValues* for the *Property* security mechanism. To show which security mechanism a service uses, a PropertyInstance with the chosen security mechanism is associated with the service. An example for a resource is the *WSDL-File* which is usually part of the description of a web service. In our example, the *CustomerSearchService* is implemented as a web service and this web service (*CustomerSearchWebService*) is associated with a resource instance containing a link to the actual WSDL file.

Instances (installations). Service modules and clients can be installed for different customers and operating zones. The operating zone can be test, integration or production. Installing a service means creating an instance in our model. Instances are also created for other elements, like clients, service modules, and service implementations (see Figure 5). Instance elements contain installation-specific information like the JNDI name of an EJB service.

The status of a service is derived from the installation location of the service module. If the service module is installed in a test zone, the service status changes to *test*; if the module is installed in the production zone, the status changes to *production*; if a new version of an existing service is created, the status of the old version is changed to *deprecated*.

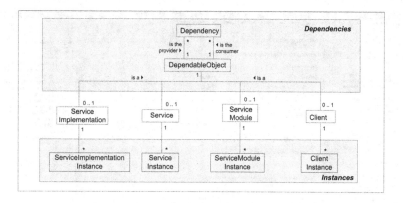

Fig. 5. Dependencies and Instances

Dependencies. Services can be used by other services and by clients. A *Dependency* is defined between two elements where one element is used by another one; one element provides information, the other one consumes this information (see Figure 5). On a more detailed level, dependencies can be defined for service implementations; on a less detailed level, dependencies can be defined for service modules. The model imposes no restrictions on the direction of the dependencies and allows incorrect dependencies such as a service using a client. Currently, such constraints have to be checked at the application level.

6   Tools

We provide two main tools, the Service Repository Console and the Service Browser, that are based on the model described in Section 5 and support the life cycle activities described in Section 4. Both tools were implemented on the basis of the Eclipse platform. This means that they can be used as standalone applications but can also be integrated into a software development environment.

The Service Repository Console is used for creating service proposals and service descriptions, for specifying service relationships, and for defining service installations. The Service Repository Console is depicted in Figure 6. The tool offers multiple views showing service proposals, services and service installations. The main area (see (2) in Figure 6) shows detailed information about the element selected in a view and can also be used for editing the element.

The Service Browser can be used for searching and browsing the service repository and for investigating service details, service relationships and service status. The browser, shown in Figure 7, offers a view for browsing products and services, a search view for searching services according to various criteria, a view for browsing the structure of a particular product, and a view for browsing client-to-service and service-to-service dependencies.

In the following, we illustrate the usage of the tools in the service life cycle presented in Section 4.

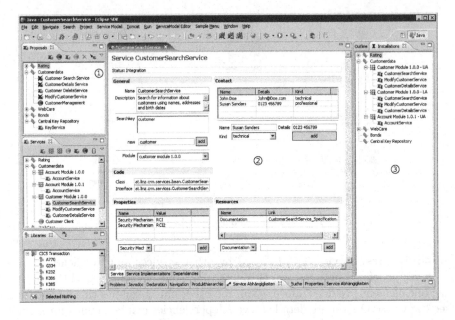

Fig. 6. Service Repository Console

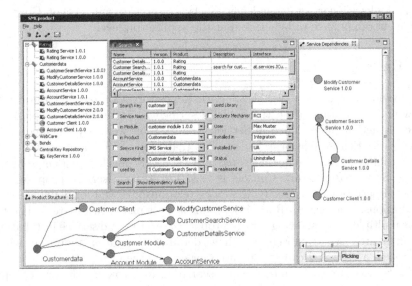

Fig. 7. Service Browser

The process is typically started by the product manager, who is responsible for defining a product and for determining product requirements, product development and other product related tasks through the complete product life cycle. The product manager can define products, clients and services using the repository console, specify new services and new clients, and propose their realization by creating service and client proposals (see (1) in Figure 6). The product manager can also define dependencies on existing services and thus propose the services that should or might be used by the new service. The icons of the displayed service proposals show whether the proposal is a client or a service proposal and whether it has been processed, accepted or rejected. The product manager can create a proposal from an existing, similar service or client. This activity is supported by the repository console. To find appropriate services, the product manager can use the service browser depicted in Figure 7. He can also use the service browser to study the existing services and their dependencies in more detail.

The proposals and their states can be viewed by the development team. If the team decides to implement a service, they must create a new service entity in the repository. Services can be created from a proposal or directly without a proposal. Services without proposals are typically created if the product has been restructured or if internal services are needed. If a service is created on the basis of a service proposal, the state of the proposal is automatically set to *accepted*. The proposal already contains suggested elements and dependencies on the new service. This information is automatically transferred to the service metadata and can be modified and extended by the service developer. At this stage, the service is already part of the repository and assumes the state *development*. Using this feature, other product managers and developers can keep track of planned services and release dates. The developer can also define service modules as the units of versioning and deployment and assign services to service modules, as shown in (2) in Figure 6. During development, the metadata of a service is continually extended. In particular, the actual dependencies, properties and resources of the chosen service implementation are provided. If a service is completely described, it can be released for installation in the test zone.

The Service Repository Console is also used for managing information about service installations (see (3) in Figure 6). The installations are organized by products and show the installed service modules along with version, location (operator), and installation zone. Installations can also be queried using the Service Browser. Together with the information about service dependencies, this information can be used to check which clients and services are affected when updating a service or when releasing a new version of a service.

7   Discussion and Further Work

We decided to create a very generic model. Properties and resources are stored as instances of the Property and Resource model elements; this facilitates adding and removing properties and resources without changing the model; only the data must be changed. Dependencies have also been modeled in a generic way. Dependencies can exist pairwise between services, clients, service modules and service implementations. The advantage of this approach is flexibility. The drawback is that certain constraints are not enforced by the model; for example, incorrect dependencies, such as a service using a client, must be prevented by the tools. Other approaches would be to specify such constraints using the Object Constraint Language (OCL) [20] in the model or to split the model into a metamodel and a model. Classes like *Property* and *Resource* could be elements of the metamodel and the concrete instances of a property such as the security mechanism could be elements of the model (i.e., the metamodel instance). This would lead to a richer but also heavier and more complex model with the advantage that more semantic information would be expressed in the model and the disadvantage that the model must be changed when data changes or new properties are needed. In our approach, all special model elements and constraints were implemented by the tools on the basis of the generic model.

Currently, the tools provide support for various activities in a service life cycle. For example: Services can be specified with service proposals; service proposals can be accepted or rejected; services can be added to products; dependencies on other services can be described and analyzed; services can be installed only if they are completely described. This means that the tools provide passive support for service governance activities by providing and validating useful information and by offering context-dependent functionality for the various roles and activities. The tools currently provide no active support for modeling a specific process or notifying specific users in case of process- or state-specific events. The latter could be realized through a notification mechanism (publish/subscribe) that informs users in case of changes. Additional useful and partly necessary enhancements include role-based authentication and authorization.

Since the tools are implemented as plug-ins, they can be integrated in an Eclipse-based workplace or development environment. Additional integration with development tools would be desirable. For instance, deployment information could be generated out of service metadata and parts of the service metadata (e.g., the class name of a service implementation) could be derived automatically from the development environment.

In Section 3, we posed 6 important questions that need to be answered for a successful SOA implementation. In the following, we outline how these questions are answered by our approach. Available services (q1) are described in the service element of the model and the Service Repository Console and the Service Browser offer lists with filter and grouping options to browse those services. The *Instance* concept of the model describes deployed services (q2) and attributes of those service instances hold information about the location of a service. The Service Repository Console provides a view containing a list of deployed services for each product. The person responsible for service development and evolution (q4) is described in the owner attribute of the service module element in the model. This information can be viewed and edited in the Service Repository Console. Dependencies between internal and external services and applications (q5 and q6) are modeled by the *Dependency* concept of the model. The Service Repository Console offers a list of services, dependent services and clients and required services. The Service Browser provides a graphical representation of the dependencies. The role of a service in a relationship (q3) is modeled in the role attribute in the *Dependency* concept. When creating a dependency between two elements in the Service Repository Console, this role attribute must be defined.

8   Related Work

Web Service Distributed Management (WSDM) [11] by OASIS comprises two sets of specifications: management using Web services (MUWS) and management of Web services (MOWS). The first specification addresses the use of Web services as the foundation of a distributed management framework [21]. The use of Web services for creating a governance or management infrastructure is not the focus of our approach. The second WSDM specification, MOWS, concentrates on managing Web services themselves, which usually means controlling and monitoring Web services as resources. This also differs from our approach, since we focus on controlling and governing the process of establishing a service-oriented architecture, which includes the process of developing a service, but not controlling the service itself. In fact, a service management approach is complimentary to governing service life cycle activities and might provide valuable information for governance activities. Both approaches are needed to successfully install an SOA governance framework.

The Common Information Model (CIM) [12] by the Distributed Management Task Force (DMTF) describes managed elements across an enterprise, including systems, networks and applications [21]. CIM contains a metamodel and generically managed object classes. The purpose of CIM is to integrate different management approaches and to allow the exchange of management information between systems throughout the network. DMTF does not intend to support the reuse of services and the governance of service life cycle activities.

The MNM Service Model [9][10] is a reference model for service management. The model is intended to describe a typical service life cycle. The life cycle phases described include design, negotiation, provisioning, usage and deinstallation. The model includes typical roles participating in the service life cycle, such as user, customer and client. It also identifies typical interactions and life cycle activities, such as contract management, problem management, security management, usage, customer care and change management. The interactions and activities are not described in detail, however; their refinement is stated as an open research issue. The MNM Service Model is intended to provide a conceptual model for describing the relationship of artifacts, roles and activities in the service life cycle. It can be used to analyze service-oriented solutions and architectures and as a conceptual model for implementing governance and management processes. It is not intended for storing actual service-related information or as a basis for governance and management tools.

UDDI [13] is a specification for (Web) service registries. It provides a standardized API for publishing and discovering services and defines registry entries. UDDI supports especially Web services through tModel registry entries. UDDI can be used to implement private and public registries. A public registry is a global directory for business services and is intended to support global service reuse. A private registry supports service reuse within one organization and the establishment of business-to-business transactions with selected partners. The main goal of UDDI is service advertisement and discovery. Its primary aim is not governance of service life cycle aspects such as service definition, implementation and evolution, though it could be used to store certain information for such activities. Contrary to service repositories described below, a UDDI registry stores only information that is needed for service (re)use, not for service development and maintenance.

Manolescu and Lublinsky [14] describe service repositories as a solution for the problem of finding service information and for supporting design, implementation, testing and reuse of services. They identify roles using the repository, such as service developer, service designer, architects and infrastructure specialists. The repository is intended to support the inception, design, implementation, deployment, enhancements, versions and discovery of services with the goal of reuse. Dependency management, versioning and change notification are mentioned as functionalities that should be supported by a service repository. This is an indication that service repositories are seen as a central element for SOA governance and reuse.

A number of commercial registries/repositories exist. Most of them are based on UDDI, some on ebXML. Examples include Systinet 2 [7], Centrasite [8] by Software AG, X-Registry by Infravio [16] and the SUN Service Registry by SUN Microsystems [23]. The functionality typically provided by such commercial approaches includes service discovery, dependency management, change notification, authentication and identity management, policy management, and federation with other repositories. In some areas the functionality clearly exceeds the functionality provided by our approach, including features such as security (authentication) and change notification. Some features are similar, like support for service description, service discovery and dependency management. Some registries like the Sun Service Registry support phased deployment to different zones, which is also supported by our approach. Some products support additional features such as impact analysis and support for tracking and analyzing processes. Competing standards for repository interoperability are emerging. Examples include the Governance Interoperability Framework (GIF) [2] and SOALink [22]. Noteworthy features of our approach are support for product management, versioning and evolution, IDE and workplace integration, a rich user interface, different kinds of services, and implicit state tracking of services. The last feature implicitly derives the life cycle status of a service (development, test, active, deprecated, etc.) from the metadata provided. The status of a service cannot be changed if not the all elements of required information have been provided to advance the service to the next state in the life cycle.

9   Conclusion

We have presented an approach for supporting service reuse and service life cycle activities. The approach is based on a generic model for describing SOA artifacts in the various stages of the service life cycle. The model contains elements for describing client and service proposals initiated by the product manager. These proposals are eventually transformed to client and service descriptions and instances. The model also contains elements for products and service modules, which are used for representing the units of product management and the units of versioning and deployment, respectively. Two tools are presented that use a service repository that is based on the model presented. The Service Repository Console is used for creating service proposals and service descriptions, for specifying service relationships, and for defining service installations. The Service Browser is used for searching and browsing the service repository and for investigating service details, service relationships and service status. The tools can be used for service reuse and for coordinating and governing the activities of product managers, developers and administrators. Together the repository and the tools represent an important step towards SOA governance and management.

Acknowledgments. The presented approach was developed as part of a joint project of the Software Competence Center Hagenberg (SCCH) and the GRZ-IT Center Linz. Both authors were members of the SCCH project team. We wish to thank Hermann Lischka, Thomas Kriechbaum and Johannes Mayr from the GRZ IT Center Linz and Thomas Ziebermayr from the SCCH for their cooperation and support.

References

1. Borges, B., Holley, K., Arsanjani, A.: Service-Oriented Architecture. WebServices Journal 4(9) (2004)
2. Systinet: Governance Interoperability Framework (2006), Retrieved June 29, 2006, from http://www.systinet.com/products/gif/overview
3. Motahari Nezhad, H.R., Benatallah, B., Casati, F., Toumani, F.: Web service interoperability specifications. IEEE Computer 39(5), 24–32 (2006)
4. McGovern, J., Ambler, S.W., Stevens, M., Linn, J., Sharan, V., Jo, E.K.: A Practical Guide to Enterprise Architecture. Prentice Hall PTR, Englewood Cliffs (2003)
5. Erl, T.: Service-Oriented Architecture: Concepts, Technology, and Design. Prentice-Hall, Englewood Cliffs (2005)
6. IBM: Customer Information Control System (2006), Retrieved June 26, 2006, from http://www-306.ibm.com/software/htp/cics/
7. Systinet: Systinet 2 Overview. (2006), Retrieved June 26, 2006, from http://www.systinet.com/products/systinet_2
8. Software AG: Software AG brings governance to SOA (2006), Retrieved June 26, 2006, from http://www.softwareag.com/Corporate/Solutions/soa_governance/default.asp
9. Garschhammer, M., Hauck, R., Kempter, B., Radisic, I., Roelle, H., Schmidt, H., Hegering, H.-G., Langer, M., Nerb, M.: Towards Generic Mananagement Concepts: a Service Model Based Approach. In: 7th IEEE/IFIP Symposium on Integrated Network Management, Seattel, Washington, USA (2001)

10. Garschhammer, M., Hauck, R., Kempter, B., Radisic, I., Roelle, H., Schmidt, H.: The MNM Service Model - Refined Views on Generic Service Management. Journal of Communications and Networks 3(4) (2001)

11. OASIS: OASIS Web Service Distributed Management (WSDM) (2006), Retrieved June 26, 2006, from http://www.oasis-open.org/

12. DTMF: Common Information Model (CIM) Standards (2006), Retrieved June 26, 2006, from http://www.dmtf.org/standards/cim/

13. OASIS: OASIS Universal Description, Discovery and Integration (2006), Retrieved June 26, 2006, from http://www.uddi.org/

14. Manolescu, D., Lublinsky, B.: SOA Enterprise Patterns - Services, Orchestration and Beyond (DRAFT). To by published by Morgan-Kaufman Publishers in 2007 (2006), Retrieved 29, 2006, from http://orchestrationpatterns.com/

15. Brauer, B., Kline, S.: SOA Governance: A Key Ingredient of the Adaptive Enterprise. HP & Systinet White Paper (2005), Retrieved June 20, 2006, from http://www.systinet.com/resources/white_papers/

16. Infravio: X-Registry Platform Overview (2006), Retrieved June 26, 2006, from http://www.infravio.com/products/

17. W3C: SOAP Version 1.2 Part 1: Messaging Framework. W3C Recommendation 24 June 2003 (2006), Retrieved June 28, 2006, from http://www.w3.org/TR/soap12-part1/

18. W3C: Web Services Description Language (WSDL) 1.1. W3C Note 15 March 2001(2006), Retrieved June 28, 2006, from http://www.w3.org/TR/wsdl/

19. OASIS: Web Services Business Process Execution Language, Version 2.0. Committee Draft, 17th May, 2006 (2006), Retrieved June 28, 2006 from http://www.oasis-open.org/

20. OMG: Object Constraint Language (2006), Retrieved June 28, 2006, from www.omg.org/docs/ptc/05-06-06.pdf

21. Papazoglou, M.P., van den Heuvel, W.-J.: Web Services Management: A Survey. IEEE Internet Computing (2005), (November/December 2005)

22. Soa Link Organization: SoaLink (2006) Retrieved June 29, 2006, from http://www.soalink.com/

23. Sun Microsystems: Effective SOA Deployment using an SOA Registry Repository, A Practical Guide (2005), Retrieved June 29, 2006, from http://www.sun.com/products/soa/registry/

24. OASIS: Web Services Security Username Token Profile 1.1. OASIS Standard Specification, 1st February, 2006 (2006), Retrieved October 28, 2006, from http://www.oasis-open.org/committees/download.php/16782/wss-v1.1-spec-os-UsernameTokenProfile.pdf

25. OASIS: Web Services Security Kerberos Token Profile 1.1. OASIS Standard Specification, 1st February, 2006 (2006), Retrieved October 28, 2006, from http://www.oasis-open.org/committees/download.php/16788/wss-v1.1-spec-os-KerberosTokenProfile.pdf

Generating Systems from
Multiple Levels of Abstraction

Martin Girschick, Thomas Kühne, and Felix Klar

Technische Universität Darmstadt, Germany
{girschick,kuehne}@informatik.tu-darmstadt.de
felix@klarentwickelt.de

Abstract. We describe our prototype implementation for Architecture Stratification supporting system descriptions at multiple levels of abstraction for developing complex software systems. Our tool transforms both model and code fragments in parallel using refinement transformations which are specified with a combination of "Story-Driven-Modeling" and Java code. Multi-level editing is enabled by allowing additive modifications at lower abstraction levels that are retained on re-generation.

We present a case study illustrating the application of a number of design patterns and show how our approach can be used to tie in a generic framework by automatically generating the corresponding glue code.

1   Introduction

Large and complex systems cannot be adequately captured with a single description only. If the level of abstraction is high—so that an overall architecture can be recognized—too little can be said about important details of the system. If the level of abstraction is low—so that these details can be examined—it is difficult to see high-level structures among the low-level details.

Architecture Stratification [1], therefore, uses multiple system descriptions at the same time, each fully specifying the system at a given level of abstraction. Thus, single levels do not only present an optimal mix of overview and detail for various stakeholders, but also separate and organize a system's extension points, patterns, and cross-cutting concerns.

In this paper we briefly introduce the stratification approach and our current implementation, a plugin for the Fujaba CASE tool (section 2). We then demonstrate the utility of our current implementation by means of a small case study (section 3). Subsequently, we discuss issues of enabling multi-level editing in a stratified architecture (section 4) and, finally, address related and future work (sections 5 & 6) before concluding in section 7.

2   Architecture Stratification

Most model-driven approaches and supporting tools interpret the transformation from a source model to executable code as a monolithic step. Only a few tools actually support this transformation as a series of model-to-model transformations (see section 5).

D. Draheim and G. Weber (Eds.): TEAA 2006, LNCS 4473, pp. 127–141, 2007.
© Springer-Verlag Berlin Heidelberg 2007

In [2] Atkinson and Kühne introduce the concept of Architecture Stratification in which a system is described on several levels of abstractions. Each level (called a stratum) introduces additional concepts to a software system until the most concrete stratum describes the final system. Note that each stratum describes the entire system, with respect to the level of abstraction it addresses. Conceptually, editing of all strata is possible at all times and changes in one stratum are propagated both upwards and downwards along corresponding refinement relations within the stratified architecture. Our current research, however, focuses on the downward propagation using model transformations.

While we are currently describing systems with UML class diagrams plus associated code, this does not exclude other forms of behavior specification or the use of domain-specific languages. One can easily imagine a gradual transformation of a system description in a domain-specific language at the top-level stratum into a specification expressed in a standard language (such as the UML) for which standard code generation techniques exist.

2.1 Refinement Annotations

We guide, and in fact trigger, model transformations by annotating models with so called "refinement annotations" which are linked to corresponding "refinement transformations". As these transformations typically need to consider multiple model elements at a time and sometimes even need information that is not present in the model, the corresponding annotations feature "links" to other model elements (e.g., enumerating the observers for a given subject in the context of the Observer pattern [3]), and can be further parameterized using basic types (e.g., a string specifying the name of a class that will be generated).

We chose a notation for refinement annotations similar to UML collaborations used within UML class diagrams. Both notations share the need to specify which elements form a structure and what role the referenced elements play. In our case, we need to designate which element(s) should be involved in a single refinement transformation, which element(s) are to be used as a parameter to the transformation, and what their corresponding role is. Compared to stereotypes which are commonly used to guide transformations, our refinement annotations enable much more explicit control and use a visual approach to specifying transformation parameters. Obviously, our notation is less space efficient than stereotypes, but we support a "collapsed" presentation mode that is visually as non-intrusive as stereotypes.

Our prototype tool supporting Architecture Stratification has been implemented as a plugin—called SPin (Stratification PlugIN)— for the CASE tool Fujaba [4]. It supports the introduction and parameterization of annotations using an annotation editor. Once a model is completely annotated, the user may use the context menu of an annotation to initiate the corresponding transformation process. Further automation steps, such as a persistent selection of a set of annotations to be unfolded for a particular stratum and the recursive unfolding of strata until the most detailed level has been reached, are not yet implemented but will be supported in future versions of SPin.

2.2   Refinement Transformations

Refinement transformations, triggered by an unfolding of an annotation, are completely user defined. SPin only provides the machinery for *transformation rule authors* to create transformation rules and *stratum designers* to make use of the transformations. The transformation rules themselves are part of a transformation rule library, which can be extended dynamically while the Fujaba environment is being used.

Transformations may be specified using a visual *Story Driven Modeling* (SDM) [4] approach based on graph transformations and/or Java code, which in combination results in a maximum of flexibility but also limits the automatic support— e.g., regarding traceability—the system may currently provide (see also section 6).

In order to facilitate the creation of new transformation rules, SPin provides wizard-like functionality, automatically creating necessary elements for the transformation specification: After entering the transformation name and further data, SPin generates the body of an SDM diagram, which is responsible for checking the applicability of the transformation rule. This check is specified using Fujaba's SDM graphical notation for pattern matching, which is more self-explanatory and easier to maintain than Java code.

In addition to the graphical notation, however, SDM diagrams can also contain source code fragments (see the next section for an example). Of course, the transformation rule author is not only able to fill in the main transformation part, but also free to completely change and amend the generated transformation specification template. Once the transformation rule has been completed, it can be exported to the transformation rule library.

3   Case Study

In the following we demonstrate Architecture Stratification and our corresponding prototype tool by applying three well-known design patterns [3] and by generating "glue" code, tying a general visualization framework into a main application in order to add automatic visualization support.

3.1   System Description

Our case study concerns the simulation of the quality control aspects of an assembly line. The most abstract stratum is shown in Figure 1 and represents a high-level view on the system's structure. The system has a main quality control unit (QualityControl) that must be accessible as a singleton instance, hence the corresponding annotation. It controls an assembly line that consists of a variable number of control stations (ControlStation). The method process checks a given item passed to it by the single instance of class QualityControl. Items are represented by the abstract class Item and the concrete classes Nut and Screw. Adding a new item at the beginning of the assembly line shifts the existing items to the next control station (QualityControl.processOne).

Each control station is attached to a tester which checks the current item. For each tested item, a test report (ItemTest) is created. Testers come in two kinds:

manual testers (here, **Human**) that are able to perform very complex tests, and automatic testers, e.g., industry-robots that are specialized for testing a single property of an item (here, **Scale** and **Extensometer**). The purpose of class **ItemFactory** is to create objects of type Screw and Nut in a random fashion, in order to test the quality control features. All mentioned methods already contain Java code which represents the application specific functionality for this (comparatively high) level of abstraction.

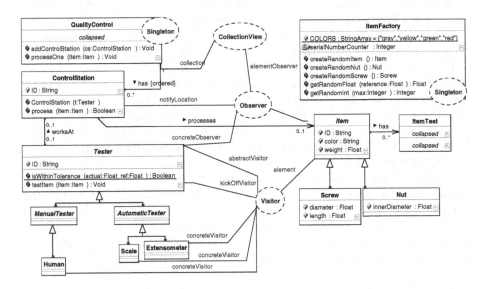

Fig. 1. Case Study: Most Abstract Stratum

3.2   Annotations

Both **QualityControl** and **ItemFactory** are annotated with a *Singleton* refinement annotation to make sure that only one instance of these classes exists respectively.

The *Visitor* annotation defines which product hierarchy (see the link *element* to **Item**) is inspected by which measurement facilities (the leafs of the **Tester** hierarchy, see the link *abstractVisitor*). The three *concreteVisitor* links designate the methods that need to receive an implementation in a stratum lower down the hierarchy. Finally, link *kickOffVisitor* defines the method that shall invoke the visitor.

The *Observer* annotation defines **Tester** to be an observer of **ControlStation**. Link *notifyLocation* defines the method which triggers update notifications to attached observers, whereas *state* refers to the state to be observed.

Annotation *CollectionView* is special in the sense that it refers to another annotation (see section 3.4) and in the sense that it does not represent a standard pattern application but is responsible for attaching a generic visualization framework to the system. This way, we obtain a rather fancy visualization of our sample system (almost) for free.

3.3   Generic Visualization Framework

Attaching a framework, which supports some subsystem functionality, to an application usually involves creating "glue code" which somehow connects the application to the framework. We have created a simple visualization framework in order to demonstrate how to use Architecture Stratification for integrating such supporting frameworks. Our sample framework is specialized to visualize collections of objects. The observer pattern is used to observe changes on this collection. When a new object is added to the collection, its visual representation is also added to the visualization and a new observer instance is created in order to watch for changes within the added object so that they can be visualized accordingly.

There is no need to specify which attributes exist within the visualized object. Our framework uses (Java-) introspection[1] to determine all attributes and their associated values and renders them in a table format. In addition, the class name is used to load a representing icon, if available, which is shown within the visualization. If an attribute named "color" is found, the icon also reflects the current "color" of the object.

By using introspection we offer a simple, generic solution to visualize object attributes. Note, however, that this technique has two disadvantages: First, introspection is not very efficient and may slow down an application considerably. Second, more complex data structures, e.g., with nested objects, cannot be rendered adequately by just using generic strategies.

Yet, these shortcomings are a phenomenon of the particular approach used for the visualization framework. All it takes to address them is an alternative approach to tying in a less autonomous version of the framework into the application. Instead of using a set of refinement annotations (*CollectionView* being one of them), which straightforwardly map the application to the framework which then uses introspection, it is of course possible to generate specialized code that specifically renders some object properties and others not. We are currently working on parameterized refinement transformations to better control the visualized information and make it more efficient at the same time.

3.4   Refining the System

There are several alternatives to start refining the most abstract stratum of Figure 1, but let us begin by unfolding annotation *CollectionView*. The associated refinement transformation first creates a new *Observer* annotation. In the final system it is responsible for updating the visualization when new objects are added to the collection. Based on its *collection* link the "Collection View" annotation unfolds to a new *Observer* annotation with three links:

---

[1] Incorrectly, referred to as "reflection" by the corresponding Java API.

- *notifyLocation*, referencing the `addControlStation` method within class `QualityControl`.
- *state*, referencing a freshly created association between `QualityControl` and `ControlStation`, named `lastItemOfControlStations`.
- *concreteObserver*, referencing the `CollectionVisualizer` class, which is part of the already existing visualization framework and is therefore included using a "reference" stereotype.

Subsequently, the "Collection View" transformation checks for an *elementObserver* link, referring to an *Observer* annotation. If this exists (as in our example), the transformation adds a second *concreteObserver* link to it, linking it to the class `ElementVisualizer`, which is also part of the visualization framework. If no link named *elementObserver* is found, the transformation will search for links *state* and *notifyLocation* which are used to parameterize a new *Observer* annotation. The link *concreteObserver* will again refer to the class `ElementVisualizer`.

Finally, class `QualityControlVisualizerStartup` is created so that it may set up the visualization framework and attach it to the quality control system.

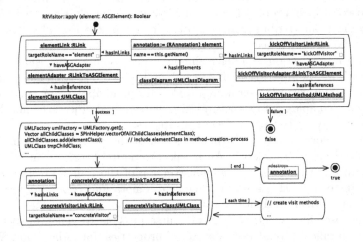

Fig. 2. Excerpt of Visitor Refinement Transformation

In addition to the two visible annotation links, shown in Figure 1, annotation *CollectionView* contains three string parameters, which may only be inspected with the annotation editor. They define the labels of three buttons, which are shown below the visualization. The refinement transformation generates the respective code fragments, which create the buttons and add them to the visualization window. A stratum designer will eventually also have to provide appropriate behaviour for each button into the generated code. Following our philosophy to enable editing on all strata, this additional code is maintained so that it is retained on re-generation, i.e., re-application of the *CollectionView* transformation rule. We will elaborate on this functionality in section 4.

What remains to be done, in order to completely refine the system description to its most detailed level, is to unfold both *Singleton* and the *Visitor* annotation. The latter is associated with a refinement transformation that nicely illustrates how transformations involving iteration over model elements can still rather concisely be captured using Fujaba's Story driven modelling (see Figure 2). The transformation's first activity matches the annotation links *element* and *kickOf-fVisitor*, then the necessary model elements are created (omitted for brevity from Figure 2). The next two activities create the visit... methods: The bottom left-hand side activity iterates over all *concreteVisitor* links, executing for each the bottom right hand side activity (of which we will see a detailed version in section 4). After all visit... methods have been created, the annotation is removed from the diagram, resulting in the final system structure as shown in Figure 3.

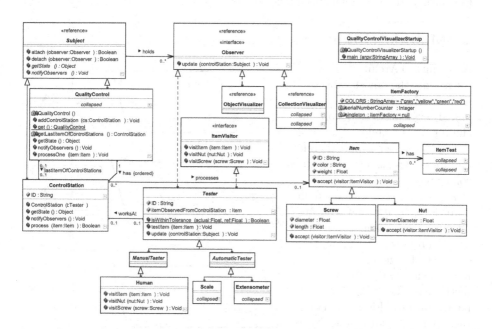

Fig. 3. Case Study: Most Detailed Stratum

3.5   Generating the System

Once the most detailed stratum has been obtained by unfolding refinement an-notations, Fujaba's codegenerator may be used to generate the executable code. This involves converting all model-related constructs (classes, associations, etc.) into plain Java code and combining it with the code that has been accumulated by all strata refinements.

Note that the most abstract stratum already contains code that defines the behavior for a simple system at this (high) level of abstraction. The methods process and processOne belong in this category, as they contain the application

specific code which cannot be generated automatically. In lower strata this code
is enhanced to support functionality, such as observer notification.

It is important to point out that our approach allows *generating* code without
compromising the need to add *hand-written* code. In addition to modifying existing code, refinement transformations create code blocks which are later filled
with custom code by the developer. Examples for such code blocks are the behavior for the visualization buttons and the implementation of the `visit...`
methods of the Visitor pattern. The absence of such code blocks—which allow
stratum designers to fill in behavior that cannot possibly be generated—will be
the rule rather than the exception. Only transformations as simple as those implementing the Singleton pattern, will be executable without further assistance
by stratum designers. How to support the persistence of stratum designer supplied code blocks, i.e., how to make them survive future regeneration steps, is
the subject of the following section.

4   Multi-level Editing

According to Architecture Stratification, the most abstract
stratum already contains a simplified system description including its behavior. Figure 4
shows these user-supplied code
and model fragments using the
color green.

As the system is refined in
lower level strata, however, additional classes and code have
to be provided. Some of this
code can be generated by the
refinement transformations directly (e.g., the "Singleton" implementation). Figure 4 shows
such parts in dark blue. Note
that generated elements (dark
blue) or user-supplied elements
(green) at one stratum will be

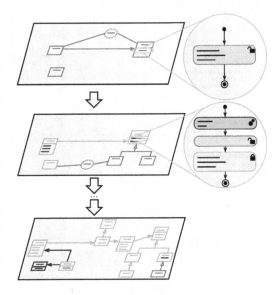

Fig. 4. Transformation with Hook Spots

treated as predefined/old elements (bright orange) at the stratum below.

A simple example for the user-supplied (green) category are the `visit...`
methods (see classes **Human** and **Scale** in Figure 3). These are relatively easy to
deal with, since they are uni-colored green, i.e., their method bodies contain new
code only. In general, methods may contain a mixture of old (orange), generated
(blue), and new code (green). Consider the lower circle in Figure 4 which starts
with a generated fragment (cogwheel symbol) followed by a green user supplied
fragment (open padlock symbol) ending with an orange colored fragment (closed
padlock symbol) which has been transferred from a stratum above.

4.1   Preserving New Parts

Even with a straightforward case, such as the Visitor methods, one still needs to take measures to prevent the new methods from being overridden upon re-generation steps. If a new unfolding of the *Visitor* annotation (e.g., since the original system or the refinement transformation rule was changed) creates new visit... stubs, we do not want to loose the existing method bodies. Three main strategies exist for dealing with this problem:

Free Editing. Any change in a stratum is possible and supported by making all such edits persistent. If a re-generation occurs, its resulting elements must change only those (orange & blue) parts in a stratum, which are controlled by the stratum above.

This approach has a certain appeal as it allows full control at each stratum without loosing edits upon re-generation. This, of course, only works if one does not allow editing of orange parts, or finds a strategy to communicate any operations on orange parts to the stratum above.

Despite the fact that this strategy would have been very difficult to implement with the current Fujaba version (which does not support multiple projects (strata) at a time and is not yet well-equipped to support consistency updates between strata), there is another good reason against such an "anarchistic" approach to stratum modification: If any of the refinement transformation rules have to be changed, e.g., since a supporting technology—such as a certain middleware solution—changes, the "free edits" in all strata below this point are potentially subject to change. Even with a good traceability mechanism in place (which would be able to locate all such parts) and an interactive scheme (allowing one to adapt the "free edits" to the new situation) one still faces a maintenance challenge. As there is no way to restrict the edits, these may aggravate the maintenance challenge by exhibiting more dependencies on provided elements in their stratum than strictly necessary.

No Editing. A solution to the problem outlined above is to disallow any editing in a stratum (except the top stratum) and to provide any extra parts in parameters of refinement annotations. This ensures full top-down re-generation without any danger of loosing extra (green) parts. However, this implies that, e.g., the visit... methods need to be written as code snippets supplied to the Visitor annotation. This is not only artificial, as the code cannot be written in its natural context, but also gets more difficult when dealing with a mixture of existing, generated, and extra code.

Constrained Editing Based on the above observations we chose a compromise and restrict editing to a few, well-known parts in a stratum. These parts are identified by the refinement transformations and, possibly, by the stratum above. Consider Figure 5, which shows how we exploit Fujaba's SDM feature that enables users to provide code (or alternative ways of describing behavior) within blocks of activity diagrams. The upper part of Figure 5 shows a method body that has been split into two blocks on purpose (see the next paragraph below). The lower part shows the result after a refinement transformation, which inserted a number of new code bits (blocks *generated.1* & *generated.2*) and supplied the block *generated.2* with two user definable pre- and post code blocks. This way, a designer may insert any appropriate code at this stratum and can be sure that these additions will not be lost upon re-generation. Any extra (green) blocks are saved in addition to the standard Fujaba model and are retrieved once a re-generation occurs.

The green *new.1* block has been inserted by the refinement step not because the refinement transformation rule author has foreseen the need to provide extra code (as with the *pre-* & *post*-blocks), but since the original method at the stratum above contained a block transition between *original.1* and *original.2*. This way, a stratum designer can induce the creation of free-editing blocks and, hence, add to the ones already created by the refinement transformation.

Since the green parts designate areas of variability (just like "*hot spots* in frameworks" [5]) and fill in parts as predetermined by the stratum above (just like "*hook* methods" in the design pattern "Template Method" [3]) we call them *hook spots*. Note that while our implementation currently supports such green parts for code fragments only, they are, in general, also applicable for any other modeling element types, e.g., classes and associations.

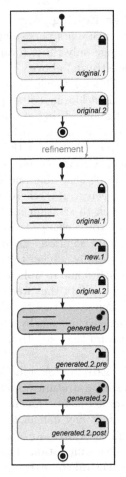

Fig. 5. Code Block Categories

4.2   Completing the Case Study

We can now describe how to use hook spots to complete the case study from section 3. Of particular interest is the **update** method of **Tester** (see Figure 3), since it contains a mixture of generated and custom extra code. This method needs to react to notification messages from subject **ControlStation**, i.e., test an item whenever it has arrived at a control station. Figure 6 shows the generated **update** method, featuring a first (blue) part which a) makes sure that the subject can be accessed, b) that indeed a change in the control station occurred, and c) sets up two variables for further use. The second (green) part then has to be implemented by a stratum designer and will be retained upon re-generation.

The visitor refinement transformation supports hook spots for the method referenced by *kickOffVisitor* and for all **visit...** methods of concrete visitor classes. The transformation code is called for each *concreteVisitor* link, adding the necessary `visit...` methods (including the respective hook spots) to the linked classes.

A third example for hook spots can be found in the framework integration annotation *CollectionView*. The current implementation of our visualization framework uses Java Swing as the GUI toolkit. If the implementation were adapted, e.g., in order to support the Eclipse SWT toolkit, then parts of the generated "glue code", which are responsible for creating and adding the buttons, would need to be modified. As these orange code blocks are maintained by the refinement transformation, they can easily be exchanged leaving the green user-supplied code blocks (containing the action code for the buttons) unchanged.

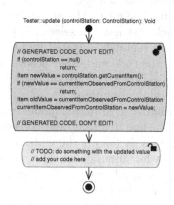

Fig. 6. Observer Hook Spot

5   Related Work

Most tools for model-driven development specialize on generating code from a model or migrating models in one modeling language to another, i.e., they specialize on *exogenous* transformations [6]. Tools that support model refactorings can—according to [6]—be classified as supporting *horizontal* endogenous transformations, whereas Architecture Stratification realizes *vertical* endogenous transformations. In other words, refactorings maintain the same level of abstraction whereas architecture stratification creates different levels of abstraction expressed in the same modeling language. Only few tools provide basic support for defining vertical endogenous transformations as well. The following paragraphs shortly describe related commercial and academic tools, comparing them with our approach.

Together Architect[2] provides an extendable template-based mechanism for defining patterns, which can then be applied to class diagram elements. In contrast to SPin, however, these transformations are executed in a step by step fashion, whereas SPin automates the transformation process and will eventually support fully automated refinement from top to bottom. Together Architect follows a purely generative approach and hence neither supports SPin's re-generation facility nor its *hook spot* approach to protect user edits from being overridden.

OptimalJ[3] from Compuware is a Java-oriented model driven development environment specialized to generate J2EE applications. Similar to SPin, it supports

---

[2] http://www.borland.com/us/products/together/
[3] http://www.compuware.com/products/optimalj/

adding editable regions (so called "free blocks") in the source code which are re-tained upon re-generation. Generated source code fragments are automatically locked and cannot be edited. Although model-to-model transformations are sup-ported, true multi-level modeling in the style of Architecture Stratification is not available. OptimalJ imposes a rather guided development process on its users, which first have to select a type of application and then have to complete the model templates created by OptimalJ. The transformation process then gener-ates the code and other needed artifacts. This approach is useful, if the needed application types are supported by OptimalJ, but fails if requirements dictate alternative solutions.

Similar to SPin, the model transformation framework "Mercator" [7] also uses UML class diagrams and corresponding model annotations to control transfor-mations. It follows the UML standard for profiles, and hence uses UML stereo-types for annotations. Our notation, similar to UML collaborations, is more expressive, directly indicating all involved elements in a visual fashion. Merca-tor provides both model to model and model to code transformation but does currently not offer the capability to add user provided code.

The "Bidirectional Object-Oriented Transformation Language" (BOTL) [8] also uses stereotypes as annotations. The pattern matching process in the source model is similar to ours whereas the generation of elements in the target model is always specified visually. Although this is also possible with SPin using Fujaba's SDM graph transformation scheme, our experience has been that Java code often enables a more direct and concise definition of transformations. Automatic code generation within BOTL is planned but not implemented yet.

The MDA tool ArcStyler[4] follows the MDA approach where a platform-independent model (PIM) is completely parameterized and then transformed to a new platform-specific model (PSM). If this approach is used in a staged, incremental manner, it very much resembles the abstraction level stratification approach of SPin. ArcStyler defines transformations using "cartridges", UML stereotypes may be used to guide the transformation process. In addition so called *marks* are used to allow further parameterization of the model. Transfor-mations are defined using the script language JPython, which is similar to our Java code definitions, however, less than the SDM capabilities that are available in Fujaba and SPin. This is supplemented by the so called "blueprints" which are similar to model templates. ArcStyler features protected code fragments, similar to SPin's code blocks. However, the latter offer more flexibility by supporting a mixture of existing, generated, and extension code fragments within the same method.

Microsoft's vision for MDSD is based on domain-specific languages (DSLs) instead of UML. So called "Software Factories" [9] are presented as an ex-tension to integrated development environments and add support for DSLs and model transformations. Both techniques share the ability to define cus-tomization points. However, the "variability points" of Software Factories only add to the domain-specific behavior of frameworks, which need to (pre-)exist.

---

[4] http://www.interactive-objects.com/

Software Factories are supposed to support advanced ways of performing multi-level modeling with a grid of models in the future, but many of the details and the implementation status remain unclear.

Czarnecki et al. propose the novel concept of "staged configuration" for feature modeling [10]. This multi-layered modeling approach exhibits some similarities to stratification. The annotations within a stratum can be compared to the features which can be selected in staged configurations. While annotations allow more flexibility, staged configurations are easier to create and use as the features are limited to a defined set and less complex than arbitrary refinement transformations.

Almeida et al. approach system design through multiple levels of abstraction, not dissimilar to Architecture Stratification [11]. They present a number of "design operations" for describing the transformations between abstraction levels. They, however, are not concerned with an automated transformation process, as the selection of elements plus the invocation of transformations are performed manually.

None of the above mentioned approaches support Fujaba's *Story-Driven-Modeling* feature [12], which is not only very useful for the semi-graphical specification of refinement transformation rules as usable in SPin, but also provided us with the basis for creating hook spots that survive re-generation steps.

6   Future Work

Although the rule library is user extensible, the utility of SPin would be increased if it already came with a rich set of ready-to-use rules. We plan to extend the library with further refinement transformation rules concerning other areas like security patterns, aspects and the integration of more complex frameworks.

Employing stratification in its intended form with SPin is currently hindered by the fact that only manual, stepwise initiations of transformations are supported. In order to fully automate the generation of a complex system from a simple system, it is necessary to automate the process of unfolding annotations. This also includes the specification of the order in which annotations are to be unfolded. Annotations exhibit natural dependencies and lend themselves to generate levels of system concerns [1]. It is therefore the task of the stratum designer to select which of the annotations are addressed at each specific abstraction level. As a result, future versions of SPin will provide a configuration system, allowing users to specify and store their annotation processing orders.

The current approach to specify refinement transformations with imperative instructions, including unconstrained Java code, implies that there is no easy way to automate traceability, e.g., supporting forward updates or backward-navigation. We are therefore investigating the usage of graph rewriting approaches [13], e.g., Triple Graph Grammars [14], to automatically maintain consistency links between adjacent strata. Such bi-directional refinement transformations would also represent an attractive facility for reverse engineering, i.e., starting from a complex system and simplifying the system by either using refinement transformations in the "reverse" direction or specifying and applying dedicated "abstraction transformations".

We plan to expand on our synchronized model and code transformation approach by looking at more sophisticated code transformations, i.e., strengthen the support for more involved code transformations. We will, moreover, provide hook spots for general model elements, over and above code fragments.

7   Conclusion

In this paper we have demonstrated the utility of Architecture Stratification, and our SPin prototype tool supporting it, by means of a small case study.

The basis of creating a hierarchy of abstraction levels, all individually describing the intended system, are model transformations. The corresponding SPin refinement transformations are user-definable, typically by using a convenient mix of SDM (for pattern matching and creation of model elements) and Java (for an unconstrained definition of transformations). Their usage is indicated by employing a concise—collaboration-like—notation for refinement annotations that enables transformation parameters to be specified both visually (through labeled links to any modeling element, including attributes and methods) and non-visually (through primitive parameter types entered into corresponding dialogs).

The creation of new transformation rules using SPin is heavily assisted by a number of convenient utilities, such as support for modifying method bodies, element creation, and synchronization with the UML metamodel. SPin also allows immediate testing and application of newly created annotations and associated refinement transformations.

Of particular value is our approach of transforming both model elements and associated code in sync with each other. We can thus obtain a *fully* specified, complex system by starting from a simple system and applying a succession of refinement steps. Such refinement steps may involve refinement annotation that in turn unfold into further refinement annotations. It was thus possible to tie in a generic visualization framework to an application with minimal effort and minimal conceptual pollution of the top-level stratum.

We have furthermore presented a useful compromise for multi-level editing, ranging between anarchistic "free-editing" and obstructive "no editing", based on the concept of *hook spots* which enable controlled amendments to both model elements and code. The combination of transformation-defined and stratum designer inducible hook spots provides a scheme that is a) implementable within the current limitations of our plugin environment Fujaba and b) more than sufficient for providing extra information at lower strata.

Despite the limitations of the current Fujaba version, i.e., the lack of support for multiple projects (strata) and, consequently, missing support for maintaining consistency between model contents (strata elements), we have managed to draw on its fine parts, e.g., *Story-Driven-Modeling* for pattern matching and an adaptable UML metamodel for supporting refinement annotations, to create a prototype supporting Architecture Stratification.

As a result our concepts and tool support go some way towards helping to deal with the complexity of today's applications. By capturing recurring software aspects by reusable transformation rules, such systems can be built faster and more reliably.

References

1. Atkinson, C., Kühne, T.: Aspect-Oriented Development with Stratified Frameworks. IEEE Software 20(1), 81–89 (2003)
2. Atkinson, C., Kühne, T.: Separation of Concerns through Stratified Architectures. In: Bertino, E. (ed.) ECOOP 2000. LNCS, vol. 1850, Springer, Heidelberg (2000)
3. Gamma, E., Helm, R., Johnson, R.E., Vlissides, J.: Design Patterns: Elements of Object-Oriented Software Architecture. Addison-Wesley, Reading (1994)
4. Nickel, U., Niere, J., Zündorf, A.: The FUJABA Environment. Technical report, Computer Science Department, University of Paderborn (2000)
5. Pree, W.: Meta patterns - a means for capturing the essentials of reusable object-oriented design. In: Tokoro, M., Pareschi, R. (eds.) proceedings of the ECOOP, Bologna, Italy, pp. 150–162. Springer, Heidelberg (1994)
6. Mens, T., Czarnecki, K., Gorp, P.V.: A taxonomy of model transformations. In: Bezivin, J., Heckel, R., (eds.): Language Engineering for Model-Driven Software Development. Number 04101 in Dagstuhl Seminar Proceedings, Internationales Begegnungs- und Forschungszentrum (IBFI), Schloss Dagstuhl, Germany (2005)
7. Witthawaskul, W., Johnson, R.: An object oriented model transformer framework based on stereotypes. In: Baar, T., Strohmeier, A., Moreira, A., Mellor, S.J. (eds.) UML 2004. LNCS, vol. 3273, Springer, Heidelberg (2004)
8. Marschall, F., Braun, P.: Model transformations for the MDA with BOTL. In: Proceedings of the Workshop on Model Driven Architecture: Foundations and Applications, CTIT Technical Report TR-CTIT-03-27, University of Twente (2003)
9. Greenfield, J., Short, K.: Software factories: assembling applications with patterns, models, frameworks and tools. In: OOPSLA '03: Companion of the 18th annual ACM SIGPLAN conference on Object-oriented programming, systems, languages, and applications, New York, NY, USA, pp. 16–27. Addison-Wesley, Reading (2003)
10. Czarnecki, K., Helsen, S., Eisenecker, U.: Staged configuration using feature models. In: Nord, R. (ed.) Proceedings of the Third Software Product-Line Conference, September 2004. LNCS, Springer, Heidelberg (2004)
11. Almeida, J.P., Dijkman, R., Pires, L.F., Quartel, D., van Sinderen, M.: Abstract interactions and interaction refinement in model-driven design. In: Ninth IEEE International EDOC Enterprise Computing Conference (EDOC'05), Twente, Netherlands, September 19-23, 2005, pp. 273–286. IEEE Computer Society Press, Los Alamitos (2005)
12. Fischer, T., Niere, J., Torunski, L., Zündorf, A.: Story Diagrams: A new Graph Rewrite Language based on the Unified Modeling Language and Java. Technical report, AG-Softwaretechnik, Fachbereich 17, Universität Paderborn (1999)
13. Königs, A.: Model transformation with triple graph grammars. In: Briand, L.C., Williams, C. (eds.) MoDELS 2005. LNCS, vol. 3713, Springer, Heidelberg (2005)
14. Schürr, A.: Specification of Graph Translators with Triple Graph Grammars. In: Proceedings of the 20th International Workshop on Graph-Theoretic Concepts in Computer Science, London, UK, pp. 141–163. Springer, Heidelberg (1994)

Using Mobile Architecture Modeling and Simulation for Enterprise Applications*

Volker Gruhn and Clemens Schäfer

Chair for Applied Telematics/e-Business
University of Leipzig, Germany
{gruhn,schaefer}@ebus.informatik.uni-leipzig.de

Abstract. Mobility–be it physical device mobility or logical code mobility–also influences enterprise application architectures. In this paper we
show how mobile software architectures can be modeled in a way that the
emergent behavior (availability, response times) of such a system can be
simulated by using an architectural model of the system and applying an
simulation approach where a network model and a user interaction model
are used for providing the contextual information. This approach can be
applied to service oriented systems and mobile applications like workforce
supporting systems, facilitating design decisions and predicting system
behavior at design time.

1 Motivation

More and more enterprises tend to mobilize parts of their information systems.
This is at least true for enterprises with sales personnel visiting (potential) customers at customer sites or with field services, who are responsible for repairing
and maintaining infrastructure of any kind. Mobilizing trends in industry can be
observed for business-to-business applications as well as for business-to-consumer
applications [18].

However, it has to be considered that design and implementation of mobile
solutions are risky and a number of mobile business cases did not work properly
in the past [17]. Reasons for failed mobile solution projects are missing knowledge
about the business processes to be supported, low level of integrations between
software systems and telecommunication infrastructure, and wrong distribution
of software components and data. Current trends in enterprise applications focus
on explicit separation of interfaces from implementations, which is quite the
essence of the Service Oriented Architecture approach: Complex systems are
built by means of building blocks (e.g. services) which are composed in order to
create new functionality. This composition is done by loose coupling, allowing
changes in the system quite easily.

If the idea of loose coupling is driven forward more radically, the application
of mobile paradigms is allowed as well. Why should it not be possible to execute

---

* The chair for Applied Telematics / e-Business has been endowed by Deutsche
  Telekom AG.

D. Draheim and G. Weber (Eds.): TEAA 2006, LNCS 4473, pp. 142–157, 2007.
© Springer-Verlag Berlin Heidelberg 2007

a certain service on a client device instead of the host system, if the service composition facility provides the necessary flexibility, and the client's device has enough computational power to run the service locally. Such dynamic reconfigurations of loosely coupled parts of the system during runtime can lead to better performance and better overall utilization of available computing power.

The idea of distributing code and data among computational nodes also gains in importance as large companies aim at restructuring and distributing their centralized infrastructure in order to decrease their vulnerability and remain able to work even if their staff members cannot use the fixed infrastructure in central offices anymore. The question of how to distribute code and data and to which extent migration of code should be allowed is not trivial. The sole possibility of distribution code and data and the existing technical capabilities are no guarantee for success, because distribution highly affects the Quality of Service: Availability and performance of such a system depend on the distribution patterns applied and the characteristics of the underlying communication networks. This problem is being solved in the area of mobile computing by using architecture description and simulation for mobile systems. In this paper, we present this approach and show how it can be applied to enterprise applications.

Previous works [2] showed, that is it generally possible to derive architectural patterns for mobile commerce applications from a classification of device mobility, user mobility and service connectivity. However, deeper analysis shows that also the architecture of a system has to be taken into account if the fitness-for-purpose of the system shall be determined. Modeling the architecture of mobile distributed systems (sometimes such an architecture is called *mobile architecture*) using a domain-specific architecture description language (ADL) is considered as an useful approach [4], since the influence of mobility emphasizes the necessity to examine functional properties of software architectures as well as non-functional properties. This corresponds to the fact that "mobility represents a total meltdown of all stability assumptions ... associated with distributed computing" [15], which subsumes the problems software engineers have to face in practice when they build mobile distributed systems. Examples for these problems are network structures, which are no longer fixed and where nodes may come and go, communication failures due to lost links over wireless networks, or restricted connectivity due to low bandwidth of mobile communications links. These all have in common that they affect the emergent non-functional properties of a system like performance, robustness, security, or Quality of Service. Besides non-functional properties, these intrinsic challenges of mobile systems may also affect the functional aspects of a system, since a mobile system may have to provide extra functionality (like replication facilities or caching mechanisms) in order to ensure usability in situations where the aforementioned problems occur. With our ADL *Con Moto* (Italian for "with motion") we propose a language which enables system developers to address these issues during the early stages of system development in order to allow them to make appropriate design choices for the mobile system.

2   Introduction

Mobile systems show complex emergent behavior due to the combination of software aspects with telecommunication issues and the therefore eroding stability assumptions. In order to determine whether a mobile system fulfills non-functional requirements like response time or availability of service, a quite complex model of the system is needed.

1. The model must reflect the system's physical structure, comprising physical components (devices) and physical connectors (communication links, network topology) as well as the properties of these items like bandwidth or bandwidth distribution and computational resources, since e.g. a (mobile) service might take more time being executed on a mobile client compared to the execution on a server.
2. The logical structure of the system must be modeled in detail, comprising information about software components, their dependencies and deployment on the physical components and the possible changes in the deployment structure.
3. The model has to reflect the dynamics of the system, i.e. the behavior of the logical components, their interactions and the exchanged information.
4. Finally, user interaction with the system must be expressed, specifying how many users are existing and how these users interact with the system.

These aspects show that the challenge in modeling mobile system lies in the need to find an appropriate level of abstraction, since over-simplification will cause meaningless analysis results; however, too detailed models are not practical during the design process. Any modeling approach should remain as abstract and as free from technological implementations of real mobile systems as possible; nevertheless, realistic assumptions about the technological implementation of a mobile system are sometimes necessary to yield feasible simulation results.

The remainder of this paper is structured as follows. First, an overview about related work is given. Next, our approach for modeling mobile systems using Con Moto is presented. After depicting an example system and simulation results for this system, results are discussed.

3   Related Work

ADLs in general have been a topic of research in previous years. The necessity for modeling non-functional properties in architecture description has been recognized by Shaw and Garlan [16]. The classification work of Medvidovic and Taylor [9] presents a sound compilation of properties of existing ADLs. From their work it becomes obvious, that none of the ADLs presented there is suitable for modeling dynamic aspects of mobile systems. In the past, this fact lead to the development of mobile ADLs which have recently been presented. The ArchWare project with its π-ADL [13] is one result of these efforts. Another mobile ADL can be found in the works of Issarny et al. [6]. Both present an ADL for mobile systems based on Milner's π-calculus [10]. These two ADLs have in common that they are able to model the dynamics of mobile systems, which is due to their theoretical foundation in the π-calculus. Although they vary in terms of elaboration and tool support, the fundamental difference—from the perspective of this paper—is the treatment of non-functional properties, which is absent in the π-calculus ADL approach. Issarny et al. address non-functional properties in their work, but the treatment of non-functional properties is bound to a global conformance condition, which must hold for a predefined set of non-functional properties assigned to components and connectors, and does not allow the composition of non-functional properties, which is novel in our approach. Besides the design of mobile ADLs there is other research in the area of non-functional properties of software systems. This work is mainly based on the Lamport's TLA+ language [7], which is a logic for specifying and reasoning about concurrent and reactive systems. Zschaler [19] presents a specification of timeliness properties of component based systems, but these as well as the underlying work of Aagedal [1], where the integration of TLA+ approach into architectural description is proposed, are not regarded further in our context, since the models in TLA+ lack the support for mobility. Other approaches based on Markov Chains and process algebras (e.g. the work of Hermanns and Katoen [5]) are not promising for out purposes, since these fall short of the support for mobility.

4   Approach

Our overall goal is the assessment of Quality-of-Service parameters of a mobile system already at design time. Formal approaches like model checking can be used to prove certain properties of a system, e.g. that a given system is deadlock-free. Unfortunately, such properties are usually less relevant in the designers daily work. Therefore, we strive to answer questions like e.g. "will a transaction complete in less than two seconds in at least 98% of all cases". To answer such questions by simulation, a rather complex model of the system is needed: Besides the architecture of the mobile system we also need to specify which communication networks the system uses and how many users interact in which ways with the systems, since our desired result is influenced by all these dimensions. Therefore, all these aspects have to be modeled in a Con Moto model, which will act as basis for later simulation.

The core architectural model is made from a behavioral and a structural specification of the system. This is due to the fact that in addition to the obviously existing structural model of mobile systems their behavior influences evolvement of the architecture and thus has to be modeled as well. Together with instantiation information, the simulator can create instances of the architectural model for simulation purposes. During simulation, communication network structures will be provided for the system as they are modeled in the network model. By applying user interactions by instantiating the Usage Patterns, the modeled system can evolve in the simulator and the evaluation results can be calculated.

In the following, we will present the different aspects of this model and exemplify their use by showing an example.

4.1 Behavioral Model

Mobile systems have to react to external conditions; the dynamically changing configuration is inherent to mobile systems. Therefore it makes sense to base architectural modeling on a behavioral model, assuming that structural aspects like components or connectors can be seen as constraints for the behavioral model of the system.

Like other ADLs for mobile systems [13], we build our behavioral model on π-calculus. π-Calculus [11] is a process algebra with explicit support for mobility. It is based on communication primitives which allow the exchange of processes or communication nodes among processes. However, π-calculus in its full beauty offers features which are not necessary for our approach. Since we build a simulation environment, only constructs which reflect typical programming situations are used; others are discarded for the sake of simplicity. Such a restriction has also been performed by the work of Pierce and Turner: with Pict [14] they present a π-calculus-based programming language, where they also omit some features of core-π-calculus, slightly reducing expressive power, but removing nondeterminism and making it appropriate for programmers.

As shown in Table 1, Con Moto provides different constructs for modeling processes: The output action allows the communication of an object over a so-called *Pin* in Con Moto (in π-calculus, the pins are called *names*). Other than in Pict, we only allow the synchronous output like in π-calculus, since we decouple in- and output by means of connectors.

Similar to Pict, we restrict π-calculus's replication prefix to input statements. Hence we do not allow the replication of processes; nevertheless, new processes can be created together with input operations, which is a quite realistic assumption, as it allows the easy creation of processes which respond to input data. The choice operator as a source for nondeterminism is omitted, but a if/then/else construct is added.

Modeling behavior includes that messages exchanged by processes need to be implemented in Con Moto. Usually, abstractions of real-world messages are used in such situations: Only that portion of a message is modeled, which is absolutely necessary to reflect the message's impact on control flow and behavior of the system. In Con Moto, we also specify meta-information about the size of

Table 1. Notation

π-Calculus	Con Moto	
$\overline{x}y$	out(x,y)	synchronous output
$x(y)$	in(x,y)	input
$e_1 \mid e_2$	par e1, e2	parallel composition
$(\nu x)e$	new x; e	channel creation
$!x(y).e$	rep in(x,y) e	replicated input

messages, because in simulation situations the real-world size of such objects is necessary for supporting non-functional properties, since these meta information can be used e.g. by the network part of the model to calculate transmission times et cetera.

4.2   Structural Model

Having identified the processes as basis for the model of a mobile system, structural information needs to be added since a solely behavioral view is unappropriate. Therefore, a structural model of the mobile system is set up. The challenges are twofold: on the one hand we need an abstraction which allows us to set up a decomposition of a mobile system and on the other hand we need some decision on what the smallest entity of mobile code is.

Structural aspects have been considered in all ADLs so far. It is commonly accepted, that an structural model comprises components, connectors and configurations. The components are the *locus computandi*: Calculations are preformed on the components, whereas connectors model the communication relationships among components. Configuration can be seen as the state of a system and represents all interconnections between components by means of connectors.

Components. For modeling mobile systems we have to clarify the notion of components and connectors. In Con Moto, we distinguish between *physical components* and *logical components*. Physical components are devices like PDAs or servers, are constrained in their resources (memory size, CPU power etc.) and act as execution environment for logical components. Logical components, in contrast, model software components. They do not have resource constraints in our understanding and can occur as components and component instances, where the first ones are stateless and the latter ones are stateful. In order to allow communication, physical as well as logical components have ports, which are aggregations of ports and pins, allowing the interconnected processes to communicate.

Connectors. In Con Moto there are two different kinds of connectors, namely *physical connectors* and *logical connectors*. Logical connectors are used for communication between logical components and are ideal: They have an unbounded bandwidth and zero latency. In contrast, physical connectors connect physical components and are not ideal, having a limited bandwidth and a latency time greater than zero.

Logical connectors can be embedded in physical connectors. This is necessary, if logical components on different physical components shall communicate. The logical connector between the two connected logical components is embedded in the physical connector between the two physical components, which act as the execution environments for the two logical components.

Mobility. Components are the smallest entity of mobile code in Con Moto. We assume that the *component* should be the element which is mobile. We do not take the extreme view of Mascolo et al. that every line of code is potentially mobile [8], because we aim at modeling enterprise application systems, where this assumption would be unrealistic.

We allow logical components as well as logical component instances to be communicated among processes. The same is true for logical connectors. This allows us to cover all kinds of mobility which are shown in the work of Fuggetta et al. [3]:

- *Client-server*, where a data file f is transferred from a node n_u to a node n_p. A program p executes on node n_p and the results are transferred to node n_u. The client on node n_u controls the operation. This is the situation as shown in our example and typical for enterprise applications, e.g. applications in Service Oriented Architecture style.
- *Remote evaluation*, where a program p is transferred from node n_u to node n_p, and executed there. Results are returned to n_u. The client controls the operation. Using Con Moto, this can be expressed by sending a logical component (which is the program p) to the computing node.
- *Code-on-demand*. Data file f and program p are transferred to n_u and executed there. The user demanding the code controls the operation.
- *Mobile agents*. Program p is transferred to n_f and executed there. Results are transferred to n_u. The agent itself controls the operation.

Configuration. It is obvious that configurations of mobile systems evolve over time, since components can connect and disconnect to other components due to their behavior. For mobile systems, however, developers usually express constraints on the possible configurations which might occur. By means of deployment diagrams like in UML 2.0 [12], developers of systems can express where components are deployed, hence which logical components are placed on which physical components. However, to be able to express constraints for configuration evolvement, this is not sufficient. Besides expressing an initial state of the deployment, there should be the possibility of expressing where components may be deployed during runtime, because then and only then runtime checks are possible whether the configuration of an mobile system evolves correctly.

Architectural Connection. Architectural connection, i.e. the way how components are connected to each other by means of connectors, is a crucial aspect for mobile systems, since here all imponderabilities of mobility arise. For realistic systems, there may be many and complex dependencies among logical components leading to many logical connections. Physical connections are fewer: usually only a small number of physical connectors connect the physical components.

In our system, logical connections must be embedded in physical connections; logical connections hence cannot be ideal–there is no synchronicity or parallelism. In order to allow different communication protocols like synchronous calls (e.g.

Remote Procedure Calls, Service Invocations) and asynchronous communication (events), our approach using pins where processes can exchange information is sufficient. Nevertheless, when a system is modeled on a quite high-level basis, there is the requirement for provides- and uses- interfaces and for services.

In order to provide a general basis, we introduce in Con Moto the possibility of ports which can consist of other ports and pins. By expressing binding rules, high-level ports can be connected and by resolving the port hierarchy and subsequent application of binding rules various pins will be connected.

5   Example System

For illustration purposes we will use a simple example system. This example system is a mobile client/server system. The users of the mobile system carry mobile devices, which are connected to a server via mobile communication links; in our example, we provide either an GPRS link, which has a rather low bandwidth, and an UMTS (3G) link, which has a higher bandwidth. There are three software components in the example system: a user interface component (UI) is deployed on the mobile devices; a database component (DATA) is deployed on the server. The actual business logic of our system is captured in the component BUSINESS, which is a mobile component and thus can be deployed either on the server or on the mobile devices. When the user invokes a service of the UI component, a request is sent to the BUSINESS component (either on the mobile device or on the server). This component itself invokes a service of the DATA component before it returns its calculation results to the UI component. The structure of the example system is shown in Figure 1.

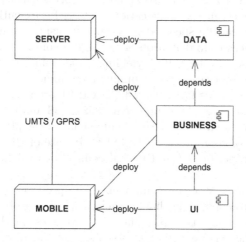

Fig. 1. Example system

5.1   Modeling in Con Moto

At the end of this paper, the Con Moto code, which is actually a document in an XML dialect, of the described example is shown. The section <physical-components> declares two hardware components, namely MOBILE and SERVER. For both, their CPU power is set and the possible connections to the network (which ends up in physical connectors during simulation) are defined. The <network- access> for MOBILE allows connection either to UMTS or GPRS network, the SERVER can only connect to the WAN.

The actual network model is given in the section <network-config>. Here, the network types UMTS, GPRS and WAN are defined. For all these network types, the bandwidth is specified (10.0, 2.0 and 1000.0 kBit/s). Latency times are not given in this example for the sake of simplicity. An additional network node named backbone is also given. All network connections via UMTS, GPRS and WAN automatically connect to this backbone, allowing to address any device from any other device which is connected to the network, i.e. physical components can communicate when they have connected to the network. This is a model similar to the internet and reflects the communication relationships in Service Oriented Architectures. For the UMTS and GPRS nodes in the network we define that these nodes are equally distributed, which is necessary information if during simulation the number of network nodes is increased.

By introducing ports and port hierarchies in the section <connection> it is possible to have complex ports which act as an method provider interface or method invoker interface and hence represent published and used service definitions. By specifying macros for ports a certain behavior can be implemented in the port definition and easily be reused in the actual process definition. In the example, the invocation of a service is modeled as a macro in port methodInvoker. Since port methodsProvider has an extendable process which provides the counterpart for this macro, method invocation, waiting for execution and returning of a method result can be specified in π-calculus using in and out command on pins. In the processes in definition of the logical components, however, these macros and processes can be reused, yielding a code which is structurally equivalent to code in an imperative programming environment.

The logical components DATA, BUSINESS and UI are specified in the section logical-components. For the components BUSINESS and UI startup processes are defined, which execute when the components are deployed. During these processes, lookups of components (BUSINESS in case of UI and DATA in case of BUSINESS) are performed and logical connections to the components are established.

For implementing services on components, the processes of the methodProvider ports are extended, such that the action which is to be undertaken after a service has been called is implemented in processes on the logical components. On DATA the service getData sets a size of the return package of 100 bytes and blocks the CPU for 100 milliseconds. This return package size is used by the simulator to calculate the transmission time through the network.

On BUSINESS the service getInfo makes a call to getData before a return package size of 5000 bytes is set and the CPU is blocked for 500 milliseconds.

5.2 Simulation

We have simulated the example system using our Con Moto simulator for user counts ranging from 10 to 150, respective 10 to 150 MOBILE devices. The users use the system as modeled by a Poisson-process with an arrival rate of 10 per hour. The simulation has been performed for an time resolution of 1 millisecond. Figure 2 shows the simulation result, meaning that starting with 90 users the system gets increasingly congested and the response times of the services at the UI component increase drastically. Differences can be seen in the response times of GPRS and UMTS, which is due to the higher bandwidth of UMTS compared to GPRS.

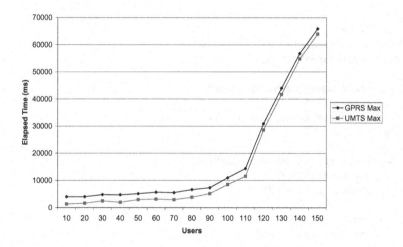

Fig. 2. Simulation result

6 Discussion

In this paper we have described how mobile systems can be modeled using the Con Moto approach with the goal of determining Quality of Service parameters during design time by means of a simulation approach. By basing an architectural description on π-calculus and making a clear distinction between logical and physical components and connectors, modeling of mobile systems on a quite high level is possible with feasible effort. First simulation results on an toy example system, which structurally resembles an enterprise application system built in a service oriented style, show that the general approach is promising and can be applied to enterprise application systems. Nevertheless, further formalization of the approach is necessary and subject to ongoing work.

Areas of further work are the discussion of models for physical communication channels. So far, we assume just a constant bandwidth and latency time, but more complex models of modeling transmission characteristics of communication channels are necessary for realistic simulation results. The area of user interaction with a mobile system is also part of further investigation, since not only the stochastic processes for user behavior need careful consideration–also the question how to derive user interaction patterns suitable from simulation from business process models is interesting. Ongoing work is the creation of an environment allowing designers specifying Con Moto models not only in XML-documents but also by means of more comfortable editors. Finally, evaluation of the approach by comparing simulation results to real-world measurements is a future task.

7   Example Code

```
<system>
  <connection>
    <port-role name="in" />
    <port-role name="out" />

    <port-role name="methodsInvoker"
      extends-role="out" >
      <ports name="methodInvoker" />
    </port-role>

    <port-role name="methodInvoker" >
      <pin name="call" />
      <pin name="return" />

      <macro>
        <parameter name="argument" />
        <result name="result" />
        <pi>
          out(call, argument);
          in(return, result);
        </pi>
      </macro>
    </port-role>

    <port-role name="methodsProvider"
      extends-role="in" >
      <ports name="methodProvider" />
    </port-role>

    <port-role name="methodProvider" >
      <pin name="invoke" />
      <pin name="response" />
```

```
      <process>
        <pi>
          object arg, result;
          rep in(invoke, arg) {
            <extension-point />
            out(response, result);
          }
        </pi>
      </process>
    </port-role>

    <bind-rule>
      <scope>
        <from>methodsInvoker</from>
        <to>methodsProvider</to>
      </scope>
      <bind>
        <from>methodsInvoker.methodInvoker</from>
        <to>methodsProvider.methodProvider</to>
      </bind>
    </bind-rule>

    <bind-rule>
      <scope>
        <from>methodInvoker</from>
        <to>methodProvider</to>
      </scope>
      <bind>
        <from>methodInvoker.call</from>
        <to>methodProvider.invoke</to>
      </bind>
      <bind>
        <from>methodInvoker.response</from>
        <to>methodProvider.return</to>
      </bind>
    </bind-rule>
  </connection>


  <network-config>
    <passive-node name="backbone" />

    <active-node name="UMTS">
      <multiplicity>0.5</multiplicity>
      <auto-link>
        <node>backbone</node>
        <bandwidth>10.0</bandwidth>
      </auto-link>
    </active-node>
```

```
<active-node name="GPRS">
   <multiplicity>0.5</multiplicity>
   <auto-link>
     <node>backbone</node>
     <bandwidth>2.0</bandwidth>
   </auto-link>
</active-node>

<active-node name="WAN">
   <multiplicity>unbounded</multiplicity>
   <auto-link>
     <node>backbone</node>
     <bandwidth>1000.0</bandwidth>
   </auto-link>
</active-node>

</network-config>


<logical-components>
  <component name="DATA">

    <port type="methodProvider"
      name="getData">
      <extend-process>
        <pi>
          result.size = 100;
          useCpu(100);
        </pi>
      </extend-process>
    </port>
  </component>

  <component name="BUSINESS">
    <size>200</size>

    <start-process>
      <pi>
        PhysComp remoteHW =
          lookupPhysComp("SERVER");
        LogComp remoteSW =
          remoteHW.lookupLogComp("DATA");
        connect(this.getData,
          remoteSW.getData);
      </pi>
    </start-process>

    <port type="methodInvoker"
      name="getData" />
```

```xml
      <port type="methodProvider"
        name="getInfo" >
        <extend-process>
          <pi>
            object res;
            object par;
            res = getData(par);
            result.size = 5000;
            useCpu(500);
          </pi>
        </extend-process>
      </port>
  </component>


  <component name="UI">
    <port type="methodInvoker"
      name="getInfo" />

    <start-process>
      <pi>
        PhysComp remoteHW =
          lookupPhysComp("SERVER");
        LogComp remoteSW =
          remoteHW.lookupLogComp("BUSINESS");
        connect(this.getInfo,
          remoteSW.getInfo);
      </pi>
    </start-process>

    <pin name="action">
      <process>
        <pi>
          object dummy;
          rep in(action, dummy) {
            getInfo(dummy);
          }
        </pi>
      </process>
    </pin>
  </component>
</logical-components>

<physical-components>
  <component name="MOBILE">
    <memory>unbounded</memory>
    <cpu>10</cpu>

    <network-access>
      <xor>
        <type>UMTS</type>
```

```
            <type>GPRS</type>
          </xor>
        </network-access>

        <logical-component-deployment>
          <name>UI</name>
          <instance>on-start</instance>
        </logical-component-deployment>

        <logical-component-deployment>
          <name>BUSINESS</name>
          <instance>client-controlled</instance>
        </logical-component-deployment>

      </component>

      <component name="SERVER">
        <memory>unbounded</memory>
        <cpu>1000</cpu>

        <network-access>
           <type>WAN</type>
        </network-access>

        <logical-component-deployment>
           <name>BUSINESS</name>
           <instance>on-start</instance>
        </logical-component-deployment>

        <logical-component-deployment>
           <name>DATA</name>
           <instance>on-start</instance>
        </logical-component-deployment>
      </component>

    </physical-components>

  </system>
```

References

1. Aagedal, J.Ø., Quality of Service Support in Development of Distributed Systems. PhD thesis, University of Oslo (2001)
2. Book, M., Gruhn, V., Hülder, M., Schäfer, C.: A Methodology for Deriving the Architectural Implications of Different Degrees of Mobility in Information Systems. In: Fujita, H., Mejri, M. (eds.) New Trends in Software Methodologies, Tools and Techniques, IOS Press, Amsterdam (2005)
3. Fuggetta, A., Picco, G.P., Vigna, G.: Understanding Code Mobility. IEEE Transactions on Software Engineering 24(5), 342–361 (1998)

4. Gruhn, V., Schäfer, C.: Architecture Description for Mobile Distributed Systems. In: Proceedings of the Second European Workshop on Software Architecture (EWSA 2005), pp. 239–246. Springer, Heidelberg (2005)
5. Hermanns, H., Katoen, J.-P.: Performance Evaluation:= (Process Algebra + Model Checking) × Markov Chains. In: Larsen, K.G., Nielsen, M. (eds.) CONCUR 2001. LNCS, vol. 2154, pp. 59–81. Springer, Heidelberg (2001)
6. Issarny, V., Tartanoglu, F., Liu, J., Sailhan, F.: Software Architecture for Mobile Distributed Computing. In: Proceedings of the Fourth Working IEEE/IFIP Conference on Software Architecture (WICSA'04), Oslo, Norway, pp. 201–210. IEEE Computer Society Press, Los Alamitos (2004)
7. Lamport, L.: Specifying Systems: The TLA+ Language and Tools for Hardware and Software Engineers. Addison-Wesley, Reading (2002)
8. Mascolo, C., Picco, G.P., Roman, G.-C.: A fine-grained model for code mobility. In: ESEC/FSE-7: Proceedings of the 7th European software engineering conference held jointly with the 7th ACM SIGSOFT international symposium on Foundations of software engineering, London, UK, pp. 39–56. Springer, Heidelberg (1999)
9. Medvidovic, N., Taylor, R.N.: A Classification and Comparison Framework for Software Architecture Description Languages. IEEE Transactions on Software Engineering 26(1), 70–93 (2000)
10. Milner, R.: Communicating and Mobile Systems: the π-Calculus. Cambridge University Press, Cambridge (1999)
11. Milner, R.: Communicating and Mobile Systems: the π-Calculus. Cambridge University Press, Cambridge (1999)
12. OMG. Unified Modeling Language (UML) Specification: Superstructure, Version 2.0 (formal/05-07-04)
13. Oquendo, F.: π-ADL: An Architecture Description Language based on the Higher-Order Typed π-Calculus for Specifying Dynamic and Mobile Software Architectures. ACM Software Engineering Notes 29 (2004)
14. Pierce, B.C., Turner, D.N.: Pict: A programming language based on the pi-calculus. In: Plotkin, G., Stirling, C., Tofte, M. (eds.) Proof, Language and Interaction: Essays in Honour of Robin Milner, MIT Press, Cambridge (2000)
15. Roman, G.-C., Picco, G.P., Murphy, A.L.: Software Engineering for Mobility: A Roadmap. In: Proceedings of the Conference on the Future of Software Engineering, pp. 241–258. ACM Press, New York (2000)
16. Shaw, M., Garlan, D.: Formulations and Formalisms in Software Architecture. In: van Leeuwen, J. (ed.) Computer Science Today. LNCS, vol. 1000, pp. 307–323. Springer, Heidelberg (1995)
17. Türker, C.: Mobilität und Informationssysteme. Technical Report 422, ETH Zürich, October (2003)
18. Wichmann, T., Stiehler, A.: Process Optimisation with Mobile Solutions. Berlecon Research (March 2004)
19. Zschaler, S.: Formal specification of non-functional properties of component-based software. In: Bruel, J.-M., Georg, G., Hussmann, H., Ober, I., Pohl, C., Whittle, J., Zschaler, S. (eds.) Workshop on Models for Non-functional Aspects of Component-Based Software (NfC'04) at UML conference 2004, September 2004 (2004)

An UML-Based Approach for Validation of Software Architecture Descriptions

Mohamed Hadj Kacem[1,3], Mohamed Jmaiel[1],
Ahmed Hadj Kacem[2], and Khalil Drira[3]

[1] University of Sfax, Laboratory ReDCAD-ENIS, B.P. 3038 Sfax, Tunisia
mohamed.hadjkacem@fsegs.rnu.tn
[2] University of Sfax, Laboratory MIRACL B.P. 1088, 3018 Sfax, Tunisia
[3] LAAS-CNRS, 7 Avenue du Colonel Roche 31077 Toulouse, France

Abstract. UML became a standard for modeling distributed architectures. The development process produces models representing architecture according to different views and different abstraction levels. These models must be valid and coherent together, so the architecture description and its evolutions have to be logical and interpretable. This paper, proposes to define intra and inter profile validations rules enabling one to define the basic elements of each profile, to minimize the modeling errors and to ensure the architecture conformity to its meta-model.

1   Introduction

Current applications are more and more distributed, large and complex. Such applications are generally composed of a significant number of networked software entities, cooperating to provide user required services. This complexity is related to the great geographical and structural dispersion of the various parts constituting the application. It is also related to hardware and software heterogeneity, the network extension and the necessary and permanent system software requirement evolution. In order to answer the needs of the software, various programming paradigms were proposed. But needs remain important for design support that helps mastering architectural complexity.

In order to face this complexity, the OMG proposed the Model Driven Architecture [1]. In the MDA approach, all descriptions are considered as models. MDA appears to be one of the most likely approaches for providing satisfactory answers to these new requirements [2]. In this approach, models constitute the layer necessary to provide the abstraction level required today. MDA approach recommends using UML for model development. Thanks to its version 2.0, UML became a widely used standard for architecture design and modeling. However, even with this intention to be general with various diagrams offered, UML cannot cover all the description requirements. UML offers a mechanism of extensibility based on profiles [2]. A UML profile allows the customization and the adaptation of UML to deal with specific fields that cannot be represented with UML in its original basic notation.

Our research work fits in this context and consists in proposing modeling solutions in conformance with the MDA approach. Our research consists in providing

D. Draheim and G. Weber (Eds.): TEAA 2006, LNCS 4473, pp. 158–171, 2007.

modeling solutions allowing to guide and assist design activities of the dynamic architecture. Our approach consists in extending UML2.0 notation to describe dynamic software architecture. We define three UML profiles. The first, the structural profile, which extends component diagrams and allows basic elements of an architecture to be designed; as well as connections that associate them. The second, the dynamic profile, which extends the first profile and allows to describe transformation rules of an architecture in terms of addition and/or suppression of components and/or connections (reconfiguration rules). The third, the coordination profile, which extends activity diagrams and describes the coordination between various reconfiguration rules. Moreover, to get models correct by design, we define a validation approach based on intra-profile and inter-profile rules. Intra-profile rules allow checking the specification coherence compared to its profile. Inter-profile rules allow assisting the passage from a profile to another.

The rest of this paper is organized as follows. In the second section, we present the related work. We present in the third section, a general overview of our three profiles. We define intra and inter-profile rules in order to validate the model and to assist architects to make the passage from one profile to another. In the fourth part, we describe extensions we implement on top of FUJABA. In the fifth part, we present our conclusion and current and future prospects.

2   Related Work

Considering the complexity and the cost of distributed architectures, a new orientation of research works consists in exerting checking and validation tasks of conceptual models before deeply advancing in the development process [3], [4]. There are principally two approaches adopted and used: the meta-modeling approach, and the UML verification through formal methods.

2.1   The Meta-modeling Approach

MOF (Meta-Object Facility) [5] is a set of interfaces allowing to define the syntax and semantics of a modeling language. It was created by the OMG in order to define meta-models and their corresponding models. Four levels characterize this meta-modeling standard. The M0 level is the real data level, composed of information that we wish to model. This level is often regarded as being the real world. If we describe the information contained in the M0 level, this activity gives birth to a model belonging to M1 level. A UML model belongs to the M1 level. The M2 level is composed of models definition languages, also called meta-models. A meta-model defines the model structure. The M3 level defines the elements used to specify meta-models. It defines basic concepts allowing the representation of lower levels as well as itself. In the MOF, the model validation is done with the lower level model. The meta-model concept is fundamental. It not only helps to reduce the notation ambiguities and inconsistencies, but it also constitutes a precious advantage for designers. The major disadvantage of MOF compared to our objectives is that it does not offer passage rules from a model to another.

2.2   UML Verification Through Formal Methods

The objective of this research orientation [6], [7] is to propose a formal base for UML models. It proposes translation of a subset of UML diagrams into various formal languages such as Z [8], [9], B [10], LOTOS [11], PROMELA [12]. These languages offer a formal base that is more solid than UML. Moreover, they have some integrated tools allowing an automatic error detection (simulators, proof obligation, ...). The objective of this approach is to formally express various elements of diverse diagrams as well as intra-diagram relations. This translation gives semantics to diagrams. It also gives a formal technique offered by associated tools.

Dupuy and al. [13] propose a method with a support tool for generating formal specifications from informal object-oriented notations. This work consists of translating an UML application, described with the Rose toolkit, into Z specifications. It is focused on the generation of basic operations and their preconditions from a class diagram. More complex operations are not considered. The method is not dedicated to a specific domain.

Kim and al. [9] present a formal Object-Z model of the UML State Machine. They encapsulate the abstract syntax and the static and dynamic semantics for each individual model constructed as a single Object-Z class. To formalize the dynamic semantics, a denotational semantics of the construction is given first ignoring detailed operational sequences. Based on this denotational semantics, an operational (execution) semantics is then defined in terms of (Object-Z) class operations and invariants constraining the operation sequences. The timed refinement calculus is used to define the operation sequences within Object-Z. Finally, integrity consistency constraints with other models constructed are formalized in terms of invariants defined in the state machine.

Varro and al. [12], [14] propose the VIATRA framework. It is the core of a transformation-based verification and validation environment for improving the quality of systems designed using the UML by automatically checking consistency, completeness, and dependability requirements. In VIATRA, the static syntax of a modeling language is specified in the form of UML class diagrams and formalized by typed, attributed and directed graphs. They present a tool for model checking dynamic consistency properties in arbitrary well-formed instance models of any modeling language defined visually by meta-modeling and graph transformation techniques.

Latella and al. [15] present a translation from a subset of UML Statechart Diagrams into PROMELA. They defined a base translation which allows for the automatic verification of UML Statechart Diagrams. The basic notion in the UML Statechart Diagrams, can be dealt with in a clean and modular way by defining a deduction system for modeling completion steps. Compton and al. [16] present a toolset which can validate both static and dynamic aspects of a model defined with UML. This toolset is based on the semantic model using Abstract State Machines (ASM). Based on the schema for generating ASM specifications for a UML model, their approach allows to build a toolset helping software developers find errors during their early stages of software development.

Apvrille and al. [11] propose a UML profile called TURTLE. The profile proposes a coupling between UML1.5 notation and formal language RT-LOTOS. It gives a formal semantics to associations between UML classes. It defines temporal operators of non deterministic time type and offers facilities of temporal constraints validation. Formal semantics of this profile is given by the translation in the formal language RT-LOTOS and simulated and checked by using the model checker RTL.

These works constitute the most interesting used for checking UML models. They propose, on the one hand, the UML diagrams transformation towards a formal language, and on the other hand, they transform UML diagrams into a formal language and then reason about the resulted specifications. These works generally offer tools allowing automating the transformation and checking process. According to this study, we noted that the suggested approaches consider only object oriented models. Generally, few diagrams are considered. Some other works tried to deal with static and dynamic aspects as well. However, they restricts their interest to object oriented approaches.

3   The Validation Approach

In our approach [17], [18], the architecture modeling is conducted following three steps. The first step describes the structural aspect in terms of components and connections. The second step describes the dynamic aspect in terms of reconfiguration rules allowing the architecture evolution to be modeled. The third step describes the application order of reconfiguration rules. These three steps are in link and the passage from a stage to another is conditioned by applicability of rules.

We propose in the sequel, a framework for validating the generated specifications according to their profiles. Our approach offers intra-profile validation rules allowing to check coherence between a specification and its profile. These rules are used to facilitate the identification of possible inconsistencies, to detect and correct specification errors and to ensure thus the specification conformity compared to its profile. Our approach also offers inter-profile validation rules allowing to assist the architect to make the passage from an aspect to another. These rules allow to reduce the errors and to automate the passage process. We describe in the following, some of these rules.

3.1   Intra-profile Validation

As described in equation (1), our model is defined by three profiles "StructuralProfile", "DynamicProfile", "CoordinationProfile" and by inter-profile rules.

$$Model \stackrel{\text{def}}{=} < StructuralProfile, DynamicProfile, CoordinationProfile, R_{interProf} >$$
$$(1)$$

3.1.1   The Structural Aspect

The structural profile defines component types used in the system and types of connections linking these components. It also defines architectural properties which must be satisfied by all configurations belonging to the architectural style. This profile extends the UML2.0 component diagrams. As depicted in figure 1 (a), the structural profile is described by a set of concepts allowing to describe the architecture structure. To describe the structural aspect, we propose a new notation depicted by figure 1 (b).

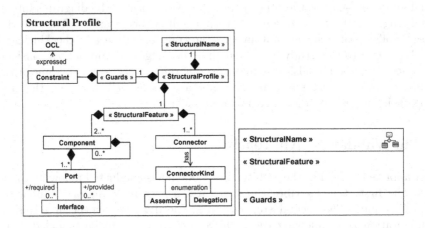

Fig. 1. (a)The Structural Profile and (b)The Structural Notation

– **Meta-model rules**

As described in equation (2), a "StructuralProfile" is composed of a "StructuralName", a "StructuralFeature", a "Guards" and a set of intra-profile rules. The "Guards" part is expressed by zero or several constraints described using OCL.

$$StructuralProfile \stackrel{\text{def}}{=} < StructuralName, StructuralFeature, Guards, R_{intra} > \tag{2}$$

The "StructuralFeature" is composed of two or several "Components" and one or several "Connectors" (3). A "Component" can be composed of zero or several "Components" and it contains one or several "Ports".

$$StructuralFeature \stackrel{\text{def}}{=} < Component, Connector > /$$
$$Component = \{Cp_1, Cp_2, ..., Cp_n\} \text{ With } n \geq 2 \text{ and} \tag{3}$$
$$Connector = \{Ct_1, Ct_2, ..., Ct_m\} \text{ With } m \geq 1$$

A "Connector" establishes the link between two "Components" via two "Ports" and it can be of "Assembly" (4) or of "Delegation" type (5).

A "Port" must have an "Interface" of required and/or provided type. The Interface type is given by the "*TypeI*" function.

$$\forall \, Ct \in Connector/ \ TypeC(Ct) = \ assembly \Rightarrow$$
$$\exists \, Cp_1, Cp_2 \, \in \, Component \, .$$
$$\exists \, P_1 \in \, PortComp(Cp_1) \text{ and } \exists \, P_2 \, \in \, PortComp(Cp_2) \, .$$
$$\exists \, I_1 \, \in \, InterfacePort(P_1) \text{ and }$$
$$\exists \, I_2 \, \in InterfacePort(P_2) \text{ and }$$
$$TypeI(I_1) \neq \, TypeI(I_2) \text{ and } (I_1, I_2) \, = \, Ct$$

$$(4)$$

$$\forall \, Ct \in Connector \ /Type(Ct) = \ delegation \Rightarrow$$
$$\exists \, Cp_1, Cp_2 \, \in \, Component \text{ and }$$
$$\exists \, P_1 \, \in \, PortComp(Cp_1) \text{ and }$$
$$\exists \, P_2 \, \in \, PortComp(Cp_2) \text{ and } \quad (5)$$
$$\exists \, I_1 \, \in \, InterfacePort(P_1) \text{ and }$$
$$\exists \, I_2 \, \in \, InterfacePort(P_2) \text{ and }$$
$$TypeI(I_1) \, = \, TypeI(I_2) \text{ and } (I_1, I_2) \, = \, Ct$$

– **Model rules**

Other rules independent of the profile can be also added in order to better specify an architecture. These rules are related to the specification.
A "Component" (6) and a "Connector" (7) in an architecture are each identified by one name. The Component name is given by the "*NameComp*" function and the Connector name is given by the "*NameConnect*" function.

$$\forall \, Cp_1, \ Cp_2 \, \in \, Component \, . \ NameComp(Cp_1) \, \neq \, NameComp(Cp_2) \quad (6)$$

$$\forall \, Ct_1, \ Ct_2 \, \in \, Connector \, . \ NameConnect(Ct_1) \, \neq \, NameConnect(Ct_2) \quad (7)$$

A "Port" is identified by one name within a "Component". Within a "Port", an "Interface" is identified by one name (8). The interface name is given by the "*NameI*" function. The "*PortComp*" function gives the list of the ports within same Component.

$$\forall \, Cp \in Component \, /$$
$$\forall \, P, \in \, PortComp(Cp) \text{ and }$$
$$\forall \, I_1, I_2 \in \, InterfacePort(P) \text{ and } \quad (8)$$
$$NameI(I_1) \neq \, NameI(I_2)$$

3.1.2   The Dynamic Aspect

The dynamic profile allows to describe the various reconfiguration rules allowing to describe architecture evolution in terms of creation and removal of components and connections. This profile extends UML2.0 component diagrams. It is described by a set of concepts allowing to describe the dynamic of a software architecture depicted by figure 2 (a). To describe the dynamic aspect, we propose the new notation depicted by figure 2 (b).

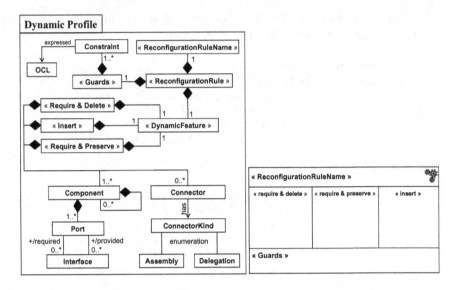

Fig. 2. (a) The Dynamic Profile and (b) The Dynamic Notation

– Meta-model rules

As described in equation (9), a "DynamicProfile" is defined by a set of "Reconfiguration Rules". Each "ReconfigurationRule" is defined by a "ReconfigurationRuleName", by the "DynamicFeature", by the "Guards" and by the Intra-profile rules (9).

$$DynamicProfile \stackrel{def}{=} < ReconfigurationRuleName, DynamicFeature, \qquad (9) \\ Guards, R_{intra} >$$

The "Guards" is expressed by zero or several OCL constraints (10).
$$Guards \stackrel{def}{=} \{C_1, C_2, ..., C_n\}/ \\ |Guards| \geq 0 \text{ and} \qquad (10) \\ \forall i \in \{1, ..., n\} \text{ . } C_i \text{ is an OCL constraint}$$

The "ReconfigurationRule" is represented by "Components", "Connectors", "Ports" and "Interfaces" instances. A "DynamicFeature" is composed of a "Require&Delete", "Require&Preserve" and "Insert" parts (11).

$$DynamicFeature \stackrel{def}{=} < Require\&Delete, Require\&Preserve, Insert > \qquad (11)$$

The "Require&Delete", "Require&Preserve" (12) and "Insert" parts are composed, each one, of zero or several "Component" instances and zero or several "Connector" instances.

$$Require\&Preserve \stackrel{def}{=} < IComponent, IConnector > / \\ IComponent = \{ICp_1, ICp_2, ..., ICp_n\} \text{ With } n \geq 2 \text{ and} \\ IConnector = \{ICt_1, ICt_2, ..., ICt_m\} \text{ With } m \geq 1 \\ \qquad (12)$$

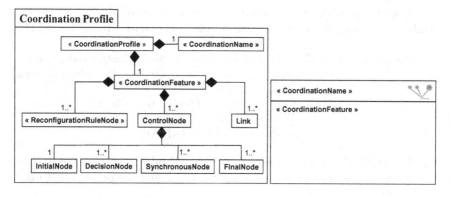

Fig. 3. (a) The Coordination Profile and (b) The Coordination Notation

– **Model rules**

Other independent profile rules can be also added in order to better specify the architecture evolution.

The "Component" instance name is post fixed by : *NameComp*. A "Component" (13) and a "Connector" instance (14) are identified by only one name.

$$\forall \; ICp_1, \; ICp_2 \; \in \; IComponent \, . \, NameComp(ICp_1) \; \neq \; NameComp(ICp_2) \quad (13)$$

$$\forall \; ICt_1, \; ICt_2 \; \in \; IConnector \, . \, NameConnect(ICt_1) \; \neq \; NameConnect(ICt_2) \quad (14)$$

3.1.3   The Coordination Aspect

The description of the structural aspect and the dynamic aspect is necessary but insufficient to describe the architecture evolution. For that, we add the coordination profile in order to describe the organization and the sequence between various reconfiguration Rules described on the dynamic aspect. This profile, as depicted by figure 3 (a), is based on UML2.0 notation and extends activity diagrams. To describe the coordination aspect, we use the UML2.0 notation proposed by activity diagrams depicted by figure 3 (b).

– **Meta-model rules**

As described in equation (15), a "CoordinationProfile" is defined by a "CoordinationName", a "CoordinationFeature" and intra-profile rules (15).

$$CoordinationProfil \stackrel{\mathrm{def}}{=} < CoordinationName, CoordinationFeature, R_{intra} > \quad (15)$$

A "CoordinationFeature" is composed of one or several "Reconfiguration RuleNodes", one or several "ControlNodes" and one or several "Links" (16).

$$CoordinationFeature \overset{\text{def}}{=} < ReconfigurationRuleNode, ControlNode, Link > /$$
$$ReconfigurationRuleNode = \{Rop_1, Rop_2, ..., Rop_n\}$$
With $n \geq 1$ and
$$ControlNode = \{Rn_1, Rn_2, ..., Rn_k\}$$
With $m \geq 1$ and
$$Link = \{L_1, L_2, ..., L_k\} \text{ With } k \geq 1$$

(16)

A "ControlNode" is composed of an "InitialNode", one or several "DecisionNodes", one or several "SynchronousNodes" and one or several "FinalNodes" (17).

$$ControlNode \overset{\text{def}}{=} < InitialNode, DecisionNode, SynchronousNode, FinalNode > /$$
$$InitialNode = In$$
$$DecisionNode = \{Dn_1, Dn_2, ..., Dn_l\} \text{ With } l \geq 1 \text{ and}$$
$$SynchronousNode = \{Sn_1, Sn_2, ..., Sn_k\} \text{ With } k \geq 1 \text{ and}$$
$$FinalNode = \{Fn_1, Fn_2, ..., Fn_h\} \text{ With } h \geq 1$$

(17)

– **Model rules**

Other independent profile rules can be added in order to better specify the coordination between various reconfiguration Rules.

A "ReconfigurationRuleNode" exists only in one occurrence and is identified by a single name. The "Link" establishes a link either between a "ReconfigurationRuleNode" and a "ControlNode", or between a "ControlNode" and a "ControlNode", or between a "ControlNode" and a "ReconfigurationRuleNode" (18).

$$\forall L \in Link. \ \exists \ Ropn_i, Ropn_j \in ReconfigurationRuleNode \text{ and}$$
$$\exists \ Rcn_n, Rcn_m \in ControlNode / \Rightarrow$$
$$(Ropn_i, Ropn_j) = L \text{ With } i \neq j \text{ or}$$
$$(Ropn_i, Rcn_n) = L \text{ or}$$
$$(Rcn_n, Rcn_m) = L \text{ With } n \neq m \text{ or}$$

(18)

A "CoordinationFeature" always starts with only one "InitialNode" and it ends with one or several "FinalNodes".

A "ReconfigurationRuleNode" can have only one "Link" in input and only one "Link" in output. A "InitialNode" admits only one "Link" in output and zero "Link" in input. A "FinalNode" admits only one "Link" in input and zero "Link" in output. "DecisionNodes" and "SynchronousNodes" admit one or several "Links" in input and one or several "Links" in output.

3.1.4   The Meta-modeling Validation

For the intra-profile validation, we used, as depicted by figure 4, the MOF approach. In the meta-model level, we define our three profiles: structural, dynamic and the coordination profile. For each profile, we define a set of rules defined according to the meta-model. On the model level, we define the three aspects: the

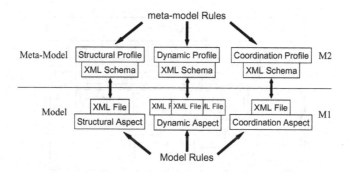

Fig. 4. The meta-modeling validation

structural, the dynamic and the coordination aspects. For each aspect, we define a set of rules defined according to the model. Based on the MOF approach, the model is validated according to its meta-model.

In this intention, we defined for each profile an XML schema which translates the M2 level of the MOF approach and implements the meta-model rules. Then, and for each profile, different XML files will be generated. One file for the structural aspect, several files for the dynamic aspect according to the number of the reconfiguration rules and one file for the coordination aspect. These files are generated automatically thus ensuring their conformity compared to their XML Schema.

3.2 Inter-profile Validation

In addition to the intra-profile validation, we define, as depicted by figure 5, a second validation type, the inter-profile validation. This rule-based validation, allows to assist architects and to automate the passage from the structural profile towards the dynamic profile and from the dynamic profile towards the coordination profile.

Fig. 5. The Inter-Profile relations

3.2.1 Structural Towards Dynamic

- Each "Component" instance in the "DynamicFeature" part corresponds to a "Component" in the "StructuralFeature" part.
- Each "Connector" instance in the "DynamicFeature" part corresponds to a "Connector" in the "StructuralFeature" part.

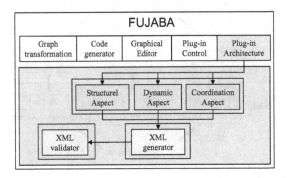

Fig. 6. Our FUJABA extension

- Each "Port" instance in the "DynamicFeature" part corresponds to a "Port" in the "StructuralFeature" part.
- Each "Interface" instance in the "DynamicFeature" part corresponds to an "Interface" in the "StructuralFeature" part.

3.2.2 Dynamic Towards Coordination

- Each "ReconfigurationRuleNode" in the "CoordinationFeature" part corresponds to a "ReconfigurationRule" in the "DynamicFeature" part after elimination of parameter names.
- Each "ControlNode" in the "CoordinationFeature" part is specified by one or several OCL constraints in the "Guards" of " DynamicFeature" part.

4   Implementation

We extended the FUJABA tool in order to support our approach. FUJABA [19], [20] is free, open source and allows modifying the source code and adding plug-in allowing to integrate our profiles and to validate our specifications. It supports UML2.0 notation.

As depicted by figure 6, the plug-in that we implemented and integrated in FUJABA offers three functions: the notation integration, the XML generator and the XML validator. It allows, to implement and to integrate our new notations in the FUJABA. As depicted in the appendix, our plug-in allows to translate the graphical notation and to generate automatically, the XML files allowing to describe the graphical specification with the new notations. Our plug-in also ensures the validation of the generated XML files. It ensures that the document is well-formed and it ensures the validation of XML file compared to its XML Schema according to the MOF approach.

5   Conclusion

Our research consists in extending UML2.0 notation to describe dynamic software architecture. We define the structural, dynamic and the coordination profiles allowing to describe the software architecture. We proposed in this paper an approach allowing to validate a software architecture compared to its meta-models. We proposed a rule-based validation approach. Our approach offers intra-profile and inter-profile validation rules allowing designers to validate a software architecture. The intra-profile rules allow checking the specification coherence compared to its profile and the inter-profile rules allow assisting the passage from a profile to another. Our approach supports the MDA technique and offers extensions to FUJABA tool and was tested with two case studies: the patients monitoring system and the co-operative review system.

Once we obtained a valid specification in accordance with the intra-profile and the inter-profile rules, we translate the generated XML files into the Z language according to a defined grammar. We currently work on the verification aspect. We seek to verify essentially two properties: the *architecture consistency* which consists in proving the existence of at least a possible architecture configuration. The *conformity* which consists in proving that the architectural style is preserved when reconfigurations are applied.

References

1. OMG: MDA guide version 1.0.1, document number: omg/2003-06-01. OMG document (2003)
2. Lopes, D., Hammoudi, S., Bézivin, J., Jouault, F.: Generating transformation definition from mapping specification: Application to web service platform. In: Pastor, Ó., Falcão e Cunha, J. (eds.) CAiSE 2005. LNCS, vol. 3520, pp. 309–325. Springer, Heidelberg (2005)
3. Bouabana-Tebibel, T., Belmesk, M.: Formalization of UML object dynamics and behavior. In: SMC'05: Proceedings of the IEEE International Conference on Systems, Netherlands, 10-13 October, pp. 4971–4976. IEEE Computer Society Press, Los Alamitos (2004)
4. Astesiano, E., Reggio, G.: Towards a well-founded UML-based development method. In: SEFM'03: 1st International Conference on Software Engineering and Formal Methods, Brisbane, Australia, 22-27 September 2003, p. 102 (2003)
5. OMG: Meta object facility (MOF) specification (version 1.3). OMG document, Object Management Group: 2001-03-08 (2000), ftp://ftp.omg.org/pub/docs/formal/00-04-03.pdf
6. Legeard, B., Peureux, F., Utting, M.: Automated boundary testing from Z and B. In: Eriksson, L.-H., Lindsay, P.A. (eds.) FME 2002. LNCS, vol. 2391, pp. 21–40. Springer, Heidelberg (2002)
7. Abrial, J.-R.: B$^{\#}$: Toward a Synthesis between Z and B. In: Bert, D., Bowen, J.P., King, S. (eds.) ZB 2003. LNCS, vol. 2651, pp. 168–177. Springer, Heidelberg (2003)
8. France, R.B., Bruel, J.-M., Larrondo-Petrie, M., Shroff, M.: Exploring the semantics of UML type structures with Z. In: FMOODS '97: Proceeding of the IFIP TC6 WG6.1 international workshop on Formal methods for Open Object-Based Distributed Systems, pp. 247–257. Chapman and Hall, Ltd., London, UK, UK (1997)

9. Kim, S.-K., Carrington, D.A.: A formal model of the UML metamodel: The UML state machine and its integrity constraints. In: Bert, D., Bowen, J.P., Henson, M.C., Robinson, K. (eds.) B 2002 and ZB 2002. LNCS, vol. 2272, pp. 497–516. Springer, Heidelberg (2002)

10. Laleau, R., Mammar, A.: An Overview of a Method and its Support Tool for Generating B Specifications from UML Notations. In: ASE '00: Proceedings of the 15th IEEE international conference on Automated software engineering, p. 269. IEEE Computer Society Press, Washington, DC, USA (2000)

11. Apvrille, L., Courtiat, J.-P., Lohr, C., de Saqui-Sannes, P.: TURTLE: A Real-Time UML Profile Supported by a Formal Validation Toolkit. IEEE Trans. Softw. Eng. 30, 473–487 (2004)

12. Csertan, G., Huszerl, G., Majzik, I., Pap, Z., Pataricza, A., Varro, D.: VIATRA: Visual automated transformations for formal verification and validation of UML models. In: ASE '02: Proceedings of the 17th IEEE international conference on Automated software engineering, Edinburgh, Scotland, UK, 23-27 September 2002, pp. 267–270. IEEE Computer Society, Los Alamitos (2002)

13. Dupuy, S., Ledru, Y., Chabre-Peccoud, M.: An overview of RoZ: A tool for integrating UML and Z specifications. In: Wangler, B., Bergman, L.D. (eds.) CAiSE 2000. LNCS, vol. 1789, pp. 417–430. Springer, Heidelberg (2000)

14. Schmidt, A., Varro, D.: CheckVML: A tool for model checking visual modeling languages. In: Stevens, P., Whittle, J., Booch, G. (eds.) UML 2003 - The Unified Modeling Language. Modeling Languages and Applications. LNCS, vol. 2863, pp. 92–95. Springer, Heidelberg (2003)

15. Latella, D., Majzik, I., Massink, M.: Automatic verification of a behavioural subset of UML statechart diagrams using the SPIN model-checker. Formal Aspects of Computing 11, 637–664 (1999)

16. Shen, W., Compton, K., Huggins, J.: A toolset for supporting UML static and dynamic model checking. In: COMPSAC'02: Proceedings of the 26th International Computer Software and Applications Conference on Prolonging Software Life: Development and Redevelopment, pp. 147–152. IEEE Computer Society Press, Washington, DC, USA (2002)

17. Hadj Kacem, M., Miladi, M.N., Jmaiel, M., Hadj Kacem, A., Drira, K.: Towards a UML profile for the description of dynamic software architectures. In: COEA'05: The International Conference on Component-Oriented Enterprise Applications, Erfurt, Germany. Lecture Notes in Computer, pp. 25–39 (2005)

18. Hadj Kacem, M., Jmaiel, M., Hadj Kacem, A., Drira, K.: Describing dynamic software architectures using an extended UML model. In: SAC'06: The 21st Annual Symposium on Applied Computing, Track - Model Transformation, ACM SIG Proceedings. Dijon, France, April 23-27, 2006, vol. 2, pp. 1245–1249. ACM Press, New York (2006)

19. Burmester, S., Giese, H., Hirsch, M., Schilling, D., Tichy, M.: The Fujaba real-time tool suite: Model-driven development of safety-critical, real-time systems. In: Proc. of the 27th International Conference on Software Engineering (ICSE), St. Louis, Missouri, pp. 670–671. ACM Press, New York (2005)

20. Kohler, H.J., Nickel, U., Niere, J., Zundorf, A.: Integrating UML diagrams for production control systems. In: ICSE'00: Proceedings of the 22nd international conference on Software engineering, pp. 241–251. ACM Press, New York, NY, USA (2000)

Appendix. The conformity between the proposed notation and XML file of the structural profile.

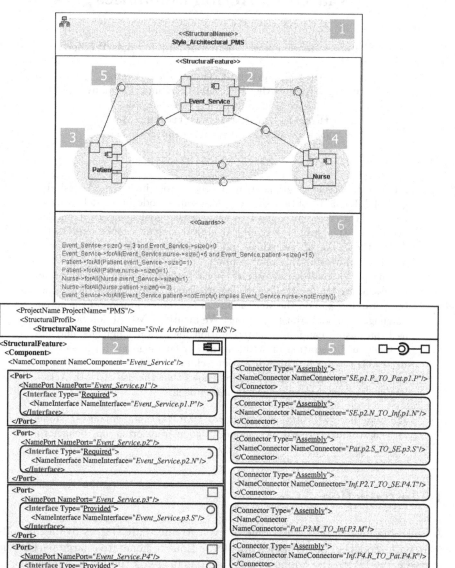

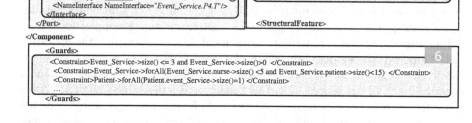

Integration of an Action Language
Via UML Action Semantics

Claudius Heitz, Peter Thiemann, and Thomas Wölfle

Institut für Informatik, Universität Freiburg
Georges-Köhler-Allee 079, 79110 Freiburg, Germany
cheitz@informatik.uni-freiburg.de
thiemann@informatik.uni-freiburg.de
thomas.woelfle@interactive-objects.com

Abstract. Transformations play a central role in MDA. A desirable goal of MDA is to obtain the complete source code by model transformations. Currently, it is hard to achieve this goal using UML models because UML's standard graphical notation alone cannot express the detailed behavior of operations and transitions. Action languages are a means of addressing this shortcoming.

The paper investigates different means of integration of action languages in an MDA development environment. The focus is on tool interoperability and on the amenability of the representation of the action language to model transformations. We identify UML Action Semantics as a promising candidate representation for action languages and implement an integration of ABL, an action language for business logic, using this approach. This integration achieves 100% code generation for a small example, but our evaluation shows that the use of UML Action Semantics is not the most practical approach.

Keywords: UML Action Language, UML Action Semantics, Model Driven Architecture (MDA), model to code transformation, behavioral modeling.

1 Introduction

A central point of MDA, the Model Driven Architecture [11], is to specify software with models and use model transformations to generate a large part of the source code. UML, the Unified Modeling Language, is the OMG's language of choice for modeling. Unfortunately, UML's notation is not sufficiently detailed to fully define the behavior of operations and transitions. Examples for the required degree of detail are attribute assignment, link creation, and the operation call. Thus, a UML model with standard graphical notation cannot completely specify the behavior of a software system so that model transformations cannot generate 100% of the source code. But the latter is a desirable goal of MDA because the current practice to insert target code fragments in generated code has its problems. Although techniques (like protected areas) exist for managing such

D. Draheim and G. Weber (Eds.): TEAA 2006, LNCS 4473, pp. 172–186, 2007.
© Springer-Verlag Berlin Heidelberg 2007

code fragments, they come with many disadvantages: the code breaks abstraction, it requires knowledge about the transformation and the target platform, and changes in the model can break the code.

In UML 1.5, the OMG introduced Action Semantics [14] to facilitate the complete description of behavior. While UML Action Semantics provides the required facilities up to a certain degree, it is also not without problems (see Section 7 for a discussion). Certainly, UML Action Semantics is too low-level to be suitable as a programming language for defining operations.

Consequently, *action languages* have been conceived as high-level programming languages for defining operations in UML Class Diagrams or transitions in UML State Machines. Currently, there are about 15 different action languages, which are often proprietary extensions of UML which are not interoperable: it is hardly possible to interchange the action language parts of models between different tools because the action languages are all different and they are integrated with UML in different ways.

The facilities to integrate action languages in UML have different properties concerning tool interoperability and the amenability to model transformations of the representation of the action language. Both are core points in the MDA approach and thus important to consider. Section 4 compares two integration paths and discusses their properties.

As a result of this discussion, we have chosen to represent actions in the model with UML Action Semantics, while presenting the developer a newly defined action language ABL (Action Language for Business Logic). In this setup, we demonstrate with an example that 100% code generation is feasible. We implemented this integration in a prototypical extension of ArcStyler. The implementation shows that the chosen integration via UML Action Semantics is currently not the most practical approach. The main reason is the low level nature of UML Action Semantics that makes some transformations very awkward.

The rest of the paper proceeds as follows. Section 2 considers the requirements of an integration of an action language in UML and an MDA development environment. Section 3 contains a brief introduction to UML's UML Action Semantics as a participant in one possible integration path. Section 4 presents two facilities to integrate action languages in UML and compares them. Section 5 introduces the action language ABL. Section 6 explains the transformations in the implementation for UML Action Semantics. Section 7 contains a final, detailed discussion of the pros and cons of using UML Action Semantics for integrating an action language. Section 8 reviews related work and Section 9 concludes.

2   Requirements for an Integration

An MDA development environment is a set of interoperable tools that support the use of models throughout the lifecycle of the software development. A key feature is the ability to transform higher-level models (specifications) into lower-level ones (*e.g.*, code) without human intervention. The range of transformations includes the generation of source code, tests, and build support. Thus, any additional kind of model in an MDA development environment has to be judged by its amenability to transformation.

A modeling language integrated with an action language also needs tool support. A good integration should be interoperable, *i.e.*, it should not depend on any particular tool implementation. Hence, models that contain action language fragments should be readable by other tools and (in the best case) even the transformations should be interchangeable. An integration may support interoperability at three different levels.

A *flat integration* includes actions in a representation the structure of which is not obvious to other tools. For example, the action language code may be a comment string in the model. Such a choice enables a minimum level of interoperability. Other tools can read UML models containing actions and process everything except the action language parts. A transformation may render actions inconsistent with the rest of the model.

In a *structured integration* other tools can parse the action language parts. This alternative requires the choice of a standardized syntax for representing the action language. After parsing, the action language parts are amenable to transformation in this approach.

Semantic integration is the third level of interoperability. In addition to the structured integration, there is a predefined semantics for the standardized syntax. This choice facilitates editing the action language parts and perform namespace and type checks, at the price of requiring a compiler for the representation of action languages.

Hence, the requirements for integrating the action language in UML and an MDA environment are:

- A representation of the action language in the model that enables one of the three integration levels; in the best case a semantic integration with full control over the representation of action languages.
- A representation that is amenable to transformations, without requiring extensions to the transformation framework.

3   Background: UML Action Semantics

Action Semantics was incorporated in UML 1.5 with the explicit goal of specifying an abstract syntax for defining low-level fine-grained behavior of operations on instances of UML Class Diagrams. At the time of designing the UML Action Semantics some action languages already existed (ASL[4], OAL[1,7], Kabira AS[6]), which had to be amenable to transformation to UML Action Semantics. Hence, the following properties of UML Action Semantics:

- possibly parallel execution of actions, driven by data dependencies and ordered by explicit control dependencies,
- no restrictions concerning the type system (static or dynamic typing),
- no predefined primitive data types and primitive functions,
- flexible messaging system (synchronous or asynchronous),

- no predefined JumpActions but facilities to define any kind of control transfer,
- flexible handling of collections.

An UML Action Semantics model consists of actions connected by data-flow and control-flow dependencies. Each action comes with a number of InputPins and OutputPins through which the action communicates with its environment. A data-flow dependency exists if an InputPin of an action connected to an OutputPin of another action. A DataFlow element models this connection[1]. There is no fan-in but fan-out is admissible. An action executes after all its InputPins have values and afterwards its result is available through its OutputPins.

All actions that have their inputs available may execute, possibly in parallel. The only ordering that must be observed is due to data-flow dependencies or to explicit control-flow dependencies expressed by separate ControlFlow elements in the model. Both kinds of dependencies together must form a directed acyclic graph. The idea is to prevent overspecification and to enable scheduling for optimization purposes.

4   Integration Paths

There are two main approaches to integrating an action language in UML and an MDA development environment. The first approach is to put an action language code fragment in the body of a UML ProcedureExpression. The second approach transforms actions into UML Action Semantics as an abstract syntax.

A UML ProcedureExpression is an uninterpreted textual statement[2]. According to the semantics, a ProcedureExpression can be evaluated in a context, possibly return values, or change the values of its environment. It may contain action language code as a string and thus corresponds to a flat integration. The integration is neither structured nor semantic because it cannot be assumed that every tool comes with a parser for the action language.

This approach is fully compatible with the UML specification and takes only little effort to implement. Without a parser for the action language, a model transformation cannot analyze the structure of the actions and, thus, cannot transform them in a nontrivial way.

Turning to the second approach, UML Action Semantics offers all constructs necessary to represent the semantics of an action language in UML. Every tool that supports UML 1.5 or higher should be able to parse UML Action Semantics. Transformations may directly access the parsed action representation and transform it into a target language. Hence, a representation of an action language using UML Action Semantics is amenable to transformation.

---

[1] In UML 2.0, the DataFlow element does not exist anymore. OutputPins can be connected directly to InputPins.

[2] UML 1.5 [14], p. 2-90. In UML 2.0 [16] the respective element is called OpaqueExpression. See UML 2.0 superstructure, p. 97.

The model elements in UML Action Semantics are already connected with respective elements in the rest of the UML model (*e.g.*, Attributes, Associations, Operations, Classifier). Like the rest of UML, UML Action Semantics is defined in MOF and has a semantics described in natural language. Hence, the integration using UML Action Semantics is a semantic integration as defined in Section 2.

The use of UML Action Semantics might also improve interoperability by serving as a common internal representation for actions across different action languages. Each action language would come with a transformation to UML Action Semantics and a common backend would generate code for different target platforms from there. Alternatively, an interpretive approach could be used to execute actions directly.

For our prototype, we have chosen the integration path via UML Action Semantics because we were aiming for a semantic integration, we hoped for the interoperability promise inherent in adhering to a standard, and we wanted to exploit the existence of the UML Action Semantics metamodel. This choice has turned out to be unsatisfactory in a number of respects which we summarize in Section 7.

5   ABL, the Action Language for Business Logic

ABL is our proposal for an action language for business logic. Many aspects of ABL are inspired by Java, which is a language commonly used for implementing enterprise systems. Its description is included mainly to shed some light on the source language of our translation to UML Action Semantics, which is covered in Section 6. Hence, we only consider parts of the language with significant differences to Java.

5.1   Types and Variables

As ABL is geared at defining the behavior of operations from a class diagram, the language has no syntax to define types (*e.g.*, classes, interfaces, enumerations), attributes, or operations. The class diagram must provide definitions for all those and ABL accesses them through the standard (package qualified) UML notation.

Local variable are considered as attributes of operation activations. Their declaration syntax extends Java's variable declarations with adornments to specify orderedness, uniqueness, and multiplicity.

[ordered] [unique] *classifier* [*multiplicity*] *var* [*initializer*]

A *classifier* from the model (or a primitive type) specifies the type of the variable, the ordered and unique adornments modify the type accordingly, and *multiplicity* is a multiplicity specification in UML 2 syntax restricted to the numbers 0, 1, and *. The default multiplicity is [0..1].

A variable (or attribute) reference in an expression may be indexed (starting from 0) to extract only some of the variable's values. For example,

```
var[0..7]        // extract the first eight values (at most)
var[1..*]        // all but the first value
var[5]           // at most one value
```

None of these expressions fails if the indices are out of range, they just return the selected elements. Assuming the declaration `T[*] var`, the first two expressions have type `T[*]` and the third one has type `T[0..1]`.

There is no type constructor for arrays. Unidimensional arrays can be expressed through the multiplicity specification of a variable. Multidimensional arrays must be constructed indirectly via an intermediate class with a sequence-valued attribute.

5.2 Assignment Compatibility

Assignment compatibility is derived from the generalization relation among model elements and from the additional multiplicity, ordering, and uniqueness adornments. It is defined as the overloaded subtyping relation $\leq$. We start with multiplicities, which are ordered as follows

$$[a..b] \leq [c..d] \quad \text{if} \quad c \leq a \text{ and } b \leq d$$

where $a, b, c, d \in \mathbf{N} \cup \{*\}$ with $a \leq b$ and $c \leq d$ with the latter defined by

$$a \leq b \quad \text{if} \quad a, b \in \mathbf{N} \wedge a \leq b \text{ or } b = *$$

Let $A(m, o, u)$ denote an adorned type with base type A, multiplicity m, `isOrdered` flag o, and `isUnique` flag u. Define the subtype ordering by

$$A(m, o, u) \leq A'(m', o', u') \quad \text{if} \quad A \leq A' \text{ and } m \leq m' \text{ and } o \leq o' \text{ and } u \leq u'$$

where $o, u \in \{\text{true}, \text{false}\}$ with $\text{true} \leq \text{false}$.

Type casts are quite important in ABL. Because of the adornments, there is a greater chance that a computed value cannot be assigned directly to an attribute or passed as a parameter.

5.3 Links

The assignment operators (=, +=, -=) also create and destroy links. The left hand side of such an operator *must* be the role name of the target end of an association. An unqualified identifier refers to an association in which the receiver object of the operation (*e.g.*, `this`) can participate at the source end. If the left hand side

Fig. 1. Shopping cart

is a navigation expression, the last part of the navigation denotes the target end of an association where the object returned by the initial part of the expression can participate in a source role.

The right hand side denotes an object to which a link is created or destroyed.

For illustration, consider the situation in the diagram in Figure 1 and suppose the `ShoppingCart` class has an operation `addItem (Item it)`. Here is its implementation in ABL, which assumes an attribute `total` in `ShoppingCart`:

```
item += it;                        // link item to shopping cart
total += it.unitCost * it.quantity; // compute the total attribute
```

ABL only supports binary associations where the association end at the navigation target has a role name.

There is a for-each loop to iterate over a collection and execute the loop body for each element of the collection. Any variable, attribute, or association end may serve as the source for a collection. For example, an operation to check the total cost of a shopping cart may be implemented by

```
checkTotal = 0;
for (Item it in item) {
   checkTotal += it.unitCost * it.quantity;
}
if (checkTotal != total) { ...}
```

5.4   Create

Many programming languages have a problem with meeting the restrictions imposed by UML's multiplicities. For example, it is not possible to create two objects which partake in a 1:1 association in a mainstream programming language because each implementation has to pick an order in which the objects are created so that the first created object always violates the 1:1 constraint on the association. UML addresses this problem by essentially ignoring the lower multiplicity and always allowing 0 participants at an association end.

ABL has a **create** statement that groups the creation of objects and links in an atomic operation. Here is an example use, which assumes a 1:1 association `hasAddress` between `Person` and `Address` :

```
create {
  Person p = new {firstname= "Gustav", lastname= "Gans"};
  Address a = new { street= "Mainstr. 54"
                  , postcode= "64400"
                  , town= "Mahlbruch"};
  p.hasAddress += a;
}
```

Create does *not* open a new scope so that p and a are accessible afterwards.

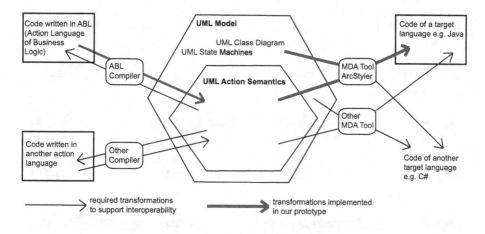

Fig. 2. Transformations for integration

6   Transformations

The integration of an action language in an MDA development environment using UML Action Semantics requires a number of transformations as illustrated in Figure 2:

1. from the action language to UML Action Semantics,
2. from UML Action Semantics back to the action language,
3. from UML Action Semantics into a target language.

We investigate each of these transformations with ABL as the action language and Java as target language. The last subsection evaluates a small example.

6.1   From ABL to UML Action Semantics

For the transformation into UML Action Semantics the parser framework ANTLR[3] serves as a foundation for creating the lexer, the parser, the type checker, and the transformation. The parser first builds an ABL-specific abstract syntax tree, performs namespace and type checking, and generates UML Action Semantics elements as specified by an attribute grammar [5]. To perform the namespace and type check, the compiler accesses the structural part of the model (Classifier, Attributes, Operation definitions, ...) through a JMI interface [3].

Practical Experiences. The transformation into UML Action Semantics is awkward because of the complexity and generality of UML Action Semantics. The required DataFlows and ControlFlows result in fairly complicated attributions in the attribute grammar.

---

[3] http://www.antlr.org

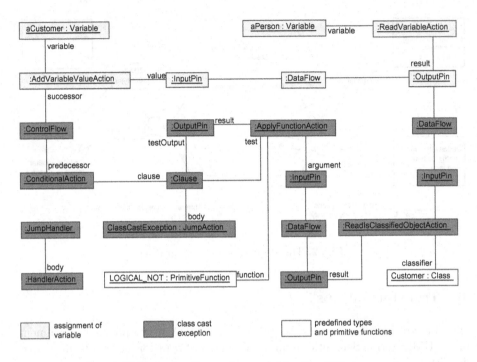

Fig. 3. UML Action Semantics model for the ABL type cast

In addition, UML Action Semantics can express some constructs of ABL only in a contorted way. As a simple example, the semantics of the model element CreateObjectAction does not include a call to a constructor. Hence, the "new" operator and the "create" statement require an explicit call of their constructor.

As a more severe example, UML Action Semantics does not have an action corresponding to a Java-style type cast operations which is also present in ABL. One candidate for representing a cast is UML Action Semantics's ReclassifyObjectAction. However, this action changes the type of the object, unlike a cast which only checks the type and throws an exception if the type does not fit the expectations. Expressing the cast operation in UML Action Semantics requires a structure of 14 elements: a JumpAction for the exception that is connected through a ConditionalAction with a ReadIsClassifiedObjectAction. Figure 3 illustrates this structure with the translation of

```
Customer aCustomer = (Customer) aPerson;
```

where `aPerson` has type `Person` which is a supertype of `Customer`.

Conclusion. The transformation from ABL to UML Action Semantics is possible. But as UML UML Action Semantics is very general and sometimes does not offer the adequate constructs, the transformation is not straightforward and leads to a large UML Action Semantics model.

6.2 From UML Action Semantics to Action Language

This transformation is important in two respects. First, as UML models are saved in their abstract syntax, there must be a transformation to recreate the action language syntax to facilitate further editing of the model. Clearly, editing the abstract syntax of UML Action Semantics is not appropriate.

Second, interchanging models between different tools with different action languages should not deprive the user from editing the model. Here the idea is to use UML Action Semantics as the common interchange format between action languages.

Unfortunately, none of the existing action languages can express all constructs of UML Action Semantics directly. Hence, it is not realistic to expect a tool to transform arbitrary UML Action Semantics models into its action language. As most existing action languages are less expressive than UML Action Semantics and differ from each other, it can be assumed that interoperation is currently not achievable. One possible solution would be to require each action language to be capable to represent every valid UML Action Semantics model. However, this requirement is counterproductive because action languages should be DSLs where full generality is often unnecessary.

In summary, UML Action Semantics is not suitable as an exchange format between different action languages. Hence, the transformation from UML Action Semantics in ABL or another action language is currently not helpful. However, it remains desirable to have an adequate concrete syntax for editing the models.

6.3 From UML Action Semantics to Java

In our prototype the transformation from UML Action Semantics to Java takes a UML model as input that contains UML Action Semantics elements. A transformation from a model into a target language requires a tool that is capable to perform model to text transformations. We use ArcStyler, a state of the art MDA tool, for performing the model to code transformation. It offers a facility to develop individual transformations from models with arbitrary MOF based metamodels into arbitrary target languages. ArcStyler's transformation engine takes a UML 1.5 model and generates the code for Class and Interface definitions as well as the whole body of Operations if they have a connected specification in UML Action Semantics.

First, we explore the feasibility of a general transformation from UML Action Semantics to Java. Then, we take a more pragmatic point and describe our implemented translation.

General Feasibility. While it is clearly feasible to implement an interpreter for UML Action Semantics that works on a generic object implementation (like an OCL interpreter; of course, a compiler might be done on similar grounds), it would be much harder to write a compiler that deals directly with native objects because there are actions in UML Action Semantics that do not have a direct Java counterpart.

For example, the CreateObjectAction can create objects with more than one Classifier; the DestroyObjectAction that destroys objects; the ReclassifyObjectAction can change the type of a given object at run time; a ConditionalAction, which has two or more Clauses and no clear ordering between them (with predecessor- / successorClause links) and the isDeterminate flag being false, executes an arbitrary Clause whose testAction results in true. Java can express none of these behaviors directly.

Pragmatic Approach. The source of many problems is that the transformation to Java is a many-to-one mapping because a Java expression, say, can cover the behavior of multiple elements of UML Action Semantics. Often, two or three elements in UML Action Semantics translate to one Java expression. The transformation engine has to navigate over Pins, DataFlow and ControlFlow elements to identify Java statements and expressions and to determine their execution order. Such a transformation is difficult to implement for an arbitrary UML Action Semantics model. Hence, our prototype transformation searches for patterns generated by the ABL compiler and translates them to Java.

For example, the transformation assumes that every ApplyFunctionAction for primitive functions like +, -, * or / has either one or two InputPins. The most complex pattern of UML Action Semantics elements that the transformation must recognize is the 14 element structure resulting from the translation of ABL's type cast operator.

To express primitive functions and jumps of an action language, the specific semantics of the UML Action Semantics elements PrimitiveFunction and JumpAction have to be defined by a UML Profile. However, UML 1.5 has no standard mechanism to import UML Profiles in model transformations. Our prototype transformation assumes the Profile of the ABL compiler, which introduces an unfortunate coupling between two tools which could be kept separate.

Finally, our transformation assumes that the model contains only a subset of all possible UML Action Semantics elements. For example, the transformation cannot transform a DeleteObjectAction or a ReclassifyObjectAction into Java.

Conclusion. The transformation that we implemented in ArcStyler performs a model to code transformation from UML Action Semantics to Java. Because UML Action Semantics has a number of constructs that cannot be expressed directly, the transformation is limited to specific patterns drawn from a subset of the UML Action Semantics. Furthermore, the model to code transformation needs to have implicit knowledge of the PrimitiveFunctions and the JumpAction types that the ABL compiler uses, to facilitate the transformation of PrimitiveFunctions and JumpActions into Java without using a UML Profile. Hence, the transformation is only applicable to UML Action Semantics structures generated by the ABL compiler. This choice is pragmatically viable, but it does not reach the goal of interoperability between different tools and action languages.

6.4   Evaluation of an Example

We implemented two of the three transformations described above in our prototype: the transformation from ABL to UML Action Semantics using ANTLR and the transformation from UML Action Semantics to Java using ArcStyler. We have tested our prototype with a small example that is delivered together with ArcStyler: the Shapes sample. It illustrates the basic modeling capabilities of ArcStyler and uses plain Java as its target language. We extend the UML model by implementing the given operations in ABL and by adding some further operations. Together with ArcStyler's capabilities to generate the infrastructure code we are able to generate the complete source code for the extended Shapes sample.

7   On the Choice of UML Action Semantics

The choice of using UML Action Semantics for our integration has a number of advantages but there are also severe limitations. The advantages are the existence of the standardized metamodel written in MOF, the (mostly) defined semantics, the tight connection with the UML model, and sufficient expressiveness for almost all action languages.

But the generality and the complex metamodel also lead to problems. First, there are neither publicly available tools that implement UML Action Semantics, nor tools that can generate UML Action Semantics models from a description in an action language. There is neither an execution engine nor a model compiler. But as UML Action Semantics is an OMG standard there is a chance that someday there are tools that implement this standard.

Second, an implementation of UML Action Semantics is difficult because it has a complex metamodel with about 60 metaclasses. UML Action Semantics is very general to offer the necessary constructs for all kinds of action languages and thus has a lot of metaclasses and features, for example for sending messages, flexible jumps, or concurrent execution.

Third, while most of the semantics UML Action Semantics is informally defined, any model using it still requires an additional Profile for JumpActions and primitive functions a. Hence, UML models with UML Action Semantics parts cannot be used in different tools because these tools cannot automatically import the required UML Profiles.

Fourth, UML Action Semantics lacks some actions to conveniently express the constructs of existing languages in a natural way. The most glaring example is the lack of a facility to express a type cast. This lack leads to bloated translations and to unreadable UML Action Semantics models.

Fifth, the flexibility of UML Action Semantics blows up the model and makes it difficult to formulate transformations. Because of its fine granularity and low level of abstraction, UML Action Semantics often needs many elements to represent one ABL construct, so that a general transformation from arbitrary UML Action Semantics to a given language can get very complicated. Furthermore, the low level of abstraction does not offer any benefit in our project because the transformation into Java has to reduce this granularity again.

8   Related Work

Other researchers also see problems with the suitability of UML Action Semantics for modeling the detailed behavior in a UML model. At the time of standardization of UML Action Semantics, Clark, Evans, Moore, Venkatesh and Weigert had severe doubts of the suitability of UML Action Semantics [12]. They raise points very similar to the problems identified in our work, for example the low level of abstraction, the problems for interchanging the models, and the effort required to implement UML Action Semantics. The research group OMEGA that defined the action language OMAL, evaluated different possibilities to integrate OMAL in UML. They dismissed UML Action Semantics right away on the grounds that "it is rather big and there is no tool support for it." [17].

In the following we give an overview on five representative action languages (out of about 15). None of the tools that support these action languages transform them into UML Action Semantics. They either store the action language code as a string in a ProcedureExpression or they use other non-standard ways for integration.

The Action Specification Language [4] developed by Kennedy Carter can be used in their tool iCCG. ASL procedures can return more than one value. This is compatible with UML where an Operation or a Method can have an arbitrary number of out Parameters (but only one return Parameter). ASL can model the identity of an object explicitly by identifying attributes.

Kabira Inc. developed Kabira AS[6] for ObjectSwitch Design Center. Its syntax is similar to C++. Furthermore, it is possible to call C++ functions from Kabira, or even include C++ code in-line.

Accelerated Technology, formerly Project Technology, developed the "Object Action Language" [1,7] (OAL) for their UML tool BridgePoint. OAL is dynamically typed and has an implicit casting between reals and integers. It does not allow an attribute to hold an object reference.

OMAL, the "OMEGA Action Language" is developed by OMEGA[4], an IST[5] research project for "Correct Development of Real-Time Embedded Systems". It is an imperative language and uses a subset of OCL as expression language [18]. OMAL offers the possibility to declare variables of the "event type" as global.

Muller, Studer, Jezequel, and Fondement et. al. developed the action language Xion [10] for their tool Netsilon, a tool for model-driven developing web applications. Xion serves for modeling the business logic and query expressions in the HTML-part and is based on OCL, but with a concrete syntax very similar to Java. The developers of Xion used it also at the meta-model level [9].

---

[4] IST-2001-33522, http://www-omega.imag.fr

[5] http://cordis.europa.eu/ist/

9   Conclusion

There are several possibilities for integrating an action language into UML and an MDA development environment. We investigate an integration using UML Action Semantics as an abstract syntax for the action language ABL. The transformation from ABL into UML Action Semantics is complex, but possible.

A main advantage is that UML Action Semantics is already defined in the UML metamodel and should thus be supported by standard-compliant tools. UML Action Semantics can also be fully integrated with the rest of the model (Classifiers, Attributes, AssociationEnds and Operations). However, there are a number of serious drawbacks (detailed in Section 7) with UML Action Semantics.

In summary, UML Action Semantics is only partly suitable for an integration of ABL and other action languages in UML. Interoperability at the expected and desired level is not possible. The effort to implement UML Action Semantics does not pay back as there is no extraordinary benefit from using UML Action Semantics.

It is an open research question how to integrate an action language in UML in a way that other tools can use it directly.

Acknowledgment. Interactive Objects provided an inspiring environment for this work.

References

1. Accelerated Technology: Object Action Language Manual. deliverd in the demo version of Nucleus BridgePoint 6.1 (2004),
   http://www.acceleratedtechnology.com
2. Interactive Objects Software GmbH Freiburg. ArcStyler Platform Guide for Version ArcStyler 5.5 (2006), http://www.interactive-objects.com/ data/ downloads/ArcStyler_DOC/doc/Platform_Guide.pdf
3. Java Community Process JSR-000040: Java Metadata Interface API Specification 1.0 Final Release (2002), http://java.sun.com/products/jmi/reference/api/
4. Kennedy Carter: UML ASL Reference Guide, ASL Language Level 2.5, Manual Revision D. (2003) Available at the OMG:
   http://www.omg.org/cgi-bin/apps/doc?ad/03-03-12.pdf
5. Knuth, D.: Semantics of context-free languages. Math. Syst. Theory (1968)
6. Kabira Technologies, Inc.: ObjectSwitch 3.2, Developer's Guide,
   http://www.kabira.com
7. Stephen, J., Mellor, M.J.: Balcer: Executable UML, A Foundation for the Model-Driven Architecture, 1st edn. Addison-Wesley, Reading (2002)
8. Mellor, S.J., Scott, K., Weise, A.U.u.D.: MDA Distilled - Principles of Model Driven Architecture. Addison-Wesley, Reading (2004)
9. Muller, P.-A., Studer, P., Jézéquel, J.-M.: Model-driven generative approach for concrete syntax composition. In: Proc. of OOPSLA Workshop on Best Practices for Model-Driven Development, Vancouvers (October 2004)
10. Muller, P.-A., Studer, P., Fondement, F., Bezivin, J.: Platform independent Web application modeling and development with Netsilon in Software and System Modeling 00, 1–19 (2005),
    http://www.irisa.fr/triskell/publis/2005/Muller05g.pdf

11. Object Management Group: Model Driven Architecture (MDA) (2001),
    http://www.omg.org/cgi-bin/apps/doc?ormsc/01-07-01.pdf
12. Object Management Group: Review of the Response to OMG RFP ad/98-11-01
    Action Semantics for the UML, Revised Submission (2001),
    http://www.omg.org/cgi-bin/apps/doc?ad/01-06-16.pdf
13. Object Management Group: XMLMetadata Interchange (XMI) Specification
    (2002), http://www.omg.org/cgi-bin/apps/doc?formal/02-01-01.pdf
14. Object Management Group: Unified Modeling Language Specification Version 1.5
    (2003), http://www.omg.org/cgi-bin/apps/doc?formal/03-03-01.pdf
15. Object Management Group: Object Constraint Language (OCL) Specification,
    Version 1.1 (2003), http://www.omg.org/cgi-bin/apps/doc?ptc/03-10-14.pdf
16. Object Management Group: Unified Modeling Language Specification, Superstruc-
    ture Version 2.0 (2005),
    http://www.omg.org/cgi-bin/apps/doc?formal/05-07-04.pdf
17. Ileana   Ober.   Action   specification   in   OMEGA,   Omega-Milestone
    IST/33522/WP2.2/M2.2.1, Revision 3-a4 (March 2004),
    http://www-omega.imag.fr/doc/d1000092_5/ASv03-a4-public.pdf
18. Marcel Kyas, Joost Jacob, Ileana Ober, Iulian Ober, Angelika Votintseva: OMEGA
    syntax for users. Omega Deliverable D2.2.3 Annex 1. January 2005 (2005),
    http://www-omega.imag.fr/doc/d1000346_2/
    WP22-D223-346-V2-D223-Annex-1-OMEGAsyntax.pdf

Software Product Lines, Service-Oriented Architecture and Frameworks: Worlds Apart or Ideal Partners?

Andreas Helferich, Georg Herzwurm, Stefan Jesse, and Martin Mikusz

Universität Stuttgart, Chair of Information Systems (Business Software),
Breitscheidstr. 2c, 70174 Stuttgart, Germany
{Helferich,Herzwurm,Jesse,Mikusz}@wi.uni-stuttgart.de

Abstract. Service-oriented Architectures and Software Product Lines are two concepts that currently get a lot of attention in research and practice. Both promise to make the development of flexible, cost-effective software systems and support high levels of reuse. But at the same time they are quite different from one another: while Software Product Lines focus on one producer alone developing a set of systems based on a common platform (often in the embedded systems-domain), most proponents of Service-oriented Architecture propose systems consisting of loosely coupled services or company-wide infrastructures including a variety of systems that are loosely coupled using services. In any case, the services are usually developed by various companies (e.g. SAP develops services for their platform itself, but explicitly allows other companies to develop and sell their services for the platform, too). Focus of this paper is the comparison of these concepts and the concept of component frameworks and show where they differ and analyze if they are mutually exclusive or (at least partially) complementary.

Keywords: Software Product Lines, Service-oriented Architecture, Enterprise Component Platforms, Business Component Frameworks.

1 Introduction

Service-oriented Architectures (SOA) and Software Product Lines are two concepts that currently get a lot of attention in research and practice: a large number of authors (e.g. [1], [2], [3]) claims that these concepts help in realizing the large-scale reuse that since the NATO-conference on Software Engineering in 1968 promises to make software development more efficient and at the same time improve the quality of the resulting software. Component Frameworks are another concept that has received quite some attention, and some of the research done on business components that could be traded on component market places and integrated into frameworks [4] is complementary to the other concepts, as will be shown.

The focus of this paper is the comparison of Software Product Lines, Component Frameworks and SOA. Specifically, to show where they differ and analyze if they are mutually exclusive or (at least partially) complementary. Therefore, we describe Software Product Lines in Section 2, Component Frameworks and Business Components in Section 3, SOA in Section 4 before comparing them using defined criteria in

D. Draheim and G. Weber (Eds.): TEAA 2006, LNCS 4473, pp. 187–201, 2007.

Section 5. Our conclusions in Section 6 answer the question if the concepts are mutually exclusive or mutually beneficial.

2 Software Product Lines

Over the last few years, Software Product Lines have developed into an approach to Software Engineering that is not only theoretically appealing, but actually in wide-scale use in practice [1]. Exploiting commonalities between different systems is at the heart of Software Product Line Engineering. Therefore, different products of one domain (also referred to as problem space or application range, e. g. operating systems for mobile telephones or software support of the sales department) are viewed as a family and not as single products. According to the Software Engineering Institute at Carnegie Mellon University, Software Product Lines are defined as "set of software-intensive systems sharing a common, managed set of features that satisfy the specific needs of a particular market segment or mission and that are developed from a common set of core assets in a prescribed way"(cf. [1], p. 5). The main elements of a Software Product Line are the product line architecture and the individual products which are part of the product line. The product line architecture describes the individual products, their common components and the differences between the products of the family (cf. [5]). These commonalities and differences are described using the core concept in Software Product Line Engineering: *variability*. Variability describes the variations in (functional as well as non-functional) features along the product line: features are either a commonality or a variation [6].

Different process models exist for the development process of product lines, e. g. those described in [8], [9] or [10]. Common to them is that the product line development process is modeled along the structure of a product line. Just as the product line consists of product line architecture and product line members, the development process also consists of the process of the development of the product line architecture and

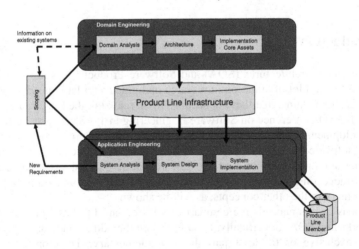

Fig. 1. The Product Line Engineering Process (modified from [7])

the development process of product line members. The development of the product line architecture is called domain engineering and the development of the product line members application engineering. Figure 1 shows the complete process.

2.1 Scoping

Scoping precedes Domain Engineering and Application Engineering. It is the process during which it is determined what to develop, i.e. which products will be part of the product line and what the commonalities and variabilities will be. At the same time – and maybe even more important – it is also determined what not to develop, i.e. the product line is bound on several levels building upon each other [11]:

- Product Portfolio Scoping – this aims at determining the range of products that shall be supported. This is mainly driven from market inputs and provides the basis for the actual domain scoping.
- Domain Scoping – this aims at identifying major functional areas (domains) that are relevant to the engineering of the product line and provides the basis for scoping the asset base or product line infrastructure.
- Asset Scoping – this aims at defining the precise functionality reusable components should support.

Currently, no single scoping approach addresses all three levels. One of the most comprehensive scoping approaches is the PuLSE-Eco approach [2].

2.2 Domain Engineering

Domain engineering consists of three steps: domain analysis, architectural design and domain implementation. During domain analysis, the analysis of the application scope of the product line that started with the scoping is continued and a requirements analysis is carried out for the complete product line. Common features among and differences between the products are defined and the so-called variation points are defined. Variation points are those system parts where the products differ from one another (see [9], pg. 20). A summary of variation points and their modeling and implementation is given in [12] (cf. pp. 13 and pp. 109).

Following domain analysis, the product line architecture is designed. The product line architecture provides the framework for reusable components. This framework describes visible properties of the components and the relations between them (cf. [5]). Reusable components are designed in the last step of domain engineering, during domain implementation. These components represent the base for the products of the product line. Together with test cases or scenarios, documentation and models they form the so-called *core assets* (cf. [13]).

2.3 Application Engineering

After Domain Engineering is finished, the members of the Software Product Line are developed in the second main part of Software Product Line Engineering called Application Engineering. During application engineering, the individual products are implemented according to the results of scoping and domain engineering. Three phases can be distinguished: system analysis, system design and system implementation.

During system analysis the requirements on the respective product gathered during domain analysis are further particularized, especially focusing on differences between variable requirements on the individual products. For every single product, those requirements are disregarded which this product does not have to fulfill. Then, the architecture of this product is derived from the product line architecture. The following steps are carried out: architecture pruning, architecture extension, conflict resolution, and architecture assessment (cf. [5], pp. 262). Next, product-specific components are implemented, using the possibilities of core asset varieties and all product specific components. Finally, the adapted core assets are tested and integrated into the designed product (cf. [9]).

3 Component Frameworks

3.1 Introduction

The term *framework* is defined in a number of ways; Mattsson [14] provides an extensive overview of existing definitions. Common to most of them is the understanding that a framework is basically a software-architecture that is meant to be reused. A framework usually consists of the design of the architecture as well as the implementation (with the source code available) of a number of functions. Johnsson and Foote for example define a framework as "… a set of classes that embodies an abstract design for solutions to a family of related problems, and supports reuse at a larger granularity than classes" ([15], p. 2). An important function of a framework is defining basic rules and services for the interplay of the components belonging to the systems that are built using this framework.

3.2 Classification and Framework Architecture

Frameworks can be classified by the reuse techniques used to extend them, which range from white box frameworks to black box frameworks to component frameworks. White box frameworks rely on inheritance and overwriting of methods in order to achieve extensibility. Therefore, it is necessary to have intimate knowledge of the structure and behavior of the framework [16], [17]. A black box framework provides classes, which can be directly initiated or parameterized since they already contain application logic [16]. Component frameworks are a special case of black box frameworks. Extensibility is here supported by defining interfaces for components that can be deployed independently and plugged into the framework via composition [17].

Turowski's BCArch (Business Component Architecture) provides a generic architecture of component based enterprise applications that consists of [18]:

- a component system framework providing application invariant generic services close to middleware (e.g. printing or saving),
- an component application framework providing services for the business software domain (e. g. mechanisms for domain specific conflict handling) and
- business components themselves providing specialized services in this domain.

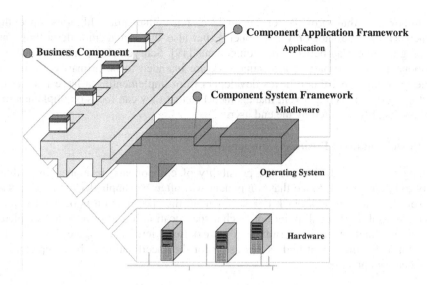

Fig. 2. BCArch (modified from [18])

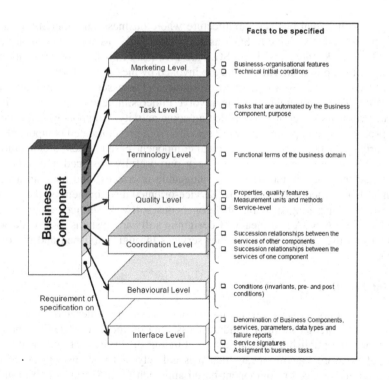

Fig. 3. Specification of Business Components (from [4])

Frameworks thus provide for higher-level reuse than class libraries since the framework provides not only components, but also the architecture describing and defining the interplay between the components [19]. Schryen [19] points out that the components that are part of the framework are intended to be primarily reused together, and adds that this relieves developers from implementing a large number of supporting functions (e.g. event management) so that they can focus on implementing the functionality required by the end user.

3.3 Specification of Business Components

Frameworks explicitly include the possibility of components developed by a third party to be integrated. Since that component will often be supplied without access to the source code, i.e. as a black box component, the specification is of great importance. As Keiblinger et al. point out, such a specification has to provide a "complete, unequivocal and precise description of its external view" [4]. Figure 3 shows the different levels they identified as necessary for the specification to be complete, unequivocal and precise

4 Service-Oriented Architecture (SOA)

"SOA is a conceptual business architecture where business functionality, or application logic, is made available to SOA users, or consumers, as shared, reusable services on an IT network. 'Services' in an SOA are modules of business or application functionality with exposed interfaces, and are invoked by messages." [20]

A SOA is essentially a collection of services. These services communicate with each other. The communication can involve either simple data passing or it could involve two or more services coordinating some activity. Component-based development proceeds by composing software systems from pre-fabricated components (often third-party black-box software). A typical component-based system architecture comprises a set of components that have been purposefully designed and structured to ensure that they fit together (i.e. have pluggable interfaces) and have an acceptable match with a defined system context. Service-oriented development on the other hand proceeds by integrating disparate heterogeneous software services from a range of providers [21]. A SOA is a means of designing software systems to provide services to either end user applications or other services through published and discoverable interfaces.

4.1 Introduction

A typical SOA comprises a service requestor, a service provider and a service broker (registry) that interact through standard messaging protocols (e.g. HTTP and SOAP) that support the publishing, discovery and binding of services. However, the diverse nature of software systems means that it is unlikely that systems will be developed using a purely service or component-based approach [22]. Rather, a hybrid model of software development where components and services co-exist in the same system is likely to emerge. One of the main goals in setting up a Service-oriented Architecture is the reuse of component-based software. But although one might, based on many articles and papers about Service-oriented Architecture, assume that by going towards a Service-oriented Architecture, reuse will automatically fall into place this is not the case. Organizational issues hold back a reuse ethic, as well as interoperability problems, poor internal communication, and lack of organizational standards [23].

4.2 Key Elements of a Service-Oriented Architecture

A Service-oriented Architecture comprises several key elements. Its elements work together to more closely link business needs with IT. The following list covers the essential ingredients of an SOA [20]:

- **Conceptual SOA vision** – An SOA is a business concept, which includes clearly defined business, IT and architectural goals.
- **Services** – An SOA enfolds all possible services in the organization alongside a service design model to assure reusability, interoperability and integration across all business processes and technology platforms. Services are indeed the central artifact of a Service-oriented Architecture.
- **Enabling technology** – The technology must ensure, that your services operate reliably and securely in support of the stated business objectives
- **SOA governance and technologies** – The SOA governance model defines the various governance processes, organizational roles, standards and policies adhered to in the conceptual architecture
- **SOA metrics** – The SOA metrics include Service-Level-Agreements (SLAs) for individual services, as well as usage metrics, business and return on investment metrics as well as process metrics
- **Organizational and behavioral model**

Generally, systems based on an SOA have many users and providers, where certain users also act as providers to other users. Most SOA- systems are considerably more complex than the one in Figure 4, which illustrates the most basic SOA architecture, but they all follow the same basic principles.

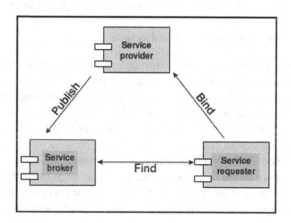

Fig. 4. Basic SOA architecture

4.3 Basic and Architectural Principles of a Service Oriented Architecture

There are several guiding principles that define the ground rules for development, maintenance, and usage of the SOA. The guiding principles cover [24]:

- Reuse, granularity, modularity, composability, componentization, and interoperability,
- Compliance to standards (both common and industry-specific),
- Services identification and categorization, provisioning and delivery, and monitoring and tracking.

The following specific architectural principles for design and service definition focus on specific themes that influence the intrinsic behavior of a system and the style of its design. They are derived from the guiding principles and cover [3]:

- **Service Encapsulation** - Accessing functionality through some well-defined interface, the application beeing seen as a black box to the user,
- **Service Loose coupling** - Services maintain a relationship that minimizes dependencies and only requires that they maintain an awareness of each other,
- **Service contract** - Services adhere to a communications agreement, as defined collectively by one or more service description documents,
- **Service abstraction** - Beyond what is described in the service contract, services hide logic from the outside world,
- **Service reusability** - Logic is divided into services with the intention of promoting reuse,
- **Service composability** - Collections of services can be coordinated and assembled to form composite services,
- **Service autonomy** – Services have control over the logic they encapsulate,
- **Service statelessness** – Services minimize retaining information specific to an activity,
- **Service discoverability** – Services are designed to be outwardly descriptive so that they can be found and assessed via available discovery mechanisms.

4.4 Outlook on Service-Oriented Architecture

SOA is the IT industry's latest attempt to promote the concept of component reusability in the development, integration, deployment and maintenance of enterprise applications. But up until today there is not even clear distinction between Service-oriented Architecture and Web Services established. Web services, in the form of SOAP-based inter-application connections, has been the headliner, while SOA — a body of application architecture and design concepts — has largely been viewed as a side effect of Web services. Since 2005, a critical mass of application architects and vendors are focusing more deeply on the foundational design value of SOA, bringing SOA to the forefront of the discussion and positioning SOAP as one (very important) way to access services, along with message-oriented middleware and other protocols [25].

The trend toward Service-oriented Architecture is growing. A Yankee Group survey of 473 enterprise decision-makers revealed that 75 percent of the participating enterprises planned to invest in Service-oriented Architecture technology in 2005. Gartner predicts that, by the end of 2009, Service-oriented Architecture will play a dominant role in new application projects. The increasing demand for SOA will have a structural impact on application outsourcing services, inducing companies to integrate SOA into their outsourcing strategies and make way for this new wave of development. [26]

5 Comparison of the Concepts

Having presented Software Product Lines, Component Frameworks, and Service-Oriented Architecture, we will now compare these concepts and investigate the commonalities and differences between the concepts, before discussing if and how they can be combined to mutually benefit each other. To facilitate the comparison, we use the following criteria:

- Goal: what exactly is the concept trying to achieve?
- Defining features: what are the characteristics of the concept that are at its heart?
- Technical methods and elements: which Software Engineering methods and elements are used to develop systems in this concept?
- Organizational methods and elements: how is software development organized according to this concept and which are the key steps in the development process?
- Field of application: in what kinds of software is this concept primarily applied?
- Reuse methods and entities: all three concepts have reuse in one way or another as their goal, but the methods and entities that are reused differ substantially.
- Abstraction level: which is the primary unit of analysis for the reuse? Not only methods and entities, even the abstraction level differs significantly.
- Examples: To illustrate the concepts, some examples for real-world application of each concept are presented here.

Table 1 provides an overview of the comparison using these criteria, whereas the in-depth comparison follows in remainder of this section.

Common primary **goal** of all three concepts is software reuse. But looking at the goals more carefully, one notices important differences: For Software Product Lines, exploiting the commonalities between related products is the actual goal. To achieve this, rather extensive analyzing and planning processes for the whole set of systems to be developed are performed. After that, the common architecture and the so-called core assets are developed in a generic way (domain engineering), before the systems belonging to the product line are developed (application engineering). Neither architecture nor core assets are to be reused outside the Software Product Line. The goal of frameworks is quite similar to that of Software Product Lines, but unlike in a Software Product Line, the systems which are to be developed using this products are not explicitly defined and planned. Instead, there is a comparably rough definition of the

Table 1. Comparison of the Concepts

Criteria	Software Product Lines	Component Frameworks	Service-oriented Architecture
Goal	Planned exploitation of commonalities within related systems	Provide a collection of functions that provide a basis for developing applications	Use of services of fine granularity within (enterprise) system landscapes
Defining features	Variability; Family of related systems based on common architecture	Components with an underlying architecture common to them	No common architecture, services are encapsulated and loosely coupled
Technical methods and elements	Variation points and mechanisms, scoping, application engineering, domain engineering	System frameworks, application frameworks, system components, business components	Reliance on generally accepted standards, additional service registration and authentication services
Organizational methods and elements	Two life cycle-model: first domain engineering to develop the assets to be reused, then application engineering to derive the actual systems	Development for reuse (for component); development with reuse (from component)	Development as well as hosting of the services can be distributed, only the light-weight interface and some additional services (registry, authentication,...) are provided
Reuse methods and entities	Reuse of all kinds of assets (components, test cases, analysis & design models), but only within the product line	Depends on the kind of the framework: white box-reuse, black-box reuse; but only within the domain	Services (simple ones or those composed of several services) are physically reused
Abstraction level	System within a family	Common architecture and components	Services
Field of application	Primarily Embedded Systems	Primarily Information Systems	Primarily Information Systems
Examples	Nokia cell phones, Cummins diesel engines	System framework: CORBA ;Application framework: IBM San Francisco	Harvard Medical School and its hospital affiliates

systems that could be developed using the framework. Following this definition, the common functions (or services) needed to develop the actual systems are developed. After this, the framework can be used/sold as a basis for other companies to develop the actual applications (e.g. a system framework acting as middleware), whereas for a Software Product Line, the same company would develop the systems that are part of the product line (possibly using components provided by a third party). The idea behind Service-oriented Architecture is quite the opposite compared to Software Product Lines: rather small services are developed (potentially totally independent from each other), published in a registry (e.g. using the Standards WSDL and UDDI) and can then be used by anyone within a company or even world-wide (the so-called service consumer). As Dietzsch [16] points out, this kind of reuse is physical rather than logical: the same entity provides the service, not a copy of the entity (a reused component is a copy of the original component used in another piece of software, the service is reused by sending a request to the very same service over the network/Internet). It is also important to point out that such a service does not have to be part of a system, but can just as well stand alone or be a connector between two independent systems.

Another difference is the fact that whereas Software Product Lines are mainly focused on Intra-Business Reuse, meaning that enterprises focus on internal reuse of components in another product, the focus of Service Oriented Architecture is the reuse of component-based software on a larger scale. The creation of SOA-compliant component-based software (e.g. Modules or Components in Enterprise Resource Planning Software like SAP) seems to become a popular business model for companies, e.g. sub-suppliers to SAP's ERP-system, that mainly focus on the creation of reusable component-based software but also for bigger companies, enabling them to sell inhouse developed SOA compliant component-based software. Problem is that although big companies have the ability and manpower to create and distribute component-based software they are afraid to do so since they don't want to distribute their business logic inherent in the component-based software to other companies working in the same business sector.

The **defining features** of the concept of Software Product Lines is variability (and vice versa commonality) as defined by the common and application-specific parts of the systems that are part of the Software Product Line, this includes defining a common architecture. Having a common architecture is the defining feature of a framework: here, this architecture is at the heart of the concept: to provide a framework for the development of certain systems. This shows the basic difference between a framework and a class library: the framework is intended to be reused as a whole, whereas a class library often contains a large number of more or less unrelated classes. This common architecture is lacking SOA, one could even say that the lack of a common architecture (since the service could be used by anyone as part of his/her system with its specific architecture) is one of the defining features together with the services being encapsulated and loosely coupled.

The **technical methods and elements** that are typical for the concepts are another criterion we used: for Software Product Lines, variation points and variation mechanisms and the distinction between scoping, domain engineering and application engineering are the defining technical methods and elements. While variation points and variation mechanisms provide the opportunity to efficiently handle the differences between the members of a product line, scoping, domain engineering and application engineering are distinct phases in the development process where special methods for Software Product Line Engineering are used (see for example [1] for details). The different kinds of frameworks and components, i.e. system vs. application frameworks, system vs. business components and the methods and elements used in component-based system-development in general are the typical technical methods and elements of frameworks. Since SOA is a concept that is rather independent of the development platform/language to be used, the reliance on the architectural principles mentioned in Section 4 need to mentioned here. Additionally, standards such as UDDI and WSDL are important and absolutely necessary elements of SOA.

Organizational methods and elements: Unlike the technical methods and elements, the organizational methods and elements define the way software development is organized. For Software Product Lines, the key question here is how domain engineering and application engineering are organized: basically, they are separate development cycles with application engineering depending on the results of domain engineering. This could for example lead to separate teams could be responsible for domain and application engineering. Another possibility would also include a separate team for domain engineering, but a member of this team being part of each application engineering teams. For an in-depth discussion of possible ways to organize Software Product Line Engineering see [27], but basically all possibilities have their own advantages and disadvantages and their suitability depends on the organization of the company as a whole. Frameworks are quite similar to Software Product Lines, some authors (e.g [28]) even use the same terminology. One important difference is that the company developing the framework is quite often not the company developing the applications, which is usually not the case for Software Product Lines. For Service-oriented Architectures, it is more difficult to make any statements concerning the organization since every service could be developed independently of all other services. But this implies a decentralized organization with no centralized coordinating unit, since there is no common architecture behind. For a company reorganizing their own infrastructure in a Service-oriented Architecture-based way, there probably will be such a centralized unit, but they might very well use services that have been provided by third parties that were not coordinated by this unit. The reliance on additional services such as a service registry and services for identification or authentication implies separate centralized organizational units providing these services to all other services.

The **reuse methods and entities** differ quite substantially: in a Software Product Line, all kinds of assets are reused, not only code, but also specifications, models (e.g. in UML), test cases and (end user) documentation, but only within the Software Product Line. In Service-oriented Architecture, the services are the main reuse entity, and interestingly, the services are physically and not only logically reused.

Thereby, logical reuse is present, if a component is replicated and delivered by the manufacturer to the application developer. By physical reuse however, the service is invoked by remote call on demand. In this case the service, e.g. a single-sign-on Web Service, is hosted by the manufacturer of the software.

This is not the case for frameworks, where architecture and components are reused within the domain for which the framework was developed, but the reuse is logical, not physical. Additionally, the reuse can be either white box or black box (via composition in the case of component frameworks regarded here) [16], which is not the case for SOA.

Taking organizational methods and elements on the one hand and the reuse methods and elements on the other hand, one gets the matrix shown in Table 2.

Table 2. Organizational Level of Reuse

Phase within the two-lifecycle model	Software Product Lines	Service-oriented Architecture	Component Frameworks
Development for reuse	within organization	within organization / outside the organization	within organization
Development with reuse	within organization	outside the organization	within organization / outside the organization

Closely related to the reuse entity is the **abstraction level:** all considerations for a Software Product Line are based on the product line as a unit of analysis, all decisions on another level (product, component or even function) are derived from the utility on the product line level. For a component framework, the common architecture and the components are the main units of analysis and as the levels of specification presented in Section 3 imply, these components should not be too small, otherwise the effort of specifying the component might be bigger than the benefit from reusing it. As the name Service-oriented Architecture already implies, single services are the main unit of analysis in this concept, since a service can theoretically stand alone.

The **fields of application**, i.e. the kinds of software where the concepts are most commonly use are embedded systems for Software Product Lines and (enterprise) information systems for Service-oriented Architecture and frameworks. Therefore, it is not surprising that the **examples** for the application of the concepts are taken from these domains: Cummins diesel engines and Nokia cell phones are just two examples taken from the Software Product Line Hall of Fame [29]. CORBA and IBM's San Francisco framework are two examples for frameworks (e.g. [16]). An SOA example for consolidating services is Harvard Medical School and its hospital affiliates, who radically streamlined their business processes around the sharing of medical data by building a SOA involving about 25 categories of Web services shared between 400 different departments with 14,000 employees. Seattle's 17-hospital Providence Health System is leveraging Web services to link its in-house legacy systems into a single patient portal, permitting online bill paying among other services[30].

6 Conclusion

The three concepts discussed in this paper, Software Product Lines, component frameworks and Service-oriented Architecture are in no way mutually exclusive, but share a number of characteristics. And where they differ, they sometimes actually complement each other, for example: while Software Product Lines do not focus on components being marketable or developed in different organizations, this is not explicitly excluded. And Knowledge gained in research on Business Component Specification (e.g. in [31], [4], [32] and [33]) can be beneficial for specifying the components used in a Software Product Line, since the company developing the Software Product Line may decide not to develop all components itself. This knowledge can also be used in combination with research on description of services in a

Service-oriented Architecture, while some of the research on authentication of web services could be used for frameworks, where components developed by third parties may (or may not) comply with their specifications.

These are just starting points for research into combining these concepts, but we think this research could be very beneficial for Enterprise Component Platforms, since such a platform shares characteristics (and therefore problems) with all three concepts.

References

1. Clements, P., Northrop, L.: Software product lines: practices and patterns. Addison-Wesley, Boston, MA, London (2002)
2. Schmid, K.: Planning Software Reuse - A Disciplined Scoping Approach for Software Product Lines. Fraunhofer IRB, Stuttgart (2003)
3. Erl, T.: Service-oriented Architecture: Concepts, Technology, and Design. Prentice Hall PTR, Upper Saddle River, New Jersey, Munich (2005)
4. Keiblinger, A., Turowski, K., Zaha, J.M.: Component Market Specification Demand and Standardized Specification of Business Components. In: 1st Int Workshop "Component Based Business Information Systems Engineering", Geneva, Switzerland (2003)
5. Bosch, J.: Design and use of software architectures. Addison-Wesley, Harlow (2000)
6. Kang, K., Cohen, S., Hess, J., Novak, W., Peterson, S.: Feature-Oriented Domain Analysis (FODA) Feasibility Study. Software Engineering Institute CMU/SEI-90-TR-21 (1990)
7. Muthig, D.: Produktlinien - Einstieg. Website of the Kompetenzzentrums Software Engineering checked (June 15, 2006) http://www.software-kompetenz.de/?2246
8. Bayer, J., et al.: PuLSE: A Methodology to Develop Software Product Lines. In: Proceedings of the 5th Symposium on Software Reusability, pp. 122–131 (1999)
9. Weiss, D.M., Lai, C.T.R.: Software product-line engineering: a family-based software development process. Addison-Wesley, Reading, MA, Bonn (1999)
10. Muthig, D.: A light-weight approach facilitating an evolutionary transition towards software product lines. PhD Thesis, Fraunhofer-IRB Verlag, Stuttgart (2002)
11. Schmid, K.: Scoping Software Product Lines - An Analysis of an Emerging Technology. Software Product Lines: Experience and Research Directions. In: Proceedings of the First Software Product Line Conference (SPLC1), pp. 513–532. Kluwer Academic Publishers, Dordrecht (2000)
12. Böckle, G., Knauber, P., Pohl, K., Schmid, K. (eds.): Software-Produktlinien: Methoden, Einführung und Praxis. Dpunkt, Heidelberg (2004)
13. McGregor, J.D.: Testing a Software Product Line, Technical Report, CMU/SEI-2001-TR-022, Software Engineering Institute, Carnegie Mellon University (2001)
14. Mattsson, M.: Object-Oriented Frameworks: A Survey of Methodological Issues. Research Paper LU-CS-TR:96-167. Lund University, Department of Computer Sc. (1996)
15. Johnson, R.E., Foote, B.: Designing reusable Classes. Journal of Object-Oriented Programming 1(2), 22–35 (1988)
16. Dietzsch, A.: Systematische Wiederverwendung in der Software-Entwicklung. PhD thesis, Deutscher Universitäts-Verlag, Wiesbaden (2002)
17. Fayad, M., Schmidt, D.C., Johnson, R.E.: Building application frameworks: object-oriented foundations of framework design. Wiley, New York (1999)
18. Turowski, K.: Fachkomponenten: komponentenbasierte betriebliche Anwendungssyteme. Magdeburg (2001)

19. Schryen, G.: Komponentenorientierte Softwareentwicklung in Softwareunternehmen. PhD Thesis, Deutscher Universitäts-Verlag, Wiesbaden (2001)
20. Marks, A., Bell, M.: Service-Oriented Architecture: A Planning and Implementation Guide for Business and Technology. John Wiley & Sons, New Jersey (2006)
21. Cerami, E.: Web Services Essentials - Distributed Applications with XML-RPC, SOAP, UDDI & WSDL. O'Reilly, Beijing (2002)
22. Kotonya, G., Rashid, A.: A Development Strategy for Minimising Risks in Component-Based Development. In: 27th Euromicro Conference: Workshop on Component-Based Software Engineering, Warsaw, Poland, pp. 12–21. IEEE Computer Society Press, Los Alamitos (2001)
23. Broy, M., Denert, E.: Software Pioneers. Contributions to Software Engineering. Springer, New York (2002)
24. Balzer, Y.: Improve your SOA project plans. IBM (2004), http://www-128.ibm.com/developerworks/webservices/library/ws-improvesoa/
25. Heffner, R.: Trends 2005: Service-Oriented Architecture And Web Services. Forester Research (2004)
26. Bissonnette, J.-F.: Service-Oriented Architecture: Changing the Landscape of Application Outsourcing, http://www2.cio.com/consultant/report3358.html
27. Pohl, K., Böckle, G., van der Linden, F.: Software Product Line Engineering. Springer, Heidelberg (2005)
28. Schmietendorf, A., Dimitrov, E., Dumke, R.: Enterprise JavaBeans - Komponentenbasierte Software-Entwicklung. Mitp, Bonn (2002)
29. Software Engineering Instute at Carnegie Mellon University: Product Line Hall of Fame last checked (July 11, 2006) http://www.sei.cmu.edu/productlines/plp_hof.html
30. Halamaka, J.: SOA Executive Forum in New York. New York (2005)
31. Ackermann, J.: Zur Spezifikation der Parameter von Fachkomponenten. In: 5th Workshops Komponentenorientierte betriebliche Anwendungssysteme, Augsburg, pp. 47–154 (2003)
32. Fettke, P., Loos, P.: Specification of Business Objects. In: Mezini, M., Aksit, M., Unland, R. (eds.) Proc. NetObjectDays 2002, Erfurt, Germany, pp. 62–75 (2003)
33. Hildenbrand, T., Korthaus, A.: A Model-Driven Approach to Business Software Engineering. In: 8th World Multi-Conference on Systemics, Cybernetics and Informatics, pp. 74–79 (2004)

Modeling the Effect of Application Server Settings on the Performance of J2EE Web Applications

Gábor Imre, Tihamér Levendovszky, and Hassan Charaf

Budapest University of Technology and Economics
{gabor,tihamer,hassan}@aut.bme.hu

Abstract. The performance of a web application is affected by several factors. In this paper, the effects of two configurable software settings of J2EE application servers are discussed: the maximum size of the thread pool and the maximum size of the connection queue. Previous work has shown that both tuning parameters have a considerable impact on the performance metrics, and both of them should be taken into account when constructing a performance model of a web application. This paper presents a queueing network-based performance model that is able to capture the effect of the connection queue limit. New performance measurements which can help improving this model are also presented.

Keywords: performance modeling, queueing networks, web applications, thread pool, connection queue.

1 Introduction

At the early stage of the Internet, the Web was mainly used to display static content. As the Web became more and more widespread, several companies realized that web applications that are able to provide dynamic content can offer a strong support for their activities. Managing business processes, the improper performance of a web application can cause serious financial loss to a company. The performance-related requirements of an Internet application are often recorded in a Service Level Agreement (SLA). SLAs can specify an upper limit for the average response time, a lower limit for availability, while the application guarantees a certain throughput level.

To meet the performance requirements of Service Level Agreements, the performance metrics of a system under given conditions can be obtained in two ways. The first method is load testing: the performance of the system is measured for all feasible client load, for all possible values of system parameters. The other method is to establish an analytical performance model of the system. This model can be solved using different techniques and an estimation of the relevant performance metrics can be provided this way. The main advantage of this latter option over load testing is that the definition, parametrization, and evaluation of a performance model has relatively low cost. In contrast to the several hours

D. Draheim and G. Weber (Eds.): TEAA 2006, LNCS 4473, pp. 202–216, 2007.
© Springer-Verlag Berlin Heidelberg 2007

or even days of an exhaustive load testing, a performance model can provide the necessary results for all values of the parameters and client load in some seconds.

The performance metrics depend on several factors, such as hardware, software, network, and client workload. This paper focuses on the settings of the application server software that serves the HTTP requests of the browsers. More precisely, the performance of a test web application is measured under different client load with different values of two parameters of the application server. These tuning parameters are the maximum size of the thread pool, and the maximum size of the HTTP connection queue. To understand the meaning of these parameters, consider Fig. 1.

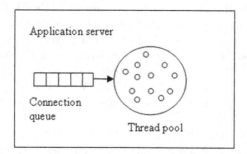

Fig. 1. The connection queue and the thread pool

In a J2EE application server, the accepted HTTP connections are placed into a connection queue. The size of the connection queue is limited by an adjustable parameter of the given application server. When this limit is reached, it is denied to serve the request. The threads in the thread pool take connections from the queue and serve the requests. The server can decide to create more threads (i.e. increase the size of the thread pool), but cannot exceed a certain configurable maximum. When the maximum thread pool size is reached, however, the requests are not dropped, as long as they find free space in the connection queue. The policy for adding new threads is typically based on the state of the connection queue.

The limit for the size of the thread pool is necessary for controlling the memory usage of the applications. When the memory requirements of serving a request is known, the maximum memory usage of a web application can be set to fit in the physical memory in order to prevent thrashing because of the size limit of the thread pool. It is important to mention that not all the application servers allow manipulating both of the settings. With IBM WebSphere [1] for example only the thread pool size is configurable. With JBoss [2] or Sun Java System Application Server [3] both parameters can be set.

The rest of this paper is organized as follows. Section 2 reviews the related work. Section 3 contains the process of the performance measurement, Sect. 4 provides a review on the proposed performance model and discusses the errors of the model. Finally, conclusions are drawn.

2   Related Work

Several papers and research projects are engaged in studying how the various configurable parameters affect the performance of web applications. Two approaches for evaluating the impact of these parameters are presented in [4] and in [5]. They use statistical methods, hypothesis testing in order to retrieve the software parameters that influence the performance. [5] investigates the average response time only, while [4] also takes the throughput and the probability of rejecting a request into consideration.

Some industry-standard benchmarks address standardizing the evaluation of application servers. In the field of Java 2 Enterprise Edition, SPECjAppServer [6] (formerly ECPerf)is the most popular benchmark. TPC-W [7] is a benchmark that is not tied to any particular implementation technology. Both benchmarks specify they own test application, and contain a driver that generates the client load and measures the performance. Furthermore, SPECjAppServer includes the implementation of the benchmark application as well. The main difference between the benchmark applications of TPC-W and SPECjAppServer is that the former one uses the database tier heavier, while the latter one stresses the EJB container.

Performance measurements can serve as the basis for performance modeling and prediction. In the past few years several techniques and methods have been proposed to address this goal. A group of them are based on queueing networks [8], or extended or layered versions of queueing networks. These methods establish a queueing network model of the system. By solving this model with analytical methods or simulation, the prediction of performance metrics is possible. Some of the proposed methods generate a queueing network model of the system based on its UML model [9] [10]. In [11], a queueing model for multi-tier internet applications is presented, where queues represent different tiers of the application. The model faithfully captures several aspects of web applications, like caching and concurrency limits at the tiers. The maximum size of the connection queue, as presented earlier, can be considered a concurrency limit of the web tier in this model, but it cannot handle the maximum size of the thread pool.

Another group of performance modeling techniques uses Petri nets or generalized stochastic Petri nets, such as [12]. Petri nets can represent blocking and synchronization aspects much more than queueing networks, which are more suitable for modeling resource contention and scheduling strategies. A powerful combination of the queueing network and the Petri net formalism is presented in [13]. Using queueing Petri nets, the authors successfully model the performance of a web application, considering the maximum size of thread pools. Their model, however, does not take the maximum size of the connection queue into account.

[14] and [15] are the first papers to best of our knowledge, where the authors show that the limits configured both for the connection queue and the thread pool have a considerable effect on the performance. The results computed by the performance model proposed in [14] and [15] do not fit accurately to the

measured data in some cases. The measurements presented in this paper aim to
help finding the possible causes of this inaccuracy.

3   The Performance Measurement

The test web application is intentionally designed to be very simple, such that
no factors other than the settings of the application server can influence the
performance. It can serve one type of HTTP requests, and is implemented with
a Java servlet. On processing a request, it loads the processor, and periodically
inserts *sleep()* calls. This emulates typical web applications, which use the processor of the machine that hosts the web container and calls services on other
machines (e.g. a database server) in a synchronous way, which blocks the caller
thread. The number of computations and the total sleep time can be defined
as parameters of the request. After processing a request, the web application
generates a small HTML file (of approximately 10 kilobytes) as a response.

The application server (Sun Java System Application Server Enterprise Edition 8.1) runs on a PC with Windows XP, and a 3 GHz Pentium 4 Hyper-
Threading processor and 1 GB memory. The emulation of the browsing clients
is performed by an open source load tester, JMeter, which runs on another PC,
with similar hardware. The two machines are connected via a 100 Mbit/s LAN.

Each test takes 30 minutes, during which the virtual clients send their requests
to the server. Each virtual client inserts an exponentially distributed thinking
time between its requests with mean 4 seconds. The virtual clients are started
gradually, in a 40 seconds interval. The system reaches a steady state after 2
minutes in terms of average response time and throughput. Between two test
runs, the application server is restarted because the new settings have to be
reloaded. The values of the two investigated tuning parameters and the numbers
of the emulated clients during the individual measurements are summarized in
Table 3. We intentionally do not cover here connection queue values that are
greater than the number of clients (i.e. no dropping of requests), since for those
cases, our performance model in [14] and [15] proved to be accurate.

During each measurement, the following metrics were registered:

- The average response time of the requests, measured at the clients. This
  includes the network time of sending the request and receiving the response,
  but this time it is negligible, since these files are small, moreover, the client
  and the server are on the same local network. This is verified by comparing

Table 1. Number of clients and values of the tuning parameters during the measurements

Maximum size of the connection queue	Maximum size of the thread pool	Number of emulated clients
50	5,10,20,30,40,44,48,50,60,70,100	10, 20,..., 100
80	40,70,90,200	10, 20,...,140

the client side response time to the response time measured at the server side. The two values differ less than 5 percent, thus, the time of the server side processing dominates the client side response time in our experiments.

- The throughput of the system, which is the number of served requests in a second.
- The rate of requests that are dropped by the server.
- The processor and memory usage of the server and the machine running the clients. We found that the memory usage does not reach the 80% of the available physical memory on either of the machines. The processor usage on the client machine never reaches 60 percent, therefore, it cannot be a bottleneck in our measurements.

The results of the measurement are analyzed in a qualitative manner in [14]. Hence, we only apply a quantitative analysis in the following section.

4   The Performance Model

In this section, we briefly review a queueing model of the performance as proposed in [14] and [15] and validate it against the results of the measurements. To specify a queueing system, it is necessary to identify the following parameters. The distribution of the interarrival time (the think time introduced by the virtual clients) is exponential with mean 4 seconds (Z). The exact distribution of the service time is unknown, but to keep our model simple, we will assume an exponential distribution with mean 0.14 seconds (S) based on measurements using one virtual client. The service rate μ is defined as $1/S$. The number of servers is one, the population size (K) is equal to the number of virtual clients. The system capacity (B), i.e. the maximum number of requests in the system is equal to the maximum size of the connection queue, because a request in the connection queue remains there until the request is served.

Using these parameters, our queueing system can be described using Kendall notation: $M/M/1/B/K$, where M stands for memoryless, a well-known property of the exponential distribution. The first M means that the distribution of the interarrival times is exponential, the second M means that the service demand of one request is also exponentially distributed. The '1' means that the system has one server, B means the capacity limit of the server, and K is the population size.

4.1   Solving the Model

The solution of the $M/M/1/B/K$ queueing system is based on *birth-death processes* which are special Markov chains in which the transitions are restricted to the neighboring states only. Figure 2 shows the state transition diagram of a general (i.e. not specific to the $M/M/1/B/K$ system) birth-death process with a finite number of states.

It can be used to model a queueing system with the state S_i meaning that there are i requests at the server. The new requests arrive with rate λ_i and

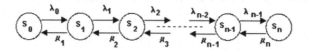

Fig. 2. A general birth-death process with finite number of states

they are served with rate μ. It can be shown (see [16]) that for the steady-state probability that there are k requests at the server (p_k), the equation

$$p_k = \frac{\lambda_0\lambda_1\ldots\lambda_{k-1}}{\mu_1\mu_2\ldots\mu_k}p_0, \ k = 1, 2, \ldots, n \tag{1}$$

holds. Because the system must be in one of the states, $\sum_{k=0}^{n} p_k = 1$, which gives

$$p_0 = \frac{1}{1 + \sum_{k=1}^{n} \prod_{j=0}^{k-1} [\lambda_j/\mu_{j+1}]}. \tag{2}$$

In the case of the $M/M/1/B/K$ queueing system, the number of possible states is $min(B, K)$, because the server cannot have more requests than its capacity limit, or the number of clients. The service rate is independent from the state, therefore

$$\mu_k = \mu = 1/S, \ k = 1, \ldots, min(B, K) \ . \tag{3}$$

The arrival rate on the other hand is state dependent, hence if k number of requests are at the server, only $K - k$ clients can send new requests, with a rate of $1/Z$, therefore

$$\lambda_k = \frac{K - k}{Z}, \ k = 0, \ldots, min(B, K) - 1 \ . \tag{4}$$

Combining 1 and 2 with 3 and 4 suggests the solution of the $M/M/1/B/K$ queueing system:

$$p_k = p_0 \frac{K!}{(K - k)!(\mu Z)^k}, \ k = 1, \ldots, min(B, K) \tag{5}$$

$$p_0 = \left[\sum_{k=0}^{min(B,K)} \frac{K!}{(K - k)!(\mu Z)^k} \right]^{-1}. \tag{6}$$

Based on these results, all other performance metrics are easy to compute, using some basic results of queueing theory. The requests are dropped, when the system reached its capacity B, hence, the error rate $e = p_B$. The throughput of the system (X) can be calculated based on the Utilization Law which states $X = U/S$, where U is the utilization of the server i.e. the probability that the server is busy, so $U = 1 - p_0$. And finally, we obtain the average response time from Little's Law $(R = N/X)$, where N is the average number of request in the system, that is:

$$N = \sum_{k=0}^{B} k * p_k \ .$$ (7)

The performance metrics obtained from this model are compared to the measured values in Fig. 3, Fig. 4, Fig. 5, Fig. 6, Fig. 7, and Fig. 8. Because of the great number of cases, we only depict 4 cases in order to keep the diagrams clear: 50 connection queue with 40 and 60 threads, and 80 connection queue with 70 and 90 threads. With these values we can observe thread limit values both greater and less than the maximum size of the connection queue.

The throughput values obtained from the model are the same for the two cases and fit quite well to the measured values, irrespectively of the number of the allowed threads. (See Fig. 3 and Fig. 4.) This is due to the fact that the maximum throughput is determined by the saturation of the server's processor: $1/S = 1/0.14 = 7.1$.

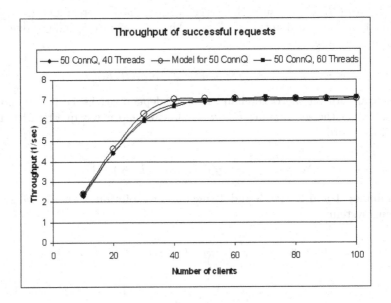

Fig. 3. Comparing the model with the measured data - throughput with 50 ConnQ

Regarding Fig. 5 and Fig. 6, one can see that the rate of unsuccessful requests depends on the number of the maximum thread number. With thread numbers higher than the size of the connection queue, the error rate is higher. The results provided by the performance model are closer to the measurements with lower thread number.

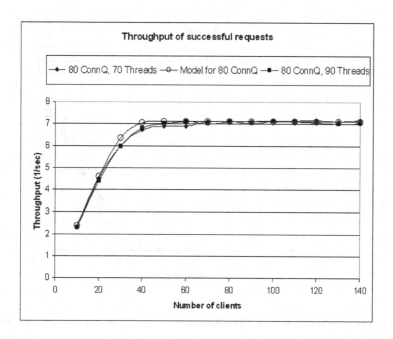

Fig. 4. Comparing the model with the measured data - throughput with 80 ConnQ

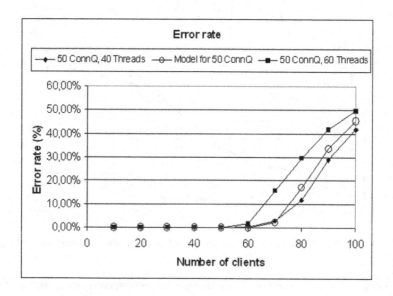

Fig. 5. Comparing the model with the measured data - error rate with 50 ConnQ

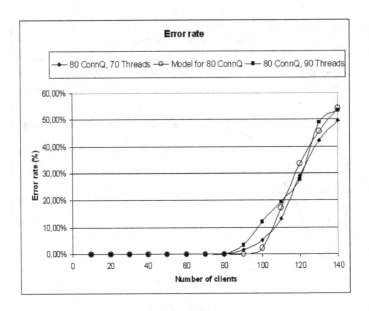

Fig. 6. Comparing the model with the measured data - error rate with 80 ConnQ

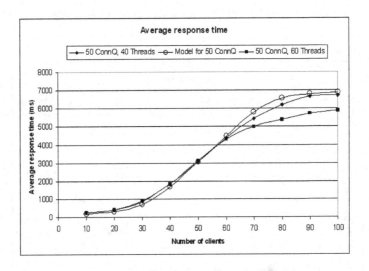

Fig. 7. Comparing the model with the measured data - response time with 50 ConnQ

The dependency on the thread numbers can be observed, with respect to the response times as well. Figure 7 and Fig. 8 show that with thread numbers lower than the maximum size of the connection queue, the measured response time is higher and is quite close to the values obtained from the model.

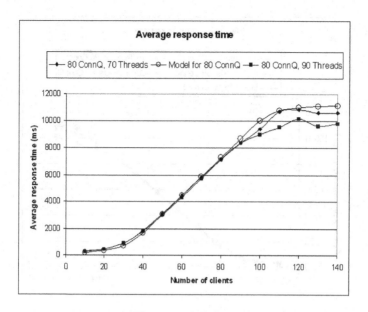

Fig. 8. Comparing the model with the measured data - response time with 80 ConnQ

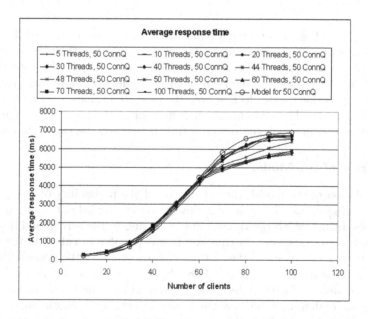

Fig. 9. Comparing all the response times with 50 ConnQ

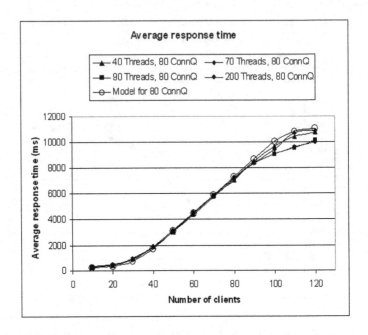

Fig. 10. Comparing all the response times with 80 ConnQ

Figure 9 and Fig. 10 discover a remarkable phenomenon: most of the configurations in which the maximum number of threads is less than the connection queue provide about the same response times which is quite close to the values predicted by the model. While the configurations with more threads allowed than the connection queue, decline from the predicted values to a significant and yet similar extent. There is only a small number of the possible configurations (e.g. 48 threads) in which the response time is between the two main curves.

4.2 Error of the Model

In the solution of the model, the calculation of the probability of k requests at the server (p_k) plays a key role. For this reason we carried out additional measurements during which the timestamps belonging to the arrival and departure of requests were registered. In this way it was possible to calculate the rate of time of having k requests at the server, as an estimate for the probabilities. We compared these results for the 100 Threads, 50 ConnQ and for the 30 Threads, 50 ConnQ configurations against the p_k probabilities predicted by the model, to obtain more details about how our model deflects from the measured results. With 10 clients, as Fig. 11 depicts, the probabilities are almost the same for 100 and 30 threads, and they do not differ significantly from the model values. This meets our expectations, since the response times are the same in these three cases. Similar results can be observed for 20 and 30 clients.

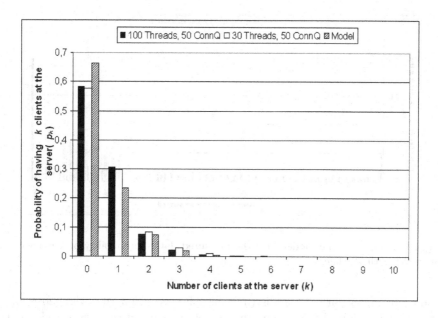

Fig. 11. Comparing the model with the measured data - probability of k requests at the server with 10 clients

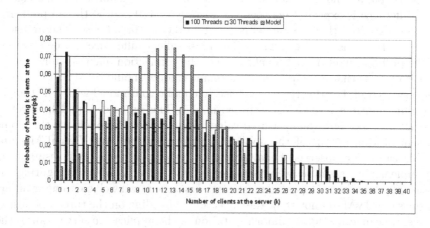

Fig. 12. Comparing the model with the measured data - probability of k requests at the server with 40 clients

The first remarkable error of the model appears at 40 clients, depicted in Fig. 12. This may be surprising, since the average response time predicted by the model matches quite well at this client number. However the distribution of the number of clients at the server is completely different in the reality and in the model. The measured values are more close to a uniform distribution, while the

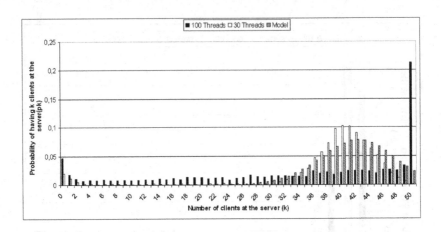

Fig. 13. Comparing the model with the measured data - probability of k requests at the server with 70 clients

model predicts a normal-like distribution. The match for the average response time can be explained that the mean number of clients at the server is about the same for all three cases (11.83, 11.3, 11.82, respectively). Similar behavior can be observed for 50 and 60 clients as well.

For 70, 80, 90 and 100 clients, based on the average response times, a significant difference is expected between the cases with 100 and 30 thread pool size, and it is expected that the model is closer to the 30 thread case. The measurements confirm this, see e.g. Fig. 13. The most salient difference can be observed at the probability of having 50 clients (i.e. the connection queue is full).

It is obvious that an improved performance model should consider the thread pool size as well. For this reason we tried to enhance our model with a method of modeling multiple threads as proposed in [17]. This enhanced model, however, was not able to follow the measured values either. Thus, we concluded that some implementation details of the application server or the Java Virtual Machine (JVM) cause the observed behavior of the system. To verify our assumption, we implemented a simple web container in Java which allowed configuring the observed parameters. Repeated measurements on our own web container running on the same JVM did not show the deflection depending on the thread pool size. Hence, we can state that an implementation of the application server causes the inaccuracy of the model.

5   Conclusions

This paper presented the results of a performance measurement that focused on two settings of the J2EE application server. A performance model was validated against the results of several measurements. We tried to obtain more details related to the fact that our simple performance model is not precise for all the configurations. We have the following important conclusions. The deviation from the model happens when the number of the allowed threads and the number of clients is greater than the maximum size of the connection queue. The absolute number of the maximum thread pool size does not play any role, only relative to the connection queue limit: note that with the connection queue sized at 50, 60 threads caused a declination, but with 80 connection queue, even the 70 threads configuration provided the results predicted by the model. Measuring the distribution of number of clients at the server provided two important results. Firstly, even in configurations where the average response time is accurately predicted by the model, the p_k probabilities of the model can be quite different from the measured values. Secondly, with clients and threads of higher number than the connection queue, the most important difference between the model and the reality appears at the probability of the connection queue being full. With our own developed web container, we have proven that application server-specific implementation details should be considered to construct an improved model. Hence, our future work will focus on investigating the source code of the Sun Java System Application Server to reveal the cause of the observed behavior and finding the way to model it.

Acknowledgement

Part of this work was funded by the National Office for Research and Technology project number NKFP 2/009/04, and the Péter Pázmány program RET-06/2005. Furthermore, the authors would like to thank EU INFSO-50883 (EGEE) program for support.

References

1. Home page of IBM WebSphere Application Server:
   http://www-306.ibm.com/software/webservers/appserv/was/
2. Home page of JBoss Application Server:
   http://www.jboss.org/products/jbossas
3. Home page of Sun Java System Application Server:
   http://www.sun.com/software/products/appsrvr/index.xml
4. Sopitkamol, M., Menascé, D.A.: A method for evaluating the impact of software configuration parameters on e-commerce sites. In: WOSP '05. Proceedings of the 5th international workshop on Software and performance, pp. 53–64. ACM Press, New York (2005)
5. Bogárdi-Mészöly, Á., Imre, G., Charaf, H.: Investigating factors influencing the response time in J2EE web applications. WSEAS Transactions on Computers 4, 179–183 (2005)
6. Home page of SPECjAppServer: http://www.spec.org/osg/jAppServer/
7. Home page of TPC-W: http://www.tpc.org/tpcw/
8. Kleinrock, L.: Theory, Volume 1, Queueing Systems. Wiley-Interscience, Chichester (1975)

9. Cortellessa, V., D'Ambrogio, A., Lazeolla, G.: Automatic derivation of software performance models from case documents. Performance Evaluation 45(2-3), 81–105 (2001)
10. Cortellessa, V., Mirandola, R.: Deriving a queueing network based performance model from uml diagrams. In: WOSP '00. Proceedings of the 2nd international workshop on Software and performance, pp. 58–70. ACM Press, New York (2000)
11. Urgaonkar, B., Pacifici, G., Shenoy, P., Spreitzer, M., Tantawi, A.: An analytical model for multi-tier internet services and its applications. SIGMETRICS Perform. Eval. Rev. 33(1), 291–302 (2005)
12. Bernardi, S., Donatelli, S., Merseguer, J.: From uml sequence diagrams and statecharts to analysable petri net models. In: WOSP '02. Proceedings of the 3rd international workshop on Software and performance, pp. 35–45. ACM Press, New York (2002)
13. Kounev, S., Buchmann, A.: Performance modelling of distributed E-Business applications using queuing petri nets. In: ISPASS'03. Proc. of the 2003 IEEE International Symposium on Performance Analysis of Systems and Software. IEEE Computer Society Press, Los Alamitos (2003)
14. Imre, G., Bogárdi-Mészöly, Á., Charaf, H.: Measuring and modelling the effect of application server tuning parameters on performance. In: 4th Slovakian-Hungarian Joint Symposium on Applied Machine Intelligence, Herl'any, Slovakia, pp. 471–482 (2006)
15. Imre, G., Bogárdi-Mészöly, Á., Charaf, H.: Performance modelling of a J2EE web application considering application server tuning parameters. In: Proceedings of MicroCAD 2006 International Scientific Conference, University of Miskolc, Miskolc, Hungary, pp. 115–121 (2006)
16. Jain, R.: The Art of Computer Performance Analysis. John Wiley & Sons, Chichester (1991)
17. Lazowska, E.D., Zahorjan, J., Graham, G.S., Sevcik, K.C.: Quantitative system performance: computer system analysis using queueing network models. Prentice-Hall, Inc. Upper Saddle River, NJ, USA (1984)

Possibilities for Advanced Dissemination and Durable Storage of Scientific Data on the Grid

Rutger Kramer

Data Archiving and Networked Services
The Hague, The Netherlands
rutger.kramer@dans.knaw.nl

Abstract. Data Archiving and Networked Services (DANS) is a new organisation in The Netherlands responsible for the archival and dissemination of scientific datasets for the humanities and social sciences. It is currently building a distributed storage system and web interface called EASY for efficient ingest and publishing of datasets for reuse in any type of setting; in scientific as well as in enterprise environments. Recently, DANS was invited to be a part of the VL-e project in which a grid environment is being set up. This opportunity presented us with a new range of possibilities both in the realm of digital durable storage and advanced dissemination. This paper gives an overview of how basic grid features can help keep data accessible for an indefinite amount of time, how the application of data mining and statistical analysis on a grid architecture can provide researchers and analists with new information and what our plans are to eventually implement all of these ideas.

1 Introduction

Data Archiving and Networked Services (DANS) is a new organisation, founded by the Royal Academy of Arts and Sciences and the Netherlands Organisation for Scientific Research in June of 2005. Its main responsibilities are to archive all available research data created in the humanities and social science fields, and to set up a data infrastructure that will enable anyone to reuse existing data.

Data submitted to DANS is generally static in nature and represents, together with publications, the end result of a research project. The actual datasets will usually not be modified or updated any further.

Apart from data experts working on its core archival task, DANS has a small Research and Development team working on software that will enable us to find new ways and use new technologies that can be used to archive and disseminate research data.

At the moment, our development team is working on the implementation of the Electronic Archiving SYstem or EASY, which will enable researchers to deposit and retrieve scientific datasets for reuse. Researchers can upload data files through a web interface and provide a minimal amount of metadata to describe its contents. As soon as the data experts have checked the data for completeness and correctness, it will be published on the web site. We aim to

D. Draheim and G. Weber (Eds.): TEAA 2006, LNCS 4473, pp. 217–225, 2007.

provide open access to as many datasets and as many people as possible, in effect releasing datasets into the public domain.

Data that is deposited into the EASY system has to be maintained and kept accessible for an indefinite amount of time, as the reusability of the datasets has an indeterminable expiration date. Economic data that may have a limited added value today (except for the research project for which it was collected), may be invaluable in fifty years time. Moreover, the added value of individual datasets can be limited since they are generally created with the sole purpose of answering research question posed in one project. Adapting datasets for use in other projects can be a daunting task for researchers working in the humanities and social science fields, because of the fact that, in general, these researchers lack the skills to restructure or reformat an existing dataset to fit their own needs. Creation of a clear data infrastructure, i.e. making clear to researchers where data relevant for their projects can be found, and making that data accessible and instantly usable for them, is just as important as actually getting the data and keeping it safe.

Making data accessible for researchers can be accomplished in a number of ways, one of which is providing data mining functionality on the data we archive. Because of the fact that DANS works for a number of disciplines, ranging from psychology to archaeology, our archives contain a wide variety of datasets. By linking individual, heterogeneous datasets (from within one discipline or across discipline boundaries), new data can be generated so that, for instance, trends, similarities and correlations can be discovered or confirmed. For example, datasets describing archaeological finds on two different locations could be cross-referenced to see whether there is a similarity in found items or stark differences in the finds. As another example, can the combination of a dataset describing macro-economical trends and data on the use of ICT in schools provide relevant new information on the sensitivity of the modernisation of education to economic prosperity?

For this to work, we have to be able to (automatically) link datasets that may be in entirely different, undocumented formats and which will generally be created in the context of different universes of discourse.

2   Requirements Surrounding EASY

Although the archival task may seem as simple as storing the data in an orderly fashion, this is not the case. A number of problems arise when dealing with the long term storage of digital material which can be categorized under the term Digital Longevity[1].

2.1   Digital Longevity

Digital longevity issues are recognised by data archives as well as scientists and governing bodies as a genuine threat to the prolonged availability of digital material. The medium on which the data is stored is susceptible to deterioration, be it on floppy, hard drive or CD-ROM. Outside influences such as magnetic fields, prolonged exposure to dry or humid conditions, and normal wear and tear greatly diminish the life expectancy of the medium. But files are not only threatened by the deterioration of the physical medium. The usability of the data is directly linked to the expected lifespan of the application used to create or open the files. A textbook example in this case is the large number of WordStar files that have been created during the early and mid 1980s. Because WordStar has been replaced by more popular word processing applications years ago, and the actual application used to create and view the files will not run on current computers and Operating Systems, it is becoming harder and harder to access these files. Old WordPerfect documents can still be opened with modern word processing software, but lose a lot of original markup during the conversion to a newer format. Although one can argue that popular formats can always be made accessible one way or another, the costs involved in making it actually happen are ever increasing. It starts getting real difficult with unpopular file formats used by custom made software or generated by old hardware. Even if a specification of the file format is available somewhere, you will need to write new software to parse the data to be able to eventually use it.

There are three strategies available to ensure accessibility of files stored in long term storage repositories: emulation, hardware conservation and migration [2]. In short, you can either provide the user with the environment needed to access the file, or you can constantly update the files to the newest available formats. Both approaches have their own specific application domain: if functionality is paramount you emulate or use the original hardware, if the data itself is paramount you migrate.

2.2   Advanced Dissemination and Data Infrastructure

Dissemination of the archived datasets poses another challenge. If the digital longevity problems with respect to digital media are taken care of, we can guarantee that whatever a researcher puts into the archive can always be taken out again. Solving the software format problem will even make the data usable for longer periods of time. This leaves us with the responsibility of creating a data infrastructure for the humanities and social sciences in which researchers are able to find, retrieve, link and analyze data using new methods and technologies. If we don't offer advanced dissemination functionality, chances are that the new data infrastructure will hardly be used by researchers. Examples of advanced dissemination functionality we are currently investigating are:

– Linking and cross-referencing different datasets to provide data mining capabilities.
– Format-on-demand: a researcher should be able to download a dataset in any (popular) data format he or she wishes, so that he or she can immediately start using it in his or her favourite software environment.

– On-line analysis: before downloading a dataset, a researcher should be able to ascertain the usability of a dataset by performing relatively simple analytical operations (such as statistical analysis) on the data. For this, we intend to use the NESSTAR[3] application for social science data.

3   Current Situation

We're currently in the first phase of the implementation of the EASY system that will not only serve as a digital durable archive, but will also be the basis for the new data infrastructure. EASY will be released during the last quarter of 2006. From then on, researchers will be able to deposit and download scientific data. In order to avoid problems of scale and especially durability, we chose to develop our own storage solution.

3.1   Storage Solution

In order to store datasets and their accompanying metadata in a digitally durable fashion, we have designed and implemented our own data repository system we dubbed AIPStore[1].

AIPStore stores the data without making any assumptions about the nature, format or contents of the dataset or the metadata. The only requirement is that the metadata is provided in XML form, but any metadata format (i.e. the tags used in the XML document) will do. It constructs an AIP out of the file data, metadata and AIP management data (for instance, creation date, categorisation, etc.) and stores this container-like construct directly on the file system.

3.2   Distributed Storage

AIPStore is designed to operate as a cluster of autonomous servers. We have decided on a distributed architecture because of the following reasons:

Storage Capacity Scalability. Although it is not yet possible to fully estimate the amount of data that needs to be stored by the system, we expect that during the first year of operations the submitted data will reach the 20 Terabyte mark. If this trend it to continue in the following years, we will need to add extra resources to be able to store all of this data. By applying a distributed storage system architecture of autonomous nodes, adding more resources will be as simple as starting a new node instance.

Shorter Response Times. Because of the fact that the metadata is spread out over autonomous nodes, queries can be distributed over these nodes. Each node will have an index built on their own domain. By distributing the query over all of the nodes, and combining the end results in one place, the response times for queries can be kept small.

---

[1] AIP stands for Archival Information Package, a concept borrowed from the Open Archival Information System (OAIS)[4] framework.

Lots of Copies Keeps Stuff Safe (LOCKSS). By applying the ideas of the LOCKSS[5] system, i.e. keeping multiple copies of one data file on several physical locations, the chances of a file completely vanishing are minimised. Whenever one of the copies gets corrupted or deleted due to malhandling, hardware failure or disasters, spare copies will be available instantly.

3.3 The DBMS Alternative

There are numerous database systems that can provide the functionality mentioned above. Open Source as well as commercial packages can take care of scalability and replication without us having to write a single line of code. So, why not use a DBMS to take care of these problems, and at the same time benefit from all the additional functionality database systems have to offer?

One of the key factors of durable long term storage is to minimize dependencies on systems and formats. Storing files and metadata in a database introduces an additional technical layer around the actual bytestream. In short, we need to have sufficient knowledge of the format in which a DBMS stores our files in order to be able to retrieve the bytestreams from the DBMS, even when the DBMS is no longer available for use. If we were to store our repositories in, for example, a PostgreSQL database and for whatever reason technical support for this DBMS is no longer available, getting to our data in case of serious system malfunction would be very difficult, as we would have to disassemble the actual database files.

Since we want to avoid dependencies on proprietary or hard to disassemble software formats, we decided to implement a storage solution that is based on filesystem storage and build functionality like querying, updating and replication around it. This way, the files would always be accessible through the file system, even if the management software would cease to be supported.

4 Possibilities for Grid Enabling AIPStore

The design of AIPStore was originally not intended to run with, on or alongside a grid. The distributed nature of AIPStore would have to handle all of the scalability issues we would encounter. This all changed when we were invited to be a participant of the Virtual Laboratories for the e-sciences project (VL-e)[6], in which the so called Big Grid is being built. Being a part of VL-e meant that we could use far more advanced storage technology to archive a multitude of datasets, and offered us a virtually unlimited amount of storage space.

4.1 Longevity on the Grid

However, we can only employ the grid as a storage alternative if it potentially offers the same functionality currently built into our own software, i.e. redundancy and scalability. As it turns out, grid storage offers some very interesting possibilities for durable long term storage:

Inherent Redundant Storage. Redundant file storage is a well known feature of data grids and can be employed to enforce the LOCKSS principle.

Migration to New Media. To the end user, the exact location where a file is stored is not important. Internally, the Storage Resource Broker decides where a file is stored. As the grid evolves, i.e. as new storage systems come available and old systems are removed from the grid, data migration strategies are automatically employed to ensure that no files will be lost. These migration activities effectively solve the durability problems concerning deteriorating media[7].

Mass Migration Capabilities. Whenever a file format becomes obsolete, the original files need to be migrated to a more up to date format. As the number of files to be managed by DANS is yet unknown but is assumed to run into the hundred thousands, migrating all of these files - even in batch - can take up an enormous amount of time. Using a cluster of worker nodes will drastically shorten the time needed to convert files.

On the Fly Conversion. Although it is not a standard feature of grid systems, the Global Grid Forum[8] is researching and designing a Data Format Description Language which could lead to the generic storage of files in an intermediate XML file format. The DFDL Working Group specifically states in its charter that they are focussing on the definition language itself, not to create a generic data representation language[9]. Moreover, the granularity the working group is aiming for in describing data elements within a file format is too small to be effectively used for any kind of generic representation of complex dataset formats.

However, datasets come in a variety of flavours including ASCII tables or raw sensor data. If the DFDL-WG activities culminate in a standard for data format description, it can be used (as the basis for) the description and documentation of the information available in these kinds of single-purpose files. Moreover, providing an XML based data definition together with the actual data can help in building applications to automatically convert from a random proprietary format to a more popular and well known format.

Metadata Storage and Categorisation (MCS). The MCS outlined in [10] is exactly what is needed for metadata storage. It supports searching and a hierarchical organisation structure, and support for multiple metadata formats. This last feature is indispensable for an archive working with data originating from different scientific disciplines. Although descriptive metadata in a general purpose format like Dublin Core (DC)[11] must be used across collections to enable search features, essential information for actual reuse must be available in discipline-specific metadata formats, such as the Data Documentation Initiative (DDI)[12] format for social science data.

4.2 Advanced Dissemination

Grid technology can also enable us to implement important features for advanced dissemination. The results of the DFDL-WG will provide us with ways to automatically annotate complex file formats, which can lead to automatic cross-referencing and linking. Using a DFDL, we can specify in a uniform manner where the values or variables are located within data files. Although variable names may not be uniform across individual datasets, the system can propose possible matches between variables using fuzzy-matching of variable names or trend similarities between value ranges.

Both annotating the data files and subsequently searching for similarities are projects that will take up enormous amounts of time. Whether the annotation process can be automated must be researched further, but the matching process definitely can be automated. A single worker node can be assigned the task to find similarities between one dataset and several (if not all) others. Distributing the work on several datasets over more than one worker node will accelerate the process of finding all possible relations between all of the datasets variables.

5 Moving to the Grid

At the time we were offered to work with the grid, the AIPStore system was not yet fully functional. Because of the proposed change in direction, further development of the system as it was originally conceived has been postponed until more is known about the technical ramifications of a possible grid implementation.

What has become apparent is that moving the AIPStore functionality over to the grid is not straight forward. Since anyone should be able to download and use the datasets, and not just researchers known to the grid user administration, a proxy system must be placed between the grid and the end-user that will act on the grid on his or her behalf. Moreover, a couple of requirements leading to the final design of AIPStore are yet to be mapped onto grid technology. Most importantly, storage of the metadata in XML because of its inherent durability, and a search and browse interface for this XML encoded metadata. We already foresee possibilities to solve these issues, but before a full fledged solution is in place we will not be able to commit entirely to the grid.

Instead, we are working on a gradual transition towards a fully grid based system. At first, AIPStore will mirror all its data on the grid for added redundancy. When we have enough experience with storing data on the grid, infrequently used datasets will be 'swapped out' of AIPStore and permanently stored on the grid. Frequently used datasets will remain in AIPStore as well as on the grid in order to ensure timely availability of popular datasets. After that, we will go into the metadata storage problem. We will be looking into the possibility of basing the metadata storage back-end of MCS on XML, or looking for possibilities of regularly exporting the metadata database to XML for long term storage.

In the end, access to the grid will always be mediated by a proxy system, but all of the data and metadata should be stored on the grid itself.

6   Future Work

We will be taking EASY and the AIPStore system on-line during the last quarter of 2006. The software itself will be released under an Open Source license during the first quarter of 2007. This software will include the basic functionality to archive and retrieve datasets from a digital durable repository.

From then on, we will be working on the advanced dissemination functionality. We will collaborate with data specialists and endusers on the design and implementation of mining systems and the linking of heterogenous datasets. Both the transition onto the grid and the implementation of automatic conversion systems start around May of 2007.

7   Conclusion

In this paper I gave an overview of DANS and its goals and purposes. The fact that data has to be stored for an indefinite amount of time is leading in the development of our own archival system EASY. We managed to implement some known best practices of digital durable storage in our AIPStore system.

The problems surrounding digital longevity that we as a data archive are facing are not new and are not confined to the realm of scientific data management. Any information intensive organization will have to have some policy on how to manage data, be it ad hoc or with Document Management Systems.

If an organization wants to keep old documents or data accessible, they will have to migrate their data at some point in time; not only from one medium to another, but also from old format to new format. As the amount of data an organization uses and generates grows, migrating the stockpile of information becomes an evermore cumbersome, time intensive and expensive task.

Grid infrastructures already incorporate a lot of functionality that can safeguard data for longer periods of time. By implementing a small amount of extra services (mass migration, conversion on-the-fly, etc.) the grid could be turned into a real digital safe haven for files. So far, the grid is the only platform on which the digital longevity problem can be sufficiently tackled for large amounts of data, be it production data, surveys, scientific data or everyone's personal digital photo album.

The VL-e project has offered us a unique opportunity to use the potential of grid technology. Virtually unlimited disk space, inherent replication and distributed computing power are resources that we are in need of to achieve our goals of providing long term access to data and building a data infrastructure enabling researchers to find new uses for existing research data and combining data from different datasets to retrieve new information.

Although much of the requirements of digital durable storage are met by current grid technology, a simple transfer of our current system to the grid is not possible. We will employ a gradual transition strategy based on an architecture in which our existing AIPStore system will act as a proxy and a cache to the grid's resources.

Eventually, we will aim for a fully grid based implementation of both the digital durable storage of datasets and the advanced dissemination functionality, both of which will be released under an open source license.

Acknowledgements. Many thanks to Jeff Templon and David Groep of the National Institute for Nuclear Physics and High Energy Physics (NIKHEF) in the Netherlands for inviting us to take part in the VL-e project and acting as guides to the world of grid computing.

References

1. Ross, S., Gow, A.: Digital Archaeology: Rescuing Neglected and Damaged Data Resources (February 1999) (2006-05-22),
   http://www.ukoln.ac.uk/services/elib/papers/supporting/pdf/p2con.pdf
2. Lee, K.-H., Slattery, O., Lu, R., Tang, X., McCrary, V.: The State of the Art and Practice in Digital Preservation. Journal of Research of the National Institute of Standards and Technology (January-February 2002) (2006-05-22),
   http://nvl.nist.gov/pub/nistpubs/jres/107/1/j71lee.pdf
3. (2006-07-21) http://www.nesstar.org/
4. Reference Model for an Open Archival Information System (OAIS), CCSDS 650.0-B-1 Blue Book (January 2002) (2006-07-21),
   http://public.ccsds.org/publications/archive/650x0b1.pdf
5. (2006-07-21) http://www.lockss.org/lockss/Home
6. (2006-07-21) http://www.vl-e.nl/
7. Moore, R.: Preservation Environments. In: 21st IEEE/12th NASA Goddard Conference on Mass Storage Systems and Technologies (MSST2004) (April 2004)
8. (2006-07-21) http://www.gridforum.org
9. (2006-07-21) http://forge.gridforum.org/sf/docman/do/downloadDocument/projects.dfdl-wg/docman.root.administrative/doc5387/1
10. Deelman, E., Singh, G., Atkinson, M.P., Chervenak, A., Chue, N.P., Chue Hong, C., Kesselman, S., Patil, L.P., Su, M.: Grid-Based Metadata Services. In: 16th International Conference on Scientific and Statistical Database Management (SSDBM04) (June 2004)
11. (2006-07-21) http://www.dublincore.org/
12. (2006-07-21) http://www.icpsr.umich.edu/DDI/

Developing Realistic Approaches for the Migration of Legacy Components to Service-Oriented Architecture Environments

Grace Lewis and Dennis B. Smith

Carnegie Mellon University, Software Engineering Institute, 4500 Fifth Ave., Pittsburgh, PA 15213, USA
{glewis,dbs}@sei.cmu.edu

Abstract. This article addresses the problem of the migration of legacy components to Service-Oriented Architecture (SOA) environments. It focuses on the development of a realistic strategy for performing such a migration, taking into account the business needs of the organization and the technical content of the organization's existing systems portfolio. It highlights the challenges of building an SOA-based system and presents development issues from three perspectives: the application developer, the infrastructure developer, and the service provider. Because there is a current trend of organizations that are leveraging the value of their legacy systems by exposing all or parts of it as services within an SOA environment, the concerns and needs of the service provider are presented in greater detail. SMART, a method for making decisions on the migration of legacy assets as services within SOA environments is presented.

Keywords: service-oriented architecture, SOA, services, Web Services, migration, modernization, legacy.

1 Introduction

Service-oriented architecture (SOA) has become an increasingly popular mechanism for achieving interoperability between systems. Because it has characteristics of loose coupling, published interfaces, and a standard communication model, SOA enables existing legacy systems to expose their functionality as services, presumably without making significant changes to the legacy systems. Migration to services has been achieved within a number of domains, including banking applications, electronic payment applications, and development tools, showing that the promise is beginning to be fulfilled [1] [2] [3] [4].

This article outlines the basic concepts of SOA at different levels of detail. Goals, challenges, and common misconceptions about the SOA approach are presented. The four pillars of SOA-based systems development are introduced as a way to address SOA challenges. Finally, the Service Migration and Reuse Technique (SMART) is presented as a method for determining the feasibility of migrating legacy components to an SOA environment.

D. Draheim and G. Weber (Eds.): TEAA 2006, LNCS 4473, pp. 226–240, 2007.

2 SOA Basics

2.1 Basic SOA Concepts

Services are reusable components that represent business tasks, such as customer lookup, account lookup, or credit card validation. Services can be globally distributed across organizations and reconfigured to support new business tasks. They are reusable in the sense that they can be used by many business processes. They usually provide coarse-grained functionality, such as customer lookup as opposed to finer grained functionality such as customer address lookup.

More formally, a service is a coarse-grained, discoverable, and self-contained software entity that interacts with applications and other services through a loosely coupled, synchronous or asynchronous, message-based communication model.

SOA is a way of designing systems composed of services that are invoked in a standard way. SOA is an architectural style, but it is not a system architecture, and it is not a complete system. In this architectural style, an SOA-based system is composed of services, applications that use services, and an SOA infrastructure that connects applications to services. This will be further explained in Section 2.3.

2.2 Goals of SOA Adoption

Common goals for the adoption of SOA are to eliminate redundancy, assemble new functionality from existing services, adapt systems to changing needs, and leverage legacy investments.

To illustrate the goal of eliminating redundancy, it is common to find that in traditional stove-piped system environments there is often duplicate functionality across systems. For example, three applications may have their own customer lookup functionality. A service with equivalent functionality can be implemented and used by all three applications. This translates into cost-efficiency because there is a single point of maintenance and can now be used by other applications that require this functionality without any additional development.

An example of assembling functionality from existing services can be illustrated by an Order Processing application that uses a set of services to implement part of its functionality. If the organization decides to go into the education business, a series of services already used by the Order Processing application would be available, such as *Customer Lookup* and *Credit Check*. The organization could move more quickly into its new line of business and the new services created specifically to support the education line of business, such as *Room Reservation*, could also be used by other applications.

The ability to adapt to changing needs is because in an SOA approach services are accessed by applications in a standard way through the selected SOA infrastructure. Therefore, as long as the interface remains stable, the logic supporting the services can change as needed and not have an effect on existing applications.

Finally, an SOA approach is an attractive option to expose functionality in legacy systems. By allowing access to the legacy system thorough a standard service interface, the details of connecting to the legacy system are the responsibility of the

SOA infrastructure and the service interface and not of the applications. As a result, the legacy platform diversity is transparent to the applications.

2.3 Building Blocks of SOA-Based Systems

An SOA-based system consists of 1) services, 2) applications that discover and use services, 3) and an SOA infrastructure that connects applications to services, as shown at a very high level in Figure 1. In this context, the SOA Infrastructure provides a standard communication mechanism between applications and services. Each application invokes the services in the same way. Each service provides an interface that is invoked through a data format and protocol that is understood by all the potential clients of that service.

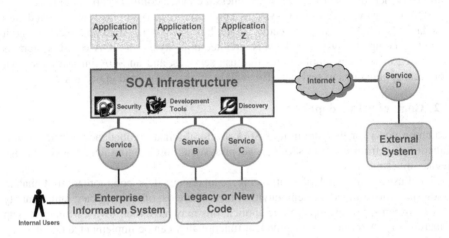

Fig. 1. Components of an SOA-Based System

Infrastructure developers focus on providing a stable infrastructure that includes standards, common services and development tools. The infrastructure supports the protocol and data formats of the service's current and potential clients.

Tasks for infrastructure developers include:

- Selecting standards to implement as part of the infrastructure
- Developing a set of common infrastructure services for discovery, communication, security, etc.
- Identifying and developing binding mechanisms to satisfy the largest set of potential service users
- Providing tools for application and service developers
- Documenting and supporting the infrastructure

Application developers focus on the discovery, composition and invocation of services, either statically at design time or dynamically at runtime. Key tasks for application developers are:

- Understanding the SOA infrastructure
- Discovering appropriate services to be incorporated into applications
- Retrieving and understanding service description documentation
- Invoking identified services in applications, including any data conversions, error handling and availability handling
- Testing services for correctness in the context of the application being developed

Service providers focus on the description and granularity of services so that applications can easily locate and use them with acceptable Quality of Service (QoS). Tasks include:

- Understanding requirements of potential service users
- Understanding SOA infrastructure
- Developing code that receives the service request, translates it into calls into new or existing systems, and produces a response
- Describing and publishing the service
- Developing service initialization code and operational procedures

With the increasing popularity of software as a service, it is becoming common for each of these components to be developed by different organizations. The tasks and risks associated with the development of each will largely depend on the distribution of the development effort across multiple organizations. If the three types of components are developed within the same organization, the challenges are less. However, if the development is distributed across multiple organizations, decisions made locally by any one of these development groups can have an effect on the other groups.

2.4 Basic SOA Operations

There are three basic operations that are required to support an SOA-based system. These are:

1. Service discovery. Service repositories are queried for services with desired characteristics. The complexity of a service repository varies from a simple directory of services categorized by type to a more complex registry where services are categorized according to a pre-defined ontology with QoS information in addition to binding information. A service registry contains basic information about available services, such as description, specification (contract), documentation; and should include more additional information such as classification, usage history, test results, and performance metrics. The major challenges of service discovery are the proper description of and the maintenance of the service repository.
2. Service composition. Services are integrated into applications to provide portions of functionality. The major challenges of service composition are input/output conversions and transaction management.
3. Service invocation. Services are invoked and the corresponding service code is executed. A service can be invoked in several ways:

- Service consumer directly invoke the service if its location is known
- Service consumer uses a discovery service to locate a service based on a specific set of criteria. The discovery service returns the location of the service so that it can be invoked by the consumer.
- Service consumer uses a service broker that passes the request to one or more discovery services.

The major challenges of service invocation are dealing with service availability and having robust exception handling in the event that services are no longer available.

3 Common Misconceptions About SOA

SOA may currently be the best available solution for achieving interoperability, agility, and other goals such as providing a technology upgrade path that preserves the investment in legacy systems and simplifies deployment of new systems. However, our experience from working with customers considering the adoption of SOA suggests that they often have a variety of misconceptions that lead them to greatly underestimate the effort required to successfully implement SOA-based systems. These misconceptions are dangerous because they make organizations more susceptible to vendor advertising and hype. In addition, these misconceptions are often embraced by internal information technology (IT) organizations, leading them to over-promise new capabilities, while underestimating the cost and effort required for achieving even modest improvements.

3.1 It Is Easy to Develop Applications Based on Services

This is also stated as "just call some services and you're done" and is obviously an oversimplification of the development process in a service-based environment. There are still many questions that need to be answered to successfully develop a service-based application. We focus here on finding services, composing and using services.

Finding services can be done using a service repository. Such a repository contains data about available services and can be part of any SOA implementation. For Web Services this could be a UDDI repository. Developers can use the search capability to find services and all the necessary information to invoke them. However, often the search capability is not sufficient if it is limited to a simple keyword search or to browsing by categories. Currently available repositories do not provide search for a service by functionality. Such a capability may be provided in the future if ontological service description approaches are added to service repositories [5]. Other challenges are level of quality, completeness and trust of the contained information.

Composing services is also not as easy as it may seem at first. While it may be easy to call one service for a specific function, such as validating a credit card or placing an order, other situations require more complex interactions. When the results of invoking service A must be fed into another service B, it is not likely that B can process the result data from A directly. In most cases, it will be necessary to develop glue code to transform the data into the correct format for B. This transformation may be simply a syntactic transformation, but may also involve the application of complex algorithms. Examples include time zone conversions, coordinate transformations, or translations between categories that do not match.

In the case of using services, it is possible that the functionality of the services does not match the functionality needed. The best available service may have the wrong granularity for the task at hand. If the service does too much, the developer needs to add post-processing of service results to get the desired functionality. If the service does too little, the developer has the choice between adding custom code in the application or finding another service to provide the additional processing. Another challenge is the determination of the resulting quality of service (QoS) characteristics, such as performance, security, or reliability, once the application is put together [6].

3.2 It Is Easy to Compose Services Dynamically at Runtime

Currently, binding to services is usually done at design time. This is referred to as static binding or fully-grounded binding. Discovery and composition of services are done at design time such that the developer can discover the syntax and semantics of the service before it is actually used. In the case of dynamic binding, discovery and composition of services are done at runtime. This is currently a very complex and poorly supported task.

In a very basic scenario of dynamic binding, service consumers retrieve the service address from a registry before each call to the service. If there are several providers of the same service the service consumer can choose at runtime which one to use. The consumer can also rank providers based on QoS criteria, choose a preferred provider, and use others as backup if the preferred service is not available.

More advanced automatic discovery and composition of new services at runtime requires the use of ontologies to describe function and usage of services. Current technologies have not advanced to a point where this is possible in production environments [7]. A potential solution requires the use of a common ontology by service providers and client applications within a domain. Given this shared ontology it would still be necessary to develop components that can construct the right queries for the discovery of services, compose services when there is not a single service that provides the needed function, and then provide the right data to invoke the discovered service. This is not an easy set of tasks to do at runtime.

3.3 SOA Is All About Standards and Standards Are All That Is Needed

This statement primarily applies in the context of Web Services because Web Services are the main standards-based technology available today for SOA implementation. This leads to a corollary misconception that SOA and Web Services are the same, while the fact is that Web Services are only one potential approach to implementing SOA.

Basic infrastructure standards that support the exchange of messages between service consumer and provider are the most developed and mature of the Web Service standards. Currently the majority of Web Services are based on WSDL Version 1.1 and SOAP Version 1.1, and these standards have been stable for a number of years.

Being stable for years does not mean that the standards are complete. For example, after adopting basic infrastructure Web Service standards, organizations building services may find that these services still cannot communicate information effectively with other services due to different design decisions and flexibility in the standards. The WS-I Basic Profile was constructed to provide better interoperability across implementations using basic infrastructure standards [8].

In addition, revisions to standards are likely in any area undergoing rapid advances in technology. This is certainly the case with Web Service standards. A new version of WSDL is currently under development. As this and other updated standards are released and become part of Web Service infrastructure products, there will likely be issues regarding the compatibility of services based on old and new versions. As an example, the SOAP 1.2 primer lists all the differences with SOAP 1.1. Just in additional or changed syntax there are 15 differences. While these changes are beneficial because they make the specification clearer and more robust, valid SOAP 1.1 messages may be invalid under SOAP 1.2 because of elements that are required in SOAP 1.2 but optional in SOAP 1.1. As a result, once tools and libraries start supporting SOAP 1.2, existing applications and services will have to make the move as well in order to continue operation.

Standards for service composition and cross-cutting concerns are less mature—and far less stable—than basic infrastructure standards. Currently, there are a number of competing proposals and standards for service composition and cross-cutting concerns that conflict and overlap. Examples of closely related capabilities that are being independently developed (and therefore are competing) include WSCL and WS-Coordination in the field of service composition. Regarding these less mature areas of Web Services, the old saying sums it up, "the best thing about standards is that there are so many to choose from." There is hope, however, that Web Service standards will evolve such that they can be combined, as in the case of WS-Security that can use SAML assertions in security token references.

3.4 Other Common Misconceptions

This list of misconceptions is not exhaustive and its intention is not to discourage the adoption of SOA. In fact, there are many success stories that prove it is a viable and real option. We have focused on those that are prevalent in the expectations of SOA customers. We hope that by recognizing these misconceptions, organizations can better understand and evaluate the promises of vendors and improve their own internal SOA expectations and planning processes. Other popular misconceptions include the views that

- SOA provides the complete architecture for a system
- Legacy systems can be easily integrated into an SOA environment
- SOA is all about technology
- The use of standards guarantees interoperability among services in an SOA environment
- It is easy to develop services anybody can use
- Services can only be business services
- Testing applications that use services is no different than testing any other application

4 Pillars of SOA-Based Systems Development

It is common to view SOA-based systems development as a technical problem with a technical solution. However, successful SOA-based systems development requires attention to four pillars as illustrated in Figure 2. These are each outlined briefly in the following subsections.

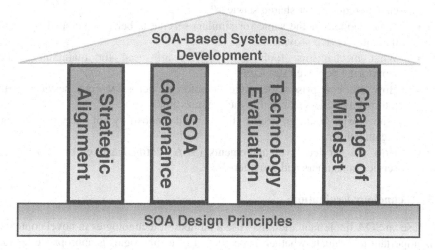

Fig. 2. Pillars of SOA-Based Systems Development

4.1 Strategic Alignment

Any successful SOA strategy has to be aligned with business goals. The high level business goals dictate the focus of an SOA implementation. For example, a goal to increase information available to business customers will focus on intuitive portals and creation of services related to customer information. A goal of integrating new business partners will focus on a flexible SOA infrastructure, a strong service repository, and clear guidelines for composition. A goal of maximizing security may lead to a proprietary SOA infrastructure.

Services are identified through a top down analysis of business processes, a bottom-up legacy system inventory, or a combination of the two. High priority services are selected based on their relationship to critical business goals.

SOA implementation starts with pilot projects that provide high impact and visibility with the lowest risk. Successful pilot projects will potentially lead to projects that integrate a single business unit, to projects that integrate multiple business units, to potentially a virtual enterprise where all applications are built based on services [9].

4.2 SOA Governance

Governance has been rated as the main inhibitor of SOA adoption [10]. A well-defined governance model is essential for SOA success and needs to answer such questions as:

- What is the process for determining what services to create?
- What is the process for evolving, and changing services if there are many consumers of the service?
- Many business services are common across several lines of business in an enterprise. Who "owns" these common services?
- Who owns the actual data if more than one service is using it?
- What is the resolution mechanism if there are conflicting requirements or change requests for shared services?
- What happens if the same (or similar) service is being developed by more than one service provider?
- What mechanisms, tools and policies are used for maintaining and monitoring deployed services?
- How are enterprise-wide policies enforced across various services both internal as well as external to the organization?
- Who owns and maintains the shared repository of services in an organization?
- How are service level agreements (SLA) defined and enforced between service consumers and providers?

4.3 Technology Evaluation

Because an SOA implementation may use a number of technologies in novel contexts, it is important to evaluate whether a specific set of technologies is appropriate for the task at hand. All technologies work well within a specific context and under certain conditions. For example, Web services work well for asynchronous communication over the Internet. In a business environment these conditions are very common. However, this may not be the case in a military tactical command and control environment where high performance and availability requirements prevail. A formal evaluation process that can allow organizations to experiment with technologies before they are inserted into organizations is necessary. This process must consider the context in which the technology will be used in order to make the right decisions.

Lewis outlines an approach for context based technology assessments that can be appropriate for SOA technology evaluations [11]. This process evaluates technologies within the context that they will be used. It includes hands-on experimentation with the technology for a greater understanding of its implications, as well as early competence development of the people conducting the experiments. An integral part of this process is the use of TechChecks (formerly known as model problems) to verify claims about different technologies and approaches. The approach involves (1) formulating hypotheses about the technology, and (2) examining these hypotheses against very specific criteria through experimentation. In this way the hypotheses are either sustained or refuted. The TechCheck approach has the advantage of producing very efficient and representative experiments that not only evaluate technologies within the context of their future use, but also generate hands-on competence with the technologies.

4.4 Awareness of a Different Mindset

There are a unique set of challenges in building SOA-based systems. These challenges require a different development approach that deals with the characteristics of SOA-based systems. Although it is difficult to generalize, some of the contrasts of SOA systems versus traditional systems are presented in Table 1.

Table 1. Differences between Traditional Systems Development and SOA-Based Systems Development

Traditional Systems Development	SOA-Based Systems Development
Tight coupling between system components	Loose coupling between applications and services
Shared semantics at design time	In the future, semantics ideally enable dynamic discovery and execution of services
Known set of users and usage patterns	Potentially unknown service users and usage patterns
System components all within the same organization	Multiple organizations providing and supporting system components

These differences impact the way software is developed throughout the life cycle. For example:

- During requirements, it is important to have close ties to business process modeling and analysis. In addition there is the need to anticipate potential requirements from unknown users
- During architecture and design, it is important to have technology evaluations and to perform explicit tradeoff analyses
- Implementation decisions will be impacted by emerging standards and may require simulation of the deployment environment
- Testing requires a strong emphasis on exception handling, and requires all users to be online
- Maintenance requires more sophisticated impact analyses and greater coordination of release cycles

5 Migration of Legacy Component to SOA Environments

Enabling a legacy system to interact within an SOA environment, such as a Web services-based architecture, is sometimes relatively straightforward. However, characteristics of legacy systems, such as age, language, and architecture, as well as of the target SOA environment, can complicate the task. This is particularly the case during migration to highly demanding and proprietary SOA environments such as those with strong requirements for security or performance. In these cases, it may not be immediately obvious how best to use legacy code—or even whether to use it. Migrations to SOA environments will likely rely less on semi-automated migration, and more on careful analysis of the feasibility and magnitude of the effort involved.

There is a need for a systematic process that addresses a wide range of considerations in order to achieve consistent results in making decisions regarding the migration of legacy components.

The Service Migration and Reuse Technique (SMART) assists organizations in analyzing legacy capabilities for use as services in an SOA environment. SMART gathers information about the migration context, potential services, legacy components, and the target SOA environment, to produce a service migration strategy as its primary product [12]. SMART also produces other outputs that are useful to an organization whether or not it decides on migration. SMART inputs and outputs are depicted in Figure 3.

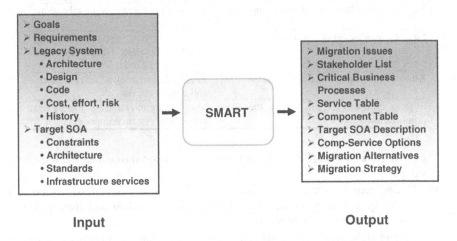

Input   **Output**

Fig. 3. SMART Inputs and Outputs

SMART consists of five major activities, each divided into several tasks. The activities and generalized process and information flows of SMART are depicted in Figure 4. Information-gathering activities for the first three activities are directed by the Service Migration Interview Guide (SMIG). The SMIG contains questions in approximately 60 areas that directly address the gap between the existing and target architecture, design, and code, as well as questions concerning issues that must be addressed in service migration efforts. Use of the SMIG assures broad and consistent coverage of the factors that influence the cost, effort, and risk involved in migration to services.

5.1 Establish Migration Context

The goal of this activity is to understand the business and technical context for migration, identify stakeholders, and select candidate services for migration. The outcome of this activity is either a reasonable set of services to be considered in the migration analysis or a decision that the legacy system is not a good candidate for migration because a reasonable set of services could not be identified.

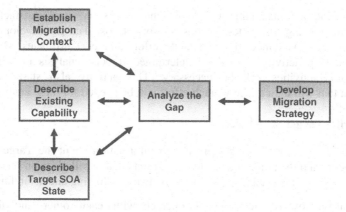

Fig. 4. SMART Activities

Understanding the migration context includes understanding the rationale, goals and expectations for migration to an SOA environment; and any programmatic constraints such as schedule and budget for migration. It also includes gaining an understanding of the system at a high level, to start identifying potential services that could be mined from the legacy system.

Identifying stakeholders to involve in the process is important because these become sources of information for the rest of the activities. It is useful to at least identify who is driving and paying for the effort, who knows what about the legacy system, and to understand the demand or need for potential services.

Once the system is understood at a high level and there is an initial idea of what services can be migrated from the legacy system and potential service needs, the next step is to select candidate services for the migration analysis. The selection process can be summarized as:

- Identify business and migration goals
- Identify key business processes that support these goals and can use functionality from the legacy system
- Identify common steps/tasks in these processes or threads
- Select a number of the steps as candidate services

If it is not possible to make a connection between goals, services, and legacy functionality, then the legacy system might not be a good candidate for migration.

5.2 Describe Existing Capability

The goal of this activity is to obtain descriptive data about the components of the legacy system targeted for migration. Basic data solicited during this activity includes the name, function, size, language, operating platform, and age of the legacy components. Technical personnel are questioned about the architecture, design paradigms, code complexity, level of documentation, module coupling, interfaces for systems and users, and dependencies on other components and commercial products. In addition, data about the relative quality and maturity of legacy components is gathered, including outstanding problems, change history, user satisfaction, and likelihood of meeting longer term needs. Historical cost data for development and maintenance tasks is collected to calculate effort and cost estimates. During the Analyze the Gap activity, it will be determined if code analysis or architecture reconstruction activities will be necessary. This activity also starts to gather information that will indicate how much effort will be needed for these analyses.

5.3 Describe Target SOA State

The goal of this activity is to gather enough information about the Target SOA in order to understand the requirements and constraints that it will place on services. The information gathered is used to answer to provide the following understanding:

- Identify how services would interact with each other and the SOA environment
- Identify the impact of specific technologies, standards, and guidelines for service development
- Determine target SOA implementation state
- Understand QoS expectations and execution environment for services
- Understand support requirements once services are in production

The characteristics of the target SOA will affect decisions about whether legacy components can be reused. The degree to which a legacy component is inconsistent with these characteristics will influence the overall migration costs.

5.4 Analyze the Gap

The goal of this activity is to identify the gap between the existing state and the future state and determine the level of effort and cost needed to convert the legacy components into services. SMART uses several sources of information to support the analysis activity. The issues, problems, and data gathered as the SMART team investigates the available components, required services, and target SOA form one source of information. A second, optional source of information is the use of code analysis and architecture reconstruction tools to analyze existing source code. Where documentation is insufficient or where there is uncertainty about code characteristics such as dependencies on commercial products or between portions of the code, tool analysis is very helpful. This option can also be used with great effect to survey representative portions of the code to verify other opinions and judgments.

5.5 Develop Migration Strategy

The final activity of SMART is the selection of a strategy to achieve the migration goal the development and presentation of the migration strategy. In many cases, the migration strategy may involve multiple steps, such as an initial wrapping, followed by restructuring of the application (now service) into appropriate layers, and finally by modification to use other services. Example elements of a strategy include

- Identities of specific components to migrate
- Recommendations regarding the ordering of migration efforts
- Specific migration paths to follow (simple wrapping vs. rewriting of code)
- Identification of increments that lead to increasing capability
- Suggestions regarding organization(s) best equipped to lead the migration effort
- Suggested coordination with related efforts, such as SOA infrastructure builds or data consolidation

There may be more than one viable alternative to achieve the migration goal. These alternatives may vary along many dimensions, such as the components selected for migration, the sequencing of migration activities, the use of external services, and the types of modifications made to the code.

The final migration strategy is prepared in two forms: a Migration Strategy Presentation for management and a Migration Strategy Report with detailed findings and steps. This latter step is optional if all that is required is a high-level analysis of migration feasibility. It should be clear that the strategy is a preliminary analysis of the feasibility but the briefing is not intended to replace system engineering activity.

6 Summary

SOA offers significant potential for leveraging investments in legacy systems by providing a modern interface to existing capabilities, as well as exposing legacy functionality to a greater number of users. The SOA approach accomplishes this by promoting assembly of applications from existing services, platform and language independence, reuse of services through loose coupling, and easy service upgrade due to separation of service interface from implementation.

An SOA-based system consists of 1) services, 2) applications that discover and use services, 3) and an SOA infrastructure that connects applications to services. An end-to-end engineering approach for SOA requires addressing the unique challenges, risks and technical issues of these three different development perspectives. In particular, the service provider that is designing reusable services requires a different approach, skill set, and mindset than in traditional development. There will be a bigger stakeholder community because services are typically reused at organization and sub-organization level. Often, the challenges provided by this fact alone, cause the cost of exposing legacy system functionality as services to be higher than actually replacing the system with a new SOA-based system. Therefore, there is a need for detailed analysis to determine the feasibility of exposing legacy functionality as services. This analysis has to include the identification of needs of the target SOA, a clear distinction between the needs that can be satisfied by the legacy system and those that cannot be satisfied, and a systematic analysis of changes that need to be made to fit into the target SOA.

SMART analyzes the viability of reusing legacy components as the basis for services by answering these questions:

- What services make sense to develop?
- What components can be mined to derive these services?
- What changes are needed to accomplish the migration?
- What migration strategies are most appropriate?
- What are the preliminary estimates of cost and risk?

With this information, an organization can then make decisions regarding the migration path to a service-oriented environment.

References

1. Polmann, M., Schonefeld, M.: An Evolutionary Integration Approach using Dynamic CORBA in a Typical Banking Environment. In: Presented at the Case Studies Workshop of the Sixth European Conference on Software Maintenance and Reengineering, Budapest, Hungary (March 11-13, 2002)
2. Radha, V., Gulati, V., Thapar, R.: Evolution of Web Services Approach in SFMS – A Case Study. In: Proceedings of the IEEE International Conference on Web Services (ICWS'04), July 6-9, 2004. IEEE Computer Society Press, Los Alamitos (2004)
3. Zhang, J., Chung, J., Chang, C.: Migration to Web Services Oriented Architecture – A Case Study. In: Proceedings of the 2004 ACM Symposium of Applied Computing, Nicosia, Cyprus, March 14 -17. ACM Press, New York (2004)
4. Chung, S., Young, P., Nelson, J.: Service-Oriented Software Reengineering: Bertie3 as Web Services. In: Proceedings of the 2005 IEEE International Conference on Web Services (ICWS'05), Orlando, FL, USA, July 11-15, 2005. IEEE Computer Society Press, Los Alamitos (2005)
5. Metcalf, C., Lewis, G.: Model Problems in Technologies for Interoperability: OWL Web Ontology Language for Services (OWL-S), Software Engineering Institute, Carnegie Mellon Unversity, Pittsburgh, PA (2006)
6. Milanovic, N., Malek, M.: Current Solutions for Web Service Composition. In: Internet Computing, vol. 8(6). IEEE Computer Society Press, Los Alamitos (2004)
7. Metcalf, C., Lewis, G.: Model Problems in Technologies for Interoperability: OWL Web Ontology Language for Services (OWL-S), Software Engineering Institute, Carnegie Mellon University, Pittsburgh, PA (2006)
8. Web Services Interoperability Organization. Basic Profile Version 1.1 (2004), Available at http://www.ws-i.org/Profiles/BasicProfile-1.1.html
9. Schulte, R.: Meeting the Challenges of SOA Adoption, Keynote at the SOA in Action Virtual Conference (November 2006)
10. InfoWorld. SOA Trend Survey (2006)
11. Lewis, G., Wrage, L.: A Process for Context-Based Technology Evaluation, Software Engineering Institute, Carnegie Mellon University, Pittsburgh, PA (2005)
12. Lewis, G., Morris, E., O'Brien, L., Smith, D., Wrage, L.: SMART: The Service-Oriented Migration and Reuse Technique, Software Engineering Institute, Carnegie Mellon University, Pittsburgh, PA (2005)

A Generic Constraints-Based Framework for Business Modeling

Min Li and Christopher J. Hogger

Department of Computing
Imperial College London
SW7 2AZ
United Kingdom
{minli,cjh}@doc.ic.ac.uk

Abstract. The potential benefits of logic-based modeling methods encourage business organizations to construct models offering flexible knowledge representation supported by correct and effective inference. However, owing to the problems of encoding expertise, the ambiguities in business concept formulation and the diversity of possible evaluation methods, there is no clear consensus on how best to apply logic-based formalization to informal or semi-formal business modeling. Our work aims to build a formal generic model framework comprised of sub-models that formulate distinct core aspects of business. The framework employs logical constraints to represent and compute the key relations among business entities, and offers scope for clarifying the semantics of other existing frameworks by translating them into this one. The paper outlines our framework and presents a synthetic case study to illustrate its nature and operation.

Keywords: business modeling, logical constraints, business concepts formulation.

1   Introduction

A business model embodies the logic underlying the operation of business organizations. It should enable one to understand and predict "how a business company is organized, what it sells, how it delivers products and services, how it adds value" [1]. Undoubtedly, business models are playing an ever more important role in the competitive, dynamic and increasingly uncertain economic society. However, owing to the problems of encoding expertise, the ambiguities in business concept formulation and the diversity of possible evaluation methods, there is currently no clear consensus on how best to formalize concepts that may be articulated only informally or semi-formally within the business community. This paper describes our attempt to represent some of these concepts in the declarative but executable framework of logic programming, including constraint logic programming. Our aim is to do this at a level of abstraction capable of representing sufficient concepts to enable useful model instances to be built

D. Draheim and G. Weber (Eds.): TEAA 2006, LNCS 4473, pp. 241–254, 2007.

and evaluated whilst at the same time not becoming so overwhelmed with detail and specificity that we forfeit generality and transparency.

While most existing research on business modeling concentrates upon very specific business domains, our interest is in conceptual and logical aspects of business in general. Our ultimate aim is to achieve a generic model which provides a semantic basis, and hence a means of comparison, for the many specialized modeling frameworks already existing.

To pursue this aim we survey some existing frameworks for business modeling and seek to capture their common essentials in our generic model. Starting with some instance of the generic model, modelers can then further instantiate and elaborate this to create their own more specific and detailed models. We outline the functions evolved in each sub-model and describe how they contribute to the overall model. In particular, we illustrate the representations and executions of business plans and constraints with simple examples. The contributions of this paper can be summarized as follows:

- a decomposition of the notion of a "business" into four separable bodies of logical constraints-covering, respectively, schedule, artifacts, finance and human organization-and a fifth body of meta-constraints expressing business rules intended to cohere the other four;
- a generic, transparent and executable scheme for representing business plans and constraints having a simple and well-defined semantics and exploiting the computational power of constraint logic programming.
- a simple and fully automatic simulator to simulate a typical business procedure, displaying required information and data through dynamically generated business assets.

In section 2 we discuss some related work. Section 3 outlines overall structure of our own model. We explain how business plans and constraints are represented and executed in sections 4 and 5 respectively. Section 6 outlines design and implementation considerations for simulating holistic business procedure. Finally, in section 7 we review the work undertaken, and our future intentions for the framework.

2   Related Work

It is evident that expressive power and logical transparency are key factors for a business company in choosing their models. Chen [2] in AIAI presented research on formal enterprise modeling using a supporting tool named KBST-BM. However, it aims from an engineering perspective at a relatively lightweight logical framework in lacking strong logical formalization of key business concepts and relationships. Gordijn [3] proposed an ontology-based conceptual model named e3value, focusing on modeling conceptualization and ontology of e-business. Loucopoulos [4] advocated the management of shared knowledge and the use of a conceptual modeling paradigm to support enterprise changes. Osterwalder [5] [6] summarized the conceptual business modeling method and presented Business

Modeling Ontology (BMO). His work connects with ours especially in relation to the components of business models, providing a good starting point in extracting the business essentials for our generic framework.

More generally, there exists a growing research community which is focusing on defining and classifying business concepts, analyzing business components, developing business representation tools [7], [8], [9], and [10]. We share a similar motivation with them in business conceptualization. Recently the Business Rules Team carried out a standard called "Semantics of Business Vocabulary and Business Rules (SBVR)" [11], which provides possibilities to share the meaning and semantics of business vocabulary and rules. SBVR is independent of any model-driven architecture and is intended to provide a common bridge between business and business models.

When investigating business modeling, it is inevitable to refer to what might be termed the "software engineering" imperatives of business analysis and design. Early approaches to this included Structured Analysis [12], [13] and the Vienna Definition Method [14]. Structured analysis is a general method for both business modeling and system modeling. It combines hierarchical data flow diagrams, sum-of-product data specification, local functionality specification and subsequently, entity-relationship diagrams. It further defines several analysis-level artifacts which together form the structured specification for models. The method provides a general bridge between business modeling and the general philosophy of disciplined software engineering. By comparison, VDM is a particular program development method based on formal specification. It begins with a very abstract specification and develops this into an implementation. Each step involves data reification and operation decomposition. Data reification develops abstract data types into more concrete data structures, while operation decomposition develops the (abstract) implicit specifications of operations and functions into algorithms that can be directly implemented in a computer language of choice. The design of our own framework was somewhat inspired by the ideas of VDM. We started from an abstract level of business concepts and their inter-functions, and then effectively performed reification and decomposition to reach a layer of acceptable detail.

More specialized frameworks exist to address particular aspects of the business modeling task. The ARIS language and tool set [15] employs so-called event process chains to capture and standardize business processes, facilitating the tasks of analyzing and re-designing them. The nearest correlate of these event process chains in our own framework is our plan structure and associated temporal constraints. Another example is Form-Oriented Analysis [16] applicable to businesses employing submit-response protocols, e.g. as seen in many web-based business applications. The interactions are modeled in a structure called form chart which effectively formalizes a finite-state machine. Through this artifact it becomes possible to elicit, in a reverse-engineering style, a semantically well-defined specification and structuring of the logic underlying the business.

However, the task of ascertaining the nature and rationale of any given enterprise through the use of systematic software engineering methodologies has not so far been our main focus. Our work could perhaps best be compared with the development of expert system shells, whose main contribution was to establish workable representations and reasoning systems capable of accommodating the rationales of arbitrary application domains, after those rationales had been elicited and shaped by domain specialists and software engineers. In short, our framework offers logical formulations and reasoning mechanisms constituting a generic approach to business modeling aiming to provide a high-level, transparent and flexible means of expressing the diverse entities and constraints typically encountered in business.

3   Model Structure

3.1   Defining the Model

A business model can be comprehended as an abstract expression of the business logic of an enterprise. The business model design translates a strategy into a business model blueprint. Then it has to be financed through internal and external funding after finally being implemented into an actual business enterprise [5]. By analyzing the existing definitions of "business" and "business model" [1], [2] and [5], we give our summarized definition of "business model" as follows:

A company's business model is a conceptual model that consists of a set of functional elements and their inter-functional relationships, representing a company's logic of business and profit making.

Here, the logic of business and profit making refers to the mechanism by which a company offers value to customers and the structure of the firm and the partner networks for creating, marketing and delivering this value and relationship capital to generate profitable and sustainable revenue streams [5].

3.2   Model Decomposition

In principle, the business of an enterprise can be formulated as a purely declarative theory expressing various business entities, their properties, inter-relationships and controls [17]. Achievable goals of the enterprise can then be identified with logical consequences of the theory, and derivations of those goals can be interpreted as particular simulations of the enterprise. However, such a theory may turn out to be highly non-deterministic in practice. A more practical approach is to replace parts of that theory by business plans which, though still expressed declaratively, are inherently more deterministic to the extent that they embody some preconceived commitments to the control and interdependence of events.

We decompose our conceptualization of a business model into five sub-models in a general manner: the business plan model, the artifacts model, the organizational model, the financial model and the business rule model. We will describe these in more detail in sub-section 3.3. Concretely, they consist primarily of logical constraints, interpreted as business requirements. For each of the first four, its constraints refer only to the particular entities associated "naturally" with it. For instance, the organization model would not normally contain constraints referring to financial assets as well as to artifacts such as physical assets. By contrast, the business rule sub-model has a more global character, containing constraints that typically refer to entities within the other four, its purpose being to integrate the overall logic of the enterprise and cohere the other four at the same time . An example of a business rule is the constraint that "this product can be sold in this period only to customers in these territories owing to licensing restrictions". It is not difficult to understand that this sample rule contains the requirements at least from organization and artifacts sub models.

Figure 1 shows the five sub-models, indicating the central role of the business rule model in cohering the other four. Its effect is to induce dependence between these other four, since their constraints must be satisfiable not only locally to themselves but also globally to the holistic business architecture.

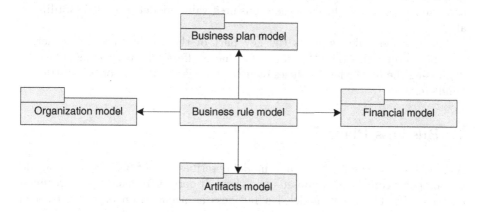

Fig. 1. A rule-centric business model framework

All these sub-models need to be further detailed and decomposed, as we shall outline and discuss in section 6.

3.3   Sub-model Features

The business plan model serves chiefly to constrain the temporal flow of actions performed as the business proceeds and, in order to anchor such constraints, it includes also a set of business plans each comprising a set of actions. Each action expresses some event that variously consults, manipulates or relates essential entities such as artifacts, finance or personnel, and is tagged by temporal parameters expressing the period over which the action is undertaken.

A plan is treated as a repeatable pattern of activity, so that multiple instances of it may arise as the business proceeds. We refer to each such instance as a process. Our representation of plans in this paper is mainly adapted from that used in [17], [18] and [19] and is described in section 4.

The organization model contains constraints expressing relationships between the participants engaged in the business. Participants include internal human resources and also external participants such as suppliers, customers and partners in other businesses.

The artifacts model constrains the non-human resources handled by the business. These resources may be physical in nature, such as materials and components used in manufacturing, or bureaucratic such as electronic records and communications. The constraints typically express, at the least, the attribute schemas of such entities but may also go further by specifying their concrete instances. The detailing of artifacts and their assumed constraints can be pursued using a variety of logical design frameworks. These include description logics [20] exploiting key relations such as "contains" - e.g. "this artifact contains these sub-artifacts" - and "is_ a" - e.g. "a house is an instance of a building".

The financial model constrains the financial aspects of the business, including its costs, profits and revenue streams. One existing method of formulating these constraints would be through the e-business value model proposed Gordijn et al [3].

The business rule model is the key part of the whole structure, cohering and interacting with the other four. It behaves effectively as their meta-theory, expressing the higher-level policies devised by senior managers or other strategy handlers.

4   Business Plans

As noted above, the business plan model describes sets of business actions and the temporal constraints imposed upon them. It derives from a simpler precursor described in [17] which modeled a business as a collection of *plans*, each of these being a logic program representing some set of actions together with some *control* imposed over that set. The output of the model, whether by inference or simulation, simply comprised the logical consequences of the union of the plans. The current framework is process-oriented, permitting each plan to spawn multiple processes.

Figure 2 shows one plan among many in a model we have recently built of a simple tool-hire company. This plan describes the logic of seeking in the company's records an existing, but as yet unprocessed, customer request for a tool of some specified type and, if finding such a request, duly processing it. Provided the request is acceptable, in that the tool type is known to the company's current inventory, the plan seeks a corresponding physical tool within its current stock. If such a tool is found then it is hired to this customer; otherwise some such tool must be already hired out to some previous customer, in which case the plan reserves it for the current customer. In either case the company incurs some administrative expense which the plan records.

Each "action" clause in a plan is a meta-declaration having an inner term, such as *hire(request, tool, hiring, t4)*, which is interpreted as an object-level predicate whose meaning is defined by some logic program held in a separate component of the model called the action knowledge base (AKB). The arguments of the predicate are treated in the implementation as ontological variables. Like

```
% plan "toolhire"

action(toolhire, 1, acquire(request, toolrequest, outcome1, t1)).
action(toolhire, 2, yes(outcome1), testacceptable).

action(testacceptable, 1, copy(inventory, t2)).
action(testacceptable,2,acceptable(request,inventory, tool), tryhire).

action(tryhire, 1, acquire(tool, any, outcome2, t3)).
action(tryhire, 2, yes(outcome2), dohire, doreserve).

action(dohire, 1, hire(request, tool, hiring, t4)).
action(dohire, 2, hireadmincost(expense, t5)).
action(dohire, 3, recordexpense).
action(dohire, 4, publish(hiring, nc, t6)).

action(doreserve, 1, reserve(request, reservation, t7)).
action(doreserve, 2, reserveadmincost(expense, t8)).
action(doreserve, 3, recordexpense).
action(doreserve, 4, publish(reservation, nc, t9)).

control(toolhire, seq).
control(tryhire, seq).
control(testacceptable, seq).
control(dohire, seq).
control(doreserve, seq).
```

Fig. 2. A tool-hire plan

action(tryhire, 2, yes(outcome2), dohire, doreserve), some "action" clauses are conditional in nature, diverting control to one or other constructs.

Figure 3 explains the relations implicated within plans, blocks and actions. Simply to put, these three objects have very similar structures in form except that if we use tree structures to express their relations, they are denoted by different types of nodes in a tree. A single plan node is denoted by the root node, a whole plan refers to the sub-tree originated from the corresponding root. The leaf nodes represent the atomic actions we mentioned above. The mid-nodes denote exactly what we call functional blocks. What worth mentioning is that the arc arrows across the sibling relations indicate the sequential order of the corresponding executions, while being concurrent without these arrows. We do not spell out here the entire grammar and surface syntax of the plan language. The essential point is that a plan establishes relations between variables as defined in the AKB.

From the operational viewpoint, execution of the model consists of spawning and running processes generated from the plans. Each process is an instance of a plan having its own binding environment for its variables. The temporal variables become bound to the times at which their associated actions are performed. Spawning and advancement of processes is controlled by constraints in the business rule model. In the present example, these constraints are such that processes are first executed to build up the company's stock of tools and to initialize such things as accounts and pricelists, after which customer request

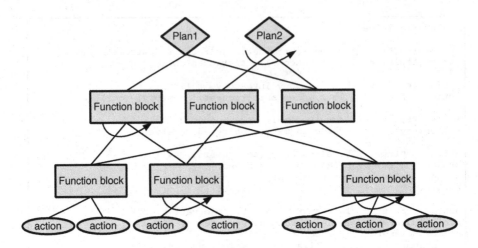

Fig. 3. A tree structure to indicate some plan semantics

processes then follow. As these get underway, other processes are spawned to deal with these requests in a concurrent but suitably-coordinated manner. The assets of the business are represented separately as structures incorporating preserved bindings of selected process variables. They function as one of the means by which processes interact and exchange resources, and they survive in the runtime environment after their originating processes have terminated. The model includes provisions for controlling the rights that processes have to access and modify existing assets.

5   Representing and Executing Business Constraints

An additional and significant control over processes' behavior and outcomes is the use of separately defined constraints over their ontological variables. These constraints are defined by, variously, Prolog programs or finite-domain constraint logic programs. They are an important means of expressing business requirements, constraining such aspects as the attributes of assets and the scheduling of process actions. They are operated on by a constraint evaluator running concurrently with the software that drives the spawning and progression of processes. The model supports a number of modes for coordinating constraint evaluation with process execution, the default mode being that which re-evaluates the constraints whenever a process action binds or further instantiates any ontological variable. However, the power of finite-domain CLP allows other modes, such as that in which constraints are evaluated (as far as they can be) in advance of process execution, for instance to restrict the possible time schedules. Figure 4 shows a simpler plan named *p1* for a manufacturing company, and will be used to illustrate the role of the constraints.

Here, *p1* starts by performing two tasks concurrently. Each one stocks and then ships a raw product. Raw product *a* is stocked by stockist *s1* from provider

```
action(p1, 1, stock).
action(p1, 2, make(m1, c, [a, b], (st5, et5))).
action(p1, 3, test (ts1, c, (st6, et6))).
action(p1, 4, dispatch(d1, ds1, c, t7)).
action(p1, 5, service).

action(stock, 1, stock_a).
action(stock, 2, stock_b).

action(stock_a, 1, stock(s1, pr1, a, t1)).
action(stock_a, 2, ship(sh1, a, (st2, et2))).

action(stock_b, 1, stock(s2, pr2, b, t3)).
action(stock_b, 2, ship(sh2, b, (st4, et4))).

action(service, 1, sell(sd1, c1, d, t8)).
action(service, 2, serve(sd2, c1, d, (st9, et9))).

control(p1, seq).
control(stock, con).
control(stock_a, seq).
control(stock_b, seq).
control(service, seq).
```

Fig. 4. A simple manufacturing plan

pr1 at *t1*, and then shipped by shipper *sh1* during the period extending from start-time *st2* to end-time *et2*. A similar treatment is applied to raw product *b*. After this, the raw products are made into *c* by manufacturer *m1* from *st5* to *et5*. Before *c* is dispatched by *d1* to *ds1* at time *t7*, it is tested by *ts1* from *st6* to *et6*. Concurrently with the above, other actions are executed which sell a product *d* from *sd1* to customer *c1* at *t8* and then provide a service by *sd2* for that product from *st9* to *et9*.

Any required constraint is identified by a logical goal of the form *rel(Args)* where *rel* is defined in a separate rulebase of business requirements. *Args* typically comprises ontological variables belonging to one or more processes. Depending on the definition for *rel*, the effect of the constraint on any one of these variables may be to restrict the variable's binding to a particular value or to restrict it to a particular finite domain of possible values. The ultimate intention of the business requirements is to ensure that its assets (which term we use in a very general sense) are generated, scheduled and managed in the manner desired. Not all constraints need to be declared explicitly. Basic temporal constraints are implicit in that we have, for instance, $start < end$ for any temporal pair $(start, end)$ in an action.

For the above plan, explicitly declared constraints and their associated definitions might appear in the requirements rulebase as shown in Figure 5.

The first two constraints require that the time spent in shipping *a* shall not exceed 3 time units and that in shipping *b* it shall not exceed 2, the possible time values being restricted to a given finite domain. They reside in the business plan model. The third constraint requires that the final product *d* be sold to customer *c1* only if *c1* is within a specified list *cl1*. This constraint refers to both an artifact

```
constraint (const1, max_duration(st2, et2, 3)).
constraint (const2, max_duration(st4, et4, 2)).
constraint (const3, to_customer(d, c1, c11)).
..
max_duration(S, E, D):- domain ([S, D, E], 1, 1000), E-S<D.
to_customer(P, C, C_List) :-
                            sell_to(P, C),
                            is_member(C, [cust1, cust2, cust4, …]).
is_member(X, [X|_]).
is_member(X, [_|T]):- is_member(X, T).
```

Fig. 5. Constraints relating to the manufacturing plan

and a human resource, and resides in the business rule model. From a technical viewpoint it does not matter how constraints are distributed among the various sub-models, which are just an aid to conceptualization. The implementation treats all the constraints as a global whole requiring to be satisfied.

In this example the constraints apply only to variables in processes spawned from plan $p1$. When constraints are required to apply across variables from different plans, disambiguation is achieved by variable annotation as in, for example, $constraint(const14, max\_duration(et2/p1, et6/p4, 5))$, which restricts the separation between the ending of some action in $p1$ and the ending of some action in another plan $p4$. At runtime the constraint is applied to the Cartesian product 1 X 4 where 1 and 4 contain all the binding environments for the currently-active processes spawned by $p1$ and $p4$ respectively. As indicated earlier, process execution and constraint evaluation need to be operated correlatively, but not necessarily synchronously.

6   Design and Implementation Considerations

The manufacturing plan $p1$ introduced in section 4 will have evolved from underlying analysis of the target business and some suitable design process. Here we shall simply outline some of the considerations involved.

We started by defining a two-dimensional structure for the model as described in Figure 6. In this structure each construct is conceptually shown as being in a specific layer and as being in a specific tree. A layer describes horizontal relationships between different sub-models, or sibling-relationships within the same sub-model. Entities which are announced in the same layer largely means that they are supposed to be discussed at the same conceptual level. A tree describes vertical relationships of constructs within a specific category. Commonly, tree structure is used to describe the affiliation dependency between different business concepts.

Figure 6.b shows three constructs named *artifacts* (in the artifacts sub-model), *role-holder* (in the organization sub-model) and *financial aspects* (in the financial sub-model). As explained in 6.a, the boxes in the graph denote the top-level

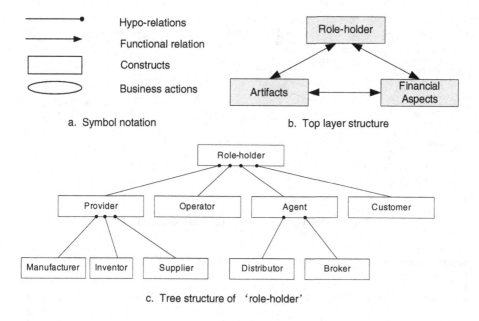

a. Symbol notation

b. Top layer structure

c. Tree structure of 'role-holder'

Fig. 6. The 2-D structure in the generic model

constructs, and the arrows denote "related_ to". At this stage, the attributes of each construct are also decided. For example, the attributes of *role-holder* could be represented by the predicate

$role - holder(Parent, Child, Entity\_type, Act\_on, Affected\_by, Constraints)$

Each abstract construct has a tree structure in which the hyper-relations indicate the sub-elements that the construct contains or the instances it has. The tree structure for *role-holder* might be as shown in figure 6.c. This tree reveals its second-layer constructs as *provider, operator, agent* and *customer* and its third layer constructs as *manufacturer, inventor, supplier, distributor* and *broker*.

We can apply an general business scenario in the second layer to develop aspects of how this business is presumed to operate, as depicted by Figure 7. First, a provider supplies an operator with the raw materials; then the operator uses the materials to produce its products. The operator sells its products to customers and provides services either by itself or by distributing it to an agent. Customers buy products and services from operator/ agent. During this business procedure, the provider, the operator and the agent can earn profit through their business activities.

At this stage constraints can be formulated to govern the business processes, as outlined in section 5. For instance, we might choose the constraint that "provider p distributes any product in domain [p1, p2, ...] to any agent in domain [a1, a2, ...]". Execution of an action such as distribute(p, product, agent) is achieved in the model by calling a definition of distribute. Whatever bindings that definition

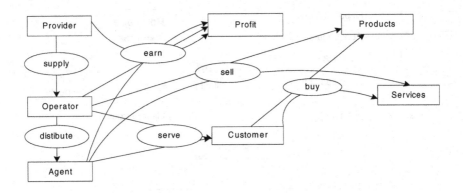

Fig. 7. Description of a simple business scenario

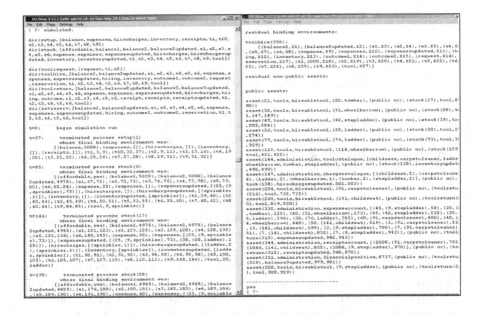

Fig. 8. An automatic business simulator: processes and assets output

yields for the variables, only those bindings that also satisfy this independently-asserted constraint will be accepted by the model.

We have developed an automatic simulator which can simulate a simple whole business procedure (rather that a single business transaction or process) by recording corresponding information possibly required by business analyzer or modeler. Originated from dealing with very simple business functions, our seventh version of simulator can do quite a lot jobs so far including system and user-defined constraints handling, parameters adjustment, full automation, the concurrency supporting of processes and so on. Figure 8 is a snapshot of the running business simulator. The left window displays the system-spawned business processes and their associated bindings recording how business runs, the right window outputs the business assets information exhibiting the business status at a specific time point. More functional extensions of the business simulator are underway.

Both the description of business plan and the simulation of our business model are implemented in SICStus Prolog 3.12.2 in Windows XP Professional on a Pentium IV 3.2 GHz CPU with 1.0 GB of RAM. SICStus is efficient and robust on this platform for handling large amounts of data and source code, besides supporting constraint processing with several powerful constraint solvers. The data we are processing are from both simple pseudo-business cases and a real business case from a tool hire company.

7   Discussions and Conclusions

We have illustrated a simple but expressive generic framework for representing and executing business models. It is generic in that it does not prescribe the particular entities, actions, variables or constraints to be used, but instead provides their general syntax, organization and means of implementation.

As practitioners in the AI and computational logic community, our work has so far focused on shaping the core logical content of our model and on producing viable execution schemes for it. Our aim has not been to produce a mature methodology for the general task of analyzing businesses and evolving robust designs for the models. Instead, we are working at a different level, seeking to establish a clear logical framework into which the results of such analysis and designs would be mapped. Our motivation in this is, in part, to achieve greater simplicity than that afforded by many other attempts to reduce business to logic, which typically resort to quite specialized logical languages lacking mature implementations. By committing to Prolog with constraint programming we benefit from a well-established formalism in which to implement our ideas. The other motivation, which flows from this simplicity, is to be able to devise schemes for systematically translating models in those other logic-based frameworks, e.g. BMO, into our own framework. The advantage in this is that the latter inherits the well-established and clean semantics for logic programs.

Every business plan of the kind we have described can be rewritten as a locally-stratified normal-clause program, as can the constraint definitions and the action knowledge base. Then, the meaning of any business model B formulated in our framework is a set of computable atomic consequences constituting the minimal stable model $\Delta(B)$ of all the normal-clause material to which B has been rewritten. This $\Delta(B)$ provides the semantics for any business model formulated in frameworks translatable to our own. It represents all the atomic outcomes obtainable by running an implementation of that business model. This paper does not afford sufficient scope for detailing this semantic scheme further, but we intend to develop and publish it presently.

References

1. Gill, H.: The Case for Enterprise Business Model Management. DM Review (2000)
2. Chen-Burger, Yun-Heh, Robertson, D.: Automating Business Modeling. Book Series of Advanced Information and Knowledge Processing. Springer, Heidelberg (2004)
3. Gordijn, J., Akkermans, H.: Value-based requirements engineering: exploring innovative e-commerce ideas. Requirements Engineering 8(2), 114–134 (2003)
4. Loucopoulos, P., Kavakli, V.: Enterprise Knowledge Management and Conceptual Modelling. In: Chen, P.P., Akoka, J., Kangassalu, H., Thalheim, B. (eds.) Conceptual Modeling. LNCS, vol. 1565, pp. 123–143. Springer, Heidelberg (1999)
5. Osterwalder, A.: The business Model Ontology- a proposition in a design science approach. PhD thesis. In: Institut d' Informatique et Organisation, University of Lausanne, Ecole des Hautes Etudes Commerciales HEC, Lausanne, Switzerland. 173 pages (2004)
6. Osterwalder, A., et al.: Clarifying Business Models: Origins, Present, and Future of the Concepts. Communications of AIS 15 (2005)
7. Afuah, A., Tucci, C.: Internet Business Models and Strategies. McGraw Hill, Boston (2003)
8. Alt, R., Zimmermann, H.: Introduction to Special Section - Business Models. Electronic Markets 11(1), 3–9 (2001)
9. Fox, M.S., Gruninger, M.: Enterprise Modeling. AI Magazine 19(3), 109–121 (1998)
10. Hamel, G.: Leading the revolution. Harvard Business School Press, Boston (2000)
11. Business Rules Team: Semantics of Business Vocabulary and Business Rules (SBVR). In: W3C Workshop on Rule Languages for Interoperability(2005)
12. Ross, D.T.: Structured Analysis: A Language for Communicating Ideas. IEEE Trans. Soft. Eng. 3(1) (January 1977)
13. Yourdon, E.: Modern Structured Analysis. Yourdon Press, Englewood Cliffs, New Jersey (1989)
14. Bjorner, D., Jones, C.B. (eds.): The Vienna Development Method: The Meta-Language. LNCS, vol. 61. Springer, Heidelberg (1978)
15. Scheer, A.W.: ARIS Business Process Modelling, 3rd edn. Springer, New York, Inc., New Jersey (2000)
16. Draheim, D., Weber, G.: Form-Oriented Analysis. Springer, Heidelberg (2004)
17. Hogger, C.J., Kriwaczek, F.R.: Constraint-guided enterprise portals. In: Proc. of 6th Int. Conf. on Enterprise Information Systems, pp. 411–418 (2004)
18. Hogger, C.J., Kriwaczek, F.R.: Extracting reusable knowledge from portal activity. WSEAS Transactions on Computers 4(2), 83–89 (2005)
19. Hogger, C.J., et al.: A flexible constraint-based portal architecture. In: Proc. of 16th Int. Conference on Computer Applications in Industry and Engineering [CAINE-2003], International Society for Computers and Their Applications, Las Vegas, Nevada, USA, November 11-13, pp. 1–6 (2003)
20. Baader, F., et al.: The Description Logic Handbook: Theory, Implementation, Applications. Cambridge University Press, Cambridge (2003)

Experimenting with the Expressive Power of an Enterprise Architecture Framework[*]

Francisca Losavio[1], Dinarle Ortega[2], María Pérez[3], and Martha González[4]

[1] Centro ISYS, LaTecS, Facultad de Ciencias, Universidad Central de Venezuela, Caracas
flosav@cantv.net
[2] Departamento de Computación, Universidad de Carabobo, Valencia, Venezuela
dortega@uc.edu.ve
[3] Departamento de Procesos y Sistemas, Universidad Simón Bolívar, Caracas, Venezuela
movalles@usb.ve
[4] Université de Versailles, Versailles, France
martha.gonzalez@prism.uvsq.fr

Abstract. Enterprise Architecture (EA) frameworks are used to model an enterprise organization; they attempt to fill the gap between the business model and the computer application model. In particular they can be used to model aspects of Enterprise Application Integration (EAI). Considering several known general frameworks discussed in this work, a new framework, called EAIF is presented, to unify different concepts and terminology concerning enterprise systems architecture and integration. EAIF, expressed in UML, extends the Brown's integration model for CASE technology, refining each abstraction level into the backward, forward and upward integration views of Sandoe's recent approach of enterprise integration. EAIF helps documenting and detecting inconsistencies in the definition of business processes, services adapted to these processes and mechanisms implementing these services. The main goal of this work is to evaluate the applicability of EAIF as an EA framework and experiment its expressive power with two enterprise systems as case studies.

Keywords: enterprise architecture, enterprise architecture integration, integration model, integration view.

1 Introduction

EAI (Enterprise Application Integration) is defined as the process of integrating Information Systems (IS) and/or existing applications. Enterprise Systems (ES) are proposed as integrated IS covering most of the enterprise business processes [25]. The term *framework* is defined as a set of *assumptions, concepts, values, and practices that constitutes a way of viewing reality* [22] and the term EAI refers to the plans,

[*] This research has been supperted by the Consejo de Desarrollo Científico y Humanístico (CDCH) of the Universidad Central de Venezuela, MODABAC project, No. 03-00-5281-2005 and by the Alma Mater OPSU program.

D. Draheim and G. Weber (Eds.): TEAA 2006, LNCS 4473, pp. 255–269, 2007.

methods and tools aimed at modernizing, consolidating, integrating and coordinating IS within an enterprise, where standards play an important role [16]. In this work, a framework considers a minimal set of architectural elements that characterize any enterprise application, hence involving adaptability or genericity aspects.

In order to fill the gap between the business processes and the computer application implementation, several frameworks modeling different aspects of business applications have been proposed: [6], [21], [22], [29], [34], [35], [36]. Most of these, called Enterprise Architecture (EA) frameworks, can also be considered for EAI modeling. EAIF (Enterprise Application Integration Framework), defined in this work, is a framework for enterprise architecture that can be used in particular to model the different integration views of EAI. The motivation was to provide guidelines to quickly design an initial architecture for the software system, derived from the business architecture (mostly expressed by business processes and rules); an instrument that can be used to define a process that has to be automated, the functionality (service) and the architectural reusable solution to accomplish the service with a certain degree of quality [14]. EAIF is independent of specific methodologies and technologies and it has been defined in previous works [13], [14], [15], [23], with the main idea of unifying terminology and characterizing the EA domain. It is an extension of the Brown's Conceptual Model of Integration (BCMI) for CASE technology [3]. The *process* and *services* levels of BCMI were extended with the three integration views proposed by Sandoe [25]: the *backward*, *forward* and *upward* views. However, the *mechanisms* level was found independent from these views [13]. EAIF also adds to BCMI a *people* level, concerning the human factors and it is specified in UML [20] as a conceptual class diagram, enriched with a detailed textual specification. It can be used as a tool to document and identify precisely central aspects of integration or other processes, functionalities and reusable architectural solutions (style, pattern, ...), at different levels of granularity if required.

The present work on one hand studies advantages and disadvantages of EAIF with respect to main EA frameworks, which are briefly presented and compared [15]. On the other hand, its main goal is to study the expressive power of EAIF using two enterprise systems. A set of features is defined to evaluate the expressiveness (adaptability or degree of genericity) of EAIF. These features can be easily reused to evaluate other frameworks related with the EA modeling. To increase legibility, the EAIF UML class diagram has been complemented with a complete textual specification to facilitate the instantiation process [23], but for lack of space it will not be presented here.

Two ES from different domains were selected as cases studies according to the underlying integration technology. The first one, SPIN, is a CORBA-based integrated environment for scientific computation. It provides backward and forward services for backward and forward processes, within an academic research organization [9]. The collaborative environment is considered a forward service and its administration represents the backward service. The second one is a J2EE-based Customer

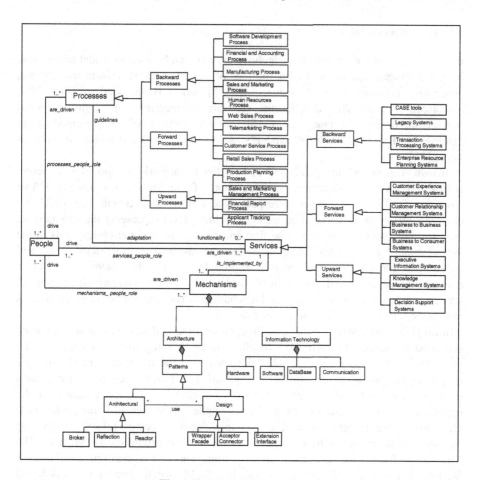

Fig. 1. EAIF UML Class Diagram

Relationship Management System, called J-énesis, for customer retention and loyalty. It follows an upward/forward process within a training organization and provides forward services [1].

This paper is structured as follows, besides this introduction: Section 2 presents a review and comparison of EA frameworks, including EAIF. Section 3 presents the two cases studies and their EAIF instantiation. Finally, Section 4 presents the features used in the evaluation, the results and the conclusion.

2 EA Frameworks

This section presents an overview of EAIF and a comparison with six EA frameworks. The common points and limitations are discussed.

2.1 EAIF Overview

EAIF is a framework for enterprise architecture that can be used to model integration. It provides organized and unified definitions of the EA elements related with people, processes, services and mechanisms [13], [15] and it is specified in UML [20]. Historically, in the 90's decade, the software engineering community proposed several approaches for integrated CASE environments. EAIF is presented as an extension of BCMI [3] with the Sandoe's backward, forward and upward integration views [25].

Brown proposes a conceptual model (three-tier framework) composed by different abstraction levels, to describe the integration of the tools constituting a CASE environment. The central level corresponds the *services* (functionality of the CASE environment) offered to the final users. The third level represents the *mechanisms* used to implement the services. The first and more abstract level corresponds to the *organizational process* providing guidelines (goals in terms of steps, tasks and constraints) for selecting the services offered by the CASE system. The relation between the services and the mechanisms levels is an *implementation* relation. A service can be implemented by several mechanisms. The relation between the process and services levels is an *adaptation* relation [13].

In order to synthesize the different integration trends, three integration views are proposed by Sandoe in 2001 [25], to allow software integration in an incremental way. The *Backward Integration* (BI) view refers to the integration of the internal organizational processes. The *Forward Integration* (FI) view refers to the integration of those organizational processes related to entities which are external to the organization, such as clients, partners and suppliers. The *Upward Integration* (UI) view means the integration of those organizational processes related to decision making. In our approach, these three views are used to extend the BCMI tiers. The Process and Services levels of the Brown's framework are refined into the Sandoe's Backward, Forward and Upward views. The BCMI mechanisms level was found independent from these views [13]. Figure 1 presents the UML class diagram of EAIF. In order to reduce complexity, only the class, relationship and role names are shown. Notice that the navigability of the associations is bidirectional and that only a limited range of very well known processes, services and mechanisms is shown, to abridge the presentation.

1. The *Processes Level*. In order to refine this level, the most commonly used organizational processes are described for each integration view. Notice that each business process has its own goals and constraints, and it depends directly from the specific functionality that is required by the computational system. *Business processes* are the activities, procedures, and rules required to complete the business tasks, independently of any information technology used to automate or support them.
2. The *Services level*. Some examples of BCMI services belonging to the three integration views are presented in Figure 1. They are represented by typical IS supporting the organizational processes.

3. The *Mechanisms Level*. According to Brown, two types of components are considered at this level: *architecture* and *technology*. Hence, a brief review on software architecture and information technology used for integration (see [14]) will be given before presenting the extension of the mechanisms level.

    a) The architectural styles considered for EAI are classical: *layers* to separate data, business logic and user interface; *repository* for data; *event-based* and *implicit invocation* for communications. This separation of concerns can be achieved through a *middleware* layer to get interoperability and flexibility to changes. In general, the architectural patterns and design patterns underlying EAI solutions are: Broker, Microkernel, Reflection, Wrapper Façade, Component Configurator, Interceptor, Extension Interface, Mediator and Publisher/Subscriber [4], [8], [26], [27].

    b) The *Information Technology* (IT) is defined as a set of resources available for managing changes and to provide support to people in the development of the activities related to an organization [12], [17], [25]. Some examples of resources considered at this level are: Hardware, Software, Database and Communication Technology.

2.2 Related Work

This section compares EAIF with other widely accepted enterprise architecture frameworks [15]. They are often used to model EAI when integrating a new application into an ES.

Zachman's framework. It allows a way of conceptualizing how the specific architecture that an organization might create can be integrated into a unique scheme [22], [36]. The overviews that allow managers to understand how everything within their organization fits together are generally called architectures. It is an analytical model or classification scheme that organizes descriptive representations in two dimensions. It does not describe an implementation process and it is independent of specific methodologies. The vertical dimension describes the perspectives of the stakeholders (Planner, Owner, Designer, Builder, Sub-contractor). The bottom row of the framework represents the "real world", the actual running elements of the organization. The horizontal dimension describes the relevant aspects or abstractions for each perspective. These abstractions (Data, Function, Network, People, Time and Motivation) are based on the widely asked questions "what", "how", "where", "who", "when", "why". To answer these questions artifacts are produced, linking perspectives and aspects. The abstraction levels of the framework are established by the stakeholder roles.

This framework is historically one of the first approaches to EA modeling [29], [35]. The strong point is that it can be used to analyze any business object or enterprise portion.

Whitten's framework. It is specific for the development of different types of IS and it specializes the Zachman's framework. Stakeholders and activities for software development play a central role [34]. It provides a unifying scheme describing the information system architecture, into which various people with different perspectives can organize and view the fundamental building blocks of information systems. The framework's perspectives are: business drivers, technology drivers, stakeholders, project and process management. These four perspectives contribute to the development of the information system. This framework emphasizes the classical activities of the information system development life cycle which can be customized.

Stojanovic's framework. It defines an integrated, effective, and flexible approach consolidated in a component-based framework providing comprehensive concepts, models, rules, methods and guidelines as a support for advanced enterprise systems development [29]. It provides a rich specification approach for defining not only behavioral and structural aspects of complex enterprise systems, but also significant human and organizational aspects. It offers an integrated view of the system through various viewpoints which evolve coordinately through time, using a consistent component-based way of thinking. It is based on the Reference Model of Open Distributed Processing (RM-ODP) [10] standardization efforts and on the Component-Based Development (CBD) approach [31]. The RM-ODP specification of a system consists of five viewpoints: Enterprise, Computational, Information, Engineering and Technology. Each viewpoint is an abstraction of the whole system focusing on a specific area of concern. The framework proposes three models to define various aspects of complex systems. These models are: Enterprise Architecture Model (related to the enterprise viewpoint), System Architecture Model (related to the computational and information viewpoints) and Distribution Architecture Model (related to the engineering viewpoint). The models are component-oriented, considering the component independent from the technology, as the integration point of business and system concerns. The aim is to provide a complete system specification, from concept to deployment, in a rigorous and consistent way. Such an integrated framework will ensure that the capabilities of distributed components are appropriately positioned in the context of the organizational structures, policies, business processes and roles. This framework, coupled with accompanying tools, should facilitate specification and building of enterprise systems that can withstand various technology and business changes, favoring flexibility.

Cummins' framework. It depicts the enterprise integration process from a management viewpoint in four different domains: users, business process, applications and infrastructure [6]. It focuses on the notion of Enterprise Integration Architecture (EIA) to establish a set of characteristics that the enterprise must posses to perform software integration. The goal of EIA is to manage the business process with workflow management facilities so that the processes are visible and manageable.

TOGAF framework. The Open Group Architectural Framework (TOGAF) is a generic framework to build different IT architectures frameworks, for example Zachman's framework can be expressed using TOGAF [21]. It provides a comprehensive approach to the design, planning, implementation, and governance of the enterprise information architecture.TOGAF considers four kinds of architectures as subsets of the Enterprise Architecture: Business, Data, Application and Technology. The combination of Data and Application architectures is also referred as the Information System Architecture. It provides a highly detailed Architecture Development Method (ADM), centered on requirements, that is tailored to the organization's needs and is then employed to manage the execution of architecture planning activities. This method is independent from tools and technologies. The TOGAF ADM graphic is dynamic; a set of circles representing the progression through the phases of the ADM and the architecture models is used and created during the phases of the enterprise architecture development (see figure 6).

Comparison of the frameworks
Common points:

- They model the whole enterprise architecture considering also software integration aspects
- Abstraction levels: people or human aspects, processes, services or information systems supporting the processes, mechanisms (architecture and technology) implementing the services
- Independent from a specific software development process. Notice that Whitten's framework considers classical methods for information systems development
- Independent from the technology
- Lack of methods to build the enterprise architecture. In general all the frameworks, excepting TOGAF, are concentrated on the artifacts and not on the description of the process to produce these artifacts.

The main limitation found was the lack of standard notation in the specification of the frameworks, even if the use of standards is suggested now, within an MDA approach [7], [19]. In response to this lack of standards, EAIF is specified in the UML notation, ensuring flexibility to changes and extensions. Another point in favor of EAIF is the reusability issue of the architectural patterns involved in the architectural mechanism specification, which can be very fine grained, if required for example to define explicitly an precisely the architectural patterns involved. This abstraction level, which is very important to model integration, is not considered in details in the other frameworks. Finally EAIF includes the backward, upward and forward integration views to enrich the framework semantics.

3   Case Studies: Description and EAIF Instantiation

In this section two case studies are described. They were developed according to different integration mechanisms, CORBA and J2EE, respectively.

3.1   CORBA Compliant Scientific Programming System Case Study

SPIN (*Scientific Programming on the InterNet*), is a scalable, integrated and interactive set of tools for scientific computations on distributed and heterogeneous environments [9], a collaborative environment allowing the access to remote resources, such as: computing resources (supercomputers, computer clusters, workstations and metacomputers), data resources (databases, directories and data services), computing services and high-performance libraries. The goal of SPIN is to provide the following advantages: platform independence, flexible parameterization, incremental capacity growth, portability and interoperability by the use of the Java [30], and CORBA technologies [18], preservation of technology investments and web integration. The potential users of a tool such as SPIN are a scientist's community which needs to implement numerical models using effective methods facilitating the data processing, after the study (modeling and discretization) of the scientific problem.

Processes. SPIN can be used by the scientists requiring the execution of numerical codes. In this case the SPIN's user interface allows: introducing the parameters required by the code, executing the code and receiving results (forward processes). SPIN allows also building new applications from predefined components ("building blocks"); the construction of new software is seen as part of the activities of the development process (backward process). These components are then shared via the Internet (forward process). SPIN's tools allow also maintenance activities (backward process).

Services. The following backward services are identified: directory facilities, servers' configuration information, resource management, tasks edition, execution services, data distribution facilities, matrix manipulation services and wrapping services to use the legacy systems.

Architecture. It follows a layers style. The architecture considers two main features: the interaction with the users, which has been defined in terms of interactive agents, according to the PAC or Mediator-based architecture [5], and the distribution of the software components on a heterogeneous environment following the CORBA specification. The three-tier architecture is composed by the Client side to manage the interaction aspects between the users and the computing services, the Middleware to manage the access to remote resources, the Server side containing the high-performance computing resources. The main architectural patterns and design patterns used were: facade, strategy, adapter, broker [4], [8], [26].

Information Technology. The *Java^{TM}* language and *Java Swing^{TM}* components were used for communication with the user interface and the middleware. The C++ language was used for the development of the wrappers objects and the ORBacus, an ORB compliant to the CORBA specification version 2.3.1.

EAIF Instantiation with SPIN. Notice that the specification is a detailed view of the UML class diagram (see figure 1), to facilitate the instantiation process. We have presented it in a textual form to abridge the presentation. Some of the instantiated classes can be seen in figure 2, showing a SPIN backward process. It is important to point out that all the activities of the processes performed by the SPIN's users can be specified using EAIF, even if some of these are not supported or partially supported by explicit services (for example the activities part of a forward process, not shown here to abridge the presentation "*test and code optimization*", related to the *structural_unit_name*="*add a new function to the library*" and "*read problem statement*", "*build the mathematical model*", both related to the *structural_unit_name*="*elicitate problem's requirements*"). However, since these activities are considered preconditions to other services, the EAIF application is useful to recommend their implementation as an extension of the SPIN services.

In what follows, the J2EE case study is presented.

SPIN_backward_process class **extends** *Software Development Process*
process_model_ name = "library maintenance"
process_model: Process_model_elements02
process_strategy = "iterative"

Process_model_elements02 class **instantiates** *Process_model_elements*
structural_unit_of_process_model: Array of
structural_unit_of_process_model02[1]="step"
table_of_process_model_elements: Array_of_structural_unit
where
table_of_process_model_elements [1] =
       (structural_unit_name = "add a new function to the library"
       structural_unit_activity: Array [1..2] of Activity **where**
               structural_unit_activity [1] = ("add function description",...)
               structural_unit_activity [2] = ("update library",...)
       structural_unit_input: Array [1..2] of Input **where**
               structural_unit_input [1] = ("new function code", "description")
               structural_unit_input [2] = ("new function code", "catalog")
       structural_unit_produc t= Array [1..2] of Product **where**
               structural_unit_product [1] = ("optimized function code
                                   description")
               structural_unit_product [2] = ("updated library")
       structural_unit_resource: Array [1..2] of Resource **where**
               structural_unit_ resource [1] = ("hardware", "software")
               structural_unit_ resource [2] = ("hardware", "updating tools")
       structural_participant: SPIN_people02)

SPIN_people02 class **instantiates** *People*
role = "System Administrator"
goals = "Maintenance activities"

Fig. 2. Instantiation of the EAIF *Software Development Process* class

3.2   CRM Case Study with J2EE

The *Customer Relationship Management* (CRM) approach is a widely used business strategy and it is still evolving. It is centered on the customer and its relation with the organization [33]. CRM addresses all the customer touch points, such as face-to-face, Internet, or phone [25]. It integrates sales, marketing and service strategies. It helps to establish collaborative relationships with customers on a long-term basis, using information technology as such as, databases, data warehouses, and data mining.

In general, CRM solutions consider three phases [32]: - Acquisition: the organization acquires new customers. The organization competes to provide better product/service according to the customer needs. - Enhancement: it increases sales per customer. It gives good supplies at low cost. It has built-in pricing flexibility. - Retention and Loyalty: it requires customer knowledge to build service adaptability and use incentives to retain customers, such as the creation of new products. The ability to retain customers is a major determining factor.

J-énesis is a CRM application for the *customer retention and loyalty phase*. It offers through Internet, registration services for different software courses; products and services offered consider customer needs (profiles) [1]. Java 2 Platform Enterprise Edition (J2EE) [31] is used as the integration mechanism.

Processes - marketing (provide data on software courses, customers' profiles and customer retention and loyalty strategies for marketing decision making; it is considered an upward process), - customer service (provide customer satisfaction using the information about products, services and customers' profile; it is a forward process), - facilities to gain customer knowledge to build service adaptability, deliver new products that meet current customers´ needs and create and transmit incentives to retain customers; it is also a forward process.

Services
- Collect, recall and update customer profile: personal information, preferences, capabilities, and markets and business environment data. These operations must be efficient, accurate and attractively presented to the user.
- Collect, recall and update software courses: information on software courses and services according to the customer's profile. These operations must be efficient, *reliable* and attractive.
- Collect, recall and update customer retention strategies: to deal with encouragement strategies to maintain customer loyalty. These operations must be efficient, reliable and attractively presented to the user.
- Historic: all transactions are stored in databases for further analysis purposes. It favors changeability.
- Subscribe/unsubscribe software courses: this service allows customer to subscribe/unsubscribe software courses according to the customer's requirements. It favors changeability.

Note that all the above are forward services. J-énesis does not support a call center service. The users of J-énesis are: customer, customer service analyst and marketing analyst.

Architecture. According to a layers style, it is a three-tier architecture: user interface, data and business logic. Some of the design patterns used are *Persistent Data*

Manager and *Observer* [24]. From the above requirements, the quality properties that must be supported by the overall architecture are: changeability, efficiency, reliability for data and business logic components; attractiveness is required for the user interface component.

Information Technology. The J2EE platform [31], the java web server is **Tomcat 4.0.x [2]**, the following J2EE 1.3 APIs were used: JDBC 2.0 (Java Data Base Connectivity) for database connectivity between the Java and MySQL; Java Servlets 2.3 extends the functionality of a Web server, generating dynamic content (HTML and XML) with Java Server Pages (JSP)1.2 and JavaMail 1.2 and interacting with web clients using Hypertext Transfer Protocol (HTTP), the Simple Object Access Protocol (SOAP) as protocol for communication between applications. SOAP is platform independent, language independent, based on XML, the Java^{TM} language to develop the application. The EAIF instantiation with J-énesis for the *Marketing Management Process* is presented in figure 3.

EAIF instantiation with the J-énesis case study. Notice that for this application, the subclass *Marketing Management Process* of class *Sales and Marketing Management Process* is instantiated as an upward process. The EAIF instantiation allows specify the complete process performed by a training organization, even if some of the processes are not supported by explicit J-énesis services, since an automatic process is not provided by J-énesis, for example, the process *"Marketing_upward_process"*. However, since this process is required by the business activity in the organization, the EAIF process instantiation can be used to recommend the implementation of additional support services. In general, we observed that the information related to the application must be available and domain experts' support is highly recommended. The goal is to avoid the modeling of unreal situations.

4   EAIF Evaluation

After having experimented on the applicability of EAIF in section 3, we proceed to state some key aspects that will outline our results. These aspects or features are selected using a feature analysis technique [11] whose main activities are: Select the framework to evaluate, decide the required features of the item being evaluated, agree on a scoring system that can be applied to all the features, analyze and interpret the results, present the results.

4.1   Features for the EAIF Evaluation

The framework to be evaluated is EAIF (see Section 2). The required features are defined in Table 2. Notice that the set of features defined for this evaluation can be easily reused to evaluate other frameworks related with the enterprise integration.

Analysis of the results. With respect to the *Precise* and *Repeatable* features, they are considered independent of the case study. EAIF provides *low support* (2) for the *Precise* feature because the EAIF semantics could be improved using a formal specification language. At present, EAIF has no automatic formal tools support; in consequence it provides *low support* (2) for the *Repeatable* feature. For *Completeness* and *Readability*, the scores were the same for both applications. In practice, even if

Marketing_upward_process class extends Marketing Management Process
process_model_name = "Marketing model"
process_goal = "this process manages the information related with software courses, customer profile and customer retention and loyalty strategies"
process_model: Process_model_elements01
process_strategy = "provide response and effective assistance to clients according to retention strategies and maintain information related with customers and courses"
Process_model_elements01 class **instantiates** *Process_model_elements*
structural_unit_of_process_model: Array of
structural_unit_of_process_model01[1]= "step"
table_of_process_model_elements: Array_of_structural_unit **where**
table_of_process_model_elements [1] =

> *(structural_unit_name = "analyze customer and software courses information for customer service analyst"*
> *structural_unit_activity: Array [1..3] of Activity* **where**
>> *structural_unit_activity [1] = ("study on customers data",...*
>> *... ... ...*
> *structural_unit_input: Array [1..3] of Input* **where**
>> *structural_unit_input [1] = ("data of customers")*
>> *... ... ...*
> *structural_unit_produc t= Array [1..3] of Product* **where**
>> *structural_unit_product [1] = ("data of customers updated")*
>> *... ... ...*
> *structural_unit_resource: Array [1..3] of Resource* **where**
>> *structural_unit_ resource [1] = ("decision tool")*
>> *... ... ...*
> *structural_participant: J-énesis_process_people01)*

table_of_process_model_elements [2] =
> *(structural_unit_name = "establish customer retention strategies for customer service analyst"*
> *structural_unit_activity: Array [1..5] of Activity* **where**
>> *structural_unit_activity [1] = ("identify customers' needs",...)*
>> *... ... ...*
> *structural_unit_input: Array [1..5] of Input* **where**
>> *structural_unit_input [1] = ("information of customer needs", "selection criteria")*
>> *... ... ...*
> *structural_unit_product= Array [1..5] of Product* **where**
>> *structural_unit_product [1] = ("document with list of customer's needs")*
>> *... ... ...*
> *structural_unit_resource: Array [1..5] of Resource* **where**

Fig. 3. Instantiation of the EAIF *Marketing Management Process* class, for J-énesis

Table 2. Feature list

Features	Definition
Extensibility	New elements can be added by specialization or by aggregation/composition at the lowest level of the framework
Completeness	All the elements of the application are represented by the framework
Readability	It has a consistent and clear structure and documentation to ease its usage
Precision	It has a non ambiguous semantic definition for each element of the framework
Repeatability	Each activity of the instantiation process can be reproduced to obtain similar results

The scale used to express the degree of adaptation of EAIF is presented in Table 3.

Table 3. Score applied for the features

Scale point	Definition of scale point
1	No support. Fails to recognize it. The feature is not supported by EAIF
2	Low support. The feature is supported indirectly by EAIF
3	Full support. The feature appears explicitly in the feature list of the EAIF. All the aspects of the feature are covered
0	The feature could not be evaluated

lacking of automated tools is a drawback, we found that the instantiation of the framework was quite easy with the guidelines provided by the textual specification, providing *full* support for *readability*. Nevertheless, it is clear that two case studies are not enough for completeness, and that further experimentation should be performed. Finally, *extensibility* could not be checked because there was no need to add new features to EAIF, all the elements could be modeled easily. However, since it is expressed in UML, extensions can be easily incorporated.

5 Conclusion

EAIF is an EAI framework, specified in UML, complemented with a textual specification and guidelines to facilitate its applicability. This work is the result of a doctoral project on EAI. Two running applications, derived from previous research projects, have been considered to experiment the applicability of this framework. In this work the instantiation of EAIF with backward/forward (SPIN) and upward/forward (J-ENESIS) integration applications as case studies is presented: a CORBA-based integrated environment for numerical computations and a J2EE-based CRM system for customer retention and loyalty, respectively. According to the evaluation with the case studies, EAIF is *Complete* and *Readable*; however the *Extensibility* issue could not be proved because no new elements were added, but the use of UML will facilitate this issue. For the features *Precise* and *Repeatable* which are independent from the case study, EAIF provided little support since formal semantics and automation are missing. However, the class specification could be easily followed as a guideline. It is obvious that the EAIF maturity will improve as more case studies will be considered. Finally, the set of features defined for this evaluation can be easily reused to evaluate other frameworks related with the enterprise architecture and integration. A strong point of experimenting with EAIF has been to point out some weaknesses of the applications studied: processes not supported by services, services without well defined processes. These aspects reflect faults in the early phases of software design. In this sense, EAIF is a useful tool to detect and document such faults, even if its purpose is not the organization itself.

Future work will focus on the formalization of the specification, the development of supporting tools and the specification of EAIF as a Platform Independent Model (PIM), according to a Model Driven Architecture (MDA) approach.

References

1. Acuña, G., Rodríguez, R.: Desarrollo de un Framework para Soluciones CRM en la Fase de Fidelización del Cliente. License Thesis, Universidad de Carabobo, Venezuela (2003)
2. APACHE, Apache Software Foundation, The Jakarta Project, Copyright 1999-2002 (2002), http://jakarta.apache.org/tomcat/tomcat-4.0-doc/index.html
3. Brown, A., Carnery, D., Morris, E., Smith, D., Zarrella, P.: Principles of Case Tool Integration, Software Engineering Institute. Oxford University Press, Oxford (1994)
4. Buschmann, F., Meunier, R., Rohnert, H., Peter, S., Michael, S.: A System of Patterns. John Wiley & Sons Ltd., New York (1996)
5. Coutaz, J.: Formal Methods in Human-Computer Interaction. In: Software Architecture Modelling: Bridging Two Worlds Using Ergonomics and Software Properties. Formal Approaches to Computing Information Technology, ch. 3, pp. 49–73. Springer, Heidelberg (1998)
6. Cummins, F.: Enterprise Integration. Wiley Computer Publishing, Chichester (2002)
7. Frankel, D., Harmon, P., Mukerji, J., Odell, J., Owen, M., Rivitt, P., Rosen, M., Soley, R.: The Zachman Framework and the OMG's Model Driven Architecture, white paper, Business Process Trends (2003)
8. Gamma, E., Helm, R., Johnson, R., Vlissides, J.: Design Patterns. Elements of Reusable Object-Oriented Software. Addison-Wesley, Reading, Massachusetts (1995)
9. González, M.: Application de Techniques Orientées-Objet pour le Calcul Réparti de Haute Performance. PhD Thesis, Université Pierre et Marie Curie (Paris VI), Paris – France (September 2002)
10. ISO/IEC 10746-1, International Standard Organization, Information Technology, Basic Reference Model of Open Distributed Processing (1998)
11. Kitchenham, B., Linkman, S., Law, D.: DESMET: A method for Evaluating Software Engineering Methods and Tools, Technical Report (TR96:09), Department of Computer Science, Keele University, pp. 1–67 (1996) [ISSN 13 53-7776]
12. Laudon, K., Laudon, J.: Management Information Systems, 8th edn. Prentice Hall, Englewood Cliffs (2004)
13. Losavio, F., Ortega, D., Pérez, M.: Modeling EAI. In: Proceedings of the XXII International Conference of the Chilean Computer Science Society (SCCC 2002), pp. 195–203. IEEE Computer Society Press, Copiapo, Atacama, Chile (2002)

14. Losavio, F., Ortega, D., Pérez, M.: Towards a Standard EAI Quality Terminology. In: XXIII International Conference of the Chilean Computer Science Society (SCCC 2003), pp. 119–129. IEEE Computer Society Press, Chillán, BÍO-BÍO, Chile (2003)
15. Losavio, F., Ortega, D., Pérez, M.: Comparison of EAI Frameworks. Journal Object of Technology 4(4), 93–114 (2005), http://www.jot.fm/issues/issue,www.jot.fm
16. McKeen, J., Smith, H.: New Developments in Practice II: Enterprise Application Integration. Communications of the Association for Information Systems 8, 451–466 (2002)
17. O'Brien, J.: Management Information Systems, 6th edn. McGraw-Hill, New York (2004)
18. OMG, Object Management Group Inc.: The Common Object Request Broker Architecture and Specification (1998), ftp://ftp.omg.org/pub/docs/formal/98-02-01.ps.gz
19. OMG, Object Management Group Inc.: 2001. MDA® Specifications (2001) Copyright 1997-2004, http://www.omg.org/mda/specs.htm
20. OMG, Object Management Group Inc.: Unified Modeling Language (UML), version 1.5 (2003) http://www.omg.org/cgi-bin/doc?formal/03-03-01
21. Open Group, TOGAF as an Enterprise Architecture Framework (2003) http://www.opengroup.org/architecture/togaf8-doc/arch/p1/enterprise.htm
22. O'Rourke, C., Fishman, N., Selkow, W.: Enterprise Architecture Using the Zachman Framework. Thomson Course Technology (2003)
23. Ortega, D.: Integración de aplicaciones empresariales, Doctoral Thesis, Universidad Central de Venezuela, Caracas (2006)
24. Rogers, G.: Framework-Based Software Development in C++. Prentice-Hall, Englewood Cliffs (1997)
25. Sandoe, K., Corbitt, G., Boykin, R.: Enterprise Integration, California State University, Chico. John Wiley & Sons, Inc, Chichester (2001)
26. Schmidt, D., Stal, M., Rhonert, H., Buschmann, F.: Pattern-Oriented Software Architecture, vol. 2. John Wiley & Sons, Ltd. Chichester (2001)
27. Shaw, M., Garlan, D.: Software Architecture, Perspectives on an Emerging Discipline. Prentice Hall, Upper Saddle River, New Jersey (1996)
28. Sowa, J.F., Zachman, J.A.: Extending and Formalizing the Framework for Information Systems Architecture. IBM Systems Journal 31(3), 276–291 (1992)
29. Stojanovic, Z., Dahanayake, A.: Components and Viewpoints as Integrated Separations of Concerns in System Designing. In: Workshop on Aspect-Oriented Design (in conjunction with the 1st International Conference on AOSD), Enschede (2002)
30. SUN, Sun Microsystems: IDL/Java Language Mapping. Technical Report orbos/97-02-01 (1997)
31. Szyperski, C.: Component Software. Beyond Object-Oriented Programming, 2nd edn. Addison Wesley, Reading (2002)
32. Tiwana, A.: The Essential Guide to Knowledge Management. Prentice Hall, Englewood Cliffs (2001)
33. Turban, E., Rainer, R., Potter, R.: Introduction to Information Technology, 3rd edn. John Wiley & Sons, Inc., Chichester (2005)
34. Whitten, J., Bentley, L., Dittman, K.: Systems Analysis and Design Methods, 6th edn. McGraw-Hill Irwin, New York (2004)
35. Zachman, J.A.: A Framework for Information Systems Architecture. IBM Systems Journal 26(3) (1987) IBM Publication G321-5298
36. Zachman, J.A.: This document is a response to the OMG BRWG RFI Version # 1b Copyright, 2003. Excerpted from The Zachman Framework for Enterprise Architecture: A Primer for Enterprise Engineering and Manufacturing (2003), http://www.zachmaninternational.com

AP1: A Platform for Model-Based Software Engineering*

Christof Lutteroth

Department of Computer Science
The University of Auckland
38 Princes Street, Auckland 1020, New Zealand
lutteroth@cs.auckland.ac.nz

Abstract. This paper gives an overview of the AP1 system, which is a platform for model-based CASE tools. AP1 is a set of libraries and tools that support different activities in the software development process, with a focus on the development of enterprise applications. It addresses some key problems of software development, like the storage and management of artefacts, their creation and modification, and the generation of artefacts from other artefacts. AP1 is based on several novel concepts, e.g. an RDB-based event-driven architecture, robust user interfaces and a generator model that offers a particularly high degree of type-safety. Due to an open architecture AP1 makes it easy to create new CASE-tools that immediately take advantage of its functionality.

1 Introduction

Many studies have shown that CASE tools have the potential to improve the efficiency and quality outcome of large software projects. It is therefore not surprising that a lot of work has been done in this field during the last three decades. However, adoption of CASE tools in industry has been slow, and the desired positive effects have not always been achieved [1]. There are many CASE tools, and most of them are not being used in industry. This is because companies trying to adopt CASE technology have to overcome different hurdles, like a steep learning curve due to technological complexity, and the need to integrate the new technology with existing resources [2]. CASE systems are enterprise applications and therefore face the same challenges as other enterprise applications, one of them being integration. Over the years, the problem of integration of different CASE tools has been addressed by many standards. But most of them – even big, government supported initiatives like the Portable Common Tool Environment (PCTE) [3] – have failed to gain widespread acceptance. This shows that integration of CASE technology is a complex problem that cannot be solved just by standardization. Despite the huge amount of work that has already been done, it is an area of ongoing research, and in need of new ideas and solutions.

---

* This work has been funded by AARN Innovation Ltd and the Foundation for Research, Science and Technology of New Zealand under grant number AARN0501.

D. Draheim and G. Weber (Eds.): TEAA 2006, LNCS 4473, pp. 270–284, 2007.

In this paper we present the AP1 system, which is a platform for model-based CASE tools. It offers the different essential parts that most CASE-tools need and thereby integrates the tools that make use of it. It is not the only system that aims to achieve this goal; there are quite a lot of others, e.g. [3]. But the architecture of AP1, which supports integration on different levels and using different approaches, is novel and mitigates many of the typical CASE issues.

Before we look into the internals of the AP1 system, we want to discuss some of the concepts and terms used in this paper in Sect. 2, and describe some of the issues motivating AP1 in Sect. 3. Then we will give a general overview of AP1's architecture in Sect. 4. In the following sections, we will look at its different parts in more detail: at the repository in Sect. 5, and at the generic editor in Sect. 6. The paper concludes with Sect. 7.

2 Terminology

We want to clarify certain terms and concepts which are relevant for this paper but are sometimes unclear or used differently. When talking about *model-based software engineering*, we mean that software engineering is done on a level of abstraction that is adequate for specifying the functionality of a system without taking into account implementation details. We concentrate on information relating to the requirements of a system, and, if necessary, also to its design. For example, we might have to specify what data should be stored in a system, but not how the system utilizes hardware resources in order to do so.

Model information can exist in different *representations*. For example, this information could be represented as text, as in in 4GLs, as graphics, as in in diagrams, or in other less human readable forms, e.g. binary code. Dealing with model information does not enforce a particular representation, however, some kinds of representations are more suitable for certain purposes than others.

When using models, we have to distinguish different levels of structural information. A model is basically a data type that allows us to specify data which adheres to certain constraints. This data, however, can in turn serve as another model description for other data. In this paper we want to use only three levels of structural information: the *metamodel*, which describes how types can be specified, *models* which are types defined by the metamodel, and *model instances*, which are data following the constraints of a particular model. Sometimes all three levels are referred to as models, and metamodels end up being called "metametamodels", which inevitably leads to meta-confusion.

Integration of models has different aspects: a syntactic and a semantic one. *Syntactic integration* means that we end up using the same metamodel for models, so that the structure of the models is defined in the same terms. This means that we can access the models in the same manner. The structure of the models can, however, be different. *Sematic integration* means the we understand not only the structure of the models but also their meaning, and that this understanding is manifested in the system. Semantic integration can be expressed, for example, in mapping information relating the models to each other or to a common "supermodel", or operations that can sensibly make use of more than one of the models. Syntactic integration is usually much easier to achieve.

3   Motivation

AP1 is motivated by some important requirements of CASE. In this section we want to outline what these requirements are and why they are so important. In the following sections we will describe in more detail how these requirements are targeted in AP1.

One of the main obstacles in CASE adoption is the complexity of CASE systems. This has been shown by several studies, e.g. [4,5], and is known to be a major cost factor when CASE technology is introduced in an industrial environment [2]. The costs of training can double the costs initially spent on CASE technology, and the usually steep learning curve can lead to an initial loss of efficiency after CASE adoption. CASE tools were frequently abandoned before a gain in efficiency could manifest. Other research points out that aspects of usability are a very important factor for the actual CASE usage [6], and that there is actually a discrepancy between the functionality developers want and the one implemented in tools [7], leaving the users dissatisfied. Therefore, one of the main goals of AP1 is to reduce complexity as much as possible, and to provide useful functionality without neglecting usability.

Another very important requirement for a CASE tool is the ability to integrate with other tools [8]. Integration and customization of CASE technology to the needs of a company can be another significant cost factor because it frequently requires the help of external consultants [2]. In order to produce the desired outcome, the tools in a software project often have to be combined, with outputs of tools forming the input of other tools. Together these tools form a tool chain. Heterogeneity of tools represents a major obstacle to this. Furthermore, it is not unusual that tools prescribe a certain software development process, which has to be adopted in order to benefit from its use [1]. This means that the decision to adopt a particular CASE technology can have a strong impact on the whole software development process. This problem can be mitigated if CASE technology offers a high degree of customizability, so that tools can be adapted to fit the desired process, and not the other way around. Unfortunately, support for integration and customizability rather add to the complexity of a system, so that these requirements are antagonistic to the aim of reducing complexity. We designed AP1's architecture so that it emphasizes support for integration and customizability, and try to solve the dilemma between complexity and lack of customizability with new, simplified user interface concepts.

4   Architectural Overview

Figure 1 gives an overview of the architecture of the AP1 system. The whole system is based on a *repository*, which is implemented on a RDBMS. The repository contains the metamodel, models and model instances, i.e. it stores all the

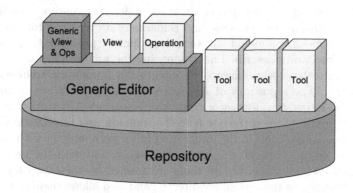

Fig. 1. Architectural overview of the AP1 system. The dark shapes represent components that are part of AP1, the light shapes components that can be built on top of it.

data used during the software development process. Besides the artefacts which are directly relevant for software development, it also stores information about changes in the data, access control information and AP1's configuration. The repository manages and protects the artefacts of software projects, and offers a notification mechanism that informs CASE tools about data changes. CASE tools can be implemented on top of the repository, taking advantage of its data management capabilities. This is reasonable because all CASE tools, no matter how specialized their functionality, need to manage their input and their output. CASE tools can access the repository either directly through the interface of the RDBMS, or through an object-oriented API. The repository supports *data and control integration.*

On top of the repository, AP1 provides a *generic editor*, which is an application for editing, analysis and processing of artefacts. The generic editor makes use of the repository's notification mechanism and provides generic views and basic operations for visualization and modification of models and model instances. The generic editor has an open architecture, which can be extended by plug-ins and configured through the repository. Plug-ins can implement new views, new operations and new data transformations. This makes it is possible to efficiently implement CASE functionality as plug-ins with a high degree of reuse. The generic editor supports *presentation integration.*

Besides data management, modification and visualization, AP1 supports data transformation by providing its own model of generators. The model is stored in the repository and the operations necessary for generation are part of the generic editor. Transformation and generation of artefacts is a very common function of CASE technology, and plays an important role in the integration of different models. Integration can be achieved by generating an instance of one model from an instance of another, with the domain knowledge about how the two models are related being programmed into the generator. Consequently, the generator model supports *semantic data integration.* This model is out of the scope of this paper; information about its underlying concepts can be found in [9]. Having means for syntactic and semantic data and control integration, AP1 provides means to model software development processes, e.g. along the lines of the procedures described in [10], paving the way for *process integration*.

AP1's architecture is similar to the integration framework architecture described in [11]. The repository of AP1 corresponds to the object management system in the integration framework, and the repository API to the integration agent. The generic editor corresponds to the common user interface component. The difference is that tools in the integration framework interact with the object management system through the integration agent, and with the user through the common user interface; i.e. all tools are framed by these two layers. AP1 allows tools to access the repository directly, and also allows them to have their own user interface. Its architecture is that of a layered platform where tools can be based on lower or higher layers, resulting in a lower or higher degree of integration, respectively.

5   The Repository

Several approaches have been proposed for the implementation of a shared repository for CASE tool integration. Some systems, e.g. the one described in [12], use relational DB technology. Other ones, e.g. PCTE [3], use object-oriented databases. And many recent approaches favour the use of XML database systems, e.g. as presented in [13]. All these approaches have advantages and disadvantages, which we will discuss with regard to AP1.

AP1 uses a relational DBMS for the repository. As already described in [12], this has the following advantages: RDBMS are a very mature technology that is widely used and highly reliable. They rely on the simple and theoretically sound relational data model (RDM). RDBMS offer a well-understood, well-known and standardized interface through the language SQL, which allows powerful operations to be specified at a high level of abstraction. A RMDB is able to check and enforce various constraints on a DB, and its functionality can usually be extended in various ways, e.g. by triggers, stored procedures and user-defined functions. Furthermore, there exist a plethora of applications supporting the creation, use and maintenance of a RDB, such as DB administration tools, backup and replication tools, application generators, and interfaces to various programming languages. Most RDBMS inherently support TCP/IP networking, so that a repository built on this technology can be accessed remotely. Furthermore, modern RDBMS offer rich features for efficient, highly concurrent transaction processing and security, e.g. encryption and access control. All these advantages can be leveraged by AP1. In comparison, object-oriented and XML-based DB technology are not as mature, much more complicated and less well supported. However, using a RDBMS also has disadvantages, and it is a challenge for AP1 to overcome these. The disadvantages are also described in [12] and include an impedance mismatch between the relational data model and the more complex data structures required for CASE, possible performance penalties when these data structures are accessed, and a lack of built-in advanced features like version management. In the following we want to address these shortcomings and describe how they can be solved.

The biggest problem arising when using a RDBMS for the repository seems to be the impedance mismatch between the relational data model and the complex data structures used for CASE. Storing such data structures in a RDB usually results in fragmentation: the data has to be spread over several normalized tables and usually comprises several rows, which have to be reconnected by joins in order to yield the original data. The schema of the DB depends heavily on the multiplicities in the represented data structure and can vary significantly, e.g. new tables can be necessary when representing many-to-many relationships. This fragmentation, the variance in schema structure and the need to reassemble data increase the complexity of the system significantly and possibly reduce its performance. AP1 solves this problem by providing an object-oriented API on top of the database, which allows to access the data in the repository in a much more convenient manner using the parsimonious data model. This API is written in the C# language and can therefore be used on all platforms that offer a common language runtime (CLR) for the .net platform. Applications accessing the repository can either access the RDB directly, using SQL, or use the API for more convenience.

As mentioned, one of the common objections against the use of RDBMS technology for repositories is performance. However, in our experiments this was not a problem. AP1 uses the Firebird DBMS [14], which uses multiversion concurrency control [15]. This means that the DBMS uses different versions of a DB in order to prevent readers and writers blocking each other. One also has to note that the additional resources used by a modern RDBMS are well-invested: relations between data can be navigated bidirectionally, and the RDMBS is able to automatically check and enforce referential integrity.

5.1   The Parsimonious Data Model

The parsimonious data model (PDM), which is described in [16], is a very simple, formally well-defined data model, which relies – similar to the relational data model – on sets and relations. It basically consists of three concepts, which can be represented visually like in the diagram in Fig. 2: *entity types*, *relation types* and *roles*. Figure 2 shows a simple model for data about customers, which can have several addresses, each address consisting of a street name and a house number, and several orders. The circles, with the labels on them that start with upper case letters, represent entity types, which are sets of values. The connections between the circles represent relation types between the entity types. The lower case labels that can be put at the ends of the connections represent roles, i.e. identifiers for the connections between entity types and relation types. Roles can be used to navigate in a PDM: if you have an element of type Customer, then accessing role "addresses" will yield all elements of type Address which are associated with that particular customer. The data elements of an entity

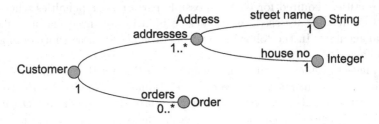

Fig. 2. Example of a PD model

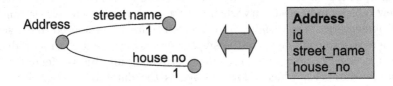

Fig. 3. Example of mapping between the PDM and RDM

type are called its *instances*, and the connections that can be made between instances according to a relation type are called *links*. Note that the same entity type can be represented in a diagram more than once, e.g. for avoiding crossing connections.

The PDM also provides notions for multiplicities and inheritance. For example, in Fig. 2 a customer can have an arbitrary number of orders, but each order belongs to exactly one customer. However, multiplicities and inheritance are optional constraints and need not be taken into account unless the designer wishes to do so. The PDM abstracts from low-level implementation details like tables, normalization, foreign keys and joins, and the repository API takes care of the mapping between the PDM and the RDM. This mapping is done on the basis of mapping rules, e.g. the one illustrated in Fig. 3, which make sure that the PDM is represented optimally.

In order to integrate different models syntactically, a parsimonious data metamodel is used. This metamodel, which is illustrated in Fig. 4, makes it possible to represent PDMs as PDM instances. In order to utilize the metamodel, the repository API provides functionality for reflection: existing models in the RDB can be introspected and read as PDM instances, and PDM instances of the metamodel can be manifested in the RDB through intercession. Compared to other metamodels, our metamodel is very simple, as it is symmetrical and comprises only very few entity types. The metaobject facility (MOF) [17], which is the metamodel for UML, comprises, in its core, a dozen interconnected classes and a variety of other related concepts. The parsimonious data metamodel is no less expressive, allowing universal definition of data types and relationally complete access, but decomposes more complex concepts into a small number of well-understood primitives. E.g. the fact that the relation types in our

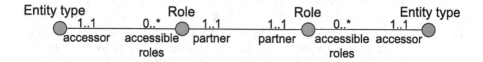

Fig. 4. The PD metamodel of the AP1 system. Entity instances are associated to other entity instances indirectly by a pair of roles, forming binary relation types.

metamodel are binary does not impose any limits on the PDMs: each n-ary relation type can easily transformed into an additional entity type and n binary relation types.

iRM [18] is a repository similar to AP1's, which is based on the MOF. Like AP1, iRM provides data management capabilities and reflection functionality for introspection and intercession of types. However, the store for metadata is separated from the data store, and thus data and metadata are not as tightly integrated. Applications can access iRM through an API, or through a non-standard relational query language similar to SQL. Despite this, iRM does not leverage existing RDBMS technology, but instead implements its own DBMS. Thus, data integration based on RDBMS standards is not supported.

5.2 Data and Control Integration

Data interchange is an important issue for CASE tool integration. If there are several repositories, it has to be possible to import and export models and model instances. AP1 uses SQL scripts for import and export. In order to support smooth integration of DBs and prevent key collisions when integrating data into the repository, non-primitive values are identified by universally unique identifiers (UUIDs) [19], also known as globally unique identifiers (GUIDs). These artificial identifiers are sufficiently small (128 bit) and can be efficiently processed and generated on the fly. If a command in an SQL script fails during an import operation because the command tries to create something that already exists in the database, it is clear that the element in the DB is the same as the one in the script, and the command can be safely ignored. Note that the SQL scripts used for import and export have a highly regular structure, even more so than XML, so that very high compression of these scripts is possible.

Another important part of AP1 is the caching and messaging architecture in the implementation of the repository API. Entity instances and links between them, as well as entity types and roles, are cached as objects in memory and updated whenever they are changed in the DB. Consequently, each application using the repository via the repository API enjoys the performance boost of an up-to-date read cache. Writes are done directly to the database (write-through), and whenever a change occurs, this change is logged in the database. Then, connected repository API components are notified by an event sent by the DBMS, and can consequently update their cache. As a side-effect, a change log is created which can be used for undo/redo and version management. The repository API allows applications to subscribe to events connected to the objects in the cache: e.g. an application can be notified when a link is deleted or added to an instance. This mechanism forms the basis of AP1's control integration, since applications are able to communicate with others just by writing to the repository. It is illustrated for AP1's generic editor in Fig. 8, which will be further explained in the next section.

The fact that SQL is such an established standard is an important factor for data integration. The schema used for AP1 is extensible and straightforward, so it is not hard to integrate existing relational data. The repository can be accessed through SQL, which makes it easier to integrate AP1 with other platforms and CASE tools. Even if tools access the repository directly, the mechanisms for notification and change management will still work. The repository also contains the program code of data operations, so that they can be used by other applications for functional integration. Data operations directly manipulate the database, which makes it possible to read their results just using SQL.

6   The Generic Editor

The generic editor can be seen as an open IDE or workbench, with an extensible plug-in architecture similar to that of popular IDEs like Eclipse [20] or MS Visual Studio [21]. It provides the basic means to view, edit, import and export model instances, invoke operations on those instances, and transform instances of one model into instances of another. In principle, modern IDEs can perform similar tasks, given a set of suitable plug-in extensions. But the way the generic editor of AP1 integrates its different components into its user interface is very different from the ones commonly used in IDEs. Most IDEs use an accumulative approach in which extensions bring their own user interface (UI) for input and output, creating their own sometimes very unique style of integration. With the addition of many extensions, this can easily result in a complex, heterogeneous, possibly cluttered UI, which is hard to access and understand. In contrast to this, AP1 aims at *conceptual integration* of different functionalities, by moving input, output and even the UI itself into the repository. In the following we will discuss this in more detail.

Figure 5 shows a screenshot of the generic editor with two work panels. Both panels use the default view, which can be used to view and edit any PD model instance. The dark text elements represent entity instances, and the light text elements represent roles. In the first line of the work panel at the top we see an entity instance representing the PD metamodel: it has the name "PD metamodel" and is of type "PD model". In the line below we see that from this instance role "entity types" can be accessed, which has multiplicity 0..*. If we navigate from instance "PD metamodel" via that role, we reach two instances of type "Entity type", which are linked to "PD metamodel": instance "Type Entity type", which is the instance representing the type "Entity type", and instance "Type Role", which is the instance representing the type "Role" (see Fig. 4 and the description in the previous section). The role in the last line in the

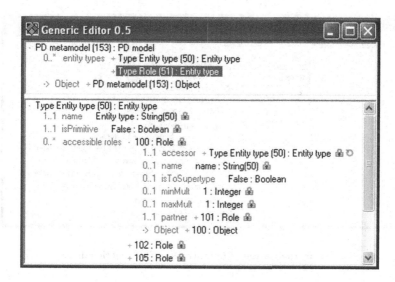

Fig. 5. Screenshot of the generic editor

top work panel refers to an inheritance relation: type "PD model" is a subtype of type "Object", and therefore an instance of type "Object" can be reached by navigating this role. The tree view supports elision, i.e. by clicking on the plus sign to the left of an instance the accessible roles of that instance and the instances connected through them become visible. The work panel at the bottom of the screenshot shows instance "Type Entity type" in more detail. Symbols on the left of an instance indicate certain properties of that instance or the link it is connected with. The padlock symbol, for example, indicates that a link is permanent and cannot be changed.

Another feature in the user interface of the generic tree view is the ability to invoke operations directly on the model. In common IDEs it is often not clear how to invoke a particular functionality: the user interfaces of the common IDEs are usually very rich and heterogeneous, with numerous buttons, menus and specialized panels. The functionality is spread out over all these different user interface elements. By contrast, operations in AP1 have a single *superparameter* (see also [16]), which comprises all information relevant for their invocation. Operations are associated with their superparameter type and invoked through its instances. Therefore, any operation can be invoked by simply editing an instance of its superparameter type and setting appropriate parameter values. Once such an instance is available, the operation can be invoked in the generic view through the instance's context menu, as illustrated in the screenshot in Fig. 6. This provides a very structured and homogeneous approach for the invocation of functionality. Specialized ways for editing superparameter instances can be realized by different views.

Robustness is the property of user interfaces to prevent data inconsistency in an application, despite a user not handling the application correctly. [22]

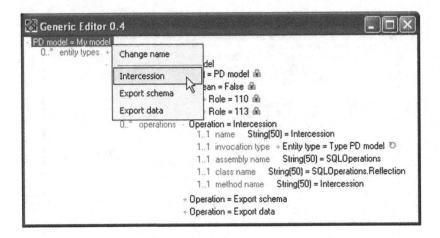

Fig. 6. Invocation of operations in the generic editor

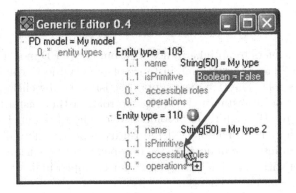

Fig. 7. Typed drag&drop in the generic editor

describes various ways for improving the robustness of a user interface, and the generic editor leverages most of them. For example, all information in the user interface of the generic editor is typed and handled in a type-safe manner. We can drag and drop instances in the default view from one place to another in order to create new links, but it is only possible to drop instances onto roles that suit their types, as illustrated in the screenshot in Fig. 7. Many constraints, like referential integrity, are enforced by the RDBMS; and since the user interface of the generic editor only reflects the state of the database, violations of those constraints in the user interface cannot occur. All operations invoked by the user are encapsulated in transactions, so that they cannot interfere with the actions of other users, and their effects become only visible after they were successfully completed.

6.1 Customizability

The generic editor is basically a configurable frame for different views on the repository. As indicated in Fig. 5, it provides a workspace which can be arbitrarily divided into non-overlapping work panels, each of which can provide a different editable or non-editable view onto the repository. The generic editor can be customized in various ways, e.g. by adding work panels or plug-ins for views and operations. All configuration information is part of the repository, and customization can therefore easily be done by editing the corresponding model instance. In contrast to this, common IDEs usually have to provide complex, nested configuration dialogues, which do not scale well and become cluttered with increasing number of features.

The storage of configuration information in the repository and its accessibility over a network have another positive effect on extensibility and maintenance: extensions and updates can be deployed centrally and activated dynamically for each user. A feature for dynamic extensibility of IDEs and its benefits have been described in [23], and AP1's repository can be leveraged in a similar way. The idea is that components of the system are themselves stored in the repository, with the repository acting as an application server. Because the code for operation and view plug-ins is bound dynamically, new plug-ins become accessible immediately for every user. But in contrast to [23], our approach is not only used for plug-ins. The program that starts the generic editor performs a simple bootstrapping process: it checks if there is a new version of the generic editor available in the repository, and if so, caches it locally and runs it. If a component of the generic editor is updated while the generic editor is running on client machines, this is immediately detected by the clients through AP1's notification mechanism. The clients will finish their pending transactions, load the new version of the updated component, and restart themselves automatically. Because all state information is stored in the repository, the client will restart in exactly the same state as it was terminated, with the user possibly not even noticing the update. After the restart, the only difference is that the local memory cache of the generic editor is empty, and its version is up-to-date. This feature, which is also known as hot-deployment, reduces the influence of maintenance on productivity to a minimum.

6.2 Distributed Synchronous Collaboration

[24] describes possibilities and benefits of the integration of features for collaborative work into an IDE. This approach, which includes the integration of chat, IM and screen sharing, has been implemented for the Eclipse IDE [25]. Interestingly, in AP1 many of these features come naturally as a side-effect: chat and IM are nothing but a list of text messages in the repository that are edited collaboratively, and all changes done in the repository can be followed live by all users. Even better: while the very nature of screen sharing is that several users see exactly the same screen, users of AP1 have the possibility to choose the view that suits their purpose best. Like in [25], data can easily be associated with other data, e.g. chats about bugs with parts of the source code. In

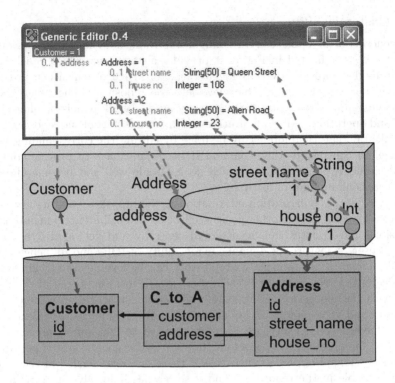

Fig. 8. Data synchronization between the RDB (bottom), the PDM API (middle) and CASE tools like the generic editor (top)

the same way, AP1 has the potential to facilitate other collaborative tasks like bug tracking and code review. Synchronous collaboration, e.g. pair programming, can effectively improve code quality, and there is evidence that this works even in distributed environments [26]. AP1 can support this in a similar way to Sangam [27], which is an Eclipse plug-in that replicates certain input events of an IDE on several clients. But Sangam can only replicate some events and conflicts with parts of Eclipse's functionality that have not been designed with synchronous collaboration in mind. AP1 supports distributed synchronous collaboration inherently and for all events affecting the repository. Possible future work is to investigate how different views for different collaborators can benefit distributed synchronous collaboration tasks, like distributed pair programming.

Figure 8 illustrates how the synchronization between the repository and the applications built on top of it works, considering as example the generic editor. At the bottom, the DB is depicted, which contains tables with all the data in the repository. When a table is changed, a trigger is fired: it logs the change into the DB and informs each connected PDM API component, illustrated above the DB, about the change, using an event mechanism that sends event messages over DB network connections. The PDM API component offers a PDM interface with event notification and a read cache. When an event is sent by the DB, a PDM API component decodes the event information and determines if it affects the PDM objects in the cache. Events are forwarded to the corresponding event handlers of those objects. The generic editor, depicted at the top of the figure, represents cached PDM instances in the views of its user interface. A view receives the events from its underlying PDM objects and can react to any change.

7 Conclusion

AP1 provides powerful features and novel concepts for the implementation of model-based CASE tools. Its architecture is, to the best of our knowledge, unique. In contrast to most other similar systems, its repository is based on a RDBMS which forms the self-contained core of the system. Additional functionality is added in layers on top of the RDBMS, such as an API that supports the more abstract PD model and an extensible user interface framework. All layers emphasize ease of integration and customizability. Currently we are working on an extension for meta-CASE functionality similar to [28,12], so that new views for different types of diagrams can be created directly.

References

1. Albizuri-Romero, M.B.: A retrospective view of CASE tools adoption. SIGSOFT Softw. Eng. Notes 25(2), 46–50 (2000)
2. Huff, C.C.: Elements of a realistic CASE tool adoption budget. Commun. ACM 35(4), 45–54 (1992)
3. Anderson, M., Bird, B.: An evaluation of PCTE as a portable tool platform. In: Proceedings of the Software Engineering Environments Conference, pp. 96–100 (1993)
4. Iivari, J.: Why are CASE tools not used? Commun. ACM 39(10), 94–103 (1996)
5. Kemerer, C.F.: How the learning curve affects CASE tool adoption. IEEE Software 9(3), 23–28 (1992)
6. Lending, D., Chervany, N.L.: The use of CASE tools. In: SIGCPR '98. Proceedings of the 1998 ACM SIGCPR Conference on Computer Personnel Research, pp. 49–58. ACM Press, New York (1998)
7. Maccari, A., Riva, C.: On CASE tool usage at Nokia. In: ASE 2002. Proceedings of the 17th IEEE International Conference on Automated Software Engineering, pp. 59–68. IEEE Computer Society Press, Los Alamitos (2002)
8. Kapsammer, E., Reiter, T., Schwinger, W.: Model-based tool integration - state of the art and future perspectives. In: CITSA 2006. Proceedings of the 3rd International Conference on Cybernetics and Information Technologies, Systems and Applications (2006)
9. Draheim, D., Lutteroth, C., Weber, G.: A type system for reflective program generators. In: Glück, R., Lowry, M. (eds.) GPCE 2005. LNCS, vol. 3676, Springer, Heidelberg (2005)
10. Bosua, R., Brinkkemper, S.: Realisation of an integrated software engineering environment through heterogeneous CASE-tool integration. In: Proceedings of the Conference on Software Engineering Environments, pp. 152–159. IEEE Computer Society Press, Los Alamitos (1995)

11. Wybolt, N.: Perspectives on CASE tool integration. SIGSOFT Softw. Eng. Notes 16(3), 56–60 (1991)
12. Gray, J., Ryan, B.: Integrating approaches to the construction of software engineering environments. In: Proceedings of the Eighth Conference on Software Engineering Environments, pp. 53–65. IEEE Computer Society Press, Los Alamitos (1997)
13. Maruyama, K., Yamamoto, S.: A CASE tool platform using an XML representation of java source code. In: SCAM '04. Proceedings of the 4th IEEE International Workshop on Source Code Analysis and Manipulation, pp. 158–167. IEEE Computer Society Press, Los Alamitos (2004)
14. The Firebird Foundation (Firebird RDBMS), http://www.firebirdsql.org/
15. Bernstein, P.A., Goodman, N.: Multiversion concurrency control -theory and algorithms. ACM Trans. Database Syst. 8(4), 465–483 (1983)
16. Draheim, D., Weber, G.: Form-Oriented Analysis - A New Methodology to Model Form-Based Applications. Springer, Heidelberg (2004)
17. Object Management Group: Meta Object Facility (MOF) Core Specification Version 2.0 (2006)
18. Petrov, I., Jablonski, S.: An OMG MOF based repository system with querying capability – the iRM project. In: Proceedings of iiWAS'04 (2004)
19. Internet Engineering Task Force (IETF) Network Working Group: RFC4122: A Universally Unique IDentifier (UUID) URN Namespace (2005)
20. D'Anjou, J.: The Java Developer's Guide to Eclipse. Addison-Wesley Professional, Reading (2004)
21. Skibo, C.: Working with Visual Studio 2005. Microsoft Press, Redmond, Washington (2006)
22. Draheim, D., Lutteroth, C., Weber, G.: Robust content creation with form-oriented user interfaces. In: Proceedings of CHINZ 2005 – 6th International Conference of the ACM's Special Interest Group on Computer-Human Interaction, pp. 2005–2006. ACM Press, New York (2005)
23. Yap, N., Chiong, H., Grundy, J., Berrigan, R.: Supporting dynamic software tool integration via web service-based components. In: ASWEC 2005. Proceedings of the Australian Software Engineering Conference, pp. 160–169. IEEE Computer Society Press, Los Alamitos (2005)
24. Cheng, L.T., de Souza, C.R., Hupfer, S., Patterson, J., Ross, S.: Building collaboration into IDEs. Queue 1(9), 40–50 (2004)
25. Cheng, L.T., Hupfer, S., Ross, S., Patterson, J.: Jazzing up Eclipse with collaborative tools. In: eclipse '03. Proceedings of the 2003 OOPSLA Workshop on Eclipse Technology Exchange, pp. 45–49. ACM Press, New York (2003)
26. Baheti, P., Gehringer, E., Stotts, D.: Exploring the efficacy of distributed pair programming. In: XP/Agile Universe 2002. Proceedings of the Second XP Universe and First Agile Universe Conference, pp. 208–220. Springer, Heidelberg (2002)
27. Ho, C.W., Raha, S., Gehringer, E., Williams, L.: Sangam: a distributed pair programming plug-in for Eclipse. In: eclipse '04. Proceedings of the 2004 OOPSLA Workshop on Eclipse Technology Exchange, pp. 73–77. ACM Press, New York (2004)
28. Zhu, N., Grundy, J., Hosking, J.: Pounamu: a meta-tool for multi-view visual language environment construction. In: Proceedings of VL/HCC'04 IEEE Symposium on Visual Languages and Human-Centric Computing. IEEE Press, Los Alamitos (2004)

A User-Oriented Design for Business Workflow Systems

Amir Pourabdollah, Tim Brailsford, and Helen Ashman

School of Computer Science and IT, The University of Nottingham
Jubilee Campus, Wollaton Road, Nottingham NG8 1BB, UK
{axp,tjb,hla}@cs.nott.ac.uk

Abstract. This paper contains some of the major design considerations which have been experienced through development of several workflow systems for business organizations and offices. These considerations, which are raised from both theoretical and practical sides, include the gathered requirements in a user-oriented iterative design, the implied changes in software architecture to satisfy these requirements and the developers' experiences on how such workflow systems can be easily adopted in typical office environments. More specifically, feedbacks of 40 users about the desired functionalities of a workflow system after using it has been compared with the initial requirements gathered before the development. This comparison shows not only the essential users' requirements from a workflow system, but also how some of the requirements can be changed through a cyclic design. The contribution of this research is a practical look at the designing implication of business workflow management system, rather than a theoretical view.

Keywords: Workflow Management Systems, User-oriented Design.

1 Introduction

The design of sustainable enterprise applications requires many concerns on usability issues. Iterative and user-centred development methods are known approaches to make such systems more user-friendly and sustainable. In these methods, users of the systems are not only those who have ordered a system (like in Waterfall Model of software engineering [16]), but those who are highly involved in the design process. Iteration here means that feedbacks from users about the designing software, as a whole or as a part, are used to re-design the system. [7]

One of the important enterprise applications are workflow management systems. Workflow management systems are being used to automate the sequence of actions or steps used in a process. This automation doesn't mean leaving computers to do tasks of workflows (even if this is possible), but using computer systems to help human resources to know and do the right action in the right time and the right place. In other words, workflow automation is distinguished from task automation, and workflow management systems are not about using computers to automate any individual task [4].

Workflow systems has two main areas of applications [14]:

a. Business/industrial processes automation, like office automation and e-commerce. Some of the benefits of using automated workflows in these

D. Draheim and G. Weber (Eds.): TEAA 2006, LNCS 4473, pp. 285–297, 2007.
© Springer-Verlag Berlin Heidelberg 2007

fields are improvement in speed, quality, reliability and flexibility [9] (The focus of this paper is on this part).

b.   Knowledge-based systems, like knowledge representation and solution processes. In the field of knowledge systems, workflows are highly combined with concepts of knowledge. Some examples are the test steps and fault detection [11]. Different user's requirements with different design consideration may be applied on this part, which are beyond the scope of this paper.

While there are hundreds of pre-designed workflow management systems being used, still many organizations need customized workflow applications to be specially designed for them concerning their special needs [18]. This paper tries to show the implications of user's requirements on the development of a workflow system through an iterative design and to show how such a design may address these requirements. It also wants to show that experiences of developers may be used to predict functionalities that the invoice user may not consider in the first stages but may realize them later.

It is observable in the workflow literature that researchers are mostly emphasis on the theory of workflow modelling and most of the efforts are devoted to technical issues or abstracted workflow modelling [9]. This is while users may have different class of concerns that may be missed in an abstracted software design. Through development and implementation of several real-world workflow systems, we believe that a main factor in making sustainable workflow system is an optimal balance between technical and practical sides of development. This paper tries to share the lesson learned when such a balance is targeted.

Another point that has been observed in organizations during this research is the existence of changes in users' expectations after deployment of workflow management systems. This can be considered as a part of organizational changes enabled by workflow systems [17].

2   Related Works

Workflow Management Coalition (WFMC) [19], is a main leading body in establishing standards in the field of workflow modelling and management. The WFMC reference model has been widely recognized and used in designing workflow systems. WFMC has also a list of software systems in the market which are completely or partially compatible with that reference model.

One of the main theoretical background in the workflow modelling is developed by Will van der Aalst (like in [3]). His model is based on a well-known information flow model known as Petri-nets (more in [13]). Workflow Patterns [1] is one of the outcome of Aalst's workflow model which can cover almost all theoretically possible situations of information flow in a workflow management system.

ADEPT [10] is a complementary framework that tries to cover more theoretical and practical sides of workflow modelling by providing more possible concepts and actions in such systems, like systematic addressing the pre-planned exceptions in order to adequately capture real-world processes (e.g. forward and backward jumps), ad-hoc derivations from the pre-modelled workflows, covering inter-workflow dependencies, advanced user interface, and some trends to optimize enterprise-wide communications. Rollback is another systematic concept that has been added to the workflow model, which has not completely covered by classic models. ADEPT has been used as a basis in other development research projects like AristaFlow [6].

Management of workflow systems while spreading them to enterprise-wide applications can raise some other concerns in software architecture that again may not be fully addressed in the classical models or in the commercial products [5, 8]. End-user access tools, workflow modelling tools, workflow instant management and project planning tools are different fields in the optimization of a workflow management system in order to make the product more sustainable in such scales.

As mentioned, different stakeholders in workflow community, i.e. academics, vendors, organizations and users, can raise different expectation from a workflow management system. Through adaptation of these stakeholders' expectations, some researches verifiy that the general results meet data from theoretical side [12], while interestingly some others believe that the theoretical side of current workflow products are quite unprepared to meet the practical users' demands [5]. We believe that this balance must be reassessed independently for each certain workflow application by making users as the centre of the design. This is why the development process of a workflow management system (which is itself a workflow) is another subject of research. Although little works has been devoted on this area, a reference workflow application development model has been introduced in [18], which is built on real-world experiences. In this model, the involvement of empirical studies, gathering users' requirements, business process modelling and workflow modelling into the design process has been studied.

Although it is observed that the details of the user-desired functionalities or features of such systems are not interested points for researchers, authors of [4] have shared some detailed experiences in implementing a workflow management system. The studied features in that work, which may consequently imply design principles, include explicit process definition tools, process enactment facilities, tracing tools, monitoring and reporting tools. The lesson they learned in their experiences are close to our results. The user's feedback on using the system was not uniformly enthusiastic in their research and they experienced negative feelings when users were presented with electronic version of their previous paper forms. Another negative users' feedback mentioned in their work is about the workflow definition tools when users need to redefine or modify the workflow. This problem comes back to this fact that many workflow definition tools or definition languages (like WPDL [19] or XRL [2]) may need certain level of computer knowledge which normal users may not have. The later point can raise many usability issues that may be addressed by introducing graphical or textual workflow definition tool. In the field of textual tools, easy process description language which are close to natural languages (like in [14, 15]) can help users in these issues.

The encountered problems that developers of workflow systems have experienced are almost same in nature. A good set of those problems has been counted in [18], like isolation of technical from organizational aspects, development without prototyping, unsuitable transfer of paper works to automatic processes and server performance in enterprise-wide applications.

3 Methodology

The method used in this research includes gathering initial users' requirements, using these requirements in the software architecture design, and gathering users' feedbacks after short-term and long-term operational phase. The development method follows the iterative design, in which the users are highly and actively involved in a cyclic process to test the system and share their views with the developers. The developers are also asked to validate the implementing system by the users' views. The details of this iteration have not been described in this paper, but the implications and learnt lessons caused by such iterations have been counted.

This method has been used in four offices of different types with different types of business: (1) TV production process in a TV program production organization. (2) Office works of a government-affiliated charity to help homeless people (3) Business processes of a multimedia advertisement company; and (4) Workflow of an international conference management company.

A total number of 40 active users in those four businesses have been selected for answering two similar questionnaires before and after using the system. The first set of questionnaires has been answered by them before starting development and the second set has been answered after having long-term (2 years) experience in using the developed system. It is also noticeable that none of these users have any previous experience with a real computerized workflow system.

4 Gathering Initial Requirements

In the initial step, general requirements of top users (or managers) are very important to be gathered. Managers in this step are usually interested to replace their manual system with a computerized workflow system, because they have some understandings about benefits of such systems. These main requirements include:

a. They usually have set of graphical flowcharts that need to be fed into new system as the raw material of workflow definition. However, these flowcharts must be re-engineered in many cases.
b. The system must be able to direct users to do what they are supposed to do, regarding to the workflow definition.
c. From a managerial point of view, the system must be able to show and trace history of processes on each case, and to show details of each user's actions to certain class of users.

The above general requirements have been studied more deeply by the developers and system designers to reach to the detailed specification. After more discussions and brain-storming sessions, some more specifications of the system have been shared between developers and users, like:

a. The system must have enough flexibility to accept frequent changes on the workflow.
b. There may be several workflows in a single organization, with or without gateways between them, while a single system is supposed to manage them together.

c. There may be several differences between the workflow designed for manual system, and those who must be used in the computerized one.

d. There may be some data forms that the users are supposed to fill before passing the subject to the next point.

e. The existence of a messaging system between users while passing the subject seems necessary. This can also be classified in public or private messages.

f. If a user wants to withdraw an already passed subject, the system must provide necessary draw-back mechanisms.

g. The workflow is defined for applying on positions (or jobs) of the users, not to users themselves. Each user may have different position in each workflow case.

5   Functionalities and Implications

Based on the requirement described in the last section, the main functionalities that need early design concerns have been extracted as different 'forms' in the system's user interface. These are as listed below:

5.1   Ready-to-Study Cases Form

A form is needed to design that contains all of the cases that the current user is supposed to do, or in other words, those which are waiting to be studied by the current user and passed to the next one. This will look like the "inbox" folder in email clients. It also must contain the detailed information about the previous study which has been done on the subject by another (or same) user. For studying a case, the user may or may not fill a data form or message to the next user. Also a confirmation about the next destination of the subject will be shown to the user before passing the subject.

5.2   Sent-Items Form

A form is needed to be designed that shows a part of sent-items which are not passed to a third party. These items are exactly those who are able to comeback to the ready-to-study cases form, if the user wishes to do so. There may be repeated items with different destination, if the current user has passed a subject through a distribution node. In these cases, drawing one of them back means withdrawal of all of them, and having them in the ready-to-study case as a single item.

5.3   History and Current-Status Forms

These two forms must be designed, preferably within a single user interface, to show where were and where are the moving subjects in the defined workflow. This has more importance from a managerial point of view to trace and investigate the stops and movements of the subjects. In some cases, these two forms may show the move of subjects from a workflow to another, if the system provides such inter-workflow jumps.

5.4 Workflow Definition/Change Interface

This form must provide the functionalities to design, review, change and update the workflow definition by certain class of users. There are two possible methods about how to manipulate the workflow definition: Textual or graphical. In the textual mode, a workflow definition language has been used. This has been called PDL (Process Definition Language) and it is a very simple language, similar to structured English and can be read and understood by normal users. A parser converts line of PDL to a set of SQL statements that can be used to define or change the data in the definition layer of the database. More details on PDL and its implementation can be found in [14].

5.5 Workflow-Bypassing Form

For escaping from happening deadlocks, or for addressing many practical issues that may happen in offices, some certain class of users must have access to this form, which is designed to bypass the defined workflow. It provides the facility that the user can pass a subject from the current node to some other node that the defined workflow doesn't allow it directly. This may practically include jumping over nodes, or taking a subject away from a certain node or acting on behalf of a user.

5.6. Drawing-Back Form

As a part of exception handling, draw-back forms are necessary to be designed. These forms will help to have limited control on sent-items to draw them back into ready-to-study forms.

6 The System Architecture

Concerning the above features, the main items about the system architecture have been concluded as:

a. The system is based on client-server architecture with a central database. The centralized database has been selected considering the size and scope of the workflows and organizations.

b. The information stored in database includes two abstracted layers, named "definition" and "execution" layers. This abstraction also complies with the WFMC reference model [19] when two different gateways are considered for definition and execution. "Definition" is the lower layer which contains all information about the definition of a workflow, and "execution" is the upper layer which contains all information about workflow cases and all processes which have been done on each task by users through the defined workflow in the lower layer. Although these two layers are dependant, this abstraction gives the system more flexibility in terms of accepting the workflow changes.

c. The required flexibility of system in terms of accepting the frequent workflow definition changes must consider keeping the execution layer information (which may be based on old definition data) always safe, integrated, valid and usable. This must be done by predicting database support to these changes.

d. The system may ask users to fill a data form associated to each node, when they want to pass a subject on that node. This implies having sub-databases for manipulating data in each data form. This also implies conjunction of the workflow database with a document management system.

e. The method of converting drawn graphical flowcharts to the information stored in the definition layer is an important stage. Some kinds of process engineering expertise need in this conversion, since a complete understanding of the organization and its process is necessary, as well as understanding of the future plan for computerizing the system. This implies graphical flow-charting tools and/or special language parsers to joint to the whole system. The next section explains this conversion in more details.

6.1 Database Design

We have reached to this conclusion that an optimal and smart database design has a very important role in making the final system reliable and sustainable. This starts from the main developers' question on "how to convert workflow graphs to data". Standardized graphs that are in use for describing workflows can be redrawn in UML standard activity diagrams [3] like the sample in figure 1. The database design is based on looking at a workflow graph as a combination of three main elements: boxes (nodes), arrows (links), and columns (groups).

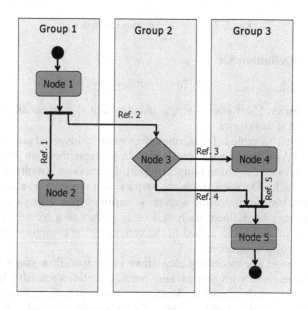

Fig. 1. A sample workflow graph

These types of graphs show the flow of operation that can be done on each subject. The rounded rectangles are processes, the diamonds are decision points and the arrows show the references. It will be shown that all processes and decisions are subclasses of "Nodes".

Based on the mentioned abstraction of definition and execution layers, Figure 2 shows the main elements in the database design and the required sets of tables.

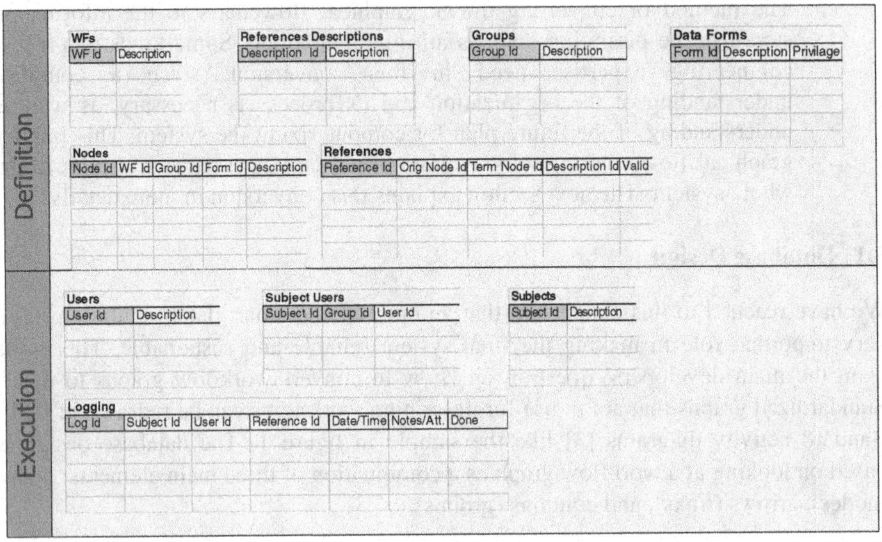

Fig. 2. The core of database tables design

6.2 Workflow Definition Set

The workflow definition set consists of the following tables:

a. **Workflows:** Used when a single management system needs to be employed for several workflows.
b. **Groups:** This table is for storing information of involved groups.
c. **Nodes:** As it can be seen from a workflow graph, there are 4 types of boxes: Start (no input), Action (single output), Distribution, (multiple outputs with same result), Decision (multiple outputs with multiple results) and Stop (no output). Instead of dealing with these various types, a single multi-purposed "node" can be defined; each will be modelled as a record in Nodes table. Their type will be identified in the system by the configuration of incoming and outgoing references.
d. **References:** For modelling each arrow in the workflow graph. Then starting nodes are those with no matching records in Reference table based on their originating node identifier. Multiple records in Reference table with same originating node identifier and different terminating node identifier means decision node, and so on.

6.3 Flexibility and Integrity of Workflow Changes

To provide enough flexibility to workflow changes while keeping all old execution layer information safe and usable (integrity), a proved solution is to keep all old records in nodes tables as "shadowed" records (called invalid mode, equivalent to a Boolean field in nodes table called 'valid'). Because Nodes table is dependant to Reference table, there will be no need to apply any validation algorithm on Reference table.

6.4 Workflow Execution Set

There will be another set of tables in the execution layer. They will be used for defining the case, the available users to the system, the involved user to each case and execution records. The details are as follows:

a. **Subjects:** This table will store a unique identifier and a name or description for each subject. There will be some application-dependant fields in this table.

b. **Users:** Regardless of the subjects of a specified workflow, the system should know about the users of the system, which this table stores them.

c. **Subject Users:** For establishing many-to-many relationship between subjects and users, this is a crossing table between the above two tables and the Groups table in the definition table set. This table tells the system that which user has which role in which subject. From a practical point of view, each user of the system can role differently for each subject.

d. **Logging:** This table contains real records of what is happening when users are dealing with subjects, according to rules of the defined workflow. It will not only contain the past records of what happened before, but also what are currently waiting to be done. A Boolean field (called "Done") represents either the relevant action has happened or waits to happen. The design is based on that a new record in this table is created when it is expected to happen, not when it happened. In this view all the identifiers are about the sender, not the receiver. This view can be changed to opposite one in developing the final application, but it is not recommended because one may not store both past and current task lists from a single table.

7 A Research on User's Requirements

A number of 40 users from different organizations have been selected for this research and they have been asked to answer a questionnaire. It is noticeable that none of these users have a real experience with computerized workflows before this research. This has been done just before designing the general specifications. The research has been repeated with the same questionnaire for 40 active users (including 3 replaced persons) after 2 years of the first user trials. During these two years the system was operational had been used actively by these users.

The result has been summarized in table 1.

Table 1. Results of a comparative research among 40 users

Issue	Options	Stage 1 (before)	Stage 2 (after)
1. How do you like the workflow system to limit the users in their office works	a. No restriction: Such systems are to answer the informational requirements of users, not to restrict them	14	5
	b. Passive: Such systems must show the users what to do, but not restrictive	15	12
	c. Active: Such systems must limit the users to do their office works in the right direction	11	23
2. The desired method for withdrawal of a subject after being passed	a. Should be impossible	9	2
	b. Users can always withdraw unwanted passing	21	12
	c. Users an withdraw unwanted passing only if the next user hasn't pass it	10	26
3. The interface for the studied cases (sent items) must:	a. Show all the sent items	15	13
	b. Show those who are ready to study by the next user	25	27
	c. Highly restricted to special users	0	0
4. Access to the history of subjects' passing	a. Show all the history	15	21
	b. Show what the current user has done	22	14
	c. Highly restricted to special users	3	5
5. Access to the current status of subjects	a. Show all the current stop points for a subject	16	28
	b. Show those who are for this user	19	4
	c. Highly restricted to special users	5	8
6. Tools for workflow definition and changes	a. Essential	5	26
	b. Good	31	10
	c. Redundant	4	4
7. Graphical tools for workflow manipulation	a. Essential	12	8
	b. Good	25	24
	c. Redundant	3	8
8. Possibility of workflow bypassing	c. Must be impossible	18	7
	a. Highly restricted to special users	12	19
	b. Must be available in some extent to all users	10	14

8   Discussion and Lessons Learnt

a.   Answers to question 1 about the desired level of general restrictive behaviour of workflow systems shows how restriction can be accepted and even been satisfied by the users, when it is used in a right direction. The point is that the general understandings of restrictive behaviour of computer systems to users are shaped when the system limits them to do what they are supposed to, but in a well-designed workflow system, this can be converted to satisfaction if they find the system allowing them what they are supposed to do and denying them otherwise.

b. The mechanism for withdrawal of the passed subjects (question 2) are mostly desired to be applicable in all situations, whether the next user has assed the subject to a third party or not. This look has been moderated in the second stage. People now mostly like to have withdrawal capabilities if the next user has not passed the subject anywhere. This is partly because of practical problems that may be caused by free withdrawal method.

c. Answers to question 3 about "sent-items" folder are almost same in both stages. Users like to have a folder called "sent items" but they mostly like it to contain the ready-to-study items, not all items. This is because they have option on seeing the history of each subject using history screen, but in sent-items screen they prefer to see those items which they can withdraw them.

d. Answers to question 4 about history page have been changed between two stages. This shows that users imagined that it is enough if they know what themselves have done in the past about a certain subject, but after experiencing the system, they feel more interested to know al the history about it. This partly shows how users need as much information as possible for decision making.

e. Similarly, the above conclusion can be said about answers to question 5 about the current status of subjects.

f. Answers to question 6 about workflow definition tools show how important are the existence of these tools. People in stage 1 had no clear idea about how frequent are the changes on the workflow definitions, or may think that such a changes are easy to apply without specific tools. This view has been corrected in the second stage.

g. Graphical tools for workflow manipulation (question 7) were an attractive idea for users in stage 1, but not so much in stage 2. This shows that in a busy office, users may have not enough time to use a graphical tool, or the textual information had enough functionality for them rather than using a graphical tool.

h. The answers to question 8 about the possibility of bypassing subjects show more restrictive views of users in stage 1 than in stage 2. This also shows that the practical situation that they may encountered in the past has guided them to consider more flexibility of the system in terms of workflow bypassing, at least for certain class of users.

9 Conclusion

The main contribution of this research is sharing some experiences through development of an operational business workflow system. Observing a gap between theoretical modelling and real-world practical problems, we tried to balance between these two sides by more focus on the details of desired workflow features. These experiences also shows how the users' requirements before and after using a system can be re-used in iterative designing stages and how the architecture of a system must obey them. The role of developers in predicting future users' requirements has also been focused, so the users' wishes can approach to the developers' ideas. Finally, it is believed that this approach can give more operational sustainability to a working management system.

Acknowledgments. The authors would like to thank Dr. Michael Hartley in the Malaysian Campus of the University of Nottingham for his valuable guidance through this research.

References

1. van der Aalst, W.M.P., Hofstede, A.H.M.T., Kiepuszewski, B., Barros, A.P.: Workflow Patterns. Distributed Parallel Databases 14, 5–51 (2003)
2. van der Aalst, W.M.P., Verbeek, H.M.W., Kumar, A.: Xrl/Woflan: Verification of an Xml/Petri-Net Based Language for Inter-Organizational Workflows. In: Proceedings of the 6th Informs Conference on Information Systems and Technology (CIST-2001), pp. 30–45 (2001)
3. van der Aalst, W.M.P., Hee, K.v.: Workflow Management. MIT Press, Cambridge (2004)
4. Abbott, K.R., Sarin, S.K.: Experiences with Workflow Management: Issues for the Next Generation. In: Proceedings of the 1994 ACM conference on Computer supported cooperative work. ACM Press, Chapel Hill, North Carolina, United States (1994)
5. Alonso, G., Agrawal, D., Abbadi, A.E., Mohan, C.: Functionality and Limitations of Current Workflow Management Systems (submitted to IEEE Expert 1997)
6. AristaFlow: Next Generation Enterprise Process Management: Component-Oriented Development of Adaptive Process-Oriented Enterprise Software Retrieved 10/2006, from http://www.aristaflow.de/
7. Baecker, R.M., Nastos, D., Posner, I.R., Mawby, K.L.: The User-Centered Iterative Design of Collaborative Writing Software. In: Proceedings of the SIGCHI conference on Human factors in computing systems. ACM Press, Amsterdam, The Netherlands (1993)
8. Bussler, C.: Enterprise-Wide Workflow Management. IEEE Concurrency 7, 32–43 (1999)
9. Choenni, S., Bakker, R., Baets, W.: On the Evaluation of Workflow Systems in Business Processes. Electronic Journal of Information Systems Evaluation (2003)
10. DBIS: Adept - Next Generation Workflow Technology (2006) Retrieved 10/2006, from http://www.informatik.uni-ulm.de/dbis/
11. Garnemark, A.: Workflow and Knowledge Management (M.Sc. Thesis), University of Goteborg, Department of Informatics, pp. 31–43 (2002)
12. Lousa, M., Sarmento, A., Machado, A.: Expectations towards the Adoption of Workflow Systems: The Results of a Case Study. In: Proceedings of the 6th International Workshop on Groupware. IEEE Computer Society, Los Alamitos (2000)
13. Peterson, J.L.: Petri Nets. ACM Computer Survey 9, 223–252 (1977)
14. Pourabdollah, A.: A User-Friendly Process Description Language Used in Creating Database Model of Workflows, M.Sc. Thesis, The University of Nottingham, Malaysia Campus (2004)
15. Pourabdollah, A., Hartley, M.: Gathering Unstructured Workflow Data into Relational Database Model Using Process Definition Language. In: Proceedings of the 24th IASTED international conference on Database and applications. ACTA Press, Innsbruck, Austria (2006)

16. Royce, W.W.: Managing the Development of Large Software Systems. In: Proceedings, IEEE WESCON, pp. 1–9. IEEE Computer Society Press, Los Alamitos (1970)
17. Sarmento, A., Machado, A.: Impact Evaluation of Organisational Changes Enabled by Workflow Systems. In: Proceedings of the 6th International Workshop on Groupware (CRIWG'00), p. 134 (2000)
18. Weske, M., Goesmann, T., Holten, R., Striemer, R.: A Reference Model for Workflow Application Development Processes. In: SIGSOFT Software Engineering Notes, vol. 24, pp. 1–10 (1999)
19. WFMC: The Workflow-Management-Coalition (2006) Retrieved 8/2006, from http://www.wfmc.org/

Olympic Agents

Nikolaos Skarmeas[1], Christos KK Loverdos[2], Katerina Tsiara[3],
Alexandros Bassakidis[4], Aris Tzoumas[4], and Dimitris Livas[4]

[1] Avaca Technologies S.A., L. Katsoni 40, Athens, GR-114 71, Greece
[2] Dept of Informatics & Telecommunications, University of Athens, Greece
[3] National Technical University of Athens, Greece
[4] OTENET S.A., Kifisias Ave. 109 & Sina Str., Athens, GR-151 24, Greece
`nskarmeas@avaca.gr`, `loverdos@di.uoa.gr`, `tsiara@telecom.ntua.gr`,
`alexbas@hq.otenet.gr`, `atzoum@otenet.gr`, `Dimitris.Livas@otenet.gr`

Abstract. We present an agent-oriented middle-tier architecture deployed during the realisation of the Athens 2004 Olympics results internet broadcasting. The system involved the online processing of messages (XML in nature) and their publishing to the www.athens2004.com internet site. Those messages were containing the Games intermediate and final results and were originated from the Olympic venues. For the accomplishment of this task a number of systems and applications needed to be integrated. Also the domain posed some unique problems regarding the fact that for the first time in the history of the Games a real time approach for broadcasting results was deployed and furthermore due to the reliability and performance requirements of the system. Various enterprise application integration patterns were used in conjunction with an agent oriented design approach. Asynchronous intercommunicating agents were deployed for realizing the architectural components of the system.

Keywords: Enterprise application integration, agent systems, pattern oriented software construction, service oriented architectures.

1 Introduction

We present an agent-oriented middle-tier architecture deployed during the realisation of the Athens 2004 Olympics results internet broadcasting. During the 2004 Olympics, for the first time in the history of the Games a real-time broadcasting of results for the Internet was introduced. The company (ATOS Origin) which was TV broadcasting the results of the Games was broadcasting the same information as an XML based real-time message feed.

The task addressed was the processing and transformation of the XML messages into HTML fragments which were published to the Athens 2004 official portal and a mobile systems operator.

The application had a number of strict requirements. Messages were real-time and they were transmitted by the ATOS platform at a rate up to 20 msgs/sec. Due to the high frequency of the messages, the system should be efficient enough to allow

D. Draheim and G. Weber (Eds.): TEAA 2006, LNCS 4473, pp. 298–310, 2007.

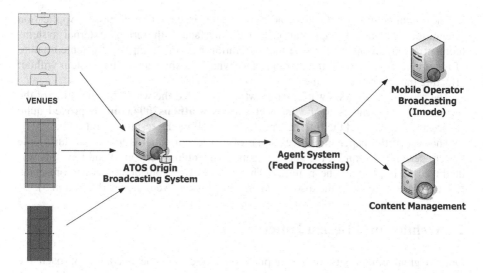

VENUES

**ATOS Origin
Broadcasting System**

**Agent System
(Feed Processing)**

**Mobile Operator
Broadcasting
(Imode)**

Content Management

Fig. 1. The overall scenario

concurrent processing of them. In addition to this, due to the large number of athletic events, the message specification was quite extensive. All information eventually published to the site was sent via this messaging infrastructure (Figure 1). The different types of messages were about 1200. Also, the real-time processing nature of the messages differed. There were message that needed immediate consideration (for example the messages containing the current score of a running basketball game which was updated every few seconds) and messages that could be postponed for a short period of time (final result messages, medal lists etc). The application should be structured in such away in order to allow for a generic and configurable modeling and processing of the messages.

Because the real-time broadcasting of the results over the Internet was introduced for the first time in the history of the Games, message structure was due to change frequently, reflecting changes to the Olympic committee specifications. Changes were even introduced during the Olympics. For instance, there were situations that two Athletes were to share a gold medal. If that case had not been predicted, the message structure would have to be altered during the games. Therefore the system should be able to adapt quickly to such changes without disrupting the overall performance and operation.

The overall system design was addressed from the multi-agent system perspective [1] in conjunction with a pattern-oriented approach [2],[3],[4],[5]. Various design patterns were identified for structuring the system. Furthermore, the constituent parts introduced were modeled as agents, communicating with asynchronous messages. Those system components should be as low coupled as possible in order to facilitate changes. We designed a generic agent architecture [6] to realize them. This architecture allowed dynamic reconfiguration of the overall system in order to deal with the uncertainty of the incoming message structure.

The architecture used, also addressed the issue of Enterprise Application Integration. Because the application had to interface with various external systems (content management etc) and be the integration bus, the component oriented nature of the application allowed the modular and dynamic expansion of the system without affecting the rest of the modules.

The result was a middleware system which mediated the whole broadcasting of the results of the Olympics to the Internet site **www.athens2004.com**. It proved quite successful and allowed the Internet spectators to follow the results in real time.

The rest of the paper introduces some of the design patterns identified during the system design (Section 2), the general agent architecture (Section 3) and how this was deployed to implement the patterns. Then some extra considerations are presented (Section 4) and finally some discussion and conclusions were included (Section 5).

2   Architectural Design Patterns

Due to great complexity of the application, there was the need to approach the problem in a generic way. During the design of the system a number of architectural patterns were identified. Those patterns were then implemented with an agent-oriented approach in order to produce loosely coupled components. The outcome of this pattern-agent marriage allowed us to deal with the unanticipated evolution of the requirements, to reduce the complexity of the implementation and to increase its adaptability. This section discusses those patterns with reference to the problems addressed.

2.1   Asynchronous Messaging

Messages arrived from the venues in an asynchronous fashion. The application received the incoming messages and forwarded it to its internal components for further processing. The internal components processed the incoming information and produced their output asynchronously. The incoming messages were in XML format. They had the header/body structure (figure 2) in the fashion of KQML [7] and FIPA [8].

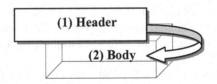

Fig. 2. Message structure

(1) Header: It identified system and communication level information like the Olympic event it referred to (basketball, swimming, athletics etc), the time of the message, the venue it originated from, the language, the internal system ID which produced the message, the type of the message (start list, final result, intermediate result, medals, weather, news etc) and other essential meta-information.

The header was mostly used for the filtering and routing of the message.

(2) Body: It contained the message content i.e. the actual event results. A result message, for example would contain the sequence of xml elements containing the athletes (in terms of their system IDs), the time information they scored, their position etc. An example of such a message taken from a real message fragment simplified for presentation purposes is included below (figure 3):

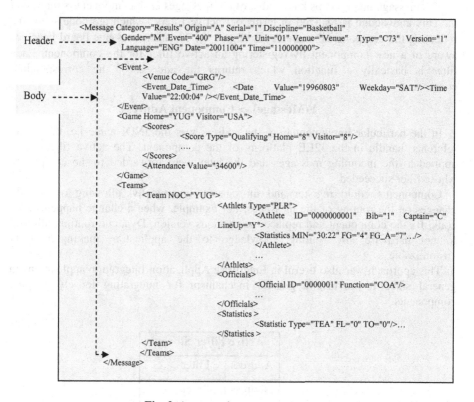

Fig. 3. An example message structure

The difference in messages was expressed at a first level by differences on the header. For instance, the discipline (**Basketball**) and message type (**C73=Final Result**). At the second level by the different content. The content was mostly determined by the discipline and message type. The combination of those two amounted to over 1200 distinct message types.

2.2   Active Message Boards and Content Based Routing

As mentioned above, one of the main problems that needed to be addressed was the existence of a large number of message types whose specification and structure might change during the application development and even the course of the Games. Hardwiring message information would cause major problems as there was the implicit requirement to be able to update the components of the system dynamically without disrupting the system's operation.

To accomplish this functionality an active message board was introduced [6]. The role of the message board is to accept incoming messages and route them to domain specific components. The routing can be either based on the processing of the headers or be "content based" via processing of the message body.

The message board keeps knowledge of the messages each component is interested in. This knowledge is realized in terms of "active filters" which are code segments reflecting the components' preferences (figure 4). Thus, the message board becomes aware of a new component by registering an active filter for the component. Each filter is basically a function which returns the address of the corresponding component:

F(Message) -> Component Address

In the particular implementation, the address was the JNDI name i.e. the object reference handle in the J2EE platform, of the component. The active filters were applied to the incoming messages and the later were forwarded to the component whose filter succeeded.

Components could register and un-register dynamically, allowing on the fly changes on the routing of the messages. For example, when a change happened, we could fix the component and replace the previous version. Dynamic routing, allowed to not hardwire any routing knowledge to the application making it fully customizable.

This approach was also useful in Enterprise Application Integration applications in general since it provides a generic mechanism for integrating loosely coupled components.

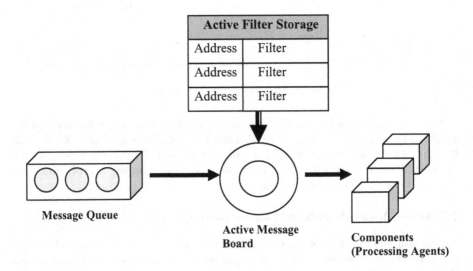

Fig. 4. The active message board architecture

2.3 Chain of Command

Messages received from the venues had to be transformed eventually to html fragments and published to the Olympics Internet site. The overall transformation was split into phases with each phase implemented by a relevant component. The overall structure was that of a pipeline (figure 5). The output of each component's processing was the input to the next. More specifically, each incoming message was initiating a thread of execution, i.e. a "chain of command process". This thread of execution had an internal processing information structure which included the original message and the results of its transformation step by step. This internal state was asynchronously communicated between the components.

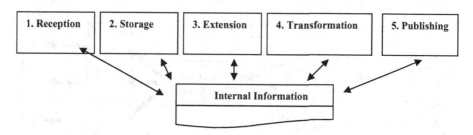

Fig. 5. The chain-of-command of message processing

After the original message reception (Step 1), Step 2 involved the storage of the incoming message and the generation of the internal representation. During step 3, the XML messages were going through intermediate transformations which enriched their content (internal representation) with extra information (figure 6). The messages, for example, contained only athlete's ID and their credential were filled in using database stored information. Therefore we needed to extend the xml with the additional information. That agent was pattern matching on the incoming xml and was inserting the missing elements.

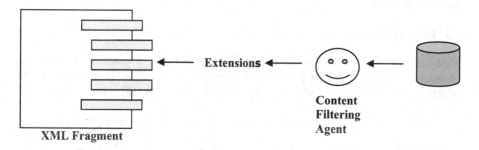

Fig. 6. Content Extension agent

The next stage of the transformation (step 4) involved XML/XSL processing in order to produce the final output. This step was used in conjunction with the final step which involved the communication with the external systems via a special set of adaptors.

2.4 Adaptors and SOA: Interfacing with External Systems

In the spirit of the EAI approach in order to interface with the external systems, a set of adaptors was created. The transformed XML messages had to be communicated to the external systems involved in the overall project. Specifically, the most significant systems were a content management system (Vignette [9]) for publishing the content to the www.athens2004.com web site and an external application, publishing content to a mobile phone operator. These systems were providing web services interface. The adaptors were acting as the interfaces to the external systems dealing with the communication and information representation differences.

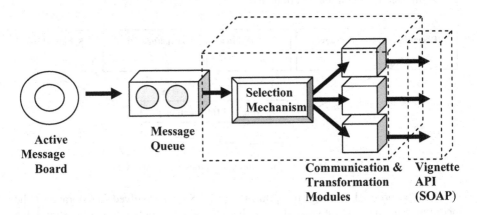

Fig. 7. External system adaptors

The routing of the messages to the appropriate adaptor(s) was performed via the active message mechanism. Internally the adaptor had a message selector for selecting the appropriate action (figure 7). This mechanism is similar to the active message board presented above and allowed the easy reconfiguration of the interaction with the external systems.

2.5 Priority Queues

Messages, as mentioned above, had different priorities. Messages of real time processing nature had higher priority than final result messages. Therefore a "queue selector" was introduced (between steps 1 and 2 in figure 5) which allowed for

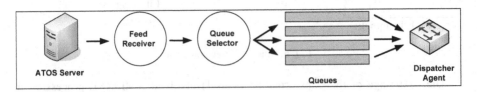

Fig. 8. Priority Queues

selectively placing messages in queues for further processing (figure 8). For example, messages depicting scores for active events had their own queue and they were getting priority over medal messages.

3 The Agent Architecture

The overall system was modeled as an agent system [6]. It received messages asynchronously (by the ATOS platform), performed complex transformations, generated subsequent information and communicated it to external systems. The agent system was designed using the patterns described above. Effectively, it was made adaptive to changes of its external environment (reflected via changes to the incoming XML messages) and reconfigurable at run-time. The overall agent architecture is illustrated in figure 9.

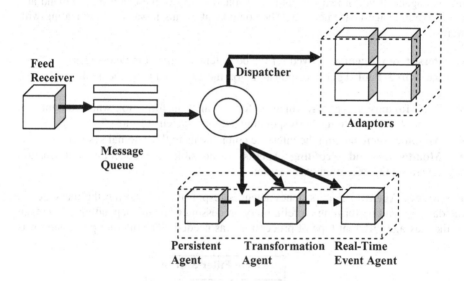

Fig. 9. The overall architecture

One of the main characteristics of this architecture is that the internal components of the agent system were also modeled as agents, thus recursively replicating the active message board pattern (as described in Section 2.2). Components for example, were implemented as message boards with subcomponents themselves.

In more detail, the system architecture consisted of the following components:

Feed Receiver Agent: It was a Servlet-based component which listened to an http port for incoming messages. Messages were received asynchronously and forwarded to the Dispatcher Agent for further processing. The feed receiver utilized the internal queue system (Section 2.5) for prioritizing the incoming messages.

In addition, the feed receiver employed a finite state machine implementation for controlling the communication buffer with the ATOS Origin results broadcasting system. The control mechanism depended on the internal state of the agent and manipulated the buffer accordingly. For example, if the agent entered a *pending* state, the feed receiver stopped consuming messages. As soon as the agent returned to the *active* state the processing of the messages resumed. The state transition was implemented using active rules in a DSL (Domain Specific Language) designed for this purpose [10]. We could temporarily "blind" the incoming xml connection from ATOS to occasionally perform internal maintenance (i.e. reconfiguring or redeploying an agent), a feature which proved quite useful during the games.

Dispatcher Agent: After the feed receiver received the message it forwarded it to the Dispatcher Agent. Forwarding was performed using the priority queues. The Dispatcher Agent was responsible for the orchestration of the subsequent processing. It monitored the processing of the messages and forwarded them to the appropriate internal agent. It performed the combined functionality of the chain of command and the active message board patterns. The component agents it was communicating with were:

- **Persistency Agent**, deployed for the persistent storage of the messages.
- **Real-time Pool Agent**, responsible for the processing of the real-time active events.
- **Transformation Agents,** which performed the transformation whose output was further forwarded to the corresponding external system adaptors.
- **Adaptor Agents,** being the interface components to the external systems.
- **Monitoring and Profiling Agents**, responsible for collecting information regarding the execution of the system.

Persistency Agent: The persistency agent is responsible for storing the messages in the database and performing a preliminary processing of them. Depending on the type of the message different type of processing was needed. The internal processing was

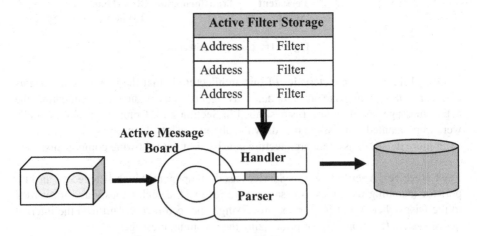

Fig. 10. The persistency agent architecture

performed by particular "handlers". The following figure illustrates the internal architecture of the persistency agent. Internally it follows the message board pattern, the "handlers" being the sub-components of the board. For each incoming message the appropriate handler is invoked (via the message board selection mechanism) for further processing and storing the message (figure 10).

Real-time pool agent: This agent was actually a pool of agents monitoring the real-time execution of the active events (figure 11). An instance of this agent type, the event agent, was actually active for as long as a particular event took place. It maintained the state of the event and the incoming messages forced it to update its state. It generated intermediate xml messages which were actually forwarded by the dispatcher to the transformation agent. For example, during a basketball match the score updates were received by that agent which would eventually update the score html fragment.

The routing to "real-time pool agent" was based on the "message category" of the message header, which signified the real-time nature of the message. Further forwarding to the sub-component was made by matching the message type and the event discipline.

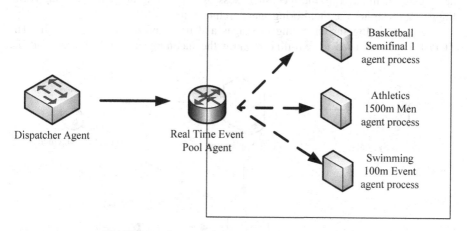

Fig. 11. The Current Event Agent Internal Architecture

Transformation Agent: This agent is responsible for transforming the message and generating the final fragment which will be forwarded to the external system(s). It also performs a transformation from the internal knowledge representation of the agent application to the external's system representation. It was actually responsible for Steps 3 and 4 of the Chain of Command (Section 2.3).

Adaptor agent: The result of the transformation is communicated to the external systems. The adaptor agent was the integration plugs to the external systems and their purpose was to hide any protocol and representation differences to those. For example, the content interface to the content management systems was a set of web services; therefore the adaptors were performing SOA calls to this system.

4 Additional Considerations

4.1 Implementation Platform

The platform was implemented as a J2EE application using the IBM Websphere application server and an IBM DB2 database. The agents were implemented as message driven beans. The communication among the components was asynchronous, using the JMS mechanism, accomplishing thus high throughput for processing the incoming messages. The communication with the external systems was accomplished via web-services. In addition, a number of open source technologies were deployed for various aspects of the system. For example, Castor was used for binding XML messages to objects.

4.2 Logging

A crucial part of this category of systems (real-time information processing and content generation) is the logging and monitoring functionality. A special agent was developed for monitoring the incoming message processing and administering them. Figure 12 illustrates the monitoring agent architecture:

The agent is logging incoming messages and trace information via TCP/IP. The TCP/IP stream is used to real-time monitor the incoming messages through all the

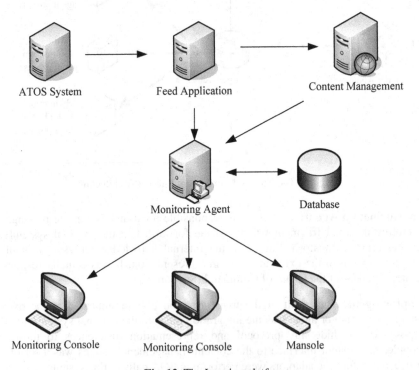

Fig. 12. The Logging platform

phases of its processing. Each agent component, as soon as it finishes processing, sends a message to inform the logging agent about the success of its processing or for any failures that occurred. The overall logging functionality was assisted by the fact that the chain of command processing was adopted.

A special graphical console application to visualize the message flow was implemented. Users could connect via this console to the logging agent and monitor the stream. In addition, this agent offered message administration functionality (via an extra graphical console). It allowed us to search over the history of messages and to possibly re-feed them, if there was such a need.

5 Summary and Conclusions

In this paper we presented the architecture and the approach for the implementation of the backend real-time Internet broadcasting system of the Athens 2004 Olympics. The application was generating the content of the www.athens2004.com web site.

We used design patterns and an agent-based approach to design and implement an Enterprise Application Integration system. This architectural approach offered a high degree of system flexibility without sacrificing performance. Just for the reference, the application was receiving messages up to the rate of 20 msgs/sec. For the broadcasting of the real-time active events, generated content was just a couple of seconds later than the TV broadcasting. The site (www.athens2004.com) is currently not available. However, the content generated by the presented system, was visited by 75 million unique users (5.2 million distinct users per day) from all over the world, amounting to a total of 800 million page views during the Olympic Games period.

The re-configurability of the system proved quite useful because during the games we managed to hot-fix various issues without disrupting the overall operation of the system. Also due to the mixture of patterns and agents the approach is also of interest from the software engineering point of view.

Currently, we are looking in applying this architecture to other applications and extending this architecture by adding other patterns as well. For example, we are looking at workflows instead of chain of command, as such systems have become more mature for production purposes quite recently.

Acknowledgements. We would like to thank for their contribution of the overall effort of this work Elias Drakopoulos, Nikos Dialektakos, Marios Koumanos, Christos Tsakiris, Kostis Panagiotopoulos, Panagiotis Tzagkarakis, Nikos Theodoropoulos, Giorgos Ploumpis, Tomas Conte, Francois Darfouille, Nicola Leclerc, Panos Pissaris, Predrac Nincovic, Aggelos Apostolatos, Giannis Giannoudovardis. We would also like to thank Otenet S.A. for allowing the publication of this material.

References

1. Huhns, M., Singh, M.: Readings in Agents. Morgan Kaufmann, San Francisco (1998)
2. Silva, A., Delgado, J.: The Agent Pattern: A Design Pattern for Dynamic and Distributed Applications. In: Proceedings of the EuroPLoP'98, Third European Conference on Pattern Languages of Programming and Computing, Irsee, Germany (1998)

3. Enterprise Integration Patterns: Designing, Building, and Deploying Messaging Solutions, Gregor Hohpe, Bobby Woolf. Addison-Wesley Professional (2003)
4. Patterns of Enterprise Application Architecture, Martin Fowler. Addison-Wesley Professional (2002)
5. Monroy, R., Arroyo-Figueroa, G., Sucar, L.E., Sossa, H. (eds.): MICAI 2004. LNCS (LNAI), vol. 2972. Springer, Heidelberg (2004)
6. Skarmeas, N., Clark, K.L.: Component Based Agent Construction. International Journal on Artificial Intelligence Tools 11(1), 139–163 (2002)
7. Finnin, T., Labrou, Y., Mayfield, J.: KQML as an agent communication language, Software Agents. MIT Press, Cambridge (1997)
8. Foundations of Intelligent Agents (FIPA), Agent Communication Language. Technical Report - FIPA Consortium (2001), http://www.fipa.org/
9. Vignette, Content Management Solutions, http://www.vignette.com/agent
10. Loverdos, C.K.K., Saidis, C., Sotiropoulou, A., Theotokis, D.: Pluggable Services for Tailorable eContent Delivery. In: Bellahsène, Z., Patel, D., Rolland, C. (eds.) OOIS 2002. LNCS, vol. 2425, Springer, Heidelberg (2002)

Relating Requirements to a User Interface Architecture for a Rich Enterprise Web Application

Rajanikanth Tanikella, Gilberto Matos, Grace Tai, and Brad Wehrwein

Siemens Corporate Research,
Princeton NJ, USA
{rajanikanth.tanikella,gilberto.matos,brad.wehrwein}@siemens.com
graceyuantai@googlemail.com

Abstract. Over the past few years, the demand for richer user interfaces and fast performance for web applications has also had its effect on enterprise web UI development. Solutions such as rich thin client frameworks and rich internet application (RIA) frameworks have emerged, alongside technologies like AJAX and Adobe Flex. At Siemens Corporate Research, our recent experience in developing a scalable enterprise web application with an agile methodology, however, has indicated that implementation decisions are often made without fully understanding the implications that the desired UI concept and look and feel have on the implementation. This paper presents a conceptual UI architecture and, for each aspect of the architecture, examines the types of requirements that should be gleaned from the various UI requirements documents. We make recommendations to help bridge the gap between user interface design specifications and user interface architectural specifications, including impacts on implementation-level architecture.

Keywords: web application, rich internet application, presentation layer, UI architecture, web engineering, agile development.

1 Introduction

Larry Constantine suggests that "In concept, perhaps, usability is the bailiwick of usability specialists. In practice, however, developers of various stripes make the vast majority of the myriad decisions that shape and determine the ultimate usability of software-based products." When software developers who are untrained in the parlance of human-computer interaction are made to translate UI concepts directly into code, it is no wonder that "Much software is designed and built with little consideration for how it will be used and how it can best support the work its users will be doing." [1]

In recent years, the Software Engineering Department at Siemens Corporate Research has personally experienced the increased demand for web applications that offer the sort of user experience associated with rich-client applications.

D. Draheim and G. Weber (Eds.): TEAA 2006, LNCS 4473, pp. 311–325, 2007.
© Springer-Verlag Berlin Heidelberg 2007

We have seen the benefit of close collaboration between user interface designers, architects, and UI implementers in the realization of such applications. We have also felt the impact of the absence of that close collaboration, when UI requirements are not properly discovered and discussed between these parties: The implementation headaches that surface from a lack of higher level guidance; the lack of awareness (on the part of various stakeholders) of the complexity that can exist in the UI architecture; and the difficulty of expressing the effort involved in making what may seem like simple changes to a UI. Our motivation for writing this paper is to stress the importance of planning the UI architecture, formalize a description of what is meant by the term "UI architecture," and provide fellow UI developers with a means of reasoning and negotiating about requirements that will affect this architecture.

In this paper we introduce a conceptual architecture that can help software developers reason about a user interface design in order to build a model of a user interface that is closer to their own domain of expertise. We use this conceptual UI architecture to help guide the software developer from a set of explicit and implied requirements expressed by UI concept documentation to a set of high-level architectural requirements that begin to direct decision making in the early stages of development. We go on to provide practical recommendations on how to better ascertain the implied requirements that must be discovered and addressed in order to fully realize the intended level of usability envisioned by the UI designers.

1.1   Terminology

Let us introduce a few terms which we will be using throughout this paper. We use the term *user task* or *task* to indicate a single, well-defined goal the end user is trying to achieve–for example, creating a new instance of object X. Designers strive to match the user interface to a user's mental model of the task.

The task-related organization of the interaction is referred to in this paper as the *UI concept*. It describes how various elements–selections from menus, form-fillin elements, dialog-boxes, etc–are used to present the interaction in a comprehensible, memorable and convenient manner relevant to the user tasks [2]. The UI concept is guidance to be applied to all use cases in the application.

A well-known UI concept both on the web and in desktop applications is the wizard-driven workflow. It organizes interactions as a linear sequence of subtasks. The interface guides the user through the subtasks, one step at a time. Each step presents only the interaction details needed for that subtask. "Next" and "Back" buttons provide a way to reach the next and previous subtasks.

We define *user gesture* as an action the user takes upon a user interface element. Examples are keyboard input, mouse clicks, mouse hovering, and dragging and dropping.

A term often heard in conjunction with user interface design is *look and feel*. The ubiquity of the term captures an intuitive notion of the appearance of an interface. As we will discuss, this could serve to disguise the complexity of the requirements involved in implementing user interfaces. In our usage, we indicate a distinction between *look* and *feel*. *Look* refers to the appearance of the view in all its states, while *feel* refers to the quality of the interactions and overall user experience.

2 Structure of the UI Architecture

When we speak of UI architecture we are referring to the portions of the web application that provide the user a visual interface by which to interact with the web application. This constitutes instances of the View and the Controller in the well known Model-View-Controller pattern. A concrete implementation of the UI architecture consists of artifacts that are delivered to the end user's web browser (e.g. HTML, CSS, and JavaScript files), the intermediate artifacts that generate them (e.g. JSP or PHP files), server-side UI logic (as opposed to application business logic) and other supporting software.

We can represent the conceptual UI architecture of a web application as comprising several pieces, which we refer to as *aspects*. These aspects are illustrated and described below.

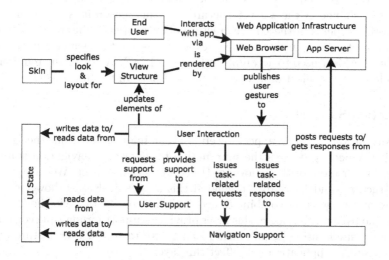

Fig. 1. Conceptual aspects of a presentation layer for rich web applications

View Structure

The View Structure organizes everything that needs to be rendered in order to provide the user with a view of the system and a way to interact with it. It defines relationships between elements that make it possible for other aspects to fulfill their respective purposes. Specifically, the View Structure is used by the User Interaction Aspect to manipulate the user interface, and by the Skin to present these elements in a usable and attractive way. Elements in the View

Structure are an answer to the question "what needs to be made available to the user to enable her to achieve her task?" Commonalities among actions and tasks drive the structuring of the elements.

Skin

The Skin is the most visible aspect of a web application's UI. It comprises the visual properties of the elements that are displayed to the user. This includes colors, fonts and styles, and layout, but excludes the screen elements themselves. Elements in this aspect are an answer to the question "How should elements in the View Structure appear to the user?" Because appearance is a concept that is easy to grasp and discuss, the Skin is arguably the simplest aspect with respect to requirements.

User Interaction

This aspect comprises features for receiving user input and propagating it to appropriate parts of the UI architecture. Events detect by this aspect are mapped to either the User Support or Navigation Support. This is the only aspect that may affect change in the View Structure. For this reason it is the interface by which other aspects in the UI architecture update what the user sees. Elements in this aspect are an answer to the question "how are the elements in the View Structure actually used to accomplish the user's goal?" As such, any requirement that relates to the effect of a user gesture will pertain to this aspect.

Navigation Support

The Navigation Support Aspect receives event information from the User Interaction Aspect, processes the information to determine navigation state and notifies one or more of the following: User Interaction Aspect, Web Application Infrastructure, and UI State. In general this aspect deals with how logical sequences of user gestures combine to accomplish a specific task via the UI. Aside from standard workflow logic, this layer provides support for multiple concurrent tasks for a single user. Requirements that relate to how a user gesture affects the state of the application will affect this layer.

User Support

The User Support Aspect enables a richer user experience by providing the user with visual guidance and support for specific UI interactions. Requirements that address accessibility, navigation guidance and contextual cues apply to this layer. In general, this layer deals with the type of interactions that do not invoke the Navigation Support. As such, these types of requirements will not impact the user workflow.

UI State

The UI State provides a memory of state that is independent of core business logic but is often required by rich interface elements. The persistence of this memory may live for any interval of time. The User Interaction, User Support, and Navigation Support aspects depend on this memory to store and provide UI information. For this reason, requirements upon these aspects might affect the UI State. The requirements as a whole should also provide an understanding of how long UI data may need to be persisted and what is the most appropriate way for data to be identified.

Web Application Infrastructure

This aspect provides the primary runtime support for the presentation layer. It is tasked with connecting the UI architecture to the user (via the web browser, for example) and to the other architectural constructs that are outside of the UI architecture (e.g. the core business logic.) It is an area of large-scale reuse primarily in the form of commercial off-the-shelf components. As such, it drives many subsequent architectural decisions. Depending on the choice of implementation technology, different breadth and depth of runtime support for the UI architecture may be available, accompanied by various constraints. Unlike the other more conceptual aspects, the Web Application Infrastructure is a more obvious proxy for the implementation technologies. These technologies tend to impose requirements and constraints independent of the user needs.

2.1 Requirements of the Different Aspects of the UI Architecture

User interface specialists have a number of tools at their disposal for conveying their designs. Documents that assist a UI designer in analyzing and managing design can be valuable for communicating the state of the design to team members and other stakeholders. At different stages of the software design cycle, these stakeholders need to know different things about the design. Concept maps, wireframes, storyboards, flow maps, detailed mockups and functional specifications each in turn provide different types of information [3]. Together, these sorts of documents convey the UI concept. At the point of constructing the conceptual software architecture, what information from UI design artifacts can support the UI architect in that task?

Our experience has been that, in the absence of a dialog between UI designers, software architects and implementers, the deeper architectural implications of these design documents can be easily missed, making it difficult to discern at the outset the lower level requirements for implementing these designs. From the top down the requirements given by UI designers can become progressively less detailed for implementers. In many instances the Skin may be very well defined. Requirements for the UI Interaction Aspect may be reasonably well described, but many details needed to inform its implementation-level architecture might not be addressed. For the Navigation and User Support and UI State, these design documents might do little to help provide detailed implementation-level requirements for developers. This is the portion of the architecture most in need of detailed requirements for the achievement of an extensible, maintainable system. Once fixed, changes to requirements that impact these aspects are very difficult and costly to make.

The apparent misalignment in the type of details provided by the UI designers and those needed by the implementers is even more paradoxical in light of the commonality in the approach to the requirement analysis: The UI designers start analyzing the requirements relevant to the deeper aspects of UI architecture very early in their work. However, their output often takes the form of static, "skin-related" wireframes, without explicitly specifying the details needed for the User Support, User Interaction and Navigation Support Aspects.

In the following sections we look at the aspects of this conceptual UI architecture and consider what clues in the UI design documents can be used to build these aspects in a manner that can clarify issues at implementation time.

2.2 View Structure

A reasonable start point for requirements gathering is with the View Structure: What elements are needed to enable the end user to accomplish a given task? What data needs to be presented? What data needs to be manipulated? What should the user use in order to manipulate the data? Although wireframe diagrams are primarily considered a description of a UI's layout, they sufficiently indicate the list of basic elements needed to present a given use case (albeit in a static way.)

But merely listing basic UI elements for a given task misses the point. Part of the richness of a user interface comes from the aggregation of basic elements–data entry widgets, buttons, and the like–into structures that match the user's semantic model of the task, and indicate well-defined relationships between those basic elements. (Let us call these aggregations *composite elements*.)

For example, a "list view" (see Fig. 2a) was a frequently occurring construct in one project. It lists a set of objects and their attributes, and allows the user to add, edit, and delete objects from the list. This description, together with its wireframe, suggests that a list view consists of a table, some checkboxes, and some buttons, each with a specific purpose.

This visual pattern was repeated in a number of wireframes. The obvious relationship that emerged was that these basic elements belong together. They are a "part of" the list view composite element.

However, just because things appear together in a wireframe does not mean they are strictly parts of a composite element. Many wireframes contained a list view collocated with primary and secondary navigation elements (see Fig. 2b.) The wireframes do not make the relationship between the navigation elements and the list view clear. But the UI concept does: User interactions upon the primary and secondary navigation elements affect which list of objects is shown in the list view. Therefore their relationship is a "cause-effect" relationship.

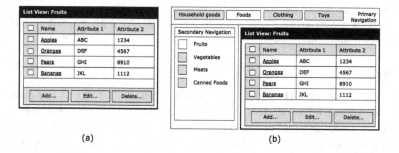

Fig. 2. (a) depicts a wireframe of a list view. A number of basic elements–text labels, check boxes, buttons, etc.–are composed to form a single composite View Structure element. (b) depicts a wireframe of a list view in context with primary and secondary navigation elements.

This is a looser structural relationship than the "part of" relationship between elements of the list view.

Which leads us to this note of caution: Hints provided by the UI concept for the View Structure should not be confused with hints provided for other aspects. In this example, the relationship between the secondary navigation and the list view composite element are of a functional nature that is more appropriately discussed in the User Interaction Aspect. They are collocated because one influences the other. The implication for the View Structure is that the user needs both of these elements to be available at the same time for this particular task.

There may be additional structural features that do not become apparent until one considers requirements of the User Interaction aspect. If elements are labeled with nouns, one might think of descriptive or state variants as adjectives. Think of an "enabled button," or a "selected object" (as opposed to one that is not selected.)

In summary, the View Structure should be concerned with making clear which basic elements are a part of which composite elements, and what of these need to be presented together. These composite elements, in turn, should represent abstractions from the user's semantic model of the task. View Structure requirements can be driven by:

– Identifying repeating (and potentially reusable) structural patterns, i.e. aggregations of basic elements
– Identifying the relationships between basic elements within a composite element. Even within a composite element there can be causal relationships. Keep in mind that such functional relationships–how one element influences another–are not a part of this architectural aspect.
– Identifying relationships between different elements. Again, keep in mind that we are looking for the "what," not the "how."
– Identifying descriptive or state variants for these elements. Note that these might also suggest additional requirements upon the UI State and Skin.
– Identifying outliers.

If the requirements gathering process is an iterative one, identifying outliers might involve comparing each instance of a pattern with patterns that have already been identified.

2.3 Skin

The Skin conveys all of the "look" and possibly part of the "feel." For each View Structure element for which it is applicable, the Skin requirements should specify its appearance. Bear in mind that the different states in which a View Structure element can exist ("enabled," "disabled," "selected," etc.) suggest requirements on the Skin.

The Skin can be discussed as a declarative aspect since, in most cases, the appearance of the UI gets mapped to attributes of the View Structure. Appearance is generally non-reactive.

There are, however, cases where code artifacts primarily targeting Skin (such as CSS) might play a more reactive role in conveying "feel." In such cases the aforementioned distinction between look and feel is important: Lumping look and feel together and making assumptions about their required interconnectivity leads to superficial requirements specifications. These fail to uncover important issues that need to be addressed where the quality of interaction is concerned. Requirements regarding the look of an application have very little direct influence on the other aspects of the architecture, while requirements regarding the feel potentially do. The implementation of feel primarily involves User Interaction, and User Support Aspects, and less frequently the Skin.

2.4 User Interaction Aspect

Features of this aspect connect user gestures upon elements in the View Structure to actions the system should take in order to achieve a designated outcome. This outcome may or may not result in changes to the application state. One side effect should always be that the UI provides an indication to the user that her input has been accepted and is being/has been processed.

One thing that is implied is that there is a mapping between user gestures and stimuli to the system to issue forth an appropriate result. This mapping is essentially the web application's way of "understanding" a user's request.

The task of understanding a user gesture is complicated by recently added user gestures that add to the richness of the interface. Traditionally, web applications did not recognize dragging and dropping gestures, or right-mouse-button clicks. These were reserved for the web browser itself. However, emerging AJAX libraries are making such gestures available to web application developers. This can dramatically increase the complexity of implementing constructs in the User Interaction Aspect.

A less obvious aspect worthy of note is that a user gesture's mapping may target any of a number of architectural constructs: It may impact elements in the View Structure, interact with other elements in the User Interaction Aspect, make requests of the User Support features, save or retrieve UI state, request navigation, or trigger core business logic.

Once View Structure elements have been identified, the cause-effect relationships are the starting point for requirements elicitation for this aspect: What user gesture upon View Structure element A causes an effect upon architectural element B?

Analysis of the cause-effect relationship between the secondary navigation element and the list view might proceed as follows: Suppose the UI concept indicated that selecting an element from the secondary navigation should provide the user with a list view of the corresponding object. This suggests a number of requirements for a number of aspects:

- The elements of the secondary navigation must be responsive to user gesture. This specifies the cause. As such, it is a requirement on the User Interaction Aspect. (Note that there may be multiple gestures assigned to an element.)
- For each (structural) element in the secondary navigation there is an associated list view. This is a requirement on the View Structure.
- There is a distinction between elements in the secondary navigation that are selected and those that are not. This is a requirement on the View Structure.
- If the aforementioned selection state has a visual distinction, then that constitutes a requirement on the Skin.
- If the selected navigation element needs to be remembered, then it contributes requirements upon the UI State Aspect.
- The user gesture upon the secondary navigation maps to the action of presenting the appropriate list view. This specifies the effect, and is therefore a requirement on the User Interaction Aspect.

It also leaves open questions: Can multiple elements within the secondary navigation be selected? Where does the selected list view come from? (The fact that the cause of the interaction is from a secondary navigation element suggests that the Navigation Support Aspect might be involved.)

To generalize from these examples, requirements for the User Interaction Aspect can be exposed by considering each element in the View Structure keeping the following questions in mind:

- What are the cause-effect relationships between its component parts?
- Is it involved in any cause-effect relationships with other elements?
- What user gestures does the element respond to?
- For each gesture
    - What is the intended target(s) in the high-level UI architecture?
    - What data does it provide to the target for processing?
    - How does the gesture provide that data to the target?
    - For each target, is there an expected response?

Keep in mind that this analysis will likely add to the list of requirements for other aspects of the UI architecture as well.

2.5 Navigation Support

The Navigation Support aspect provides the mechanisms for determining the next "place" to which to navigate in an application–the next step in the current user task. The most ostensible source of requirements for this aspect come from storyboards or flow maps that indicate navigation sequences [3]. However, requirements for deeper navigation capabilities (as opposed to a mere indication of how state transitions map to destinations) are driven primarily by the UI concept. Therefore, elements in this aspect must take into consideration the type of workflow logic illustrated in the UI concept, as well as what interactions or events affect change in the UI. For example, is the navigation concept sequential or non-sequential? Does the workflow contain optional sub-workflows that may affect the main workflow in some way? Are these presented in a single window or multiple communicating windows? Will events that are not initiated by the user affect the navigation logic?

Other pieces of information that complicate matters include the consideration of multiple windows, concurrency of workflows, and interaction between concurrent or embedded workflows. While the UI State aspect is concerned with how to use contextual information to store and identify information, the Navigation Support aspect is more focused on using these clues to correctly determine the next destination. Thus, once the requirements for the Navigation Support Aspect are agreed upon, design decisions made at this level are likely to generate functional requirements for the UI State Aspect, in terms of data structures that should be stored there. These requirements are not qualitatively different from the requirements that the UI State already handles, but represent a refinement which is straightforward to add.

Requirements on this aspect might also suggest requirements upon the User Interaction and User Support Aspects. To support wizard-driven workflows, for instance, the User Interaction and User Support Aspects would need to allow for a sequential set of actions by the user and conditional enabling of UI elements. On the other hand, for embedded workflows, the User Interaction Aspect may need to support multiple windows and the transfer of information from one window to another; the User Support Aspect may need to help the user understand how each embedded workflow relates to the main workflow; both of these may in turn suggest further requirements on the View Structure Aspect. Since the Navigation Support Aspect affects most of the other UI aspects, it should be one of the first pieces of the UI architecture to be explored and defined.

2.6 User Support

The emergence and evolution of so-called "Web 2.0" functionality, AJAX and related technologies is highlighting improved richness of user experience in web applications. One important aspect of this is the increased interactivity that provides guidance and support to the user.

User Support functions cover a wide range of needs, from customizing the contents of the navigation tree according to specific user access rights, to widget-specific tool tips, to providing inline help without impacting the user workflow. Looking at both web-based and native applications, the user support area is a critical component of competitive differentiation in the UI area.

This aspect is distinct from the Navigation Support which deals with the completion of actions/steps that directly lead to a change of state for some artifacts handled by the application. In contrast, User Support only deals with the level of support needed for the completion of one user gesture, and generally does not result in changes to application state.

Seen in another light, requirements on the Navigation Support Aspect tend to be functional requirements. User Support, as a look and feel enhancement, tends to be described by nonfunctional requirements (e.g., relating to usability.) The implementation of User Support functionality is not likely to be encapsulated in a standalone set of components, or a logical implementation layer. Rather, such requirements are likely to be orthogonal to UI elements.

Other requirements that should be discussed for this aspect are contents of tool tips, object-dependent context menus, progress or completion indicators, conditional enabling of widgets, indicators of the "droppability" of an object that is being dragged, etc. Each of these are important productivity features which are likely to increase in importance as web application UIs mature.

Since the support role of this layer is generally a passive one, it is likely that requirements for this layer receive less attention than those of features that actually achieve a user's goal. But elements in the User Support are intimately related to View Structure elements (by definition they are "in support of" those elements), and are triggered by mechanisms of the User Interaction Aspect. As such, it is natural that requirements for this aspect should be elicited alongside requirements for the View Structure and User Interaction Aspects. Furthermore, User Support requirements will, in turn, result in additional requirements for these aspects. However, let us reiterate the warning: This commingling should not result in a blurring of the architectural distinctions between them.

2.7   UI State

The UI State Aspect is responsible for maintaining the state of its user interface. Every piece of information that other UI aspects provide to the View Structure is ultimately stored and retrieved from the UI State. This aspect does not contain business logic, nor does it affect the underlying application state maintained in the Web Application Infrastructure. Although the concept of remembering information is straightforward, the complexity of this layer lies in the ability to define and maintain different spaces of information based on a number of possible constraints. These constraints help to indicate the proper context for storing data.

The proper context may be defined by the time interval in which the data must be remembered, the user or users to whom the data may be specific, the differentiating factor for data related to multiple instances of a UI element, or the sharing of data across multiple windows. As the user interacts with the application, this context ensures that the experience is consistent regardless of the resulting View Structure, concurrent user workflows, multiple-window interactions or multiple user sessions.

Time intervals that are commonly supported in web applications are the duration of single HTTP request, or a user's logged-in session. The boundaries of these intervals are well understood. However, with richer web applications, the desire for more intelligent interface elements can lead to time boundaries that may complicate implementation. For example, one requirement might state that for a given wizard-driven workflow, the last step in the wizard that was viewed must be maintained across user sessions until the workflow is completed or abandoned. This information must therefore be uniquely identifiable across multiple user sessions. Achieving a unique identifier requires having an early concept of what types of data will last in similar time spaces, and devising a proper naming convention accordingly.

Now, take the last example and combine it with another requirement that states for each user, multiple instances of this particular wizard-driven workflow can be run concurrently. This introduces a new kink to the time space originally defined for storing the last-visited page. The naming convention that was devised must now additionally support the differentiation of the last-visited page of one instance of the workflow from that of another. This is crucial for the integrity of your UI State. When such changes are made to the UI concept, it is important to determine whether this layer is also affected.

In general, the trend in providing richer functionality in web applications adds complexity to this layer. If a web application supports multiple-user interactions or multiple windows with some form of interaction, there must be consideration for defining separate and shared memory spaces. Furthermore, as richer interactions are described, we see an increase in UI State data, as well as in increase in the portion of that residing closer to the client-side and further from the core business logic.

2.8 Web Application Infrastructure

It is often not so easy to discuss how the Web Application Infrastructure is impacted by the UI concept. Clearly the Web Application Infrastructure is a very implementation-sensitive aspect. The semantic gap between a conceptual UI architecture and such an implementation-specific aspect is a difficult one to bridge.

In our experience, requirements upon this aspect are rather subtly suggested by the UI concept. How does a task decompose into parts? How reusable are these parts? How much interactivity can exist between these parts? How receptive are these to other stimuli (e.g. unsolicited events)? These questions are examples of things that can be taken for granted in describing the UI concept, but pose potentially difficult solutions to achieve in implementation. By considering these deeply architecturally relevant questions we can begin bridging the gap from the conceptual side.

From the implementation side, the availability of commercial off-the-shelf packages presents a compelling way to save on development costs. Whereas the notion of allowing a choice of technology to dictate high-level architectural concerns may seem to fly in the face of some software engineering principles, the capabilities and liabilities of technology choices are a principle architectural constraint. All but the simplest components have a presumed architectural pattern that is difficult to violate. If the architecture you design conflicts with the architecture assumed by a component, you will be shifting effort and resources toward integration. In [4], Bass et. al. provide a useful discussion about detecting and dealing with the architectural implications of OTS components.

3 Recommendations for Requirements Gathering

Based on our experiences, there are several points with respect to requirements gathering that we would like to be takeaways from this paper. These are presented below in order of importance.

The best way to refine UI requirements is to support and encourage closer collaboration between UI/HCI designers and implementers

One of the most valuable facets of agile methodologies, especially in comparison to plan-driven approaches, is their flexibility in the face of changing requirements. Having the UI designers work closely with the implementers in developing the UI concept along-side the conceptual architecture allows the two to mature in synch, rather than requiring significant rework to either. A shared boundary object, such as a storyboard as described in [5], allows both parties to bring their expertise and point of view into a discussion. The subtle implications that a UI concept has upon the UI architecture (even at a high level) can be exposed and discussed in a manner that does not stray significantly from the comfortable languages of either the UI designers or the implementers. The outcomes of this activity might be two separate documents specifying two different aspects of the system–the UI concept, and the UI architecture–but they will be well synchronized and of greater use later in the software lifecycle than if they are developed independently, one as a consequence of the other. In the event that the UI concept is beyond what can be created with the given resources/technologies/time constraints, then such a close collaboration offers the most expedient way to pinpoint that fact early on in the project time line. In this way each expertise can inform the other, and both views of the system can be enhanced for it.

Consider requirements in the deeper parts of the UI architecture before addressing requirements in less architecturally relevant parts

Only within the context of the capabilities and constraints of the deeper portions of the UI architecture can we form a realistic notion of how implementable the UI concept is. Failing to detect the mismatch between the requirements suggested by a rich UI concept and the capabilities and (perhaps more importantly) the constraints of the Web Application Infrastructure risks either increasing the effort of implementation significantly, or failing to adequately realize the UI concept. The later this mismatch is detected the greater the likely effort required to correct it. In the very least, an architectural treatment of the UI provides a basis for the realistic estimation of the effort involved in such a change.

Treat the organization and structure of the UI architecture with the same respect as that of the overall system architecture

It is a well-established practice in software engineering to document the system architecture of a software system upfront ahead of the start of development. From that view of the system, where the UI is likely referred to as a single component described in a high level manner, everything seems in perfect order; the trusty MVC pattern and its derivatives provide the basic structure for the UI, and at such a high level view no more detail is needed. Especially with respect to complex rich client-side interactions (User Interaction and User Support Aspects) this is not sufficient, as the functionality required by these aspects alone may warrant equating the UI to its own application. In these cases, especially in long term or large-scale projects with expectations of maintenance, it is recommended to approach the architectural design of the UI with similar diligence.

Mind the gap between the conceptual and the implementation architectures

The View Structure, User Interaction Aspect, User Support, and Skin are heavily related to each other. Part of what makes it difficult to distinguish them is that they can be heavily commingled in an implementation. However, allowing that commingling to suggest that these are not in fact distinct parts of an architecture risks coupling them in a way that ignores the separation of their concerns. This results in software that is difficult to comprehend, maintain, modify, and extend.

4 Conclusion

Companies continue to push the envelope of web development and redefine what users can do with their web applications. The success of the early purveyors of the so-called "Web 2.0" was largely due to its ability to provide a user experience approaching that of non-web-based applications, to which users have been accustomed for a long time. As richer user experience becomes an increasingly important product differentiator, software developers are hard-pressed to keep learning new technologies at the same unrelenting pace. Moreover, as tool vendors increase the number of offerings targeting these developers, one thing will remain the same: Developers, not UI specialists, will continue to bear the load of complex issues involved in developing the UIs of enterprise web applications, supporting and organizing conclusions drawn from analysis of the UI concept documentation, and addressing a need to more seriously consider the demands of bleeding-edge rich thin enterprise web applications (not to mention implementing, maintaining and extending them!).

The key to successful decision-making is communication in all facets of the software development process. In this paper we have discussed a specific instance of communication–that between UI designers and implementers–with the hope of helping to bridge the gap between their respective conceptual languages. Toward that end, we have outlined a conceptual architecture for rich web-based UIs. We intend for this architecture to help provide a mental framework for reasoning about UI requirements. Based on our own experiences, we have highlighted the portions of that architecture that shoulder the brunt of delivering a rich user experience. We have also suggested practical measures to aid in the elicitation of requirements for these aspects from analyzing UI design artifacts.

Although using this conceptual architecture can go quite a way toward organizing the development of user interfaces in a rich web application, it would still remain to elaborate a more detailed implementation architecture. However, even more so than in traditional web applications, the number of ways to map these conceptual elements to elements in a run-time view or a code view of an implementation architecture is quite varied. Conceptual elements will likely map to implementation elements in any of a number of languages. These elements, in turn, map to run-time elements that may reside on the client, the server, or cooperating elements on both. Even the nature of a user gesture has grown more complex: Whereas in traditional web applications the only architecturally significant user gestures were those that resulted in HTTP requests and responses, rich web applications offer a great deal more sophistication.

It is clear that this increase in sophistication suggests the need for clearer guidance in decision-making related to fleshing out an implementation architecture from the conceptual architecture presented here. We identify this as a topic for further study.

References

1. Constantine, L., Lockwood, L.: Software For Use. Addison Wesley, New York (1999)
2. Schneiderman, B.: Designing the User Interface. Addison-Wesley, Reading (1998)
3. Fulcher, R., Glass, B., Leacock, M.: Boxes and Lines over Bullets and Arrows: Deliverables that Clarify, Focus, and Improve Design. In: Presented at Usability Professionals' Association Annual Conference, Orlando Florida (2002) Available online: http://www.leacock.com/deliverables/
4. Bass, L., Clements, P., Kazman, R.: Software Architecture in Practice. Addison Wesley, New York (2003)
5. Gunaratne, J., Hwong, B., Nelson, C., Rudorfer, A.: Using evolutionary prototypes to formalize product requirements. In: Presented at Workshop on Bridging the Gaps II: Bridging the Gaps Between Software Engineering and Human-Computer Interaction, ICSE 2004, Edinburgh, Scotland (2004)

FJM2 - A Decentralized JMS System

Ruey-Shyang Wu[1], Kuo-Jung Su[1], Fengyi Lin[2], and Shyan-Ming Yuan[1]

[1] Department of Computer Science
National Chiao Tung University, Hsinchu , Taiwan, R.O.C.
{ruey,is85061,smyuan}@cis.nctu.edu.tw
[2] Department of Accounting Information Systems,
Chihlee Institute of Technology, Taipei, Taiwan, R.O.C.
O100@mail.chihlee.edu.tw

Abstract. With the growth of internet, the requirement for the communication and message exchanges between programs becomes more and more important. The Message-Oriented Middleware (MOM), such as Java Message Service (JMS), could not only greatly reduce the technical learning curve for programmers but also have some amazing characteristics: such as reliable, secured, and event-driven. In the traditional client-server architecture, not only the client side program has to maintain the resource for connections and memory management, but also the server side has to send out several copies of duplicated messages per amount of connected clients. It not only wastes the system resource but also the network bandwidth. A system this paper developed is Fast Java Messaging 2 (FJM2), it's a enhancement version from Fast Java Messaging (FJM). It creates a whole new JMS provider which is distributed, high performance, reliable, and easy to use and deploy. While compared with FJM, FJM2 adapts a more efficient communication protocol - Negative-acknowledgment (NACK)-Oriented Reliable Multicast (NORM), and does not adapt topic addressing. Moreover, FJM2 has the ability to work across WAN environment to extend the system coverage, and could be adapted for more different application scopes. It would benefit those who want to create a MOM system based on Java and multicast protocol.

Keywords: Message Oriented Middleware, Multi-cast, Enterprise Application Integration, Java Message Service.

1 Introduction

Network technology progresses very quickly in recent years. In wired environment, the bandwidth today has already been improved to 1Gbps. On the other hand, in wireless network, the 802.11n, which proposes some new physical transmission technologies, has improved the transmission rate up-to 300Mbps. Therefore, applications like digital home, VoD (Video on Demand) would no longer be a utopian idea, but a reasonable application to the real world.

With the advancements of the physical networking technology, more and more applications are trying to take the advantage of the network to establish a large-scale system. However such systems have many development issues. They include higher

D. Draheim and G. Weber (Eds.): TEAA 2006, LNCS 4473, pp. 326–340, 2007.
© Springer-Verlag Berlin Heidelberg 2007

technical learning curve and difficult to debug, comparing with traditional applications. To simplify developing effort, some kinds of distributed architectures, like MOM (Message-Oriented Middleware), has been proposed. MOM is a technology which hides the technical complexity from programmers to make system developing become much easier and quickly to create a large-scale, reliable, and secured applications. There are many MOM systems today, such as IBM WebSphere MQ, TIBCO RV, JMS (Java Message Service) [8], etc. JMS is one of the most popular and widely deployed systems in the world.

In the traditional client-server model, UNICAST transmission is widely used, because it fits human's instincts much well. It is also easier to debug and manage than other transmission technology. However, there is only one destination at a time in UNICAST transmission mode, so that if we want to broadcast a message to everyone interesting about it, we have to send out several copies of the duplicated messages. With the receivers growing, it would become a serious problem. In contrast to the UNICAST, there is another technology named MULTICAST, which could have multiple destinations for a message at a time. The management and debugging process would be much more complicated than UNICAST and requires much more software efforts because of multiple destinations capability. Moreover, the routing of MULTICAST protocol is also a difficult course to solve. It is not only a technical issue but also a policy issue to ISP (Internet Services Provider). Most of the existing routers and gateways do not support these MULTICAST routing features, so that the MULTICAST applications are usually constrained into LAN environment only. The limitation causes MULTICAST applications to develop extra functions so that they can exchange information when they are not in the same LAN.

To archive reliable service, the traditional solution is through positive ACK (Acknowledge). It sends out a positive ACK to sender whenever receive any messages. However, the ACK itself could be the performance bottleneck. It is the root cause of the relative longer message latency which constrains the overall system performance. In contrast, there is a technology called – NACK (Negative Acknowledge). It sends out only the information about the lost messages to sender, not positive acknowledges to every received messages to reduce both the number of control message and the transmission latency. In a network environment with a lower packet loss rate, the better performance we could gain through Negative Acknowledge (NACK). In this paper, we will adopt the technology into the JMS layers to improve data transmission. Unlike the traditional TCP-based JMS server, we will use MULTICAST with NACK to create best performance JMS server.

The paper is organized as following: Section 2 shows the backgrounds. Section 3 has whole design of FJM2. Section 4 introduces the protocol in FJM2. Section 5 shows the performance evaluation. Finally, section 6 is the conclusion and future work.

2 Backgrounds

2.1 Java Message Service (JMS)

Java Message Service (JMS) [8] proposed by Sun Microsystems is a set of Java API allows applications to read, write, and deliver messages. It defines only a common set of application programming interfaces and associated semantics that allow programs written in Java to communicate with each other via JMS architecture. JMS hides the network complexity from application programmers to make it become much easier for programmers to create large-scale, efficient, cross-platform and reliable messaging applications.

Figure 1 shows the abstract of JMS programming model, JMS application could play as a Message Producer or Consumer or even both of them at a time. And no matter which role they are, they must create the Connection and Session object instance through Connection Factory Object, and once Session object instance is ready, they could create Message Producer or Consumer object instance through Session object according to its requirement, and finally create the Message object instance for delivery and notification. Message Producers usually deliver messages to a specific Queue or Topic, and the JMS system would monitor such virtual destination object and notify the registered Message Consumers.

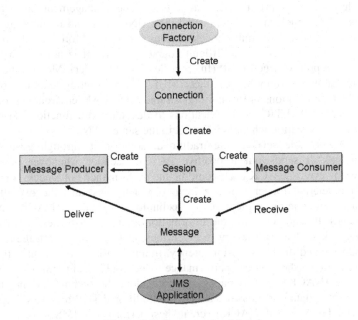

Fig. 1. JMS Programming Model

2.2 FJM

FJM (Fast Java Messaging) [9] is a former reference design of FJM2. It is a JMS system based on IP multicast protocol, negative acknowledgement and has a NACK based flow control. FJM offers only the publisher/subscriber model of JMS and its major objective is to provide a fast and reliable Java Message Service. There are several key characteristics of FJM architecture:

1.   It is a distributed system. There is no centralized management node in the entire system.
2.   It adapts NACK (Negative Acknowledgement) for message reliability. Under NACK approach, subscribers send out NACK to publisher only when message was lost.
3.   It provides a NACK based flow control. When publisher receives NAK from subscribers, it will slow down the message transmission rate to let subscriber catch up with it. If publisher has not yet received any NAK message for a period, it may speed up the transmission rate to gain a better throughput.
4.   It has membership management and multicast-based leader election protocol. While a new publisher or subscriber wants to join the system, it must first communicate with a FJM daemon to get system information. Because the FJM daemon is not dedicated to any participant, it is chosen from all the existing Topic Managers based on the election protocol.
5.   It has topic address binding. FJM binds up the topic by a specific multicast group address to reduce software overhead.

2.3 Objective

Although FJM performance is good and it simplifies programming overhead, it still has some disadvantages:

1.   The performance of FJM is not good enough while adapting into 100Mbps network environment. It requires at least 50 millisecond delay in inter message gap.
2.   The FJM cannot make the clients belonged to different subnet to communicate. The UNLICAST protocol is limited in a LAN.
3.   Programmer must be aware of the limitation described in (1), and a reasonable delay must be applied into every message publish routine.
4.   When the FJM member-ship changes, the FJM program would hang up and consume the entire system resource. (CPU utilization is almost 100%)
5.   Topic address binding would never benefit from the hardware dispatch for (Address, Port) binding. Because most of the Ethernet adapters in the world could only handle layer two (MAC Layer) protocols, while IP address is the layer three, and port number is in the layer four. Even in the recent system-on-a-chip (SoC) router design, layer four switching functionality is rarely available and never be implemented in a full specification.

We will reduce the delay in FJM2 system. Application developers will on longer notice the issues again. Besides, we develop a new addressing method to replace Topic address to gain better performance.

3 FJM2 System Architecture

FJM2 is a pure Java system so it can be cross-platform. Its major objective is to provide a de-centralized, reliable, efficient, multicast based Java Message Service (JMS) with minimal configuration overhead. To provide the WAN traversal ability for this multicast based system, Fast Java Message 2 Daemon (FJM2D) is proposed. There is also a small web based administration program - FJM2Admin, which provides FJM2D node list exchanging service. FJM2D could automatically communicate with each other across the world to provide a large-scale coverage for this multicast based FJM2 system.

3.1 FJM2 Architecture

Fast Java Messaging 2 (FJM2) is a Message Oriented Middleware (MOM) that abstracts the complexity of network programming to shorten the time for a robust

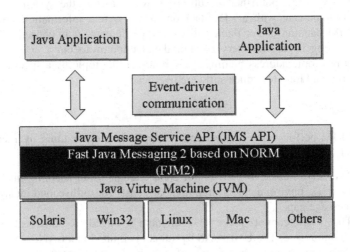

Fig. 2. FJM2 Architecture Overview

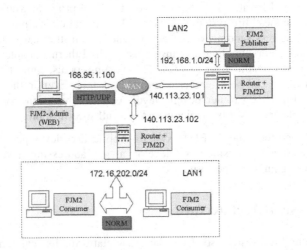

Fig. 3. FJM2 Physical Architecture

network application development. The only thing that application developers need to know is the set of JMS API. All the underlying technology is hidden as a black-box called JMS. Programmers could even change the underlying products for better performance or stability. Only few program modifications are needed. In other words FJM2 does not only provide the solution for the rapidly development, but also have the benefits of cross-platform or product characteristic.

Figure 3 shows a rough abstraction of the entire FJM2 physical architecture. Each LAN can deploy a complete FJM2 environment. All applications in the same LAN can communicate with each other. If one client wants to exchange message with another that is at another LAN, the FJM2D can carry those messages to another LAN. FJM2D is deployed at each LAN and connect to other FJM2Ds belonged to other LANs. With properly configuration, each FJM2D can decide the destination of each message; some message can be sent to another LAN, but some are not.

3.2 FJM2 Message Transmission Model

The FJM2 message transmission model is showed as Figure 4. The FJM2 publishers and consumers can communicate with each other if they are in the same LAN. However, if the message is needed by the consumers at another LAN, the FJM2D will recognized it and carry them to another FJM2D. After received the message, the FJM2D will multicast the message so that the FJM2 consumer will get the message. In the architecture, we could realize:

1. It is unnecessary to have a centralized daemon to let FJM2 publishers and consumers to communicate with each other inside LAN environment.
2. It is necessary to install a FJM2D on the edge gateway of the local network to make it possible to forward the FJM2 message to another FJM2D.
3. FJM2-Admin serves only FJM2D and never communicates with FJM2 daemons directly, so that the configuration requirement could be minimized.
4. The communication protocol between FJM2 daemons (publishers and/or subscribers) is a NORM protocol based on IP multicast and NACK.

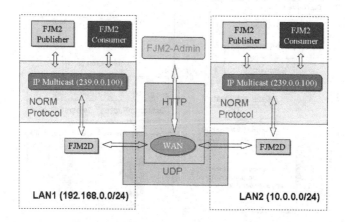

Fig. 4. FJM2 Message Transmission Model

5.   The communication protocol between FJM2 and FJM2D is a NORM protocol based on IP multicast and NACK.

6.   The communication protocol between FJM2D daemons is a NORM message delivered by UNICAST.

7.   The network behind FJM2D could be a different subnet.

3.3 FJM2 Message Publish Program Flows

Figure 5 shows the flows in FJM2 software components while publishing messages. It does not include the procedure of message repair process. It is merely a general program flow upon message publishing. It is unnecessary to determine a multicast leader (Guide) as what FJM1 does. The FJM2 daemon could immediately enter normal message handling procedures after startup. When the membership changes, there is only a little redundant message and few incomplete cache would be occupied in consumer/subscriber's memory for a period of time. It would be free upon cache expire. For the reason, the entire system overhead is much lower than the previous FJM. It would be much easier for FJM2 to develop a stable messaging service than FJM. Its flow is listed as followed:

1.   Publisher creates a Message object instance and puts data into its body.

2.   Publisher de-queue a NormDataMessage object instance from the message pool. This object instance is the container for the message.

3.   FJM2 segments the message to fit in the message payload that best fits in current network environment. However, the segmentation here generates only the marks about how the fragments should be taken.

4.   FJM2 copys the segmented message into the NormDataMessage object instance which de-queued from the pool in step (2). Finally, it will build up the header for it.

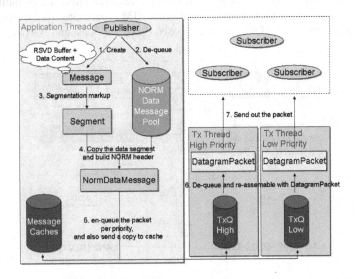

Fig. 5. FJM2 Message Publish Program Flows

5. FJM2 en-queue the prepared NormDataMessage object instance into the proper transmission queue according to its message priority, and makes a copy of the message into the MessageCaches for a possible message repair process that might be initialized later.

6. Each transmission queue has a dedicated stand-alone monitoring thread that has a proper thread priority. When the queue is not empty, the thread would de-queue a message from it and process a generic transmission routine

7. Once the transmission thread de-queue a message from the queue successfully, it will send it out through the socket library.

3.4 FJM2 Message Subscribe/Consume Program Flows

Figure 6 shows the flows of FJM2 software components while subscribing/consuming messages. It also includes the procedure of message repair process. It is unnecessary to determine a multicast leader (Guide) and the registration processes those are necessary in previous FJM. The FJM2 daemon could enter normal message handling procedures immediately after startup. During the membership changes, the incomplete message cache will be occupied in consumer or subscriber's memory. It would be free upon cache expire. So the entire system overhead is lower than FJM, and thus it would be much easier for FJM2 to develop a stable messaging service than FJM. Now let's take a look at the flows:

1. Application receives a packet (symbol) from the network, and then put it into the packet buffer.

2. Build a key for message cache from the header of the received packet, and the use for the cache lookup. If there is a corresponding cache to this key, the program flows to step (5). Otherwise, it will go to step (3).

3. Poll out a message container from the message pool. The message pool would be selected according to the total message size recorded in header.

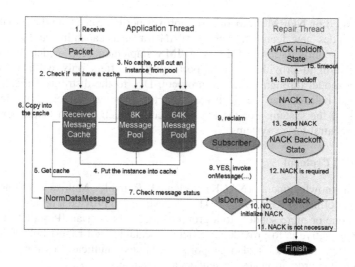

Fig. 6. FJM2 Message Subscribe/Consume Program Flows

4. Put the message container instance into the message cache.
5. Treat the object which is just fetch from message cache or polled from the message pool as a NormDataMessage object.
6. Copy the data inside the packet buffer into the NormDataMessage object.
7. Check if the message is complete or not, if it's true then flows into step (8). Otherwise, program will go to step (10).
8. If the message is already a complete one, invoke onMessage(...) of all the registered subscriber applications.
9. When onMessage(...) returns, reclaim the message object to the pool.
10. If the message is not yet complete, it would try to initialize NACK process. If the NACK process is really necessary, it then flows into step (12). Otherwise, go to step (11)
11. Although the message is incomplete, the NACK process is still not yet necessary in this case. Then, FJM2 will terminate this receive event handle.
12. If the message is incomplete and it is time for NACK process, initializes NACK process and enters NACK back-off state.
13. During NACK back-off state, the subscriber would monitor the NACK appears on the network. If it matches the one recorded in its own NACK items, it suppresses the NACK for that item. When back-off timeout occurs, the program would enter NACK transmission state.
14. In NACK transmission state, the program would send out the NACK message through socket library, and then enter hold-off state.
15. The hold-off state is the way to avoid repeated NACK message in a given delay timeout.
16. When hold-off timeout occurs, the program would flows back to NACK decision state to determine the next step is (11) or (12).

4   FJM2 Protocol

FJM2 is based on NORM protocol and improves performance than the previous FJM. It also includes new features, such as WAN traversal capability and automatically FJM2D self-configuration. FJM2 is a JMS implementation which is pure java implementation to provide the best portability. It offers only publish /subscriber messaging model through multicast protocol. Due to the distributed architecture of FJM2, load balance can be achieved, and the message server is no longer the bottleneck of the system. For the reason, it could reach a much better performance than other central server systems.

4.1   NORM Protocol

Negative-acknowledgment (NACK) Oriented Reliable Multicast (NORM) [16] Protocol is defined in RFC 3940, 3941. It's designed to provide a reliable transport of data from one or more senders to a group of receivers over an IP multicast network. Its major objective is to provide an efficient, scalable, and robust bulk data transfer over multicast network. It also supports distributed multicast session participation with minimal coordination among senders and receivers.

A NORM protocol instance (NormSession) is defined within the context of participants communicating connectionless packets over a network using pre-determined addresses and host port numbers. Generally, the participants exchange packets using an IP multicast group address, but UNICAST transport may also be established or applied as an adjunct to multicast delivery. In the case of multicast, the participating NormNodes will communicate using a common IP multicast group address and port number that has been chosen via means outside the context of the given NormSession.

Group communication scalability requirements lead to adaptation of negative acknowledgment (NACK) based protocol schemes when reliability feedback is required. NORM is a protocol centered on the use of selective NACKs to request repairs of missing data. NORM provides for the use of packet-level forward error correction (FEC) techniques for efficient multicast repair and optional proactive transmission robustness. FEC-based repair can be used to greatly reduce the quantity of reliable multicast repair requests and repair transmissions in a NACK-oriented protocol. The principal factor in NORM scalability is the volume of feedback traffic generated by the receiver set to facilitate reliability and congestion control. NORM uses probabilistic suppression of redundant feedback based on exponentially distributed random back-off timers. NORM dynamically measures the group's roundtrip timing status to set its suppression and other protocol timers. This allows NORM to scale well while maintaining reliable data delivery transport with low latency relative to the network topology over which it is operating.

4.2 NORM Protocol in FJM2

In FJM2, we adapts Compact No-Code FEC scheme in the low level transport protocol – NORM Protocol. It's a Fully-Specified FEC scheme corresponding to FEC Encoding ID 0. It does not require FEC encoding or decoding. Instead, each encoding symbol consists of consecutive bytes of a source block of the object. The FEC Payload ID consists of two fields, the 16-bit Source Block Number and the 16-bit Encoding Symbol ID.

Figure 7 is the fec_payload_id format used for Compact No-Code FEC in FJM2, it is one word smaller than Small Block, Systematic ("fec_id"=129). This is why choose Compact No-Code FEC is due to performance consideration. Generic FEC Encode/Decode is really a time consume process.

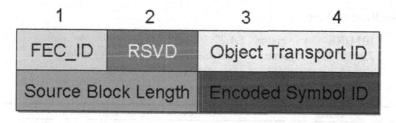

Fig. 7. Compact No-Code FFC("fec_id"=0) "fec_payload_id" Format

Table 1. Testing Environment

Item	Description
CPU	Intel Pentium M 740 (1.73 GHz)
Memory	1 Giga-Bytes SDRAM
Java Runtime	Sun Microsystems 1.4.2_04
Java FEC Library	Onion Networks Java FEC Library v1.0.3

Table 2. Performance Matrix

Symbol / Source Data	512 Bytes	1024 Bytes	1440 Bytes
1 Kbytes	0 ms	0 ms	0 ms
2 Kbytes	0 ms	0 ms	0 ms
4 Kbytes	0 ms	0 ms	0 ms
8 Kbytes	0 ms	0 ms	0 ms
16 Kbytes	1 ms	0 ms	0 ms
32 Kbytes	6 ms	2 ms	1 ms
64 Kbytes	35 ms	11 ms	7 ms

Therefore, in best case, Java FEC library could encode (1000 / 7 = 142.8) 64Kbytes Message per second, while 100 Mbps = (100 / 8 * 1024 / 64 = 200) 64Kbytes Message per second. And thus we could have a conclusion that while Java FEC is adapted, the overall system would never exceed 100 * (142.8 / 200) = 71.4 Mbps.

The NACK Algorithm used in FJM2 is almost exactly the same as the one described in NORM protocol, except the sender NACK process. Because in FJM2 we adapt Compact No-Code FEC scheme as the symbol algorithm, sender NACK suppress is meaningless to FJM2.The sender NACK algorithm in FJM2 is merely sending out a repair symbol as soon as possible when the it got NACK message. It still has the message symbol cache for this lost message, and there is no any timer used in sender NACK process.

5   FJM2 Performance Analyses

5.1   Testing Environment

Java Runtime Version:

- IBMJRE - java version "1.4.2"
- Java(TM) 2 Runtime Environment, Standard Edition (build 1.4.2)

Table 3. Testing Environment

ID	Processor	Memory	Operation Systems
PC1	Pentium M 740 (1.74GHz)	1 GB	Windows XP Home SP2
PC2	Pentium 4-M 1.80GHz	512 MB	Windows XP Professional SP2
PC3	Pentium®4 1.80Ghz	256 MB	Windows 2000 Professional SP4

- Classic VM (build 1.4.2, J2RE 1.4.2 IBM Windows 32 build cn1420-20040626 (JIT enabled: jitc))

WIN32 Compiler

- The tool-chain used in WIN32 test program is lcc-win32.

5.2 UDP Performance Benchmark on 100Mbps Ethernet Interface

Figure 8 shows the connection topology in this test. The test scenario starts from launching program at PC1. After the test program launches at the PC1, it will generate fixed-size message buffer with a randomly generated content. Then, it will try to send the whole message in a single socket function to the receiver. After the receiver receives the message, the receiver calculates the performance value without message verification. In this test scenario, there are C and Java implementation. The result is shown as Figure 9.

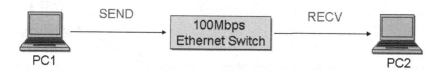

Fig. 8. 1-to1 performance test connection topology

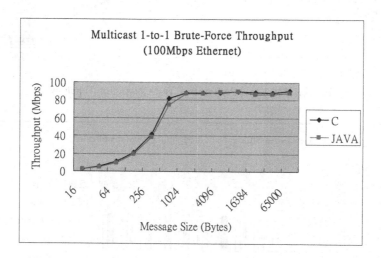

Fig. 9. UDP Multicast Throughput on 100MB

After the performance test, Java could work almost as good as C under 100MbpsEthernet network. The throughput grows very fast in the range from 256 to 1024 Kbytes. The best performance is at the range from 1024 to 2048 Kbytes. The best throughput under 100Mbps Ethernet is around 90Mbps.

5.3 One-to-Two Benchmark on 100MBps Ethernet Interface

Figure 10 shows the connection topology in this test. There are four JMS systems to be tested: FioranoMQ 2006, SonicMQ v7.0, iBus//MessageBus 5.0, and our FJM2. FioranoMQ and SonicMQ are server based products, while iBus and FJM2 are multicast based. The test scenario is as followed:

1. Launch the test program. Then, follow the parameters to generate a fixed-size message buffer with a randomly generated content.
2. The sender program would try its best to send out the whole message in a single JMS function - publish(...)
3. The receiver program would be notified through the JMS callback function - onMessage(...) to receive message, and then calculate the performance value without message verification.

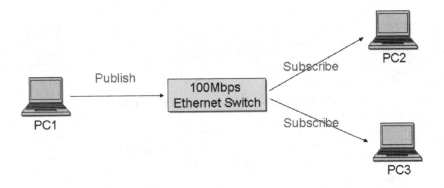

Fig. 10. JMS 1-to-2 Performance Test Connection Topology

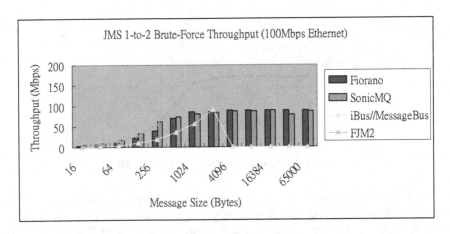

Fig. 11. JMS 1-to-2 Throughput on 100Mbps Ethernet

FJM2 obviously outperforms all the other JMS system while message size equals or larger than 512 bytes, and more subscribers grows. SonicMQ outperforms all the other JMS systems while message size is less than 512 bytes. Although iBus/MessageBus is the only one multicast based on JMS system except FJMS, it has a poor performance and serious problem on memory management.

6 Conclusion and Future Works

Publisher/Subscriber Model is a popular communication model in the world. Most of existing JMS products adapt centralized rather than a distributed architecture. Besides, most of them do not use pure Java implementation. They usually deploy a native program for the critical section for performance reason and thus lost the ability of cross-platform. Here, we introduction a possible method to implement a decentralized JMS system base on NORM protocol by pure Java.

From the benchmarks in this paper, we could conclude that FJM2 is a successful design that has took a great advantage from multicast to have a dramatic performance improvement when the number of receivers grows. On the other hand, when compared with centralized design, FJM2 could be even better than centralized products for several times. So, it also has a good performance value in 1-to-1 transmission. While compared to the existing multicast based JMS system – iBus, FJM2 is very stable and every publisher or subscriber could dynamically join or leave the topic and the action would not system to waste too much resource. However in iBus, it has not only a memory management issue on rapidly message publishing, it would even crash the topic publisher while any one of the subscribers leaves.

Acknowledgments. The Ministry of Education of the Republic of China partially supported this work under grant nos. NSC94-2725-E009-006-PAE (Advanced Technologies and Applications for Next-Generation Information Networks (II)) and NSC94-2213-E009-026 (A Research on Next-Generation Massive Multiplayer Virtual Environment Platform). We thank the anonymous reviewers and editors for many useful comments.

References

1. The Institute of Electrical and Electronics Engineers, Inc., IEEE P802.11n./D1.0 Draft Amendment to STANDARD [FOR] Information Technology-Telecommunications and information exchange between systems-Local and Metropolitan networks-Specific requirements-Part11: Wireless LAN Medium Access Control (MAC) and Physical Layer (PHY) specifications: Enhancements for Higher Throughput (March 2006)
2. Liang, D., Fang, C.-L., Yuan, S.-M., Chen, C., Jan, G.E.: A fault-tolerant object service on CORBA. Journal of Systems & Software 48(3), 197–211
3. Yue-Shan, C., Kai-Chih, L., Ming-Chun, C., Shyan-Ming, Y.: Prototyping an Integrated Information Gathering System on CORBA. Journal of Systems & Softwares 72(2), 281–294
4. Armstrong, S., Freier, A., Marzullo, K.: Multicast Transport Protocol, RFC 1301 (February 1992)

5. Braudes, R., Zabele, S.: Requirements for Multicast Protocols. RFC 1458, (May 1993)
6. Whetten, B., Montgomery, T., Kaplan, S.: A High Performance Totally Ordered Multicast Protocol. In: Proc. of Int'l. Workshop on Theory and Practice in Distributed Systems, pp. 33–57 (1995)
7. Obraczka, K.: Multicast Transport Protocols: A Survey and Taxonomy. IEEE Communication Magazine (January 1998)
8. Sun Microsystems. Java Message Service, Version 1.1 (April 2002)
9. Chuan-Pao, H., Hsin-Ta, C., Yue-Shan, C., Tsun-Yu, H., Tzu-Han, K., Shyan-Ming, Y.: FJM: A Fast Java Message Delivery Mechanism based on IP-Multicast. In: Third International Conference on Communications in Computing (2002)
10. Ruey-Shyang, W., Shyan-Ming, Y., Anderson, L., Daphne, C.: iCell: Integration Unit in Enterprise Cooperative Environment, Grid and Cooperative Computing, pp. 962 – 969 (2004/04)
11. Deering, S.: Host Extensions for IP Multicasting, RFC 1112 (August 1989)
12. Hsin-Ta, C., Shyan-Ming, Y.: An Enhanced Thread Synchronization Mechanism for Java. Software – Practice and Experience 31(7), 667–695
13. Cain, B., Deering, S., Kouvelas, I., Fenner, B., Thyagarajan, A.: Internet Group Management Protocol, Version 3, RFC 3376 (October 2002)
14. Quinn, B., Almeroth, K.: IP Multicast Applications: Challenges and Solutions, RFC 3170 (September 2001)
15. Fenner, B., Meyer, D. (eds.): Multicast Source Discovery Protocol (MSDP), RFC 3618 (October 2003)
16. Adamson, B., Bormann, C., Handley, M., Macker, J.: Negative-Acknowledgment (NACK)-Oriented Reliable Multicast (NORM) Building Blocks, RFC 3941 (November 2004)
17. Java FEC Library: http://onionnetworks.com/developers
18. Modarres, M., Ardekani, M.B.: Enterprise support system architecture: integrating DSS, EIS, and simulation technologies. International Journal of Technology Management 31(1/2), 116–128 (2005)

Implementing Automated Analyses in an Active Data Warehouse Environment Using Workflow Technology

Michael Zwick, Christian Lettner, and Christian Hawel

Software Competence Center Hagenberg GmbH
Hauptstrae 99, 4232 Hagenberg, Austria
{michael.zwick,christian.lettner,chrisitan.hawel}@scch.at

Abstract. A major goal of active data warehouses is to automatically perform analysis tasks. However, this goal is only insufficiently implemented in current active data warehousing architectures. For end-users, it is not possible to design and modify such automated analysis tasks, as the needed tools are not seamlessly integrated into common business intelligence environments. As analysis tasks can be modeled as workflows in a natural way, we propose to use workflow technology to close this gap. Furthermore, workflow engines provide a graphical user interface that can be extended to allow end-users to assemble and manage complex analysis tasks. A prototype that builds up the foundation for this new active data warehousing architecture is implemented using Microsoft Excel^{TM}, SQL Server 2005^{TM} and Windows Workflow Foundation^{TM}, providing end-users with the environment to design automated analyses.

1 Introduction

Today, many organizations are using *data warehouse* (DWH) technology to support their decision making process. Data warehouses [1] serve as a central data store loaded from operational systems and enable organizations to interactively analyze huge amounts of data by allowing them to create different scenarios to investigate a current business problem and subsequently choose the most suitable one. Traditionally, data warehouses are used to support non-routine decision making tasks within the strategic decision making process (e.g. the decision to set up a new brand or the decision to abandon a whole production process due to severe deficiencies in output quality).

On the other hand, routine decision tasks are more likely to be found at the tactical and operational level of an organization. They emerge from well structured problems where generally accepted procedures can be applied [2]. For example, failure ratio in manufacturing is monitored on a daily basis, in order to detect problems early in the production process. Although these routine decision tasks are well structured, they can be complex and may require detailed domain knowledge (e.g. if the defects rise above certain thresholds a more detailed analysis has to be performed. The exact value of the threshold is only known by the analyst himself and not stored in the DWH).

D. Draheim and G. Weber (Eds.): TEAA 2006, LNCS 4473, pp. 341–354, 2007.
© Springer-Verlag Berlin Heidelberg 2007

As these levels within the organization are more closely connected to the daily business, the requirement for more accurate data along with more frequent updates to the DWH emerges. Batches that update the DWH on a daily basis can not be used anymore. In some cases, updated data needs to be made available in the DWH as soon as an event occurs in an operational system (i.e. in real-time). In general, the data must be available at *right-time*, which is specified by the specific business demand. Right-time availability is defined by the rate of information delivery needed for a certain analysis [3,4,5]. To meet this right-time requirement, all major *extract-transform-load* (ETL) and *enterprise application integration* (EAI) tool suppliers provide solutions today [6].

Another characteristic of routine decision tasks is that the same analyses are repeated rather frequently. In conjunction with the clear scope that routine decision tasks comprise, these tasks are ideal candidates for automated analysis. This automation of decision tasks is an essential goal of *active data warehousing* [2], a goal that is barely addressed in current architectures. The needed tools are not seamlessly integrated into common business intelligence environments, which prevents end-users from designing and modifying automated analysis tasks. When the integration is accomplished, the results of automated analysis can be used to immediate trigger actions in operational systems. This implements the *closed-loop* that connects business intelligence with the operational systems [7].

An analysis can be perceived as a directed graph where each vertex represents a partial analysis and each edge a condition which connects subsequent analyses. A transition between two connected vertices (i.e. partial analysis) is performed, if the corresponding condition holds. Such a graph exhibits all properties that can be found in *workflow systems* [8]. Thus, we propose to implement an ADW architecture for automated analyses based on workflow technology. In this paper we describe why and how existing workflow technology can be used to automate routine decision tasks and subsequently implement a prototype of our proposed ADW architecture with off-the-shelf components.

The remainder of the paper is organized as follows: Chapter 2 provides an overview about related work in the field of active data warehousing. Chapter 3 introduces the proposed ADW architecture. Chapter 4 introduces primitives needed for defining analysis graphs. Chapter 5 motivates the use of workflow engines for automated analyses and presents a prototype implementation using an example taken from the quality assurance process of a sensor production line. The discussion of the achieved results and an outlook to future work is presented in Chapter 6. Finally, the conclusion is presented in Chapter 7.

2   Related Work

2.1   Combining DWH and BAM

In [9], the *event-condition-action* [10] model of *business activity monitoring* (BAM) [4] is enhanced with the powerful analytic capabilities of data warehousing. While the DWH provides access to the multidimensional cubes for complex analyses, BAM implements the closed-loop using alerts or automated actions triggered by a rule engine. A similar architecture is presented in [11]. However, the main focus of [9,11] is on right-time integration and establishing the closed-loop back into the operational systems, not on automating complex analyses tasks.

2.2 Analysis Rules

To support automated analyses, [12,2] introduces *analysis rules* that emulate the way an analyst inspects multidimensional data. Starting from a coarse-grained root cube, the analyst creates several local cubes using OLAP operators ROLLUP, DRILLDOWN, SLICE and INTERSECTION in a top-down manner. Local cubes and OLAP operators together form the *analysis graph*, where cubes represent the vertices and OLAP operators the edges of the graph. For each local cube in the analysis graph the analyst has the alternative to trigger an action, end the analysis or perform a more detailed analysis. This decision, applicable at every vertex, together with the analysis graph and the event that triggers the analysis graph, represents the semantics of the analysis rule. Each analysis rule is defined for a dedicated dimension level, the primary dimension level of the analysis rule which usually corresponds to an entity in the operational system (OLTP system). The rule will be executed for a primary dimension level element and the triggered action will be bound to the corresponding OLTP object of the primary dimension level.

Figure 1 depicts the example analysis rule *MonitorDefectiveProducts*. At the end of each quarter (the event), the rule analyzes the average number of defective products along with the trend of the last three months, in order to stop production of the corresponding product category in case the rate of defective products is above a predefined threshold (10% in this example). The primary dimension level for the rule is the dimension *Product* at the level *Category*, denoted as *Product[Category]*. Transition 1 performs a slice through the coarse-grained cube "Defects" along the dimension *Time* to get to the current quarter (in our case *Q2*). Then the average number of defects is evaluated. If the defects are below 10% for a certain product category, no further analysis is performed. If the defects exceed 10%, a more detailed analysis will be performed by drilling down to the month level within the time dimension *Time[Month]* (transition 2). Finally, the quarterly trend is analyzed by comparing the average numbers of defects for *April*, *May* and *June*. If the trend points upwards, the action to suspend production of the corresponding product categories will be triggered. If the trend points downwards, no action will be performed.

In [12,2], a proof of concept for analysis rules is implemented using triggers and SQL within an Oracle[TM] database. As end-user support was not in the scope of this work, design and modification of analysis rules needs a considerable knowledge of SQL and the underlying framework.

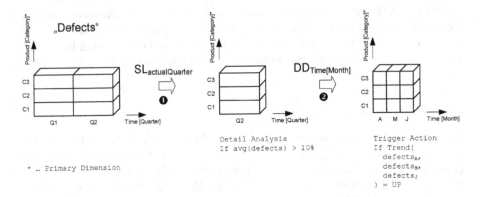

Fig. 1. Analysis Graph *MonitorDefectiveProducts*

3   Proposed ADW Architecture

We propose an active data warehouse (ADW) architecture that extends the general architecture introduced in [9] with analysis rules introduced in [2]. Figure 2 shows the resulting architecture.

The eight main components are:

1. The *OLAP Recorder* (OR), which records all OLAP queries executed by the user with an ad-hoc analyses tool. It builds up a query history which can be used to automatically generate analysis graphs.
2. The *Analysis Graph Manager* (AGM) is the glue that brings together DWH and BAM. It manages analysis graphs, which are recorded interactively by analysts using ad-hoc reporting tools or modeled directly with the Analysis Graph Manager.
3. The *Event Manager* (EM) collects events, which trigger predefined analyses in the ADW.
4. The *Right-time Integrator* (RTI) integrates the necessary data coming from different source systems. It provides a consistent view suitable for the analyses [9].
5. For each vertex in the analysis graph, the *Rule Engine* (RE) performs the corresponding analysis. Based on the results, the Rule Engine determines the next vertex in the analysis graph or triggers predefined actions.
6. The *Semantic Model* (SM) represents knowledge about processes, structures and relationships within operational systems. This knowledge will be used to evaluate decision points, trigger actions and provide explanations to the end-user.
7. The *Action Manager* (AM) stores all actions that may be performed by the ADW. Actions get triggered by an analysis graph and range from simple mail notifications to specific transactions in the operational systems.
8. The *Explanation Module* (EXM) provides the end-user with all information necessary to retrace the steps leading to the executed action.

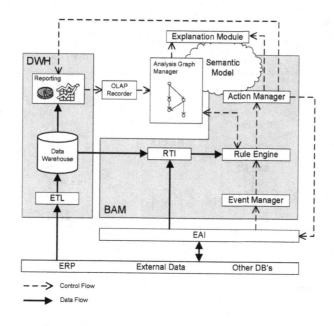

Fig. 2. ADW architecture with analysis graphs

4 Primitives for Analysis Graphs

In general, end-users analyze OLAP cubes in a top-down manner. They start
from coarse-grained cubes, inspect measures along different dimensions and make
decisions based on the information they find in the data. Decisions taken by the
end-user can be categorized into performing a further analysis or performing an
action, in case the business problem has been solved. Within the first category,
two basic patterns can be identified immediately and used as primitives for
analysis graph specifictions: *AnalysisStep* and *AnalysisLoop*. The third primitive
Action is a generic placeholder which can be configured to implement the closed-
loop e.g. via notifications or source system transactions. Figure 3 shows the
identified AnalysisStep, AnalysisLoop and Action primitives.

The AnalysisStep primitive consists of two parts: a *query part*, to get all
necessary measures, and an *evaluation part* to model decisions taken by the end-
user. The AnalysisLoop primitive selects a set of dimension members where each
member is used to execute further analysis steps in the loop. Within the branches
and bodies, all primitives can be used recursively to define more complex analysis
graphs (indicated by the question marks in figure 3).

To make analysis graphs useable for end-users, definition and recording of
analysis graphs must be preformed automatically in the background. As this is
easily possible for the queries end-users execute, it becomes even more challenging recording the decisions taken during analysis. For example, the decision to
drill-down to a certain member may be affected by implicit and domain specific

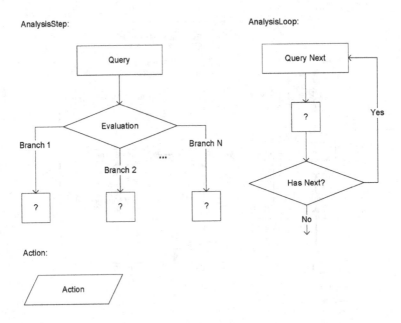

Fig. 3. Analysis Graph Primitives

knowledge of the end-user which is not automatically recordable. To capture this implicit knowledge, an adequate interaction has to take place between recorder and end-user. Domain knowledge acquired in this way could be stored in the semantic model depicted in figure 2.

5   Implementing Analysis Graphs Using Workflow Engines

5.1   Motivation

To make analysis graphs available to the analysts, we propose to implement analysis graphs based on workflow engines. As most workflow engines provide graphical user interfaces, analysis graphs can be modeled and maintained easily by the end-user. Design, modification and recording of analysis graphs within the graphical user interface of the workflow engine must be seamlessly integrated into the analyst's familiar business intelligence environment. As manual decision making generally includes a series of chronological decision steps, we think it is easier for non-expert users to navigate and understand an analysis graph modeled as workflow.

5.2   Example

In this section, we present an example that we used to implement a prototype of an ADW for automating analyses using an off-the-shelf workflow engine (i.e.

Microsoft Workflow Foundation™ [13]). The example has been chosen from the quality assurance process of a sensor production line. Within the production line, sensors run through a series of production steps followed by several electrical and optical tests. The results of these tests are collected and stored in the production process database and then transferred to the DWH, which in turn is used to continuously monitor and control the production process.

In the example, each time a sensor lot finishes testing, a notification is sent to the test operator in charge if the number of defects rises above a certain threshold. Figure 4 depicts the corresponding analysis graph *CheckDefects* as a flow chart.

Step *SelectTest* selects the first test for a detailed analysis. Only tests for the product type just finished are included. Within the first analysis step, the average number of defects for the selected test is analyzed. Step *Calculate4WeeksAverage* calculates the average number of defects based on the last 4 weeks. If the number of defects in the current week is above the 4 weeks average value, *SendBadAverage* is executed. If the number of current week defects is below the 4 weeks average, the analysis continues with a detailed analysis on the trend. Step *Calculate3DayTrend* calculates the trend of defects for the last three days. If the trend points upward, *SendBadTrend* is performed. If not, *SendGoodAverageAndTrend* sends a corresponding notification to the test operator in charge. Finally, condition *HasNextTest* repeats the analysis for all tests found in the DWH.

5.3   Implementation Overview

We implemented a prototype for the example described in the previous section using

- Microsoft Excel™ for recording end-user analyses,
- Windows Workflow Foundation Beta 2, a component of the upcoming .NET 3.0 Framework,
- SQL Server 2005™ Analysis Services as multidimensional OLAP Server and
- SQL Server 2005™ Notification Services for the implementation of the Event- and Action-Manager.

On top of the presented ADW architecture in Chapter 3, Figure 5 shows the architecture of the prototype implementation. In a first step, we concentrated on the core components needed for automated analyses: the Event Manager (EM), the Analysis Graph Manager (AGM), the Action Manager (AM) and the OLAP Recorder (OR). The Rule Engine (RE) has been implemented within the AGM.

The Event Manager has been implemented using SQL Server 2005 Notification Services. Its task is to generate an event in case a sensor lot finishes testing. In the source system, finished sensor lots are marked by a finished flag. Changes on that flag are tracked by triggers in the source system. The manager checks every 30 seconds whether the flag has changed for a certain sensor lot. If a newly finished sensor lot is thereby detected, the manager starts the ETL process which loads the new data into the DWH. After the ETL process succeeded, the manager

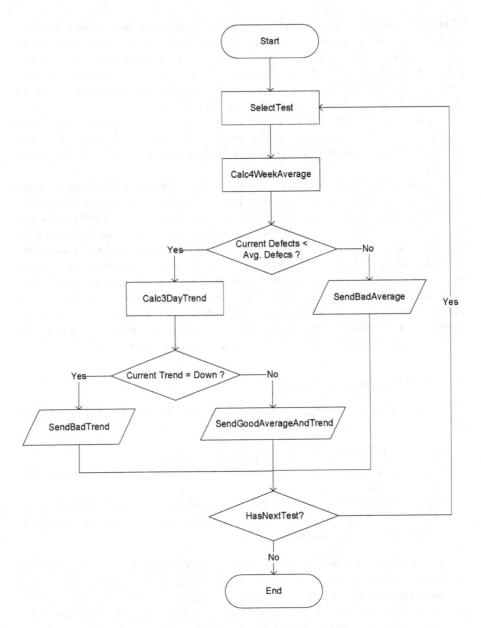

Fig. 4. Analysis Graph for *CheckDefects*

triggers all analysis graphs which are attached to this event. In our example the analysis graph *CheckDefects* will be triggered.

The Analysis Graph Manager has been implemented using WWF. Each analysis graph is modeled as a separate workflow. Analyses are performed in the vertices, while conditions are evaluated in the transitions of the workflow. If the

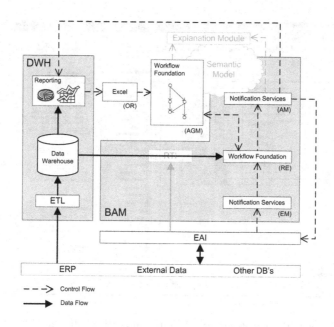

Fig. 5. Prototype architecture

execution of an analysis graph results in an action to be triggered, an event is
sent to the Action Manger. Section 5.4 provides a more detailed description of
the implementation of the AGM.

The Action Manager, like the Event Manager, has been implemented using
SQL Server 2005 Notification Services. The Action Manager evaluates the events
received from the AGM and delivers an alert to all subscribers of this event. In
our example, mail is used for notification.

So far, we implemented an OLAP-recorder (figure 6) that is capable of recording all OLAP queries conducted by the end-user in Microsoft Excel^{TM}. The condition which led to the decision to run a certain OLAP query has to be specified
textually by the end-user. Up to now, it is the task of a power-user to transform
the textually specified conditions to expressions that can be evaluated by the
computer. Based on the discussion above, this transformation may not be possible for all decision steps. As long as the needed information is not available in
a semantic model, the recorded analysis graph can not be executed in complete
automation.

5.4   Implementation Details of the Analysis Graph Manager

The AGM holds a set of analysis graphs implemented in WWF. Each analysis
graph is a composition of the three analysis graph primitives introduced in Chapter 4. For each analysis graph primitive we implemented a custom activity using
the WWF framework. In order to allow WWF to evaluate analytical expressions, we implemented the custom MDX activity. This activity is used within the

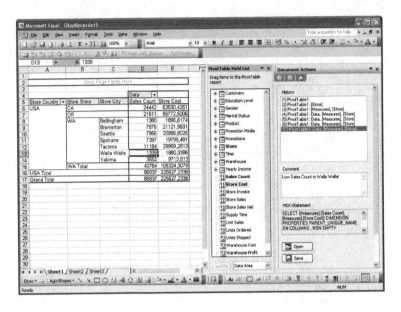

Fig. 6. OlapRecorder integrated into Microsoft Excel[TM]

analysis graph primitives to process arbitrary MDX queries and navigate to single cells returned from the queries. Access to the OLAP server is implemented using the ADOMD.NET framework which in turn uses XML/A as its communication protocol.

Figure 7 shows the analysis graph *CheckDefects* as it is implemented in WWF. When the graph is invoked by the Event Manager, the product type of the sensor lot just finished as well as the current date and week are passed as parameters to the analysis graph.

The AnlysisLoop activity *LoopTests* loops through all tests performed by the just finished product type. The MDX query used has been recorded by the OLAP recorder in Microsoft Excel and was populated with two parameters (product type and current week) that are passed to the analysis graph. As you can see in figure 8 and 9, the bind variables *:1* and *:2* are used therefore. Queries used in AnalysisLoop activities return a set of tuples which can be processed in the subsequent steps. The *CurrentItem* property of the AnylsisLoop activity gives access to the current selected tuple.

Within *LoopTests*, the AnalysisStep activity *AnalyseTest* performs the detailed analysis as described in section 5.3. The number of defects for the last 4 weeks is retrieved by 4 separate MDX activities. Figure 9 shows how the MDX activity *Defects3WeeksAgo* is configured. The results from the MDX activities are propagated to the AnalyseTest activity. There, the average number of defects for the last 4 weeks is calculated in the *Result* property.

In the evaluation part of AnalyseTest the 4 weeks average is compared to the current week defects. The right branch (current higher than 4 weeks average)

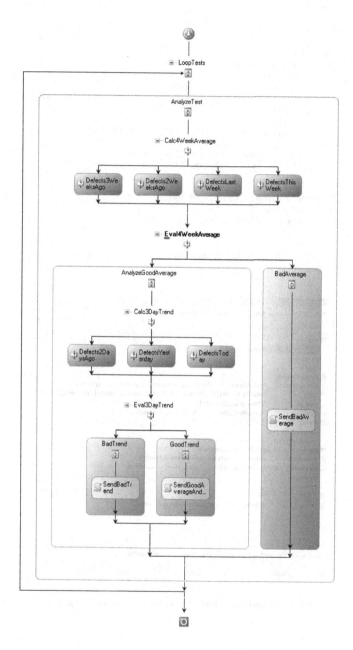

Fig. 7. WWF implementation for *CheckDefects*

contains an Action activity that sends a message to the responsible operator. The left branch is comprised by another AnalysisStep activity labeled *Analyse-GoodAverage*.

```
SELECT
  NON EMPTY HIERARCHIZE(
    Except(
      ( AddCalculatedMembers(
          Except(
            ( AddCalculatedMembers(
                DrillDownLevel(({[Defect].[DefectByGroup].[All]}))
              )
            },
            {[Defect].[DefectByGroup].[Test].&[0]}))
      },
      {[Defect].[DefectByGroup].[Test].&[0],
       [Defect].[DefectByGroup].[All]
      }
    )
  ) DIMENSION PROPERTIES PARENT_UNIQUE_NAME ON COLUMNS
FROM [Production]
WHERE ([Measures].[Rate], :1, :2)
```

Fig. 8. MDX statement for *LoopTests*

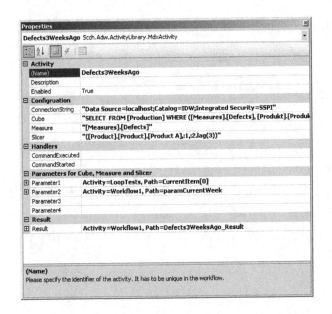

Fig. 9. Configuration of activity *Defects3WeeksAgo*

6   Discussion

Providing analysts with the appropriate tools to design automated analyses based on workflows has a series of advantages:

- the analyst will be released from routine decision tasks,
- analysis graphs can be specified in the same way manual decision making takes place; the business problem does not have to be transformed into a single complex statement,
- the workflow steps of an analysis graph are much more readable and maintainable as a single complex query,
- workflows make the analysts domain knowledge explicit,
- the domain knowledge of the analyst will be documented,
- design and modification of analysis graphs can be accomplished by the analyst himself using graphical editors and last but not least,
- through automation of routine analysis tasks, a continuous and proactive monitoring of production processes is guaranteed.

The prototype presented in this paper builds up the fundamental architecture. In contrary to [12,2], our approach strongly advocates to integrate end-users into the definition process of analysis graphs. Further, we could not identify the need for a dedicated primary dimension level as it is introduced in [12,2]. The main reason therefore is, that we are not strongly binding actions for the OLTP system to the corresponding dimension element in the DWH.

There are a lot of open issues for future work in this area. First, a practical evaluation of the proposed approach is needed. Key aspects will be how end-users cope with design and modification of analysis graphs and whether the approach scales up well for real world applications. Other issues are how to automatically transform recorded analysis into analysis graphs, how to identify and merge identical analysis graphs and which optimizations can be accomplished to improve execution performance. Finally, specification of decision points by end-users will likely become the most challenging issue. As decisions are also driven by implicit knowledge of end-users, the semantic model will probably become a central component in the architecture. An interesting approacch to avoid the semantic model would be to interrupt the execution of the analysis graph and prompt for user interaction. How far this approach is viable for practical applications has to be investigated.

7   Conclusion

Considering the tremendous amount of data that will be generated in future, we believe automated analysis will become a key technology to integrate data warehousing into the operational business. Compared to classical data warehouses, active data warehouses are used for day-to-day business tasks, which affect a growing number of users. These new users are experts in there respective domain but typically no IT professionals and therefore need user-friendly tool support.

To address these issues, we presented an approach for implementing automated analyses in ADW systems using workflow engines. An example taken from the quality assurance process of a sensor production line was implemented using Windows Workflow Foundation and SQL Server 2005.

Acknowledgement. The authors gratefully acknowledge support by the Austrian Government and the State of Upper Austria in the framework of the Kplus Competence Center Program.

References

1. Kimball, R., Ross, M.: The Data Warehouse Toolkit. Wiley Computer Publishing, New York (2002)
2. Thalhammer, T., Schrefl, M., Mohania, M.: Active data warehouses: Complementing olap with analysis rules. Data & Knowledge Engineering 39 (2001)
3. Agosta, L., Gile, K.: Real-time data warehousing: The hype and the reality. Technical report, Forrester Research (2004)
4. Dresner, H.: Business activity monitoring: Bam architecture. In: Gartner Symposium ITXPO (2003)
5. Nguyen, T.M., Tjoa, A.M.: Zero-latency data warehousing for heterogeneous data sources and continuous data streams. In: Proceedings of the Fifth International Conference on Information and Web-based Applications & Services (iiWAS 2003) (September 2003)
6. NCR/Teradata: http://www.teradata.com/
7. Agosta, L.: How to tell if your data warehouse is active. Technical report, Giga Research (2004)
8. Coalition, W.M.: Workflow management coalition terminology and glossary. Technical report, Workflow Management Coalition (1999)
9. Golfarelli, M., Rizzi, S., Cella, I.: Beyond data warehousing: What's next in business intelligence. In: Proceedings of the Seventh ACM International Workshop on Datawarehousing and OLAP (DOLAP '04), pp. 1–6. ACM Press, New York (2004)
10. McCarthy, D., Dayal, U.: The architecture of an active database management system. In: Proceedings of the 1989 ACM SIGMOD International Conference on Management of Data, pp. 215–224. ACM Press, New York (1989)
11. Nguyen, T.M., Schiefer, J., Tjoa, A.M.: Sense & response service architecture (saresa): An approach towards a real-time business intelligence solution and its use for a fraud detection application. In: Proceedings of the Eighth ACM International Workshop on Datawarehousing and OLAP (DOLAP '05), pp. 77–86. ACM Press, New York (2005)
12. Thalhammer, T.: Schrefl: Realizing active data warehouses with off-the-shelf database technology. Software: Practive and Experience 32(12), 1193–1222 (2002)
13. Microsoft: http://wf.netfx3.com/

Author Index

Lecture Notes in Computer Science

Sublibrary 3: Information Systems and Application, incl. Internet/Web and HCI

For information about Vols. 1– 4302
please contact your bookseller or Springer

Vol. 4560: N. Aykin (Ed.), Usability and International-ization, Part II. XVIII, 576 pages. 2007.

Vol. 4559: N. Aykin (Ed.), Usability and International-ization, Part I. XVIII, 661 pages. 2007.

Vol. 4558: M.J. Smith, G. Salvendy (Eds.), Human Interface and the Management of Information, Part II. XXIII, 1162 pages. 2007.

Vol. 4557: M.J. Smith, G. Salvendy (Eds.), Human Interface and the Management of Information, Part I. XXII, 1030 pages. 2007.

Vol. 4541: T. Okadome, T. Yamazaki, M. Makhtari (Eds.), Pervasive Computing for Quality of Life Enhancement. IX, 248 pages. 2007.

Vol. 4537: K.C.-C. Chang, W. Wang, L. Chen, C.A. Ellis, C.-H. Hsu, A.C. Tsoi, H. Wang (Eds.), Advances in Web and Network Technologies, and Information Management. XXIII, 707 pages. 2007.

Vol. 4531: J. Indulska, K. Raymond (Eds.), Distributed Applications and Interoperable Systems. XI, 337 pages. 2007.

Vol. 4526: M. Malek, M. Reitenspieß, A. van Moorsel (Eds.), Service Availability. X, 155 pages. 2007.

Vol. 4524: M. Marchiori, J.Z. Pan, C.d.S. Marie (Eds.), Web Reasoning and Rule Systems. XI, 382 pages. 2007.

Vol. 4519: E. Franconi, M. Kifer, W. May (Eds.), The Semantic Web: Research and Applications. XVIII, 830 pages. 2007.

Vol. 4518: N. Fuhr, M. Lalmas, A. Trotman (Eds.), Comparative Evaluation of XML Information Retrieval Systems. XII, 554 pages. 2007.

Vol. 4508: M.-Y. Kao, X.-Y. Li (Eds.), Algorithmic Aspects in Information and Management. VIII, 428 pages. 2007.

Vol. 4506: D. Zeng, I. Gotham, K. Komatsu, C. Lynch, M. Thurmond, D. Madigan, B. Lober, J. Kvach, H. Chen (Eds.), Intelligence and Security Informatics: Biosurveillance. XI, 234 pages. 2007.

Vol. 4505: G. Dong, X. Lin, W. Wang, Y. Yang, J.X. Yu (Eds.), Advances in Data and Web Management. XXII, 896 pages. 2007.

Vol. 4504: J. Huang, R. Kowalczyk, Z. Maamar, D. Martin, I. Müller, S. Stoutenburg, K.P. Sycara (Eds.), Service-Oriented Computing: Agents, Semantics, and Engineering. X, 175 pages. 2007.

Vol. 4500: N.A. Streitz, A.D. Kameas, I. Mavrommati (Eds.), The Disappearing Computer. XVIII, 304 pages. 2007.

Vol. 4495: J. Krogstie, A. Opdahl, G. Sindre (Eds.), Advanced Information Systems Engineering. XVI, 606 pages. 2007.

Vol. 4480: A. LaMarca, M. Langheinrich, K.N. Truong (Eds.), Pervasive Computing. XIII, 369 pages. 2007.

Vol. 4473: D. Draheim, G. Weber (Eds.), Trends in Enterprise Application Architecture. X, 355 pages. 2007.

Vol. 4471: P. Cesar, K. Chorianopoulos, J.F. Jensen (Eds.), Interactive TV: A Shared Experience. XIII, 236 pages. 2007.

Vol. 4469: K.-c. Hui, Z. Pan, R.C.-k. Chung, C.C.L. Wang, X. Jin, S. Göbel, E.C.-L. Li (Eds.), Technologies for E-Learning and Digital Entertainment. XVIII, 974 pages. 2007.

Vol. 4443: R. Kotagiri, P. Radha Krishna, M. Mohania, E. Nantajeewarawat (Eds.), Advances in Databases: Concepts, Systems and Applications. XXI, 1126 pages. 2007.

Vol. 4439: W. Abramowicz (Ed.), Business Information Systems. XV, 654 pages. 2007.

Vol. 4430: C.C. Yang, D. Zeng, M. Chau, K. Chang, Q. Yang, X. Cheng, J. Wang, F.-Y. Wang, H. Chen (Eds.), Intelligence and Security Informatics. XII, 330 pages. 2007.

Vol. 4425: G. Amati, C. Carpineto, G. Romano (Eds.), Advances in Information Retrieval. XIX, 759 pages. 2007.

Vol. 4412: F. Stajano, H.J. Kim, J.-S. Chae, S.-D. Kim (Eds.), Ubiquitous Convergence Technology. XI, 302 pages. 2007.

Vol. 4402: W. Shen, J.-Z. Luo, Z. Lin, J.-P.A. Barthès, Q. Hao (Eds.), Computer Supported Cooperative Work in Design III. XV, 763 pages. 2007.

Vol. 4398: S. Marchand-Maillet, E. Bruno, A. Nürnberger, M. Detyniecki (Eds.), Adaptive Multimedia Retrieval: User, Context, and Feedback. XI, 269 pages. 2007.

Vol. 4397: C. Stephanidis, M. Pieper (Eds.), Universal Access in Ambient Intelligence Environments. XV, 467 pages. 2007.

Vol. 4380: S. Spaccapietra, P. Atzeni, F. Fages, M.-S. Hacid, M. Kifer, J. Mylopoulos, B. Pernici, P. Shvaiko, J. Trujillo, I. Zaihrayeu (Eds.), Journal on Data Semantics VIII. XV, 219 pages. 2007.

Vol. 4365: C.J. Bussler, M. Castellanos, U. Dayal, S. Navathe (Eds.), Business Intelligence for the Real-Time Enterprises. IX, 157 pages. 2007.

Vol. 4353: T. Schwentick, D. Suciu (Eds.), Database Theory – ICDT 2007. XI, 419 pages. 2006.

Vol. 4352: T.-J. Cham, J. Cai, C. Dorai, D. Rajan, T.-S. Chua, L.-T. Chia (Eds.), Advances in Multimedia Modeling, Part II. XVIII, 743 pages. 2006.

Vol. 4351: T.-J. Cham, J. Cai, C. Dorai, D. Rajan, T.-S. Chua, L.-T. Chia (Eds.), Advances in Multimedia Modeling, Part I. XIX, 797 pages. 2006.

Vol. 4328: D. Penkler, M. Reitenspiess, F. Tam (Eds.), Service Availability. X, 289 pages. 2006.

Vol. 4321: P. Brusilovsky, A. Kobsa, W. Nejdl (Eds.), The Adaptive Web. XII, 763 pages. 2007.

Vol. 4317: S.K. Madria, K.T. Claypool, R. Kannan, P. Uppuluri, M.M. Gore (Eds.), Distributed Computing and Internet Technology. XIX, 466 pages. 2006.

Vol. 4312: S. Sugimoto, J. Hunter, A. Rauber, A. Morishima (Eds.), Digital Libraries: Achievements, Challenges and Opportunities. XVIII, 571 pages. 2006.

Vol. 4306: Y. Avrithis, Y. Kompatsiaris, S. Staab, N.E. O'Connor (Eds.), Semantic Multimedia. XII, 241 pages. 2006.